Energy Security and Sustainable Economic Growth in China

The Nottingham China Policy Institute series brings together cutting-edge scholarship, policy relevance and accessibility. It includes works on the economics, society, culture, politics, international relations, national security and history of the Chinese mainland, Taiwan and Hong Kong in the twentieth- and twenty-first centuries. Books in this series are written in an accessible style, although they are based on meticulous research. They put forward exciting ideas and research findings that specialist academics need to take note while policy-makers and opinion leaders will find inspiring. They represent innovative multidisciplinary scholarship at its best in the study of contemporary China.

Series Editors: **Shujie Yao** and **Steve Tsang**

Titles include:

Shujie Yao and Maria Jesus Herrerias (*editors*)
ENERGY SECURITY AND SUSTAINABLE GROWTH IN CHINA

Jing Zhang
FOREIGN DIRECT INVESTMENT, GOVERNANCE, AND THE ENVIRONMENT IN CHINA
Regional Dimensions

Steve Tsang (*editor*)
THE VITALITY OF JAPAN
Politics, Economics, Society and Culture

The Nottingham China Policy Institute series
Series Standing Order ISBN 978–0–230–36922–1

You can receive future titles in this series as they are published by placing a standing order. Please contact your bookseller or, in case of difficulty, write to us at the address below with your name and address, the title of the series and the ISBN quoted above.

Customer Services Department, Macmillan Distribution Ltd, Houndmills, Basingstoke, Hampshire RG21 6XS, England.

Energy Security and Sustainable Economic Growth in China

Edited by

Shujie Yao and Maria Jesus Herrerias
School of Contemporary Chinese Studies, University of Nottingham, UK

palgrave
macmillan

Softcover reprint of the hardcover 1st edition 2014 978-1-137-37204-8

First published 2014 by
PALGRAVE MACMILLAN

Palgrave Macmillan in the UK is an imprint of Macmillan Publishers Limited, registered in England, company number 785998, of Houndmills, Basingstoke, Hampshire RG21 6XS.

Palgrave Macmillan in the US is a division of St Martin's Press LLC, 175 Fifth Avenue, New York, NY 10010.

Palgrave Macmillan is the global academic imprint of the above companies and has companies and representatives throughout the world.

Palgrave® and Macmillan® are registered trademarks in the United States, the United Kingdom, Europe and other countries

ISBN 978-1-349-47595-7 ISBN 978-1-137-37205-5 (eBook)
DOI 10.1057/9781137372055

This book is printed on paper suitable for recycling and made from fully managed and sustained forest sources. Logging, pulping and manufacturing processes are expected to conform to the environmental regulations of the country of origin.

A catalogue record for this book is available from the British Library.

A catalog record for this book is available from the Library of Congress.

Transferred to Digital Printing in 2014

Contents

List of Figures

List of Tables

Preface

China has overtaken the United States as the world's leading producer and consumer of energy since 2009. The significant increase in the demand for energy, especially for coal and electricity, in this country has triggered an international debate as well as within the domestic economy for its enormous implications on the sustainability of growth and climate change agreements. On the one hand, the sharp increase in energy consumption from China has raised international commodities prices, giving rise to inflationary effects in developed and developing countries. On the other hand, and from a domestic perspective, such a demand has led to an electricity shortage, especially in the summer period, in the majority of regions in addition to a significant increase in environmental damage.

As it is well known, the Chinese economy has its own specific characteristics, such as the presence of the state sector and a concentration of economic activities in the coastal areas. This phenomenon is not significantly different as far as energy demand is concerned. However, energy supply is highly concentrated in Shanxi and Inner Mongolia in terms of coal and Sichuan and its neighbouring provinces in terms of hydro-electricity generation. This imbalance between energy supply and demand, along with a primitive transmission grid, is influencing the overall performance of the energy industry in China. Therefore, an essential investigation of the current situation of the energy market in the Chinese economy at both national and provincial levels is important when it comes to designing energy policies. In addition, the role played by institutions in a broad sense, renewable energies, ownership and open-door policy reforms will be investigated as suitable mechanisms to reduce energy consumption and consequently to prevent climate change. The implications of such policies on economic growth will also be assessed critically.

This book is a collection of 14 papers produced by different authors who have been invited by the editors to make a contribution in different aspects of the Chinese energy industry. It aims to present a comprehensive picture on the energy situation in China, covering the issues of energy security, institutional reforms, international relations, environmental implications at present and the development prospects in the future.

Without any doubt these works are an important reference for the study of the Chinese energy industry as this is the first book in the literature which addresses a comprehensive set of issues of such an important industry in the rapidly growing Chinese economy.

Chapter 1 by Carlos Aller and Lorenzo Ductor analyses the Chinese energy sector in comparison to other developing economies. They examine the relationship between energy consumption and economic growth in these countries and the main characteristics of their energy sectors, including energy dependency and current energy policies. They present an outlook on the expected energy consumption and carbon dioxide emissions for the next decades in China and in other big economies like Brazil, India and Mexico. Finally, the authors provide some policy recommendations to reduce carbon dioxide emissions and achieve a sustainable economic growth.

Chapter 2 by Atanu Ghoshray and Javier Ordóñez considers China as a major participant in the world commodity markets. China's spillovers of aggregate activity and commodity-specific demand shocks may have a large impact on commodity prices and terms of trade at the global level. Although there is a vast literature trying to quantify the driving process of commodity prices and the impact of economic activity on these prices, the analysis of the changing role of China in the world commodity market has been rather scarce. In this chapter, the authors discuss the scale of China's impact on energy markets. For this purpose they ask whether the apparent increase in commodity intensity demand is linked to the structure of Chinese economic growth and its fast expansion in the tradable sector and large-scale fixed asset investment.

Chapter 3 by Elzbieta Maria Pron studies the Shanghai Cooperation Organisation (SCO), which was established in 2001 by China, Russia and four Central Asian republics as a security mechanism. Although little progress has been made since then, in 2011 the SCO announced that the Club creation was entering "its final strait [sic]". This chapter uses a foreign policy-oriented approach to address the question: what role will SCO energy multilateralism play in China's cooperation on energy with Central Asia? The analysis of the geo-political obstacles to the foundation of the club and China's stakes in the SCO energy multilateralism reveals that China will continue to access energy resources bilaterally, while the SCO energy club will play a role as a political agent for promoting cooperation on the energy issues.

Chapter 4 by Karolina Wysoczanska aims to shed light on the institutional context of China's energy policy and further the understanding of the institutions and players in the formulation of energy policy in China. This chapter reviews the evolution of the institutions in China regarding energy policy and examines the current institutions. Institutions here cover the organizational structure governing China's energy policy, the relations between the main governmental organizations, the relations between these governmental organizations and the major national oil companies (NOCs), and main policy tools. The first major part of the chapter is an overview of the changes in these governmental organizations with regard to energy policy in the past decades since 1949, with an emphasis on the post-1978 era. The second major part of the chapter contains an examination of the current organizational structures governing energy policy and government-NOCs relations, as well as an exploration of the possible role of NOCs in China's energy policy.

Chapter 5 by Shujie Yao and Dan Luo discusses the advantages and disadvantages of different renewable energy sources, aiming to provide an overall picture of China's energy security situation and to explore alternative ways to improve energy supply and efficiency. Fast economic growth in the past three decades has led to a rapid growth of energy demand in China. This has a number of implications on sustainable economic growth, energy security, environmental damage and climate change. China has relied heavily on coal, which is highly polluting, as its most important source of energy. Rapid growth in car ownership has also led to a huge and rising demand for oil, which has become increasingly more dependent on imports. To reduce the dependence on coal and oil, apart from improving energy efficiency and industrial restructuring, China has to develop renewable energies such as wind, solar, hydro and nuclear powers. Each of these sources has its advantages and limitations. This chapter offers a comprehensive study on all these issues.

Chapter 6 by David C. Broadstock explores the nature of oil markets within China. In recent years domestic demand for oil products has been exceeding supply, creating imbalance and a supply gap in the domestic market as well as a dependency on oil imports. The sustainability of these trends, and in particular the market imbalance, is examined from a number of perspectives. There are important questions that must be considered, such as how much will future demand for oil rise? How long will oil supply last? Does the global political economy of oil have implications for the supply gap in China? Does China have an appropriate social and/or physical infrastructure to substitute oil for alternative energy sources?

Chapter 7 by María J. García focuses on China's current reliance on fossil fuels which has led to three major challenges: environmental degradation, pressure to reduce carbon emissions and external reliance for oil. This chapter reviews key actions and milestones achieved in China's quest for cleaner and independent energy focusing on renewable energy sources (hydro, wind, solar, biomass power), as well as the recent impetus to pursue alternative energy sources such as natural gas, unconventional gas and coal-to-liquid and coal-to-gas technologies that are placing China at the forefront of these technologies. China's renewable energy potential and vast reserves of shale gas and coal technologies could guarantee its future energy independence. However, coordination and investment obstacles remain, and the recent emphasis on gas and coal technologies, whilst ensuring security, does little to alleviate environmental problems.

Chapter 8 by M.J. Herrerias and Roselyne Joyeux studies regional electricity consumption and economic growth in China. Since the seminal paper by Kraft and Kraft in 1978, the relationship between energy consumption and economic growth has been widely investigated in the energy economics literature. While the majority of work focused on country level, this chapter investigates the regional dimension and potential spillovers through cross-sectional dependence at the prefectural level of China, using panel data techniques for 1996–2010. The empirical results indicate that there is uni-directional causality from per capita GDP to per capita electricity consumption for all the transmission grids except for the east in the long-run. This finding suggests that energy conservation policies can be adopted without interrupting the path of growth, and in consequence, there is scope for the implementation of policies in China to mitigate climate change.

Chapter 9 by M.J. Herrerias studies the relationship between energy intensity and productivity across the Chinese regions during 1995–2008. It argues that if lower energy intensities are related to productivity improvements, energy-saving measures may be viewed as a policy guide for economic performance. The unbalanced growth and the uneven distribution of energy resources across regions justify the need to investigate this relationship at provincial level as well as at the industrial level. Energy intensity is measured differently, including total energy intensity, electricity intensity, coal intensity and oil intensity. The relationship between each of the energy intensity measurements and productivity has its own economic meaning.

Chapter 10 by Ana Cuadros and Vicente Orts studies energy intensity and its policy implications in China. A simple way to explore the efficient use of energy resources in China is through the examination of energy intensity. The Chinese case is attractive because the economic reforms initiated at the end of the 1970s, along with the massive foreign direct investment and trade flows in the 1990s, have helped to decrease energy intensity. This open-door policy has been complemented by reform of state sector, allowing the emergence of new forms of investment ownership, and by energy price deregulation. In this chapter, a close look at this topic is taken by reviewing those factors that may have a major influence on the energy situation in China.

Chapter 11 by Maoliang Bu and Huajiang Luo studies globalization and energy consumption in the Yangtze River Delta. It is a big concern to question how globalization impacts the environment, especially towards developing countries like China. To date, however, few studies have explicitly analysed for the influence of globalization on the energy consumption. This chapter analyses the influence by taking the case of Yangtze River Delta, which not only contributes mostly to China's manufacturing, but also ranks possibly at the top level of globalization involvement across the Chinese regions. The results reveal that foreign investment plays a leading role in the decline of energy intensity in the Yangtze River Delta, whether it is total energy, coal or electricity under consideration.

Chapter 12 by Evan B. Hills and Zhengxu Wang studies the institutional barriers to China's renewable energy strategy. It examines the effects of various institutional inefficiencies on the implementation of China's renewable energy policies. It focuses on three major causes of institutional inefficiencies. Firstly, it examines the role that state-owned enterprises play in the production and transmission of renewable energy. Secondly, it addresses the fragmentation of central government agencies associated with renewable energy, along with the subsequent creation of special interest groups that undermine central government policy initiatives. Thirdly, it examines the inherent conflict of interests between central government policies and local government incentives. It is concluded with some suggestions as to how to best eliminate these inefficiencies, so as to improve the effectiveness of China's renewable energy policies in the future.

Chapter 13 by Chaoxian Guo and Yanhong Liu studies the demand effects on CO_2 emission in China. In the past decade, China's fast economic growth was achieved at the expense of a faster increase of carbon emission and deterioration of the environment. The structural decomposition analysis (SDA) approach is employed in this chapter based on the 1992–2007 input/output data in China. It reveals that its economic growth pattern of over-dependence on investment and export, and the internal structures of high carbon intensity, constituted the major determinants for the rampant carbon emission expansion in China since 2002. It is suggested that, to mitigate this problem, efforts should be taken in the direction of effectively expanding domestic consumption, restructuring the investment with priorities on the new energy and circular economy, and optimizing the export structure by developing manufacturing sectors and industrial chains with international competitiveness.

Chapter 14 by Xiumei Guo and Dora Marinova studies environmental protection and sustainability strategies in China. Due to its remarkable economic rise in the last three decades, China is now the world's second-largest economic power. The country however has also become the world's largest greenhouse gases emitter and its growth continues to contribute to global and local environmental issues related to climate change, pollution, biodiversity loss and ecological deterioration. As China's industrialization, urbanization and agricultural modernization persist, developing a green energy-saving economy is becoming more important for the country and the world. This chapter examines China's major policies for environmental protection and current orientation towards a more sustainable development, including analysis of the relationship between GDP growth and carbon emissions. Sustainability strategies for policy-makers are proposed to better direct the green growth path and achieve a secure clean energy future for an environmentally friendly society.

Professor Yao gratefully acknowledges the financial support of a China's National Natural Science Foundation research grant (No.71133007/G0301).

Notes on Contributors

Editors

Shujie Yao is Founding Head of the School of Contemporary Chinese Studies at the University of Nottingham, UK, and Special Chair Professor of Economics, Chongqing University and Xi'an Jiaotong University, China. An expert on economic development in China, he has written 10 research monographs, edited books, and produced more than 90 refereed journal articles. He was ranked eighth among the world's China scholars specializing in the study of the Chinese economy in a recent article published in the *Journal of Asian Economic Literature*. Professor Yao has published widely in many top economics and development journals, including *Journal of Political Economy, Journal of Comparative Economics, Economic Development and Cultural Change, Journal of Banking and Finance, World Economy, China Quarterly* and *Journal of Development Studies, China Economic Review*, among others. He is the founding editor of *Journal of Chinese Economic and Business Studies*, chief economics editor of *Xi'an Jiaotong University Journal* (Social Sciences), editorial member of *Journal of Comparative Economics, Food Policy* and *Journal of Contemporary China*. He is also coordinator of the China and the World Economy Programme at the Globalisation and Economic Policy Centre of the University of Nottingham. He has had a wide range of consultancy experience with major organizations including the UNDP, FAO, World Bank, ADB, DFID, EU and the UNCDF, working in many less developed and transitional economies in Africa, Asia and Eastern Europe.

Maria Jesus Herrerias is Lecturer of Economics in the School of Contemporary Chinese Studies, University of Nottingham. She is an expert on Chinese studies on economic growth, international trade and regional development. Recently, she has started to work on energy and environmental issues in the case of developed and developing countries with emphasis on China. Her main works have been published in *China and World Economy, Economics of Transition, Empirical Economics, Economic Modelling, Papers in Regional Science, Annals of Regional Science, Energy Policy, Applied Energy, Energy Journal, Energy Economics, Regional Studies, Journal of Policy Modelling, Pacific Economic Review* and *China Economic Review*. She has presented her works in conferences such as the

Royal Economics Society, the Chinese Economic Association (UK), the European Trade Study Group, among others, and has received invitations to participate in conferences including the Asian Economic Panel in Tokyo in 2011.

Contributors

Carlos Aller is Teaching Fellow at the University of Alicante, Spain. His PhD dissertation focused on household and corporate finance. His research interests include banking, energy and applied microeconometrics. He has participated and presented his work at conferences including the Annual Meeting of the Association of Southern European Economic Theorists (Portugal) and Simposio de la Asociación Española de Economía (Spain) and at seminars.

David C. Broadstock is Associate Professor at Research Institute of Economics and Management based in the Southwestern University of Finance and Economics in Chengdu, China. David is an expert on transport- and energy-related issues, particularly focusing on aspects relating to empirical modelling of demand from a consumer perspective. Prior to moving to an academic post in China, David was an economic consultant within a global engineering firm and undertook private and government based transport/energy projects from around the world. David has published in an array of international journals including the *Economics Bulletin*, the *Journal of Economic Studies*, *Energy Economics*, *Energy Policy*, the *International Journal of Transport Economics*, *Transportation Research Part A: Policy and Practice*. He participates regularly in domestic and international meetings, recently including the 23rd CEA (UK) and 4th CEA (Europe) Annual Conferences (UK); the international Workshop on Empirical Methods in Energy Economics (Germany); the Chinese Economists Society Annual Conference (China); the International Conference on Financial Management and Economics (China – Hong Kong, receiving the Excellent Paper Award of the conference).

Maoliang Bu is Assistant Professor at the School of Business, Nanjing University, and Lecturer at the SAIS Nanjing Center, Johns Hopkins University. He was a post-doctoral researcher at the University of Goettingen, Germany in 2011–12. His main research interest concerns environmental economics in an open economy. His papers have appeared in both Chinese and international journals such as *China and World Economy*, *Energy Policy* and *Journal of Cleaner Production*. He has received research grants from the European Union and the Chinese government.

Ana Cuadros is Lecturer at the University Jaume I of Castellon, Spain. Her research focuses on the effects of foreign capital inflows and international trade in developing and emerging economies. She has recently started to work on energy issues in the case of developing countries with special emphasis on China. Her papers have been published in the *Journal of Development Studies, Economic Letters, Journal of International Development, Review of Development Economics, Journal of Policy Modelling* and *Energy Economics*. She has participated in conferences such as the European Trade Study Group Conference, the Annual Congress of the European Economic Association, International Atlantic Economic Conference and the Chinese Economic Association (UK/Europe) Conference, among others.

Lorenzo Ductor is Lecturer in Economics at Massey University, New Zealand. His research focuses on co-authorship networks and their effects on individual academic productivity. He also investigates the negative effects of the excess of financial development on economic growth. His areas of specialization include applied econometrics with research interests in economic growth, financial development, energy and applied microeconomics. Lorenzo has presented his work at conferences such as the 26th Annual Congress of the European Economic Association (University of Oslo, Norway), the Interdisciplinary Workshop on Information and Decision in Social Networks (MIT, USA) and the Workshop on Advances in Business Cycles and Economic Growth Analysis (The Rimini Center for Economic Analysis, Italy), among others, and in seminars at the University of Cambridge, St. Gallen, Valencia and Alicante and many other institutions.

Maria J. Garcia is senior Marie Curie fellow at the School of Politics and International Relations at the University of Nottingham, UK. Her research interests focus on the dynamics of free trade agreement proliferation in the Asia Pacific and the European Union's relations with Asia. Her work has appeared in various journals including *Journal of Common Market Studies, Journal of World Trade and Cambridge Review of International Affairs*.

Atanu Ghoshray is Senior Lecturer at the University of Bath, UK. He has undertaken research as Consultant for the Asian Development Bank (ADB) and has been a visiting scholar at the United Nations University, World Institute for Development Economics Research (UNU-WIDER). Atanu was educated at the University of Calcutta in India where he obtained his BSc degree in Economics. He went on to study at Birkbeck College, University of London and the University of Nottingham in the UK where he was awarded MSc and PhD degrees respectively. Atanu's interests are in the field of primary commodity markets and macroeconomics. He has published in the *Journal of Development Economics, American Journal of Agricultural Economics, Economics Letters* and *Energy Economics* among others.

Xiumei Guo is a research fellow at Curtin University Sustainability Policy (CUSP) Institute in Australia. Her research interests are in the areas of demography, economic development, energy efficiency, low-carbon economy and sustainability studies with a focus on China. She has published widely in international journals and conference proceedings. Recent work has appeared in the *Journal of Contemporary China, Journal of Cleaner Production* and *Environment, Development and Sustainability*.

Evan B. Hills is currently a student at the University of St Andrews, majoring in International Relations. He has also attended the Contemporary China Studies program in the School of International Studies, Renmin University of China. Evan's main research interests are terrorism studies, Sino–US relations, and international environmental policy. Additionally, Evan is a marketing associate at a San Francisco-based software company.

Roselyne Joyeux is Associate Professor at Macquarie University in Sydney. She received a PhD in Economics and a master's in Mathematics from the University of California at San Diego. She has held positions at Cornell University, the University of Auckland, the Centre for Operations Research and Econometrics at the University of Louvain-la-Neuve and the GREQAM at the University of Provence. She has published widely on both econometric theory and economic modelling. Recent papers have been published in the *Energy Journal*, the *Journal of Financial Econometrics, Applied Financial Economics* and the *Economic Record*. Her interests include time series analysis and its applications to macroeconomic modelling, energy economics, carbon emission trading and finance.

Yanhong Liu is Lecturer at the Graduate School, Chinese Academy of Social Sciences (CASS) and currently a Marie Curie research fellow at the China Policy Institute (CPI), University of Nottingham. Her fields of research and teaching include the theory of public choice, corruption in the higher education sector, public opinions and democratization, etc. Her publications appeared in referred academic journals in China, such as *Journal of Chinese Academy of Governance*, and *Journal of the Party School of Central Committee of CCP*.

Dan Luo is Lecturer in Business and Finance at the School of Contemporary Chinese Studies (SCCS) and senior research fellow of the China Policy Institute (CPI) at the University of Nottingham. She previously worked as a research fellow in the Centre of Global Finance, University of the West of England. She obtained her MA in Finance and Investment from Nottingham University Business School in 2006 and her PhD in Finance in 2009 at the School of Contemporary Chinese Studies, University of Nottingham. She has also been a member of the Association of Chartered Certified Accountants (ACCA) since 2007. Dr Luo's major research interests focus on the Chinese financial market, in particular the banking sector and stock market. She has also conducted intensive research on asset pricing, stock market volatility, income inequality and energy efficiency. Her work has been published in journals such as *The World Economy* and *Applied Financial Economics*, *Journal of Contemporary China* and *Journal of the Asia Pacific Economy*.

Huajiang Luo is currently a student at the School of Business, Nanjing University. He won a national scholarship from China's Ministry of Education. His main research interests include applied econometrics, energy economics and labour economics. In 2011, he published a paper in *Journal of Southern Population*.

Dora Marinova is Professor of Sustainability and Deputy Director of the Curtin University Sustainability Policy (CUSP) Institute in Australia. Her current research relates to the role of new technologies for sustainability, technology policy, energy efficiency and economic development in Australia and China. She has more than 300 publications and has supervised to completion more than 40 PhD students.

Elzbieta Maria Pron is PhD candidate at the School of Contemporary Chinese Studies, University of Nottingham. She holds two MA degrees – from Adam Mickiewicz University in Poznan (Poland) in Sinology, and from National Taiwan University in National Development. Elzbieta has worked on China's foreign policy, China's relations with Central Asia and China's engagement in international institutions.

Javier Ordóñez is Lecturer at the University of Bath, UK and at University Jaume I, Spain. He has also held a position as Assistant Research Professor at the School of Economics, University of Copenhagen, and has been a visiting professor at the Universities of Nottingham, Rome and Bologna, among others. He obtained his PhD from University Jaume I. Javier's research interests are in the fields of applied economics, focusing on economic and regional integration, real exchange rates, oil and unemployment. He has published in *Empirical Economics*, *Southern Economic Journal*, *Energy Journal*, *Economic Modelling* and *Economic Letters*, among others.

Vicente Orts is Professor of Economics, Department of Economics and Institute of International Economics in the University Jaume I of Castellon (Spain). His research has focused on the determinants of international trade flows, relationship between foreign direct investment and trade, economic geography, openness and growth and economic development. Recent work has appeared in the *Journal of Developments Studies, Journal of International Development, Review of Development Economics, Economics of Transition, Scandinavian Journal of Economics, Southern Economic Journal, International Review of Law and Economics, Journal of Economics and Management Strategy, Economic Modelling, Empirical Economics, Journal of Policy Modelling,* and *Papers in Regional Science and Energy Economics*.

Zhengxu Wang is Associate Professor at the School of Contemporary Chinese Studies and Senior Fellow and Deputy Director of the China Policy Institute (CPI), the University of Nottingham. He researches citizen values and political behaviours in China and East Asia, institutional changes and political reforms in China, perceptions of other powers in international politics, and elite politics in China, among other topics. He publishes widely in major academic journals, including *The China Quarterly, Governance* and *International Review of Sociology*. He works with internationally renowned think tanks and supplies timely and sharp analyses of political events and international affairs of China to a wide range of media outlets as well.

Karolina Wysoczanska is PhD candidate at the School of Contemporary Chinese Studies, University of Nottingham. In 2009 she obtained a master's in Management in Contemporary China. She obtained a scholarship from the Confucius Institute to study Chinese language at Fudan University, China. She has worked in China's political institutions, and its oil and gas industry. She has published in the *Journal of Contemporary African Studies*.

List of Abbreviations

BP	British Petroleum
BTU	British thermal units
CCP	Communist Party of China
CNOOC	China National Offshore Oil Corporation
CNPC	China National Petroleum Corporation
CO_2	Carbon Dioxide
COP	Conference of the Parties
CPCIF	China Petroleum and Chemical Industry Federation
CTGPC	China Three Gorges Project Co.
DEA	Data Envelopment Analysis
DOLS	Dynamic Ordinary Least Squares
EI	Energy Intensity
EIA	Energy Information Administration [US]
EKC	Environmental Kuznets Curve
FDI	Foreign Direct Investment
FYP	Five-Year Plan
GDP	Gross Domestic Product
GHG	greenhouse gas
GW	gigawatt
IEA	International Energy Agency (US)
KMG	KazMunaiGaz
KP	Kyoto Protocol
LNG	liquefied natural gas
MLNR	Ministry of Land and Natural Resources
MLTPRE	Medium and Long-term Development Plan for Renewable Energy
MOF	Ministry of Finance
MOFCOM	Ministry of Commerce
MTCE	metric tons of carbon dioxide equivalent
MUV	Manufacturing Unit Value
MW	Megawatt
NEA	National Energy Administration
NEC	National Energy Commission
NDRC	National Development and Reform Commission
NOCs	National Oil Companies

NPU	Nuclear Power Unit
OECD	Organisation for Economic Cooperation and Development
OPEC	Organisation of the Petroleum Exporting Countries
PLA	People's Liberation Army
PPP	purchasing power parity
PRC	People's Republic of China
PV	Photovoltaic
REL	Renewable Energy Law
R&D	Research and Development
SASAC	State Asset Supervisory and Administration Commission
SAFE	State Administration of Foreign Exchange
SEPA	State Environmental Protection Agency
SERC	State Electricity Regulation Commission
SBPCI	State Bureau of Petroleum and Chemical Industry
SCE	Standard Coal Equivalent
SCO	Shanghai Cooperation Organisation
SEC	State Economic Commission
SELG	State Energy Leading Group
SEO	State Energy Office
SETC	State Economic and Trade Commission
SDPC	State Development and Planning Commission
SINOPEC	China National Petrochemical Corporation
SOEs	State-owned Enterprises
SPC	State Planning Commission
TERI	The Energy and Resources Institute
TFP	Total Factor Productivity
TBEA	Tebian Electric Apparatus Stock Co. Ltd.
UNFCCC	United Nations Conventions on Climate Change
UNSC	United Nations Security Council
URR	Ultimate Recoverable Resource
USD	United States Dollar
WTI	West Texas Intermediate
WTO	World Trade Organization
XUAR	Xinjiang Uyghur Autonomous Region

1
International Comparison in the Energy Sector

Carlos Aller and Lorenzo Ductor

This chapter analyses the Chinese energy sector in comparison to other developing economies.

1 Introduction

Developing countries that are experiencing high economic growth have to face the subsequent environmental problems, exacerbated by the increase of their population and improved living standards. Kyoto Protocol (KP) did not bind developing economies (or the United States (US)) but the majority of them adopted the compromise of reducing carbon emissions in order to mitigate greenhouse gas (GHG) effects since then.[1] Currently, developed economies emit sensibly more GHG emissions per capita than developing economies. However, the predictions about developing economies are not optimistic. It is expected that the emissions of counties that are not members of the Organisation for Economic Cooperation and Development (OECD) will reach 28.9 billion metric tons in 2035, 73 per cent above the 2008 level (US Energy Information Administration (EIA), 2011).

Enkvist et al. (2007) estimate the costs of mitigation and abatement of GHG and conclude that developing economies have a greater potential of abatement at low cost for a number of reasons, like their large populations or the lower cost of mitigating new growth as opposed to reducing existing emissions.

Traditionally, developing economies have been reluctant to commit to reducing emissions as it can be observed in the successive United Nations Framework Convention on Climate Change (UNFCCC) where those emerging economies have shown their fear of emission restrictions on the basis that they will curtail economic activity. The eighteenth session of the Conference of the Parties (COP18) at Doha (Qatar) on December 2012, ended with approval of an extension of the KP from 2013 to 2020 rather than a new one. Furthermore, a number of countries (Japan, Russia, Canada and New Zealand) have refused to sign the protocol again and there are no additional "committed" members.

Economic growth and its influence on the environment has been an object of study by numerous researchers. The so-called "Environmental Kuznets Curve" (EKC) postulates an inverse U-path from pre-industrial to post-industrial economies that suggests increasing environmental damages at the early stages of economic development followed by improvements in subsequent rising levels in per capita income.

Such hypothesis has been tested in several studies for industrialized countries. For example, the studies by Canas et al. (2003), who examine the EKC for 16 developed economies in the second half of the 20th century, and Galeotti et al. (2006) who, for a similar period of time, find evidence for the hypothesis in OECD economies, but not for the rest.

Notwithstanding, the EKC hypothesis is not highly supported when it is tested in developing economies, as in the paper by Focacci (2005) who tests the hypothesis for China, Brazil and India, three big emerging economies. Narayan and Narayan (2010) perform estimations on 43 developing economies to conclude that the hypothesis holds only in 35 per cent of them, in which the three countries mentioned above are excluded. By regions, the hypothesis would only hold in the Middle East and South Asia.

These results reveal the necessity of a better understanding of the energy sectors of developing economies in order to make environmental policy recommendations, given the important asymmetry across those economies and with respect to the developed ones. In this chapter, we provide a detailed description of the energy sectors of a selected group of developing economies, each of very different characteristics in energy resources and volume, but with the common feature of having high Gross Domestic Product (GDP) growth rates in the last decade. We put special emphasis on China and some other highly populated emerging economies like Brazil, Mexico, India or Russia. The objective is to provide a good understanding of the problems faced by these countries regarding energy supply and environmental issues in the short–medium term in order to search for the appropriate policies that Chinese authorities must follow to achieve sustainable economic growth in the forthcoming years.

The remainder of this chapter is organized as follows. Section 2 reviews the nexus between energy consumption and economic growth.

Section 3 describes the characteristics of the energy sectors: energy dependency, consumption and Carbon Dioxide (CO_2) emissions; and current energy policies. Section 4 provides an international outlook on expected energy consumption and CO_2 emissions in forthcoming decades and section 5 concludes and suggests some recommendations for policy makers.

2 Energy use and economic growth

There is a general consensus that energy plays an important role in the production process. However, empirical results on the causal relationship between energy and growth have yielded mixed results. For example, in a survey of the electricity consumption-growth literature, Payne (2010b) finds that for the 74 countries studied, 31.15 per cent supports the neutrality hypothesis, that is the absence of Granger causality between electricity consumption and economic growth. In 27.87 per cent of the countries studied, a unidirectional Granger causality from economic growth to electricity consumption is found. A unidirectional Granger causality from electricity consumption and economic growth is also found in 22.95 per cent of the surveyed countries. Therefore, for 60 per cent of the countries surveyed, the studies did not find a causal relationship from electricity consumption to economic growth. This suggests that conservation policies to reduce or constraint the consumption of electricity would not have an impact on economic growth for at least 60 per cent of the countries surveyed (Payne, 2010b).

The mixed empirical evidence is also found in China (Yuan et al., 2008; Yuan et al., 2007; Chen et al., 2007 and Shiu and Lam 2004). Most of these studies use a small sample (30–40 observations) and implement a bivariate error correction model (energy consumption and GDP), which can lead to spurious correlations and erroneous conclusions through omitted variables and small sample problems. In this section, we do not focus on the causal relationship between energy consumption and economic growth. We instead present a descriptive analysis of the current and past situation of the Chinese energy sector relative to the main developing economies.

We start our analysis by comparing the GDP per capita (constant 2000 US$) and the Energy use per capita (kg of oil equivalent per capita) of China with respect to the main developing economies: Argentina, Brazil, Chile, Colombia, India, Indonesia, Malaysia, Mexico, Peru, Poland, Russian Federation, Thailand, Turkey and Venezuela. We select these economies because the composition of their energy sector is very different but they share positive economic growth during the last decades.

China shows more rapid growth in real GDP than in energy consumption. Its real GDP per capita grew on average, by about 8.19 per cent between 1980 and 1989, while energy use per capita grew by 1.6 per cent during the same decade. Between 2000 and 2009, real GDP continued to grow, on average, by 8.70 per cent, while energy use grew by about 7.05 per cent. We observe the same pattern in most of the developing economies, although the GDP per capita growth in China was significantly much higher than in the other developing countries during the whole period, between 1980 and 2010.

The gap between the GDP per capita growth and the energy use per capita growth in the South American developing economies is higher than in the non-OECD Asian economies. This may be a consequence of the different structure of their economies. Figure 1.2 shows the agriculture, industrial and service value added as a percentage of the GDP.

The industry share of GDP has declined in most of the South American economies except Chile, where the industry share is almost flat during the whole period. The industry share in China has also remained flat during the period and it represents around 50 per cent of GDP, the agriculture share has significantly decreased, while the service sector is becoming more and more important in the Chinese economy. Industry production is the most important sector in the developing Asian countries, which is more intensive in energy than services, the main sector in the South American economies. For example, manufacture-production represents 32 per cent of the Chinese GDP and 34 per cent of Thailand's GDP while it only represents 12 per cent of Chile's GDP or 21 per cent of the Argentina's GDP, Argentina being the South American economy with the highest industry share. China has the considerable advantage of being able to produce many manufacturing goods because of its low cost of labour. This has facilitated a relocation of manufacturing production to China and other Asian economies leading to a significant increase in energy demand and consequently in CO_2 emissions. We suggest that the Chinese government should tax its chemical and manufacturing production to internalize the costs of the damage caused by production, burning of fossil fuels and water pollution by those industries, which costs are now paid by all the inhabitants of China.

In the next section, we analyse the energy sector of these economies and their linkages with the GDP composition described above.

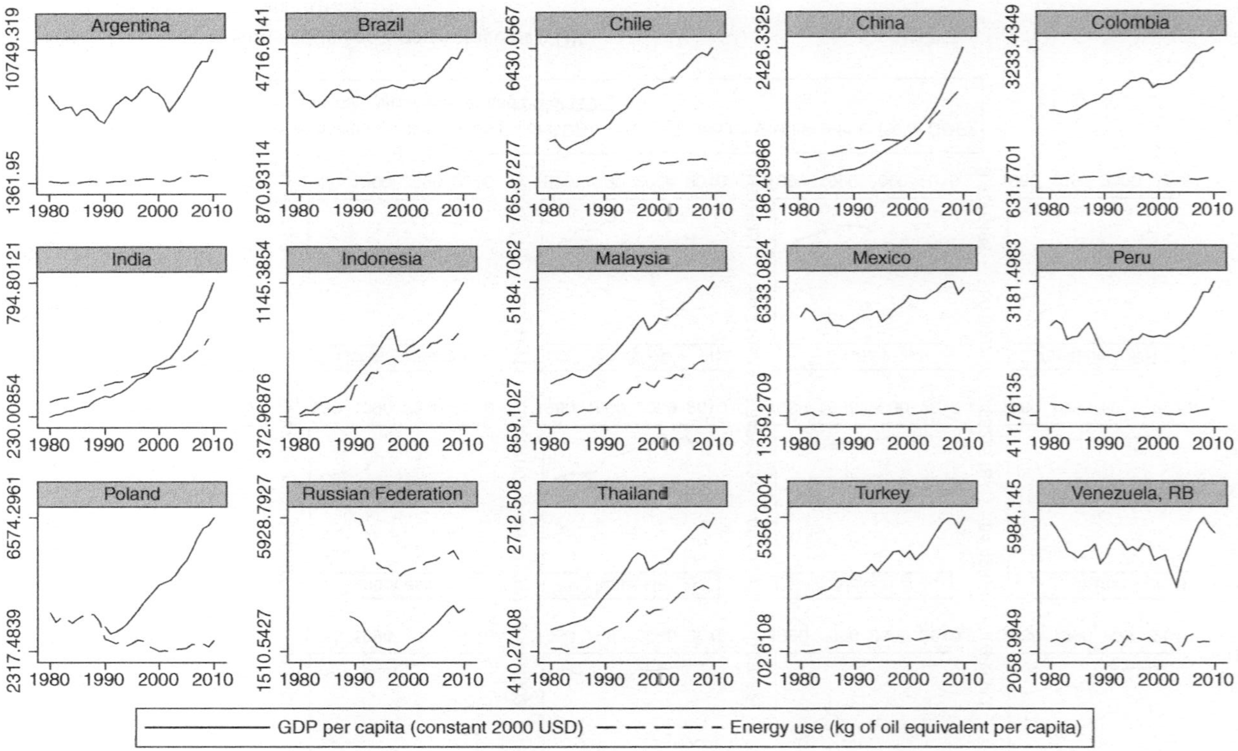

Figure 1.1 Energy use and GDP (per capita)

Source: The World Bank Data, 2012.

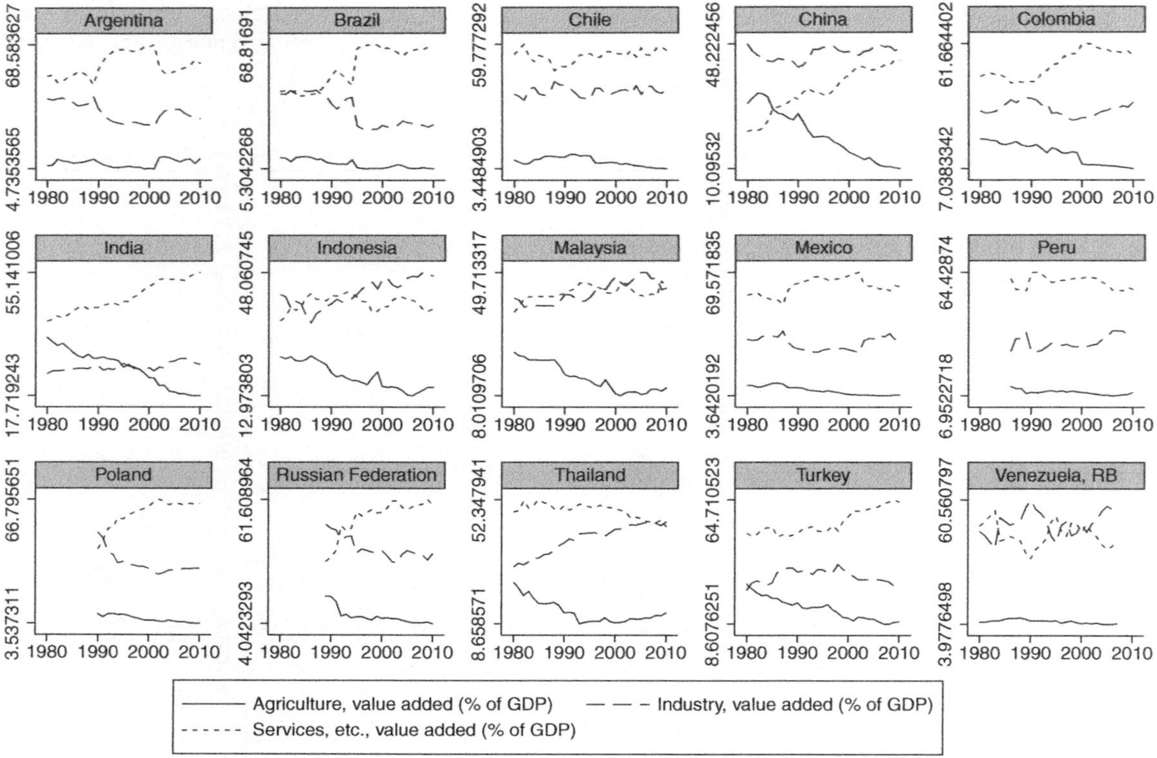

Figure 1.2 Sectors value added as a percentage of GDP

Source: The World Bank Data, 2012.

3 Energy sector characteristics

This section describes the energy sectors of the countries considered in this study. We first state in Table 1.1 some indicators of the size, the volume of energy consumption and CO_2 emissions and the degree of development of each country.

China is the world's most populous country: 22 per cent of total world population in 2009 resided in China. The consumption of energy and CO_2 emissions has increased markedly over the last decades, not only in absolute but also in per capita terms. In other developing countries with high populations, like India and Indonesia, the consumption of energy and CO_2 emissions is comparatively very low, which is partly explained in both cases by the relatively low percentage of people who have access to electricity (two-thirds against almost all the population for the rest of the countries). Furthermore, the Indian industrial sector is not as energy-intensive as the Chinese one, in which petrochemical and iron and steel production consumes more than half of the energy consumed by the industrial sector.

In the following sections we examine the degree of energy dependency, the consumption of energy disaggregated by energy source, and

Table 1.1 Population, energy consumption, CO_2 emissions and GDP per capita, 2009

	Population (1,000)	**Consumption (Mtoe)**	**CO_2 emissions (Mt) (2008)**	**GDP per capita (in constant 2000 US$)**
Argentina	40,062	74.2	192.4	9,933.23
Brazil	193,246	240.2	393.2	4,424.76
Chile	16,956	28.8	73.1	6,117.11
China	1,331,380	2,257.1	7,031.9	2,208.40
Colombia	45,654	31.8	67.7	3,152.68
India	1,207,740	675.8	1,742.7	735.63
Indonesia	237,414	202.0	406.0	1,089.72
Malaysia	27,949	66.8	208.3	4,914.91
Mexico	112,033	174.6	475.8	5,857.71
Peru	28,765	15.8	40.5	2,955.19
Poland	38,151	94.0	316.1	6,332.96
Russia	141,910	646.9	1,708.7	2,806.07
Thailand	68,706	103.3	285.7	2,531.23
Turkey	71,846	97.7	283.91	4,968.58
Venezuela	28,384	66.9	169.5	5,700.88

Source: The World Bank Data, 2012.

the volume of CO_2 emissions across the different countries over the period 1980 to 2010.

3.1 Energy dependency

Being a net energy importer or exporter economy is subject to different interpretations. On the one hand it can be said that a net importer economy is highly subject to external shocks. For example, the conflicts in the Middle East and North Africa in 2011 and 2012 shrunk the supply of crude oil, increasing the energy costs of many countries. On the other hand an alternative view is that in countries with scarce energy resources, energy independence is prohibitively costly and hence it is optimal for them to be a net importer.

For net energy exporter countries, not all the implications are necessarily good. These countries usually have deficiencies in human rights and economic development, as well as environmental problems derived from their additional energy production to be sold to other economies. In the case of China, its recent (1993) shift to being a net energy importer economy becomes of great importance, as the requirements of energy security strongly influence Chinese foreign relations (see Wu and Storey, 2008).

We measure energy dependency by net energy imports, which are estimated as energy use less production as a percentage of energy use. Figure 1.3 shows China as a net importer of energy, but the share is low compared to other countries like Turkey (great importer of Russian oil), Chile (that imports the bulk of its energy needs, specially Argentine natural gas) or Thailand (a net importer of coal and natural gas). On the other side, net exporters include countries like Colombia (China is, after the US, the second top destination for Colombia's oil exports), Venezuela (that is diversifying its crude oil destinations away from US to the benefit of, among others, China), Russia (with large coal, oil and natural gas reserves, it is a net exporter of all these sources) or Indonesia (leading exporter of natural gas and coal, it is the major source of this source Chinese imports).[2]

In the last twenty years, the increasing demand has turned China into being a net importer of coal, natural gas and oil, resulting in an economy that depends on imported sources for nearly eight per cent of its energy. The Chinese dependency is significantly lower than the Indian (25 per cent) and higher than the Brazilian (4 per cent). India is an interesting case of study for its similarities to China. This country is facing an increasing demand of energy. Despite its high reserves of coal, it had to import this source from countries like Indonesia and this pattern seems

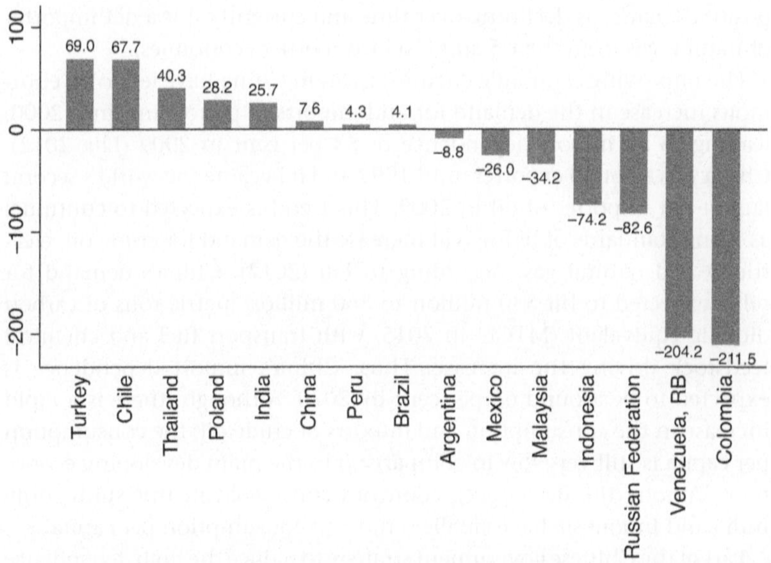

Figure 1.3 Net energy imports: energy use less production (percentage of energy use), 2009

Source: The World Bank Data, 2012.

to consolidate through the years (Parikh and Parikh, 2011). Besides, it has become a net importer of natural gas from 2004 and is an increasingly oil-dependent country, whose imports come mainly from the Middle East. For this reason, to satisfy natural gas import demand, the Indian government has considered a number of schemes including pipelines with neighbours, (Iran, Pakistan, Turkmenistan and Afghanistan) imports from Myanmar or liquefied natural gas (LNG) from Qatar.

Brazil has a different framework. To face the rise in energy demand, it has made efforts in increasing its energy production in ethanol and oil, so the volume of exports and imports in these liquids barely differ. Recent discoveries of large pre-salt oil deposits will transform Brazil into one of the largest oil producers in the world, becoming a net oil exporter in the short term, according to US Energy Information Administration (EIA) projections (2011). Additionally, these discoveries could affect Brazil's natural gas imports that come especially from Bolivia, since they will contain substantial reserves not only in oil but in natural gas as well. Regarding Mexico, it is one of the ten largest crude producers in the world and one of the largest exporters to the US. However, the positive balance is declining over time and currently it is a net importer of natural gas from the US and LNG from other economies.

The improving economic circumstances in China have led to an enormous increase in the demand for and imports of petroleum since 2000, leading to an import dependence of 53 per cent in 2009 (Liu, 2012). China was a net oil exporter until 1992 and it became the world's second largest net importer of oil in 2009. This trend is expected to continue, as rising standards of living will increase the demand for crude oil, electricity and natural gas. According to Liu (2012), China's demand for oil is expected to hit 530 million to 560 million metric tons of carbon dioxide equivalent (MTCE) in 2015, with transport fuel and chemical feedstock driving the increase. Thus, China's import dependence is expected to be around 65 per cent by 2020. Although, there is a rapid increase in the consumption and imports of crude oil, the consumption per capita is still very low in comparison to the main developing economies. Among the developing countries considered in this study, only India and Indonesia have smaller crude oil consumption per capita.

Part of the Chinese government strategy to reduce the high dependence on imports of oil consists of improving energy efficiency, diversifying import sources and increasing the investment on domestic exploration and production of crude oil. However, rising energy consumption and CO_2 emissions, as described in the next sections, demand for more ambitious efforts to achieve a sustainable economic growth in the long run.

3.2 Energy consumption

Chinese residential electricity consumption is still low in comparison to OECD countries (about one-third of the world's average level). However, among the developing countries considered (Figure 1.4), China is far from being among the lowest. The high electric power consumption in China is a consequence of the importance of the industrial sector in the Chinese economy (50 per cent of the GDP) and in particular of the energy-intense industries, such as petrochemical and iron and steel production. In addition, in some Asian developing countries, such as Thailand, India and China, an inefficient problem of wasteful electricity usage has been found (Shiu and Lam (2004) and Ghosh (2002)).

Currently, a large proportion of the population in developing countries lives in rural regions and still has no access to electricity. For example, in China low capital investment in rural areas, as well as high tariffs and fees, has been a constraint on growth of electricity consumption (Shiu and Lam, 2004). However, the expected increase in income and standards of life will increase the demand for home appliances,

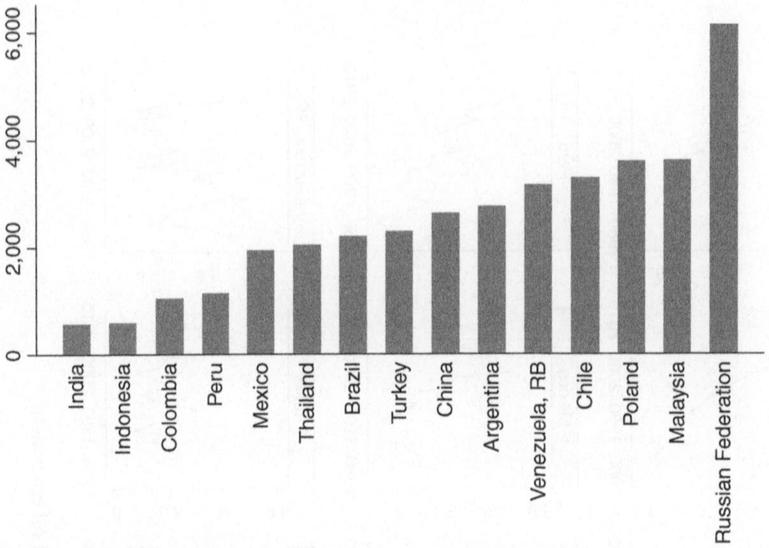

Figure 1.4 Electric power consumption (kWh per capita)
Source: The World Bank, 2012.

electronic devices and other durable goods, leading to a strong growth in electricity demand in these developing economies. According to the EIA (2012), electricity generation is expected to increase by an average annual rate of 3.3 per cent in the non-OECD economies. In contrast, the expected growth in the OECD economies is slower, around 1.2 per cent per year from 2008 to 2035.

The energy intensity, measured by the GDP per unit of energy use (constant 2005 purchasing power parity (PPP) $ per kg of oil equivalent), has declined in most of the developing countries during the last decade.[3]

Among the main developing economies, the average of GDP per unit of energy use for China during the period 1990–2009 is 2.72, the second lowest after Russia with 2.22 GDP per unit of energy use. Although, the energy intensity is much higher in China than in other developing countries, such as Peru or Colombia, there has been an important decrease of this indicator in China across the studied period. During the 1980s the average GDP per unit of energy use was around 1.17, that is to say, one kilogram of oil produced around 1.17 GDP units (in 2005 PPP $). This average increased a lot during the decade of 2000–09, reaching

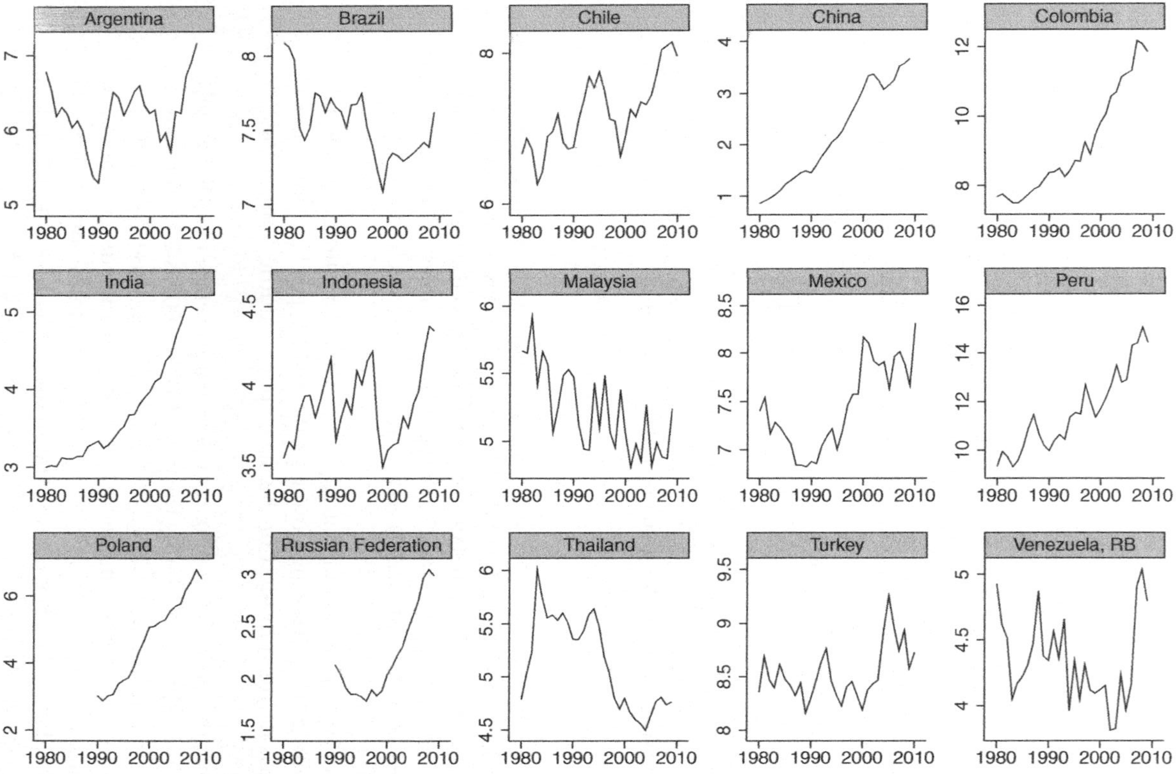

Figure 1.5 GDP per unit of energy use (constant 2005 PPP $ per kg of oil equivalent)

Source: The World Bank Data, 2012.

3.33, meaning that during this decade one kilogram of oil produced on average around 3.33 GDP units (in 2005 PPP $). Therefore, the economy of China is becoming less energy-intensive across time, but the average energy intensity is still quite high relative to the main developing economies. The decline in energy intensity is also observed in Russia, a net energy exporter country affected by severe climate conditions.

Being a net energy importer at this moment, the high energy intensity of China shows a low efficient energy usage compared to other clear net energy exporter economies like Colombia or Venezuela, which implies that there is much potential for improvements in efficiency. This inefficient energy usage is justified by the enormous relevance of the energy-intensive industries like petrochemical, steel, iron and textile. These kind of firms have been the target of Chinese government efforts to lower energy intensity and pollutant emissions and they are expected to reduce the amount of energy needed to produce a unit of gross domestic product by an average of 16 per cent in the context of the China's 12th Five-Year Plan (12th FYP), from 2011–2015 (Legget et al., 2008).

But these goals will only be achieved if traditional Chinese reliance on fossil fuels diminishes. As can be observed in Figure 1.6, the use of these

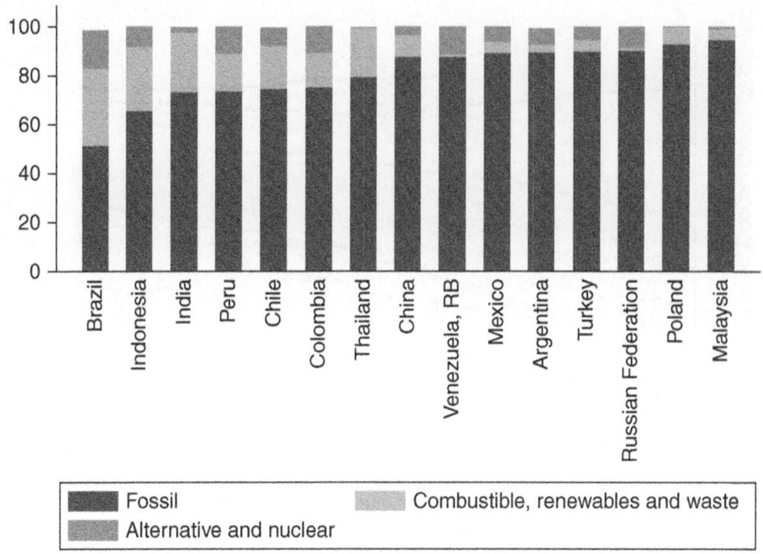

Figure 1.6 Energy consumption from different sources, 2009
Source: The World Bank Data, 2012.

energy sources, which are the most polluting ones, is much more prevalent than in other big economies, like Brazil or India where the share of total energy use of renewable energy sources is relatively high (the same happens with Chile, Indonesia, Peru and Thailand), something that is not seen in China.

In addition, as we can see in Figure 1.7, the consumption of fossil fuels exhibited a positive trend during the last 30 years (in relative and absolute terms). This increase on the consumption of fossil fuels partially explains the increasing CO_2 emissions experienced by China, as we explain in section 3.3.

In this figure we observe how the tendency of the Chinese economy is to converge to the level of fossil fuel energy consumption of Russia and Mexico. However, it is important to remember that the high level observed for these latter two countries are mainly caused by natural gas and oil respectively, two sources which are less polluting than coal. A similar tendency is observed for India. Despite it not having reached Chinese levels yet, we observe a higher yearly increment in the use of this source. India is another country with similar share in fossil fuels to China, coal being the most relevant one. India possesses one of the

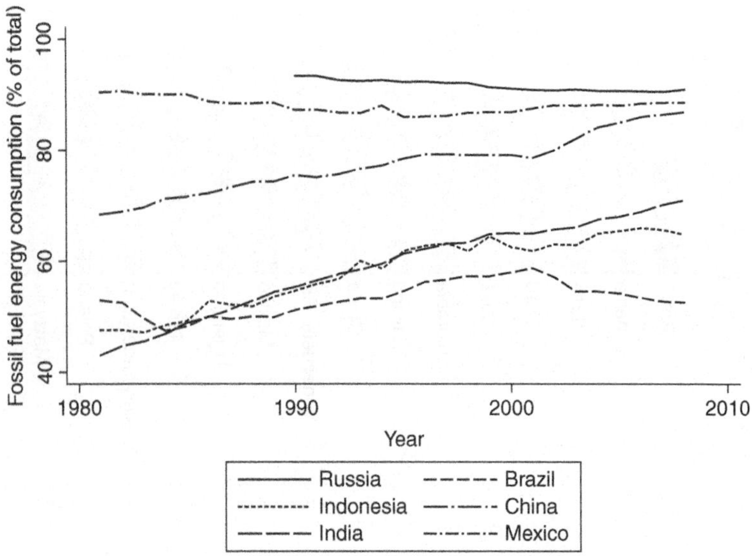

Figure 1.7 Consumption of fossil fuels in selected countries, 1980–2010
Source: The World Bank Data, 2012.

dirtiest coals in the world (Friedman and Schaffer, 2009), which makes the idea of relying in its domestic source for economic development unwise due to environmental issues. India's great potential in renewable sources like sun and wind should be seriously considered by its authorities to guarantee a sustainable economic development in the following years. Although, as said before, India is going to be a clear net energy importer in the future, this country has great potential in nuclear and solar energy, and in energy efficiency and conservation. A similar situation is faced by Indonesia, where fossils represent almost the 75 per cent of energy use (Figure 1.6), having increased at a lower rate than China and India in the last decade, but whose reserves for crude oil and natural gas are estimated to last for 23 and 52 years respectively at current production rates. However, subsidies on fossil energies and the high production cost of renewable energy sources have meant that these latter sources are not optimally used in Indonesia (Hasan et al., 2012), despite its great potential in solar, wind, micro, hydro, and biomass energies.

Finally, we observe that Brazil's reliance on fossil fuels has decreased from the beginning of this century to become one of the lowest proportions of fossil fuels among the countries considered in this study. The lower demand for energy in Brazilian case has allowed this country to have an important share in renewable sources, without the necessity of relying on fossil fuels to a great extent. This way, the Brazilian renewable energy market is one of the most important in the world, since it has abundant sources of renewable energy like wind and solar power, small hydroelectric plants, ethanol and biodiesel (Pereira et al., 2012).

Among fossil fuels, coal is the most polluting and is the main source of energy in China. Figure 1.8 shows the share of coal, natural gas and oil in fossil fuels consumption for the developing countries. Derived from the fact that China is the third-largest holder of coal in the world (behind the United States and Russia), we observe that it is clearly also the country with the largest share of coal use: 76 per cent in 2009. For this reason, government policies aimed at reducing and improving (in environmental terms) the consumption of this energy source have increased during recent years. The Chinese 12th FYP has set a target to raise non-fossil fuel energy consumption to 11.4 per cent by 2015 and the EIA projects coal share to fall below 60 per cent by 2035. Chinese energy policies are dominated by three main themes: i) growing demand for oil and reliance on oil imports, ii) increasing the use of natural gas as a proportion of energy consumption (ten per cent in 2020) by expanding domestic reserves and importing from its neighbours via pipelines, and

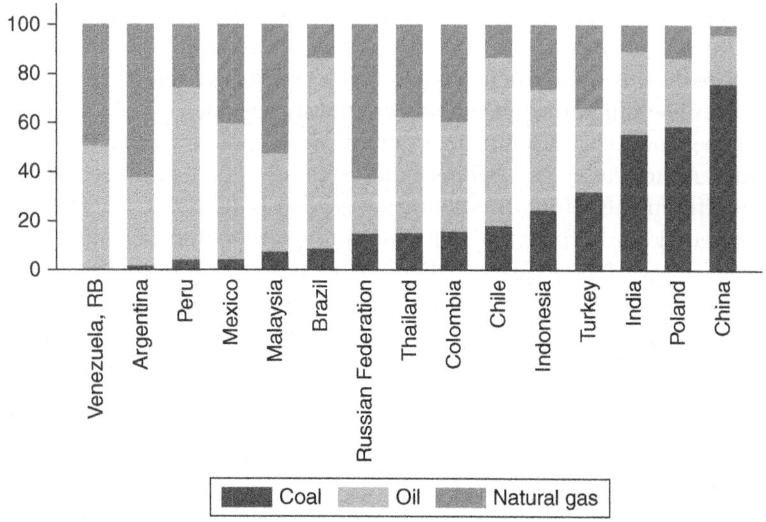

Figure 1.8 Fossil fuel decomposition, 2009

Source: The World Bank Data, 2012.

iii) controlling the growth in coal production and promoting the development of a large coal-to-liquids industry. Additionally, the Chinese government aims to generate at least 15 per cent of total energy output via renewable energy sources by 2020. However, nuclear energy development has been somewhat interrupted due to the Fukushima accident (see Section 4).

3.3 Carbon dioxide emissions

Per capita CO_2 emissions stemming from the burning of fossil fuels and the manufacture of cement show (Figure 1.9) the pollution intensity of the energy sector of a country. These CO_2 emissions by human activities contribute to an excess of greenhouse gases, resulting in an increase of the Earth's temperature and subsequent environmental negative effects.[4] China is among the most polluting developing countries, even in per capita terms. This is a consequence of the facts stated in Section 3.2: the importance of fossil fuels, in particular coal and oil shale, in the Chinese economy.

According to this measure, Russia is the most polluting developing economy, caused by the volume of exported energy sources and its severe climate conditions. Venezuela's CO_2 emissions are also very high

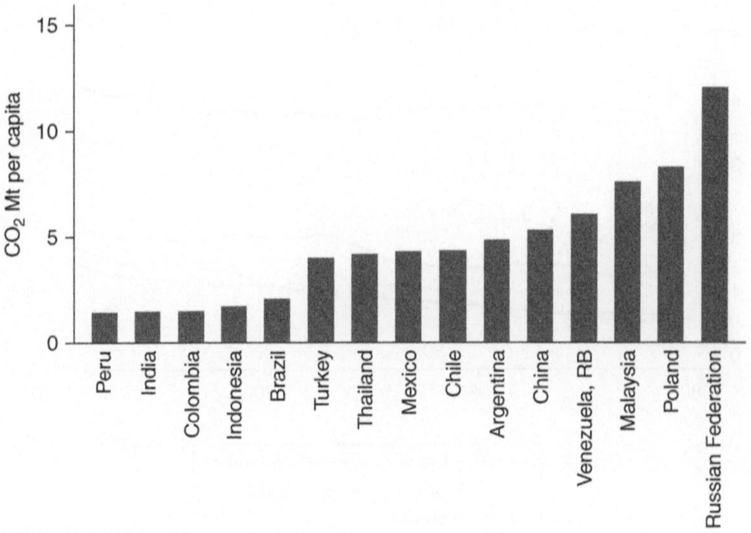

Figure 1.9 CO_2 emissions per capita, 2009
Source: The World Bank Data, 2012.

relative to its GDP. This South American country contains some of the largest oil and natural gas reserves in the world and it was the world's eighth-largest net oil exporter in 2010, which explains its intensive oil and gas production and the high level of CO_2 emissions.

It is interesting to note the data for India and Brazil, both sensibly lower than those observed in the case of China. If we look at the evolution of CO_2 per capita emissions in the last years (Figure 1.10), we realize that the last decade has been dramatic for China.

While other economies like India or Brazil have experienced a more gradual increase in this indicator, China has almost doubled its per capita emissions. Considering the total population and the volume of emissions in absolute terms, it is clear that an appropriate policy aimed to alleviate this problem is needed.

Figure 1.11 shows the CO_2 emissions per primary energy unit of consumption in 2009, where China appears as the most CO_2-intensive, closely followed by Poland, the most intensive among EU member states. Indonesia and Brazil are the least CO_2-intensive. This fact is not surprising given the large share of renewable energy sources observed in these two countries (see Figure 1.6). In 2009, 83 per cent of the total electricity production in Brazil was from hydroelectric sources.

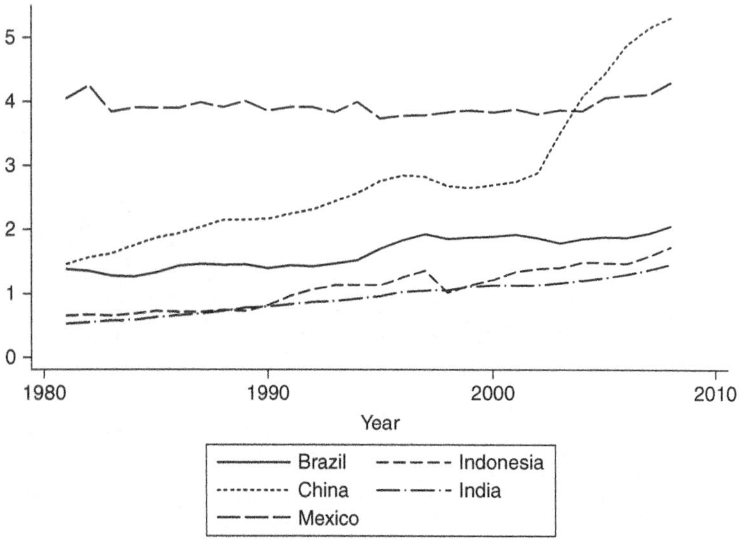

Figure 1.10 CO_2 emissions (metric tons per capita)
Source: The World Bank Data, 2012.

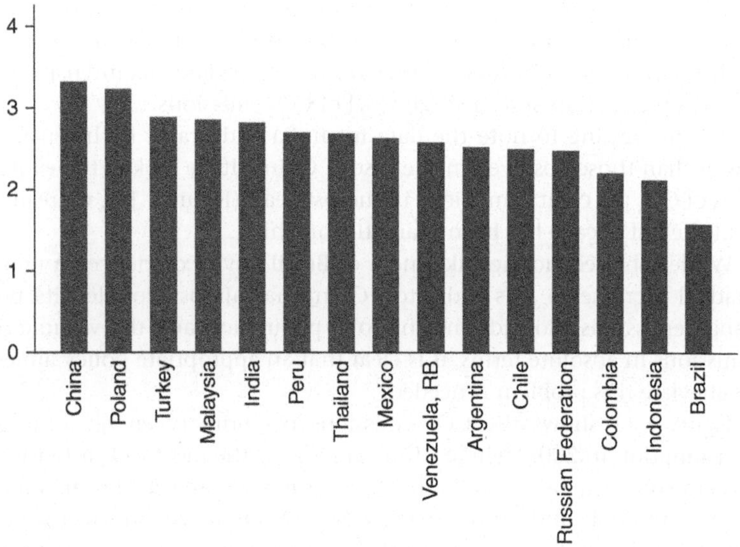

Figure 1.11 CO_2 emissions (kt) per energy use (kt of oil equivalent)
Source: The World Bank Data, 2012.

To understand the differences between the CO_2 emissions across countries, we also consider CO_2 emissions by sectors: manufactures, residential consumption, transport, electricity and heat, and others. Manufactures' CO_2 emissions contain the emissions from combustion of fuels in industry. Manufacturing industries and construction also includes emissions from coke inputs into blast furnaces. Residential's CO_2 emissions contain all emissions from fuel combustion in households; transport's CO_2 emissions are those from the combustion of fuel for all transport activity, regardless of the sector, except for international marine bunker and international aviation. Electricity and heat's CO_2 emissions are the sum of main activity producer electricity and heat, unallocated auto-producers and other energy industries.[5] CO_2 emissions from other sectors contain the emissions from commercial or institutional activities, residential, agriculture or forestry, fishing and other emissions not specified in the above categories.

We plot the evolution of CO_2 emissions from 1980 to 2009 across the different developing countries, 1980 being the reference base period (Figure 1.12a).[6] The rate of growth of electricity CO_2 emissions has increased considerably across the Asian developing countries, especially in China, where the electricity and heat emissions are more than double the reference base period in relative terms, and in 2008 represented more than 50 per cent of the total CO_2 emissions in the country (Figure 1.12b). Over the period 1980 to 2009, around 70–80 per cent of the electricity consumption was for industrial production (Shiu and Lam, 2004). If we add the electricity consumption for industrial production to the manufacture emissions, the CO_2 emissions from the industrial sector represented around 70 per cent of the total CO_2 emissions in China.

This growth is led by the energy-intensive industries, such as petrochemicals, iron and steel and non-metallic minerals, which consumed most of the energy used in the industrial sector. Petrochemical production has expanded rapidly through domestic firms such as Sinopec and PetroChina and international investment from multinational firms, such as ExxonMobil (EIA, 2012b). These companies should focus on reducing energy consumption, which represents an important proportion of their production costs, by improving the electricity efficiency of electrical equipment. The government's long-term policies should focus on improving the efficiency of public and private intensive industries (e.g. promoting recycling of materials and fuel inputs), developing new sources of energy such as natural gas and renewable energies like hydropower reserves. This trend in electricity and heat CO_2 emissions is also present in Brazil, India, Indonesia, Malaysia, Mexico and Turkey. On the

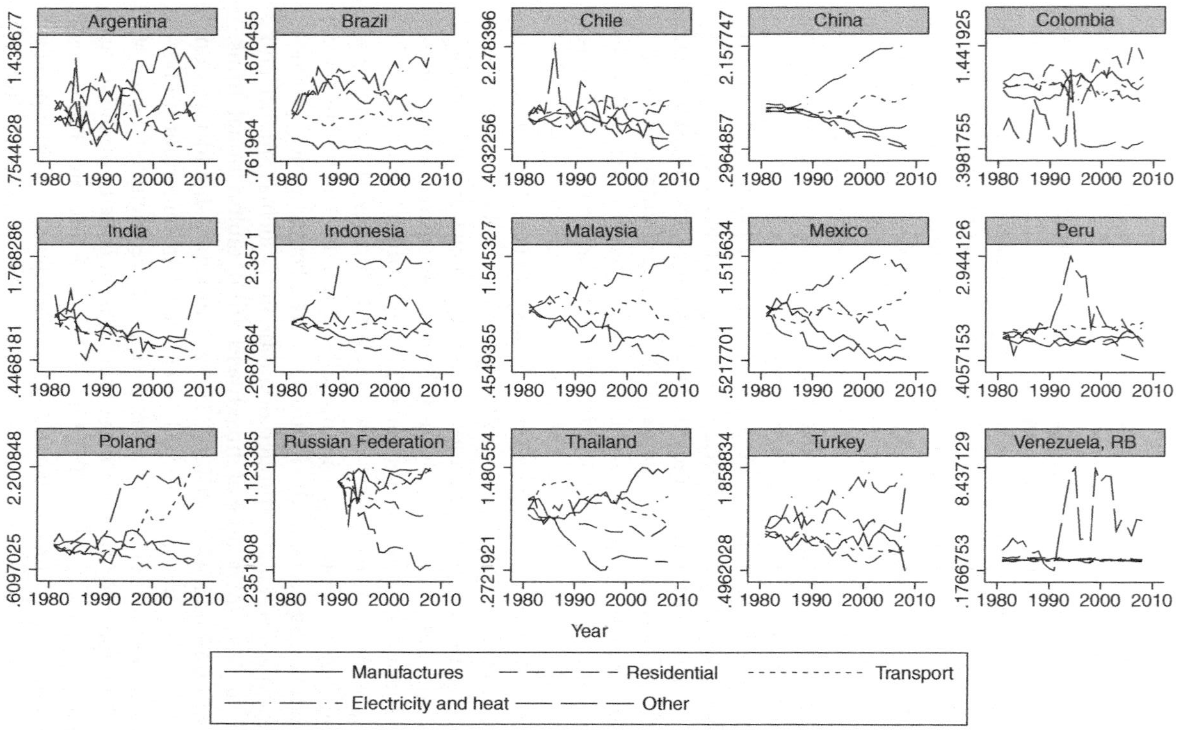

Figure 1.12a Evolution of CO_2 emissions by sector (reference year: 1980)

Source: The World Bank Data, 2012.

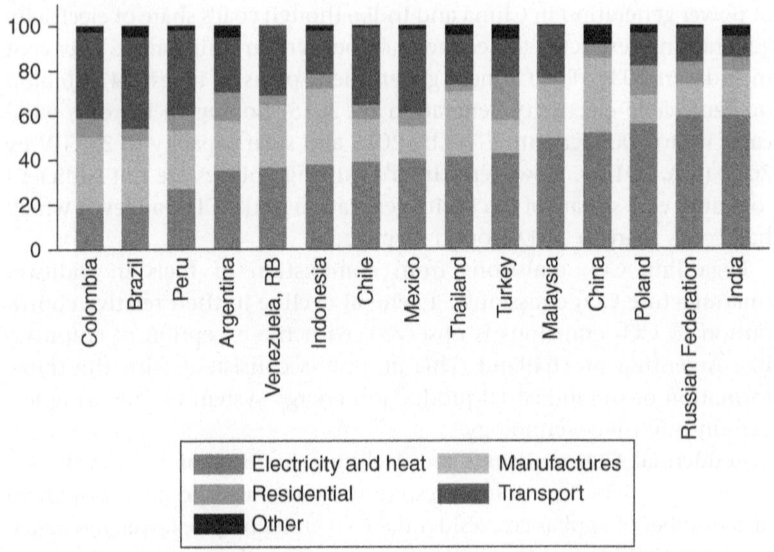

Figure 1.12b CO_2 emissions by sector, 2008

Source: The World Bank Data, 2012.

other hand, in South American developing economies (except Brazil) the electricity and heat emissions has remained constant and even decline in some countries like Colombia and Argentina. As a result of the evolution described, the current (2009) situation of CO_2 emissions by sector is shown in Figure 1.12b.

These differences between South American and Asian economies are explained by the different sources of electricity production. In 2009, the main source of electricity production in most of the South American economies was hydroelectric. For example, 72 per cent of the electricity produced in Colombia is from hydroelectric sources, 42 per cent in Chile (an economy where the industrial sector share is around 38 per cent of the total GDP). This source is significantly less polluting than coal, which is the primary source of electricity production in Asian countries. In China 79 per cent of total electricity production was from coal in 2009, 69 per cent in India, 41 per cent in Indonesia. China was the world's largest producer of hydroelectric power in 2010 (EIA, 2012b). However, this source of energy only represented 17 per cent of the total electricity production. The reference case of EIA's 2011 edition of the International Energy Outlook projected that coal would remain the predominant source of power generation in China and India, though coal's share of electricity generation is expected to decline to 66 per cent in China and 51 per cent in India in 2035. The Chinese government plans to invest $473 billion on renewable electricity generation by 2015, hoping to increase wind capacity to 100 gigawatt (GW) by 2015 and solar capacity to 25 GW by 2020 (EIA, 2011a). However, China's existing policies are not sufficient to reduce coal's share of electricity generation to the Chilean level, which had coal's share in 2009 around 24 per cent.

Regarding CO_2 emissions from combustion of fuels in industry (manufacture CO_2 emissions), a general decline in their relative contribution to CO_2 emissions is observed, with the exception of countries like Argentina or Thailand. This decline is consistent with the transformation of the industrial production energy system to one using less carbon-intensive technology.

Residential CO_2 emissions are declining in most of the developing economies, including China. Despite the continued population growth and number of appliances, residential CO_2 emissions are lower and lower, implying that improved energy efficiency offsets the growth in demand.

Transportation CO_2 emissions have substantially increased during the period 2000–09 in China, Russia, Mexico and Poland. The increasing standards of life in these economies have increased the demand for private vehicles and air transportation. Moreover, the total demand for transport linked to the industrial sector is increasing due to the rapid economic growth in these economies, especially in China. As a consequence, the demand for oil rose substantially during this period (see Section 3.1). This source of energy leads to high levels of air pollution, affecting not only the global warming but also health. Thus, governments should enhance environmentally friendly and energy-efficient means of transport (e.g. electrification of rail system and public transport, water transport) to cope the growing transport demand and reduce the oil dependency of their economies. For example, in 2005 the main energy carriers of the transport sector in China are gasoline (33 per cent), diesel (52 per cent), fuel-oil (8.7 per cent), kerosene (5.6 per cent) and electricity (1.1 per cent) (Institute for Energy and Environmental Research Heidelberg, 2008).

4 Perspectives

According to EIA (2012) projections, world energy consumption will increase by 47 per cent from 2010 through 2035. This substantial increase will be led by non-OECD economies, especially China and India.[7] In other developing economies from Europe and Asia, like Russia, improvements in energy efficiency will lower the increase in energy consumption.

In terms of sources, renewables seem to be the world's fastest-growing ones in response to international environmental concerns. Fuels present asymmetric trends: while oil will experience slow growth due to its implications for GHG emissions and expected high prices, coal and natural gas consumption will grow by 50 per cent through the period 2010–35. In the case of coal, the desirable reduction in emissions will be offset by the fact that two large economies, India and China, account for big reserves of this source, which is and will be essential in the high economic growth of these two economies. In the case of natural gas, its lower carbon intensity has led the economies to choose this source rather than coal and oil to fulfil environmental commitments. Finally, with respect to nuclear energy, a significant increase in its use by developing countries is expected. Contrary to OECD economies which, after the Fukushima nuclear power plant damage caused by an earthquake in Japan in 2011, have opted to reduce nuclear energy use, developing economies still plan to expand their nuclear power to 2035, this is the case with China, India and Russia, whose nuclear power capacity will increase by 109, 41 and 28 gigawatts (GW) respectively from 2010 to 2035.

Rühl et al. (2012) rely on historical processes of industrialization when they analyse the evolution of energy intensity to conclude that, in the next twenty years, the predicted high growth in per capita income will not necessarily be constrained by resource availability thanks to improvements in energy efficiency. Based on *British Petroleum's Energy Outlook 2030* (British Petroleum, 2012) these authors provide past and future trends of energy consumption and energy intensity for several countries, as we can see in Table 1.2 and Table 1.3.[8]

Table 1.2 Energy consumption (Million Tonnes of Oil Equivalent), 1990–2030

Year	US	Brazil	Russia	China	India	World
1990	1968	124	862	681	181	8109
1995	2122	153	664	913	236	8578
2000	2314	185	620	1038	296	9382
2005	2351	207	657	1691	364	10801
2010	2286	254	691	2432	524	12002
2015	2258	290	731	3118	676	13360
2020	2270	333	766	3688	871	14627
2025	2263	371	801	4091	1048	15635
2030	2241	407	838	4431	1262	16632

Source: Rühl et al., 2012.

Table 1.3 Energy intensity (Tonnes of Oil Equivalent/Million $2010 PPP), 1990–2030

Year	US	Brazil	Russia	China	India	World
1990	222	103	374	298	142	197
1995	213	111	485	248	151	187
2000	191	123	439	229	147	174
2005	170	119	339	227	119	165
2010	158	116	298	204	117	155
2015	139	109	260	175	107	142
2020	124	104	228	151	102	129
2025	109	97	204	128	94	115
2030	97	92	185	109	88	103

Source: Rühl et al., 2012.

These authors study the energy path followed by OECD economies to assess the perspectives of the non-OECD ones. In this way, taking into account various factors like GDP forecasts, figures for the trade of coal, natural gas and crude oil, population growth rates, and so on, they estimate an annual 3.0 per cent increase in energy consumption in China for the period 2010–30, while energy intensity is estimated to decline by 3.1 per cent per annum in the same period of time. This declining path for energy intensity is not only predicted for the Chinese economy, but to a lesser extent, for the rest of the countries considered: U.S. (2.4 per cent), Brazil (1.2 per cent), Russia (2.4 per cent) and India (1.4 per cent). Regarding total energy consumption, according to these authors, China will experience an annual increase of 3.0 per cent, only surpassed by India (4.5 per cent), and larger than Brazil (2.4 per cent), Russia (1.0 per cent) and the US, but this will decrease by 0.1 per cent per annum in the period 2010–30.

Climate change and carbon output is one of the special concerns of the international community. Broadly speaking, non-OECD economies will account for the majority of carbon emissions by 2035, when these countries will double the OECD's ones. China will experience one of the largest increases in CO_2 emissions from 2008 to 2035 (2.5 per cent per annum), similar to the predictions for Brazil (2.8 per cent) or India (2.7 per cent) and far from the ones obtained for Russia (0.2 per cent) or Mexico/Chile (1.7 per cent). Emissions increases in Asian economies are mainly due to coal, although emissions from liquids and natural gas are not negligible. In the case of Russia, its small increase in this period is explained by the expected decline in population and the higher reliance on nuclear energy to meet the future demand.

Under the expected increase in energy consumption and CO_2 emissions, how can governments mitigate GHG emissions to achieve sustainable economic growth? The next section provides a review of existing and proposed policies to reduce the energy intensity in the electricity, transportation, building and commercial and industrial sectors of China, India, Brazil and Mexico.

4.1 Potential mitigation of GHG emissions

Erickson et al. (2009) provide another outlook on GHG emissions by 2030, considering different baseline emissions scenarios for six different countries: China, India, Brazil, Mexico, South Korea, and South Africa. Using international energy, population and economic activity data from the International Energy Agency, United Nations, World Energy Council, and EIA, they estimate that baseline energy sector GHG emissions from these six countries would represent over 40 per cent of global emissions. The authors also provide a review of those studies aimed at forecasting the potential mitigation of GHG emissions by 2030. Studies about the potential mitigation of GHG in China include the following: Tsinghua (2006), Nauclér and Enkvist (2009), Vattenfall (2007) and the United Nations Framework Convention on Climate Change (2007).[9] Table 1.4 shows the minimum and maximum estimated mitigation potential, metric tons carbon dioxide equivalent (MTCE) per year, in 2030 across different sectors.

The estimated mitigation potential in 2030 differs significantly across the studies, as the methodology and underlying assumptions are not always transparent and consistent (Erickson et al., 2009).[10] Among the four developing countries, China is the one with the highest potential to mitigate GHG emissions by 2030. Most of the estimated potential mitigation in China comes from the electricity sector, with an estimated mitigation between 680 to 2800 MTCE per year. The Chinese government has the responsibility to implement and enforce energy policies to achieve such potential reductions of energy intensity in the

Table 1.4 Estimated mitigation potential in 2030, Met per year

Sector	China	India	Brazil	Mexico
Electricity	680–2800	400–410	7–8	95–140
Transportation	300–600	100–410	40–69	45–76
Building & Appliances	80–1100	0–150	4–50	3–35
Industry	300–1200	150–170	15–99	13–77

Source: Erickson et al., 2009.

electricity sector. The existing and proposed policies can be summarized as follows: renovation of existing technology in electric plants, e.g. "eliminating backward production capacity" and promoting "clean coal" (People's Republic of China, 2008), proposed research and development (R&D) to develop technology to capture carbon dioxide at power plants and storage in long-term reservoirs (Tsinghua, 2006), quadrupling nuclear production capacity by 2020 (Pew Center on Global Climate Change, 2007), developing hydroelectric plants and increasing the share in primary energy of renewables from seven per cent to 15 per cent by 2020. The Chinese government is also implementing policies to mitigate GHG emissions in the transportation sector. For example, tightening fuel economy standards to improve combustion engine efficiency, current taxes based on engine size, proposed fuel tax, and conversion of public bus transport to compressed natural gas, liquefied petroleum gas or biodiesel. These policies could help to mitigate the GHG emissions between 300 to 600 MTCE per year in this sector. There are also existing policies to reduce energy intensity in the building and commercial sector. The Chinese government target, under the 11th FYP, is to reduce the GHG emissions by 100 MTCE, through strengthening enforcement of buildings' energy standards, introducing appliance labelling and standards, reform of heat supply systems and introducing renewable energy (Price et al., 2011). The most ambitious estimated mitigation in the building and commercial sector comes from Nauclér and Enkvist (2009), who have estimated that the potential reduction of energy intensity in this sector could lead to a mitigation of GHG of around 1100 MTCE per year. According to Nauclér and Enkvist (2009), this reduction is possible if some policies are implemented to improve lighting and heating efficiency, enforce current energy efficiency building codes and retrofit existing buildings. Potential reduction in energy intensity can also be achieved in the industry sector through the closure of older and less efficient plants. For example, the *Comprehensive Working Plan of Energy Conservation and Emission Reduction* announced by China's State Council in 2007 aims at accelerating the closure of small plants and outdated capacity in several industries such as iron, steel, coal, pulp and paper. The State Council expects to save from this policy around 118 MTCE (Price et al., 2011). Nauclér and Enkvist's (2009) predictions are more optimistic, since they estimate a mitigation of GHG emissions in the industry sector by 1200 MTCE per year if his proposed policies are implemented. Among his suggestions, we emphasize the switch to natural gas from coal in the chemical industry, the increased use of combined cycle power plants in the steel industry and the capture and storage of GHG emissions in steel, cement and chemical sectors.

Overall if the above existing and proposed policies are enforced and implemented by the Chinese government, the estimated mitigation in total is around 1360–5700 MTCE per year. The successful implementation of these policies will depend on the efforts of the Chinese government, international collaboration and implementation costs. According to Tsinghua (2006) and Nauclér and Enkvist (2009) many of the existing or proposed policies are available at low or negative marginal cost.

In India the scope of potential mitigation of GHG emissions is not as high as in China. The total estimated mitigation is around 650–1140 MTCE per year, from which 400–10 MTCE come from the electricity sector. Most of the existing policies are focused on the transformation of the coal industry, for example government renovation and modernization of existing coal-fired plants (Kumar et al., 2009; Shukla et al., 2007), new price policy to price coal based on gross calorific value and not useful heat value. There are also some proposals to create new nuclear reactors (International Energy Agency, 2008), facilitate hydro resources from Nepal or Bhutan (Government of India, 2006) and increase R&D plus specific production and deployment goals for solar thermal and photovoltaic (Government of India, 2008). Some reduction of energy intensity is also expected in the transportation sector, through the promotion of hybrid vehicles (Government of India, 2006), price incentives for alternative-fuel vehicles and the existing biodiesel plantation pilots in 26 states (Government of India, 2008) and an urban planning and modal shift to public transport, including long-term transit plans. Most of these options are very likely to benefit the economy and society of India and at a low marginal cost, according to The Energy and Resources Institute (TERI) assessments (2006).

Brazil is one of the most active countries in terms of elaborating new policies to address climate change. The National Plan on Climate Change (2008) is aimed at reducing GHG emissions from forestry, land use and a low carbon economy. Although Brazil is, among the developing countries studied, the least polluting one (83 per cent of total electricity production is from hydropower sources), the use of gas-intensive fossil fuels has increased steadily. According to Erickson et al. (2009), the total estimated potential mitigation in Brazil is low in comparison to China, India and Mexico, between 66 and 226 MTCE per year. Some of the existing policies to reduce Brazil's GHG emissions are: current research by Petrobras and "Associação Brasileira de Engenharia e Ciências Mecânicas" on carbon capture and storage and other clean coal technologies (De Gouvello,

2010; Garg et al., 2007), third nuclear power plant under construction and existing efforts to switch coal for renewable charcoal in steel production (International Atomic Energy Agency, 2006).

Mexico is another active country in sustainable economic growth policies. The government elaborated a cap-and-trade program in 2012 to reduce emissions by 50 per cent in 2050. This would require structural reform of the energy supply, effort in many sectors (to reduce the energy intensity) and international and financial assistances. The estimates provided in Erickson et al. (2009) are not as optimistic as the government plan and range between 154 and 328 MTCE per year. Some of the policies in the studies reviewed by Erickson et al. (2009), and available at a low marginal cost, are the following: closure of inefficient plants in favour of high-efficiency natural gas-fired power plants, (La Comisión Intersecretarial de Cambio Climático, 2009; De la Torre et al., 2009), conversion of fuel-oil thermo-electrical plants into combined cycle to increase the plants' efficiency, increase the renewable capacity by 7,000 megawatt or develop sustainable public transport in cities with at least 100,000 residents. Clapp et al. (2009) also review some studies about the potential mitigation of GHG emissions in Mexico. At a price of USD 50 per ton of carbon dioxide equivalent, these studies estimated potential mitigation between 12–65 per cent below baseline emissions in 2020 in the electricity sector. In the transport sector, the mitigation potential ranges from six to 20 per cent.

The success of all the existing and proposed policies reviewed above is crucial to achieve sustainable economic growth in the long run in these economies. An extra effort is needed by government and international institutions to implement the policies and the success will depend on many factors: government commitment and efforts, social support, international cooperation, financial assistance (Taylor et al., 2008), energy supply and price of energy sources, among others.

5 Conclusions

The expected increase in energy consumption and CO_2 emission demands more ambitious agreements, involving not only developed economies but also developing countries. On December 2012, the only legally binding plan for combating global warming, Kyoto Protocol, was extended till 2020. A new global climate agreement replacing the Kyoto Protocol is expected in 2015, potentially restricting the CO_2 emissions of poor and developing countries like China. Most of the arguments to avoid the emissions cut in developing countries are related to the possible negative effects of these emissions cuts on economic growth. However, there is no agreement in the literature about the relationship between energy consumption and economic growth. Moreover, there are various studies proposing new environmental policies to achieve important reductions in CO_2 emission at low marginal costs. For example, if the Chinese government implements policies, such as renovation of existing technology in electric plants, developing hydroelectric plants and increasing the share in primary energy of renewables among others (see Section 4 for a review of these policies), the estimated mitigation in total is around 1360–5700 MTCE per year. Other developing economies like India, Mexico and Brazil could potentially reduce their emissions by 650–1140, 54–328 and 66–226 MTCE per year, respectively (Erickson et al., 2009). The successful implementation of these policies will depend on the efforts of their governments, international collaboration, future energy treatments and implementation costs.

Future energy agreements, like that expected in 2015, should take into account the different characteristics in energy consumption, sources, intensity and dependence of the different developing economies. As described in this chapter, there are important differences between the energy composition of South American and Asian economies. For example, in South American developing countries, most of the electricity production is from hydroelectric power while in Asian developing economies the main source of energy is the most polluting one, coal. The international community plays an important role in restructuring the energy sector of China, from a coal-intensive sector to a more renewable one. In the last agreement of December 2012, the main developed economies promised to mobilize USD 100 billion a year for poor nations to adapt to climate change. China, as the word largest emitter of CO_2 and largest producer of manufactures should be the priority of the international community.

Notes

1. KP's Annex I countries, that is, those that must reduce emissions by 5.2 per cent below 1990 levels for the period 2008–12, represent just 15 per cent of global emissions.
2. See US Energy Information Administration (EIA) (2012b) for a detailed description of the energy sector of these economies.
3. Energy intensity is measured as GDP per unit of energy use. Therefore, an increase on this measure will imply a decrease on the energy intensity.
4. There exist additional sources (e.g. deforestation) and gasses (e.g. methane) that contribute to GHG emissions, but they are not considered in this chapter.

5. See Appendix A for more details about the CO_2 emissions data.
6. Regardless of the importance of each sector in the different countries, the lines depart from the same point (1.0) at the base period (1980), so the evolution of the different sectors must be understood as relative to 1980 situation.
7. Among the economies considered in this study, only Mexico, Chile, Poland and Turkey are current OECD countries.
8. Note that this definition of energy intensity used by Rühl et al. (2012) must be interpreted in the opposite direction than the one used in Section 3: the lower the indicator, the lower the energy intensity is.
9. The studies related to Indian potential mitigation of GHG are: The Energy and Resources Institute (TERI) (2006), United Nations Framework Convention on Climate Change (2007) and Tanaka (2008). For Brazil: Centro Clima of the Federal University of Rio de Janeiro (Garg et al., 2007), United Nations Framework Convention on Climate Change (2007), Tanaka (2008) and Schaeffer et al. (2009). For Mexico: Centro Mario (2008) and the United Nations Framework Convention on Climate Change (2007).
10. See Erickson et al. (2009) for a description of the methodology used to obtain these estimates.

2
The Chinese Energy-Intensive Growth Model and Its Impact on Commodity Markets

Atanu Ghoshray and Javier Ordóñez

1 Introduction

In the early 1970s and 1980s, the western economies witnessed two oil prices booms. These two price spikes were the consequence of an interruption of supply but also were driven by the expectation that oil demand would increase for a sustained period. Expectations were not fulfilled. First, the oil cartel of the 1970s fractured and, second, the major economies were on growth paths that did not make intensive use of commodities. As a consequence, both shocks were short-lived, with prices falling back soon to their pre-boom levels (Radetzki, 2006). Since 2001 energy prices have been increasing persistently. The current upward trend may well signal a break with the experience of the 1980s and 1990s and earlier energy price booms (IMF, 2001). In recent years the expectation of an increasing and sustained growth in energy demand seems confirmed. According to the International Energy Agency forecast in Energy Outlook (2012), global energy demand will be about 30 per cent higher in 2040 compared to 2010. One of the countries responsible for such expected rapid growth in energy demand is China. This country has become a major participant in energy markets, and her resource-intensive growth path has led to the question as to what extent China's demand for commodities can be a driver of rising energy and related commodity prices.

The expected rapid growth in energy demand in emerging economies can be coupled with a downshift in the growth trend of energy supply. Medium-term forecasts on oil production by the International Energy Agency (IEA, 2010a and 2010b) suggests only modest increases in new capacity over the next five years. A constrained supply of energy commodities will induce further tension in prices. Sluggish supply responses to shifts in demand reflect that energy prices can be subject to "super cycles" caused by implementation lags for discovery, exploration, and capital investment (Cuddington and Jerret, 2008). Given the high investment costs, production levels are maintained even if the demand growth is unexpectedly low. As a consequence, energy prices may be below the total cost of production for long periods. On the other hand, if major economies growth increases, energy prices can be well above the total cost of production for a sustained period of time (Garnaut, 2012). Thus, energy price cycles have longer durations than the typical business cycle (Slade, 1982).

The effects of growth and fluctuations in demand interact with supply conditions to determine global energy prices. As a consequence of both demand and supply factors described above, the global economy may witness a structural break in the historic trend of falling energy prices. When energy supply tightened in the 1970s and oil prices rose and remained high, energy demand decreased sharply due to an intense contraction in growth and an increasing oil substitution by coal. Current upward trend energy prices can be sustained by growing energy consumption in emerging economies. High prices can have important economic repercussions to growth, inflation, external balances, and poverty.

In this chapter we seek to discuss the Chinese resource-intensive growth path and its linkages with the sustained demand for energy. We also discuss China's economic growth and consumption as a cause for the upward trend in energy and other related primary commodity prices.

2 China's role in world energy markets: long-term trends

Since economic reforms started at the end of the 1970s, the Chinese economy has undergone an exceptional growth rate, based mainly on the promotion of capital accumulation and exports (Herrerias and Orts, 2011). The Gross Domestic Product (GDP) increased from USD 189,399 million in 1980 in current prices (USD 182,941 in constant 2000 USD prices) to USD 7,318,499 in 2011 (3,547,886 in constant prices). The average annual income growth in recent years has been 9 per cent. Figure 2.1 shows per capita real GDP at constant USD for a group of selected countries. Data has been transformed to an index with 1980=100. We find that China exhibits an impressive period of

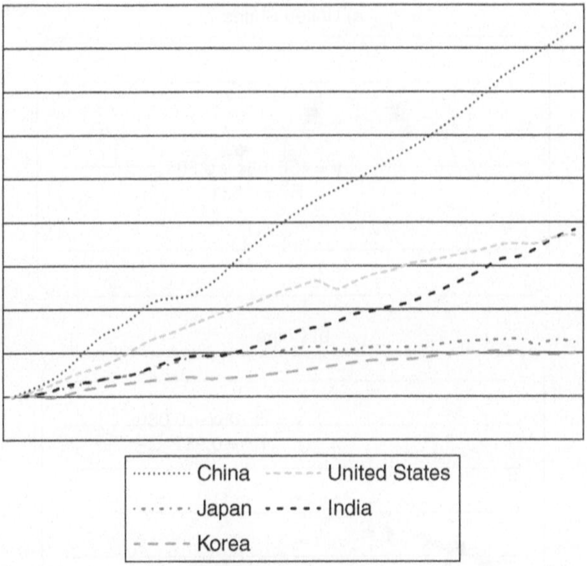

Figure 2.1 GDP (constant USD, 1980 – 100)
Source: World Development Indicators (WDI), World Bank.

sustained growth relative to other economies. However, this experience has not been unique. India and Korea have also grown rapidly and for a sustained period. The 1980s saw the rise of North East Asian economies such as Korea and Japan, whereas the 2000s witnessed the rise of two key countries influencing the global economy, China and India.

The outstanding economic performance in both China and India seems to be linked to an energy-intensive growth model. According to the World Economic Indicators of the World Bank, China is the first energy consumer in the world, with a total primary energy consumption of 2.257 million kt of oil equivalent in 2009, and India is the third-largest energy consumer behind the United States, with 0.675 million kt of oil equivalent. Figure 2.2 shows the relationship between per capita primary energy consumption and per capita real GDP for China, India and United States, which is used with comparative purposes. The relationship between GDP and energy consumption, both in per capita terms, measures the degree of energy-intensive growth. United States can sustain GDP growth without the need to increase energy consumption. Rather, the declining trend shows that this country has grown with a decrease in primary energy consumption. The scenario is completely

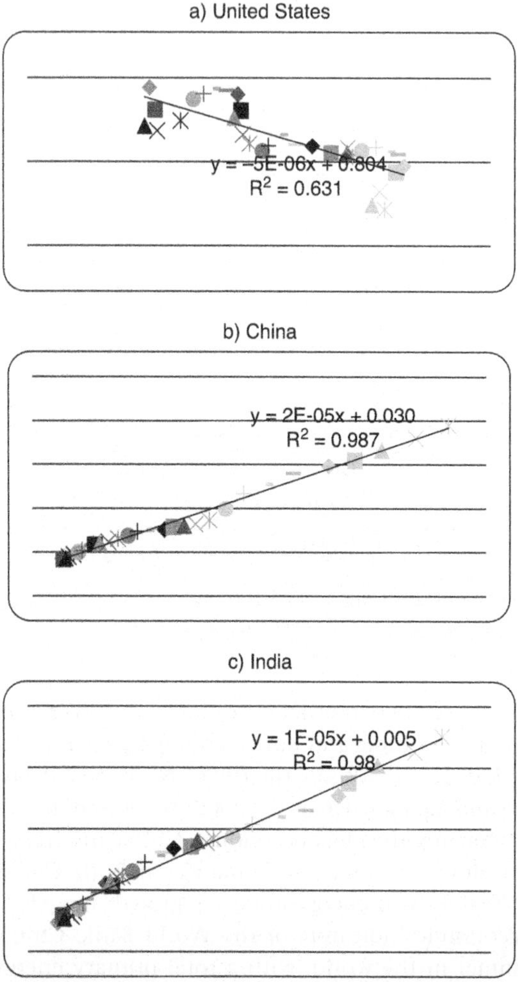

Figure 2.2 Relationship between per capita energy consumption and GDP growth

Source: World Development Indicators (WDI), World Bank. International Energy Agency, IMF International Financial Statistics and own calculations.

different in the case of China and India, growth in per capita income has closely tracked energy consumption.

The mainstream literature on economic growth and development does not consider energy as an input factor that could constrain or enable economic growth (Aghion and Howitt, 2009). The neoclassical growth model, Solow (1956), does not include resources or energy. The level of output in a country is determined by the stock of capital, the labour force and the state of production technology. In this model, growth in equilibrium is due to exogenous improvements in production technology. This leaves the economy's long-run growth rate unexplained. Endogenous growth models (Arrow, 1962) explain the long-term rate of growth in GDP per worker making the rate of technological change dependent on the basic model parameters. Adding non-renewable natural resources to the growth models means that capital needs to be accumulated to compensate for resource depletion (Stern, 2011). Hence, a higher rate of technological progress is required to outweigh the negative effect on growth from population growth and increasing natural resource scarcity.

A larger initial stock of exhaustible resource per capita should, ceteris paribus, yield a higher GDP per worker. Consequently, we should expect a positive relationship between the use of non-renewable natural resources and the level of real GDP per capita. This positive relationship is not confirmed for the case of the United States, which shows a downward trend in energy intensity.[1] This decline may be driven by several factors: substitution between energy and other inputs, technological change, shifts in the composition of the energy input, shifts in the composition of output or structural changes. The growth models with non-renewable natural resources assumed unlimited technological possibilities of substituting capital and labour for increasingly scarce resource inputs. The limiting substitution between energy and other inputs could explain the observed decline in energy intensity in the United States. However, the assumption of unlimited substitution should not be taken literally, but rather as reflecting that growing scarcity of a particular natural resource will generate an economic incentive to develop new substitute inputs. In fact, Stern (2011) suggests that the most important driver of reduced energy intensity in the United States appears to have been technological progress. In the case of China and India the switch towards coal has increased energy intensity. All in all, the increased energy intensity in emerging economies reveals that future energy consumption will depend largely on continued and rapid GDP growth in these fast-growing economies. This is specifically the case for China, which has become the largest energy consumer in the world (International Energy Agency, 2012).

The positive relationship between energy consumption and GDP growth describes the increasing path in energy intensity growth in countries like China. However, it does not provide information about whether GDP growth causes an increase in energy consumption or whether it is the energy consumption that determines the economic growth. This is an important question in the empirical energy growth literature initiated by Kraft and Kraft (1978). The direction of causality between energy consumption and economic growth is highly relevant for policy making in terms of the design of effective and prudent energy policies in the context of increasing energy prices and the need for reducing dependence on foreign energy resources. Apergis and Payne (2009a, 2009b) survey the relationship between energy consumption and economic growth and summarize the possible outcomes of causality according to four different hypotheses proposed in the literature. The growth hypothesis suggests that an increase in energy consumption causes an increase in real GDP; this implies that energy conservation policies would have adverse effects on economic growth. The conservation hypothesis states that an increase in real GDP causes in increase in energy consumption. Under this hypothesis energy conservation policies designed to reduce energy consumption and waste may not have an adverse impact on real GDP. The neutral hypothesis considers that energy consumption is a small input in the production function and thus may have little impact or no impact on real GDP. Similarly to the conservation hypothesis, energy conservation policies would not have an adverse impact on real GDP. Finally, the feedback hypothesis suggests that energy consumption and real GDP complement each other. In terms of causation this implies that both variables are interrelated and cause each other. Under this hypothesis, a shift from less efficient energy sources to more efficient and less polluting options may be a stimulus rather than an obstacle to economic growth (Costantini and Martini, 2010).

Although the causal relationship between energy consumption and income has been widely studied, no consensus regarding this so-called energy consumption–growth nexus has yet been reached (Belke et al., 2010). Ozturk (2010) and Payne (2010a) survey the empirical literature on energy consumption and GDP growth nexus and conclude that the results are mixed and inconclusive, largely dependent on different econometric methods, different time periods of study, countries' characteristics and the variables used. In the case of China, Yalta and Cakar (2012) conclude that this country is not an exception in contradicting empirical results regarding energy consumption and GDP. These authors analyse the last eight studies on the literature and found that only two of them do not fail to confirm the null of neutrality (Soytas and Sari, 2006;

Chen et al., 2007), three support the growth hypothesis (Shiu and Lam, 2004; Zou and Chau, 2006; Yuan et al., 2007), one provides evidence in favour of the conservation hypothesis (Zhang and Cheng, 2009) and, finally, two support the feedback hypothesis (Zhang and Li, 2007, and Yuan et al., 2008). Yalta and Cakar (2012) conclude that the use of aggregate data in the literature explains the contradicting results given the limited potential to observe the complex causal linkages between energy consumption and income. Recent studies achieve the same conclusion (e.g., Bowden and Payne, 2009), while the relationship between energy consumption and growth seems to be neutral on the macro level, for a lower level of aggregation causality is found (Gross, 2012). In the case of China, this result implies the need for using sectoral and provincial data to provide reliable and robust answers to questions about the energy consumption and income growth nexus in this country.

The energy-intense growth path of the Chinese economy has intensified from 2001 onwards. Figure 2.3 shows the share of primary energy consumption as a percentage of total world consumption in China and some selected countries and regions. During the 1960s and 1970s China accounted on average for 4.5 per cent of total world primary energy consumption. In the 1980s and 1990s this share increased to 8.4 per cent. In the 2000s primary energy consumption in China has risen rapidly with an average of 15.7 per cent, achieving 21.3 per cent in 2011. Panel b and c in Figure 2.3 depict respectively the share of crude oil and coal consumption in China as a percentage of the total world consumption.

Oil and coal are the two main sources of energy in China. Table 2.1 below shows the total energy consumption and composition of China. Since 1980 it is clear that total energy consumption has increased dramatically. The marked increase can be noted over the last ten years. While these increased amounts of total energy consumption have evolved over the years, the proportion of energy sources from coal and crude oil have not shown a significant variation, 19 per cent of total energy use is supplied by oil and 68 per cent is supplied by coal. Although China has made an effort to diversify its energy supplies, the participation share of China's energy consumption is relatively small; hydroelectric sources account for 6 per cent of China's energy consumption, natural gas for 4.4 per cent, wind 1.6 per cent, nuclear power for 1 per cent, and other renewables for just 0.3 per cent.

China is the second-largest consumer of oil behind the United States with a share of total world consumption of 11 per cent in 2011. China consumed an estimated 9.4 million barrels per day in 2010 (US Energy

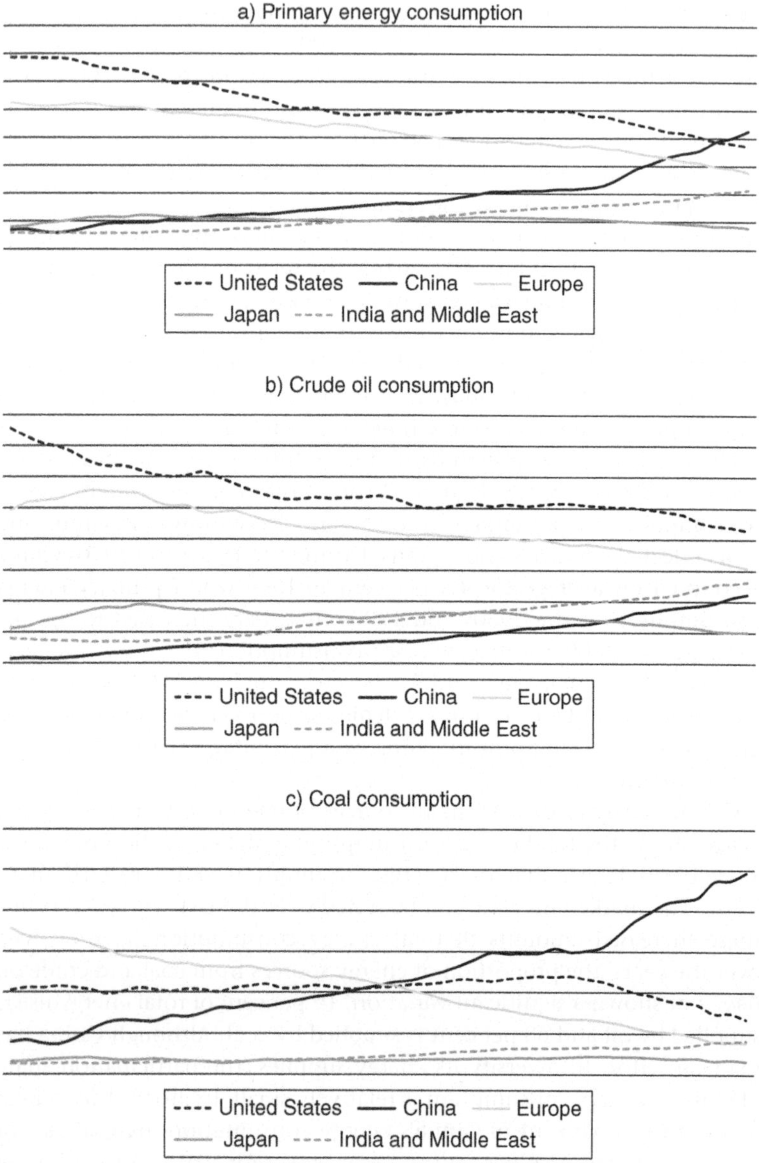

Figure 2.3 Energy consumption as a share of world energy consumption (per cent)

Source: World Development Indicators (WDI), World Bank.

Table 2.1 Total energy consumption (TEC) and its composition

		Percentage of TEC			
	TEC	Coal	Crude oil	Natural gas	Hydro/Nuclear/ Wind
1980	60275	72.2	20.7	3.1	4.0
1985	76682	75.8	17.1	2.2	4.9
1990	98703	76.2	16.6	2.1	5.1
1995	131176	74.6	17.5	1.8	6.1
2000	145531	69.2	22.2	2.2	6.4
2005	235997	70.8	19.8	2.6	6.8
2010	324939	68	19	4.4	8.6

Source: National Bureau of Statistics of China, 2011.

Information Administration, 2011b). And China is the largest consumer of coal in the world, and accounted for almost half of the world's coal consumption in 2011 with an estimated consumption of 4 billion short tons of coal. Coal consumption has increased in China from 2000. The average consumption before 2000 amounted to 18.4 per cent of world's coal consumption, in the 2000s this share is 39.5 per cent. Coal consumption in China has increased from a 30 per cent share of total world consumption in 2000 to a 49.4 per cent in 2011.

Figure 2.4 presents China's evolving share of global production and consumption of crude oil and coal between 1981 and 2009. China's share of global production is small, less than 5 per cent in 2011. China produced an estimated 4.3 million barrels per day of total oil liquids in 2011, of which 95 per cent was crude oil (US Energy Information Administration, 2011a). Since the mid-1980s China's production is roughly constant and according to the International Energy Agency (2012), over the long-term, production will remain rather flat, reaching 4.7 million barrel per day in 2035. A key observation is that the gap between China's share of global production and its consumption of crude oil has grown rapidly since 2001. In 2001 China was the world's second-largest oil importer behind the United States with 5.5 million barrels imported. According to the Energy International Agency (2012), China's oil demand was expected to grow over 0.8 million barrels per day between 2011 and 2013. Despite this moderate pace of growth, 64 per cent of world growth in expected oil demand during this two-year forecast period was expected to correspond to China (US Energy Information Administration, 2011a). China's search for oil has intensified notably

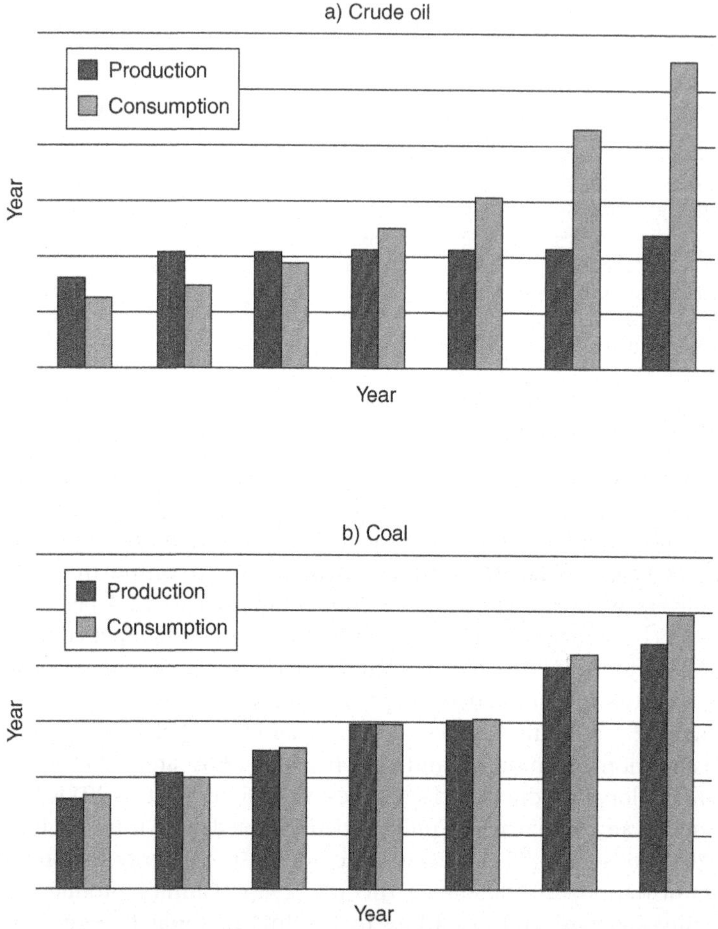

Figure 2.4 Energy production and consumption as share of world energy consumption (per cent) in China

Source: World Development Indicators (WDI), World Bank.

in the Middle East, Russia and Africa. An important part of China's foreign policy has been driven by China's search for increased supplies of energy. China prefers to import its crude from resource-rich countries such as Sub-Saharan Africa that lack the capital, finance or technology to exploit and explore oil fields (Zafar, 2007). Oil is one component of China's growing reach into Africa and as a result China has adopted an "aid for oil strategy" in which the major beneficiaries are Angola and Sudan. China has invested vast amounts of money to develop Angola's and Sudan's infrastructure.

China is the largest producer of coal in the world. Because of its abundance in proven reserves (128 billion short tons of recoverable in 2011) and stability of supply, coal will continue to be a key component of the primary energy mix in China. Production of coal has dramatically increased from 2001. In 2001 the share of Chinese coal production over the world's coal production was 29.9 per cent, whereas in 2011 this share had increased to 45.7 per cent. There are 27 provinces in China that produce coal, although it is mainly in the north of the country, Shanxi and Inner Mongolia provinces in particular, where coal is the most easily accessible. However, Chinese coal is of low-grade, meaning that it is useful for power generation but not for meeting the needs of the steel sector. As a consequence, China has become an increasingly significant importer of higher quality coking coals.

The high energy dependence on fossil fuels in China also makes this country the world's largest source of greenhouse gas emissions. As we have already discussed, emerging economies like China may face the dilemma of promoting energy-saving measures at the expense of economic growth. The 11th Five-Year Plan (2006–10) called for a reduction of energy intensity by 20 per cent during this five years period. However, as pointed out buy Zhou et al. (2010), the results are rather mixed. The delay in the recognition of energy and environmental issues as a priority and the poor effectiveness of energy policies raise important questions for the future development of China. The vast territory of China and the significant heterogeneity of its regions, urge the creation of a specific set of polices addressed to the issues of energy-saving.

A combination of environmental and financial reasons has forced China to look at other sources of energy besides coal. The data from Table 2.2 shows that the reliance on coal has been decreasing over the years since 1990 whereas other forms of energy, such as liquefied petroleum gas and natural gas, have increased substantially over the same period.

China is a large consumer of a broad range of primary commodities. The market shares of various primary commodities have increased sharply since 2000, mainly reflecting China's rapid economic growth. As a percentage of global production, China's consumption during 2010 accounted for about 23 per cent of major agricultural crops, and 40 per cent of base metals (Roache 2012). In the case of non-renewable energy resources, China's consumption as a percentage of global

Table 2.2 Average energy consumption for households in China

	Coal (10000 tons)	Kerosene (10000 tons)	LPG (10000 tons)	Natural gas (100mn cu.m)	Coal gas (100mn cu.m)	Heat (10 bn KJ)	Electricity (100 mn kWh)
1990	16700	105	159	19	29	8972	481
1995	13530	64	534	19	57	12637	1006
2000	8457	72	858	32	126	23234	1452
2005	10039	26	1329	79	145	52044	2885
2007	9761	20	1638	143	186	57689	4063
2008	9148	13	1457	170	184	62765	4396
2009	9122	19	1496	178	166	67000	4872

Source: National Bureau of Statistics of China, 2011.

production amounted to about 20 per cent in 2010 (ibid., 2012). China's growing demand for base metals has been a result of increasing investment in metal-intensive construction activity. Other resource extraction includes copper (Zambia, Democratic Republic of the Congo), and iron ore (Liberia).

Figures 2.2 to 2.4 and Table 2.1 reveal an exceptional increase in Chinese energy consumption in the early 21st century, as we have already extensively discussed. According to Garnaut (2012), two related causes explain this fact. First, rapid urbanization, and second, a high and rising investment share of expenditures, the latter being driven by a transition from strong specialization in labour-intensive manufacturing towards more capital-intensive products. Table 2.3 presents added value for the Chinese economy by sector in three different periods, mid-1990s, early 2000s and mid-2000s. The data shows the percentage share of sectorial added value over the overall economy added value. The contribution of the added value to the total economy added value for traditional labour-intensive sectors has clearly decreased. For example, in the agriculture sector the decline is 41.8 per cent, 21.5 per cent in textile, and 10 per cent in food products. In contrast, the share of added value over the total added value has increased for capital-intensive sectors: 23 per cent in mining, 65 per cent in wood, 27.7 per cent in paper products, 32.5 per cent in coke and petroleum products, 35.2 per cent in chemicals, and 34.6 per cent in transport equipment.

High rates of economic growth significantly increase the demand for oil and other energy products such as natural gas and coal. This increase in demand is faster than the capacity of mining and extraction. As a

Table 2.3 Sectorial added value

Sector	mid-1990s	early 2000s	mid-2000s	Percentage change (mid-1990s to mid-2000s)
Agriculture, hunting, forestry and fishing	21.8	18.1	15.4	–41,8
Mining and quarrying	4.6	5.5	6.1	23.2
Food products, beverages and tobacco	5.4	5.7	4.9	–10
Textiles, textile products, leather and footwear	5.2	5.5	4.3	–21.5
Wood and products of wood and cork	0.3	0.5	0.9	65.6
Pulp, paper, paper products, printing and publishing	1.3	1.4	1.8	27.7
Coke, refined petroleum products and nuclear fuel	1.2	2.4	1.7	32.5
Chemicals and chemical products	3.8	4.7	5.9	35.2
Rubber and plastics products	1.5	1.6	1.3	–13.6
Other non-metallic mineral products	3.9	2.3	1.5	–155.5
Basic metals	3.3	3.3	4.4	24.3
Fabricated metal products except machinery and equipment	1.6	1.1	1.6	–1.1
Machinery and equipment	4.2	3.1	4.9	14.8
Office, accounting and computing machinery	0.2	0.6	1.2	86.4
Electrical machinery and apparatus	1.1	3.8	2.2	49.9
Radio, television and communication equipment	1.3	1.5	0.9	–39.53
Medical, precision and optical instruments	0.2	0.2	0.4	36.4
Motor vehicles, trailers and semi-trailers	1.4	1.6	1.5	9.4
Other transport equipment	0.7	1.2	1.1	34.6
Electricity, gas and water supply	2.3	4.7	4.5	49.7
Construction	7.1	7.2	7.2	3.3
Wholesale and retail trade; repairs	7.9	7.7	8.4	6.1
Transport and storage	4.2	4.2	7.1	40.1
Post and telecommunications	1.2	2.4	3.4	64.1
Finance and insurance	5.4	4.6	4.2	–28
Other Business Activities	8.7	5.1	2.9	–199.3

Source: OECD STAN database.

result, countries that experience high rates of economic growth such as China, will continue to demand energy even in the face of rising prices. This happens as the short-term supply and demand is highly inelastic and any increase in demand leads to a sharp increase in prices. However, in the long-term, it is believed that this higher price will lead to a contraction in demand. Increasing energy prices add to higher costs which reduces demand. This leads to a gradual fall in prices. On the other hand, in the face of higher prices supply will increase and coupled with lower demand will contribute to falling prices.

In recent years a major concern of policy makers in China has been to raise energy prices to promote higher energy efficiency (Hang and Tu, 2007). Energy efficiency has been a key policy objective aiming to reduce energy consumption while preventing any slowdown in economic growth (Birol and Keppler, 2000). This requires that the links between energy prices and energy efficiency are well understood.

A number of studies (Zhang, 2003; Fisher-Vanden et al., 2004) have concentrated on energy efficiency and have focused on the decline in aggregate energy intensity, defined as the energy consumption per unit of GDP, in China over the last two decades. In the late 1970s when China initiated its economic reform program, the energy intensity for China was double that of the United States and triple that of Japan (Hang and Tu, 2007). However, by 1999 the energy intensity of China had declined to levels more comparable to those of the United States and Japan (Crompton and Wu, 2005). Although technical and structural changes have been identified as causes for this decline, the impact of energy prices on energy intensity is an area where limited research has been carried out.

3 China and international commodity markets

In recent years China has emerged as a major force to deal with in the case of international commodity markets. It has been argued that the economic and environmental policies of China have a large impact on the recent trends in commodity prices. This study which attempts to understand the impact of China's role on commodity prices can lead one to understand some of the explanations of current trends in commodity prices. Commodity prices in turn, can affect terms of trade which can then affect economic conditions in other emerging and developing countries in particular Sub-Saharan Africa.

Terms of trade have played a central role in policy making especially since the work of Prebisch (1950) and Singer (1950). Their studies involved the estimation of the trend of commodity prices relative to manufactured goods. Their conclusions were that the price of real commodities displayed a declining trend over time. More recently, another line of reasoning regarding the trend of commodity prices was put forward by Deaton (1999) who argues that prices of commodities in developing countries can be characterized as containing no significant trend by linking commodity price determination to the Lewis (1954) model. Lewis in his seminal paper states that in poor countries there is an unlimited supply of labour at a fixed subsistence wage which prevents real wages from increasing. As a result, prices of commodities are unlikely to exceed the cost of production in the long-run. Deaton (1999) claims that this is especially true for commodities produced in developing countries. Thus commodity prices may deviate in the short run from the long run subsistence wage rate, but because there is an unlimited supply of labour, prices will eventually revert to the base. Using this line of reasoning, the fact that China has a huge surplus of labour may be a reason why wages are unlikely to grow and will continue to place pressure on manufactures prices, thereby possibly reversing the trend in primary commodities in relation to manufactures.

It is not unsurprising that employment in the manufacturing sector is likely to fall in Organisation for Economic Cooperation and Development (OECD) countries where they pay high wages and are faced with cheap imports from low- wage economies. From Table 2.4 we can see that employment in the formal manufacturing sector fell by 24.62 per cent in OECD countries from 1991 to 2010. Employment in China increased roughly over the same period by 27.10 per cent. For China, we can see that the share of employment in the agricultural sector has decreased substantially by 33.6 per cent since 1991, which is lower in comparison

Table 2.4 Employment by sector (percentage of total employment)

	OECD countries			China		
	Agriculture	Industry	Services	Agriculture	Industry	Services
1991	9.66	29.69	60.45	59.70	21.40	18.90
1995	8.46	28.13	63.26	52.20	23.00	24.80
2000	7.03	26.96	65.81	50.00	22.50	27.50
2005	5.73	24.86	69.07	44.80	23.80	31.30
2010	5.11	22.38	71.84	39.60*	27.20*	33.20*

Note: *These figures pertain to 2008.

Source: World Bank (2012): World Development Indicators.

to the 47.1 per cent decrease in the share of agricultural employment in OECD countries; albeit the share of agricultural employment in OECD has a low base. While the OECD countries saw their share of employment in services increase by 18.8 per cent, the share in China has rocketed by 75.6 per cent.

The issue of whether real commodity prices exhibit a declining trend is essentially an empirical one. Since the seminal papers of Prebisch and Singer, there has been a huge volume of empirical studies that emanated over time. Most of these studies have employed the so-called Grilli-Yang Index. However, many of the past studies have overlooked an issue relating to this data. The deflator for commodity prices is the United Nations Manufacturing Unit Value index or abbreviated as the MUV. This is a weighted average of manufacturing prices from five industrialized countries being UK, USA, France, Germany and Japan (Pfaffenzeller et al., 2007). Since the 1980s China has emerged as one of the major exporters of manufactured goods. Clearly, the index for MUV would need to be updated and take China into account. Kaplinsky (2006) points out that manufactures can be differentiated into "complex production systems" which are based on cost-plus pricing and "simple" products that are sold in competitive markets. As a result, great care needs to be taken when deriving policy responses from trends in commodity prices in relation to manufactured goods.

Why is China important in relation to commodity prices relative to manufactured goods? Since the 1980s China has experienced a significantly rapid rate of economic growth surpassing the growth rates of other countries. There is evidence to suggest that this growth was trade orientated. In the 1970s, China's trade as a percentage of GDP was approximately 9.51 per cent. Since the 1980s this figure has been increasing steadily. In the 1980s the figure was 24.14 per cent, in the 1990s it grew to 37.01 per cent and over the last 10 years since the turn of the millennium it has averaged at 57.36 per cent.[2]

An interesting observation that can be made is that as China has been experiencing rapid economic growth, there have been signs of a changing trend in commodity prices. China has become a very large market for the exports of other countries. China's exports of consumer electronics have involved the assembly of components sourced from East Asia (Kaplinsky, 2006). It has been argued that China's increasing demand for hard commodities has pushed up the prices. This demand has been fuelled by domestic demand for household consumer goods, investment in metal-intensive public- and private-sector infrastructure and growing exports of metal-based products. Metal prices have generally increased quite sharply, especially copper and zinc, due to declining inventories and depreciation of the US dollar. China's share of global demand for base metals (including copper and zinc) has increased exponentially. The increased demand for these metals may have triggered a sharp increase in prices for these metals since 2000. This is reflected in Figure 2.5.

Zinc prices have displayed a sharp increase since 2003 partly because of declining inventories and partly due to the high demand for galvanized steel. Copper prices displayed a similar rise since 2003 due to the strong demand for exports of metal-based products. Also, stocks have been low due to strikes and delays that have led prices to spiral upwards.

Mostly OECD economies have seen significant gains from agricultural commodity exports to China. China's main agricultural imports are wheat, corn, beef and soybeans. Wheat is exported by Australia, Argentina and Canada; corn is exported by the US and Argentina; beef by Australia and New Zealand. Commodity prices are known to be volatile, displaying persistence and punctuated with sharp upwards spikes over time. However, with the growing demand for agricultural commodities from China, the underlying trends in these prices may well change. Figure 2.6 shows that for selected agricultural prices such as wheat, maize and beef, prices can be characterized as displaying an upward drift since 2000.

What implication does this have for commodity terms of trade, that is, the prices of commodities in relation to manufactured goods? As we have seen from Figures 2.5 and 2.6, the view that prices of real commodities have been declining may be challenged since the start of the 21st

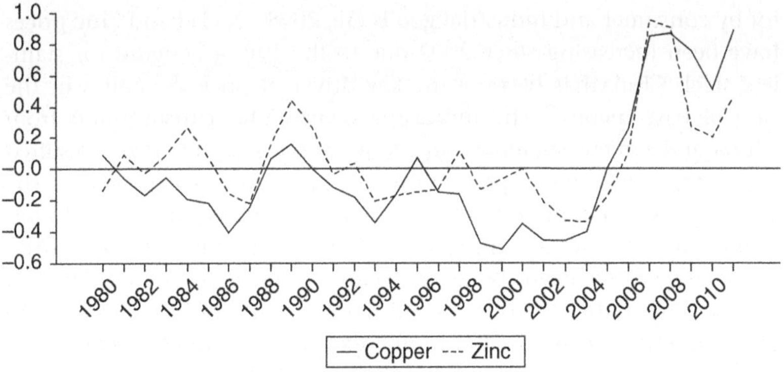

Figure 2.5 Metal prices

Source: Grilli-Yang Index from Pfaffenzeller et al. 2007.

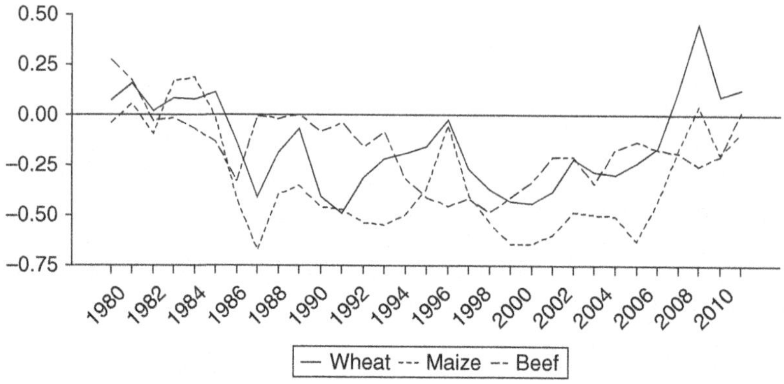

Figure 2.6 Agricultural prices
Source: Grilli-Yang Index from Pfaffenzeller et al. 2007.

century. Besides, the prices of manufactures, particularly those in which China participates, are likely to be falling over time. From the demand side an increase in incomes will lead to an increase in consumption which will lead to an increased demand for commodities, including soft commodities. On the supply side, the large labour force of China may prevent any capacity constraints and continue to make manufactured goods appear competitive on the global market.

The large increase in the demand for commodities has been a result of high investment rates to support industrialization and urbanization in China (Yu, 2011). Over half of China's copper usage is accounted for by infrastructure investment and construction, with a third accounted for by consumer and industrial goods (Ye, 2008). Nickel and Zinc prices have been increasing since 2002 due to the strong demand for stainless steel. China has become the key driver of price dynamics in the case of base metals.[3] The increasing demand for consumption from China and for raw materials for its manufacturing sector has resulted in a surge in base metal prices in recent years. As discussed earlier, the causes for recent commodity boom are partly because of low stocks but also because of China's large appetite for commodities. Other contributing factors have been the diversification of portfolios by investing in commodities rather than stocks and shares. Hedge funds have grown to be quite active on commodity futures exchanges. Given that commodities are priced in dollars, the sliding dollar has helped in contributing an increase in commodity prices.

Since 2003 a sharp increase in crude oil prices is recorded (see Figure 2.7). During this time, China's demand for oil surged. Coal prices have seen huge increases in price due to strong global demand and supply constraints from major coal-producing countries. Since 2006 prices of coal have increased rapidly due to reduced exports from China. High oil prices have contributed to similar price movements in other energy prices such as natural gas. China's natural gas production has been rising steadily during recent years. From 1980 to 2010, the average growth rate of China's natural gas production was about 6.71 per cent, and in the most recent decade the growth rate was on average around 13.36 per cent. Currently China is among the world's largest consumers of natural gas [BP Statistics 2010]. The industrial sector in China absorbs a large proportion of natural gas in its production processes. Other sectors such as the transportation sector and households are the next-largest consumers of natural gas. As a result China's imports of natural gas have been rising rapidly exerting an upward pressure on the price.

4 Concluding remarks

China has become a major participant in commodity markets, and its resource-intensive growth path has led to questions about the extent to which China's demand of commodities is a driver of rising prices. The expected rapid growth in commodity demand in emerging countries

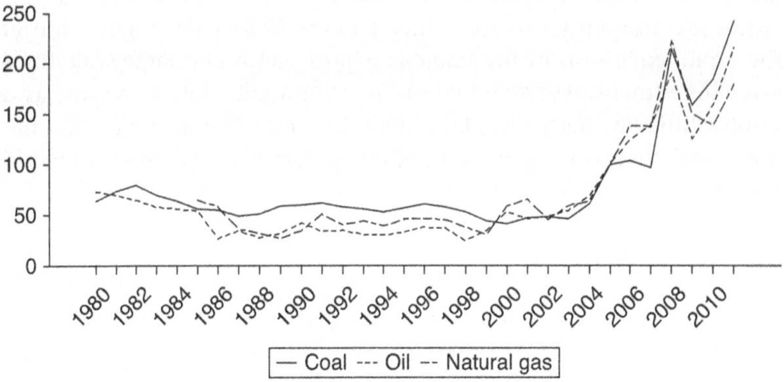

Figure 2.7 Non-renewable energy prices

Source: International Financial Statistics.

like China can be coupled with a downshift in the growth trend of energy supply, inducing further tension in prices. As a consequence, energy and other commodity prices are subject to "super cycles", that is, cycles with longer duration than typical business cycles. The fact that commodity prices can be well above the long-run trend for a sustained period of time may have negative effects on other emerging or developing economies.

The positive relationship between energy consumption and GDP growth describes the path of increasing energy-intense growth in China. Two related causes explain this fact. First, rapid urbanization, and second, a high and rising investment share of expenditures, the latter being driven by a transition from strong specialization in labour-intensive manufacturing towards more capital-intensive products. Newly emerging industries with higher technological content are growing robustly whereas the contribution of traditional labour-intensive sectors to total added value has clearly decreased. As a result, energy-intensive sectors are growing more rapidly than industry overall. This Chinese industrial "deepening" with a shift to more capital-intensive sectors has caused a surge in demand for materials, metals and energy.

Commodity prices are known to exhibit trending behaviour as well as being highly volatile. The rapid increase in the demand for commodities in China, particularly base metals and non-renewable energy, has had an impact on commodity prices and the this is expected to persist at high levels. China will play an important role in the world commodity trade as long as it affects the relative distribution of supply and demand of different commodities across countries (Roache, 2012). China's rapidly growing commodity intensity since 2000 is likely to be a reflection of the rapid expansion in the tradable export sector and large-scale fixed asset investment. These activities are commodity intensive and as a result China has started to play a dominant role in base metals and has made an impact on global food and energy markets as its share of world imports rises steadily.

Acknowledgements

The second author gratefully acknowledges the financial support of the CICYT project ECO2011–30260-C03–01 and Generalitat Valenciana project PROMETEO/2009/098.

Notes

1. In an interesting paper, Herrerias et al. (2013) suggest that the unbalanced regional growth in China has been translated into differences in the need for energy resources and therefore in energy intensity across regions in China.
2. Calculated from the World Development Indicators.
3. Source (IMF 2006) World Economic Outlook; Financial Systems and Economic Cycles.

3

China's Energy Diplomacy via the Shanghai Cooperation Organisation

Elzbieta Maria Pron

1 Introduction

In the early 1990s, China's energy security changed from one of self-sufficiency to a net importer of energy resources. China's oil imports increased five-fold between 1991 and 2012, reaching 1 million barrels per day in mid-2012. Since 2007 China has also become a natural gas importer, aiming to satisfy ten per cent of its total energy demand with gas by 2020 (EIA, 2012a). China's growing energy dependency on external resources has made Beijing vulnerable to fluctuations in global energy prices. The stability of the energy supply has been a precondition for China's economic growth and the factor ensuring socio-political stability. As a result, energy security has become a core interest of the CCP leadership and an inherent element of China's foreign policy. To address its new energy security concerns, China has pursued a long-term energy strategy. This strategy aims at reforming its domestic energy institutions and adjusting national oil companies (NOCs) to become more competitive in the global market. China has also looked to diversify energy suppliers and to secure access to oil and gas fields (Zhang, 2011, pp. 11–12).

Newly emerged in 1991, Central Asian states – Kazakhstan, Kyrgyzstan, Turkmenistan, Tajikistan, and Uzbekistan – became a focus of China's energy policy. Central Asia adjoins the western border of China and is rich in energy resources. Turkmenistan possesses the fourth-largest gas reserves in the world, followed by Uzbekistan, while Kazakhstan accounts for the eleventh-largest global oil deposits (EIA, 2012d, p. 4; EIA, 2012c, p. 9). Tajikistan and Kyrgyzstan have abundant hydro power potential, of which less than ten per cent is currently used (Daly, 2012). In addition, the post-Soviet republics have a tangible interest in diversifying their energy partners – the region had been subject to Russian price discrimination until the mid-2000s. This was a result of the former Soviet single economic space and the underdevelopment of Central Asian energy infrastructure, entirely directed northward to Russia. Constraints in the field of energy security – security of demand in Central Asia and security of supply for China – compelled both regions to further their cooperation on energy.

China–Central Asian cooperation on energy proceeded through a combination of bilateral agreements and, increasingly, the multilateral structure of the Shanghai Cooperation Organisation (SCO). The idea of the SCO multilateral cooperation on energy – the SCO Energy Club – was first initiated in 2006, but has not become effective. Chinese analysts argue that China's interest in the SCO multilateral energy institutions grows out of the challenges posed by Western involvement in the energy-rich regions in Central Asia (Wang, 2011) and the practice of translating Sino-Central Asian bilateral cooperation into multilateral one (Xu, 2012, p. 56). Nonetheless, given China's energy vulnerabilities and the relative advantage of Central Asian energy-producing countries, this argument is not convincing. As much as the proposal of the SCO multilateral energy institutions raised concerns in the West, which was alarmed by the formation of Asian "energy cartel", they have not been widely studied.

Past research on Sino-Central Asian energy relations falls into two fields of research. The first deals with the geopolitical conditions that permitted Sino-Central Asian bilateral energy cooperation (Bailes and Dunay, 2007, pp. 1–29; Clarke, 2008; Garrison, 2009; Marketos, 2009; Sutter, 2008, pp. 295–319; Yuan, 2010). The authors usually reveal the complex character of bilateral energy deals, but they neglect the SCO as a platform for cooperation on energy, limiting its role to the security organization. The SCO Energy Club is either portrayed as a Sino-Russian concept with unclear utility (Bailes and Dunay, 2007, p. 27; Clarke, 2008, p. 108), or as entirely irrelevant to the analysis of Sino-Central Asian energy links (Garrison, 2009, pp. 54–56). The second field of research looks directly at the SCO Energy Club, presenting a discrepancy between Chinese and non-Chinese authors writing on the Club. Chinese look at a variety of the functions, ranging from political institution to a confidence-building measure, which the Club can play in Sino-Central Asian cooperation on energy (Wang, 2011; Xu, 2012). Nonetheless, Chinese analysts oversimplify the geopolitical conditions in Central Asia, focusing on Sino-Russian balancing as a central factor shaping energy multilateralism. On the contrary, non-Chinese accounts of the possible functions of the SCO Energy Club reflect the complexity of Central Asian states' mutual relations, but they examine the SCO Energy Club purely from the economic-energy perspective (Kassenova, 2009; Matusov, 2007). Hence, the analysis evolves around the Club as either potential "energy cartel" or as a mechanism ineffective to further regional cooperation on energy.

To fulfil the existing gaps, this chapter uses a foreign policy-oriented approach to tackle the question: what role will SCO energy multilateralism play in China's cooperation on energy with Central Asia? To respond to the problem of energy multilateralism in Sino-Central Asian relations, this chapter comprises of three parts. The first part looks at the main channels for China's relations with Central Asia and at Chinese objectives in the region. The second part scrutinizes the development and role of the SCO institutions related to the energy sector, particularly the SCO Energy Club. The third part analyses Chinese interest, opportunities and risks in furthering the multilateral cooperation in energy with Central Asia.

2 China's relations with Central Asia until 2012

China and Central Asia, although bound together by the Silk Road trade chain for centuries, remain distant partners in cultural, ethnic and linguistic terms. When Central Asia gained independence from the former Soviet Union in 1991, it was politically unstable, had unresolved border disputes with China, and was a potential trigger for separatism in Xinjiang Uyghur Autonomous Region (Xinjiang; XUAR). Nonetheless, a sovereign Central Asia gave China a chance to develop the economies of its Western provinces and normalize diplomatic relations with its newly independent neighbours.

China has used a double-track diplomacy to further its interests in Central Asia. One track is the multilateral institution of the SCO and the other is bilateral cooperation in economic and energy sectors. This clear division arises from the sometimes contradictory approach to the SCO among its member states, varying from economic-energy angling to security. China's choice of double-track diplomacy towards Central Asia is informed by two main factors. The first is limited feasibility of multilateral projects in the region. Central Asia has had a number of unresolved ethnic, territorial, and geopolitical conflicts, which impede multi-party cooperation. The second, external factor shaping China's

Central Asian diplomacy is the Sino-Russian relationship. The SCO is one of several forums for balancing Sino-Russian relations, but without Russian approval of China's endeavours in Central Asia, Beijing has little room to manoeuvre. Central Asian states still perceive Russia as its main security guarantor, trading partner and ally at the international forum (Zhao, 2007, p. 207). On the contrary, China's post-Cold War entry to the region is seen in Central Asia with suspicion, ranging from academic assessments of China's neo-imperial policy of divide and rule (Walsh, 1993, p. 275; Laruelle and Peyrouse, 2009, p. 130)[1] to popular voices on China's "swallowing" the region (Khodzhaev, 2009, p. 17).

2.1 Shanghai Cooperation Organisation

The Shanghai Cooperation Organisation has its origin in the Shanghai Five group established in 1996 by China, Russia, Kazakhstan, Kyrgyzstan, and Tajikistan devoted to the issues of resolving territorial disputes and reducing military activeness in border areas. In June 2001, the group was reorganized as the SCO and admitted Uzbekistan as its sixth member state. Over more than a decade, the SCO has established two permanently operating bodies of the SCO Secretariat and Regional Anti-Terrorist Structure, responsible for drawing up counter-terrorist agreements and staging SCO counter-terrorist exercises. The SCO has also launched institutions in the fields of economy (SCO Business Council), financial sector (SCO Interbank Association), education (SCO University) and several working groups in culture, health, and other areas. Since the mid-2000s, the SCO has also expanded its membership to include five observer states (Afghanistan, India, Iran, Mongolia and Pakistan) and three dialogue partners (Belarus, Sri Lanka and Turkey). The SCO has held regular annual summits, which change location along with a rotating one-year chairmanship of the organization.

Over the years, the focus of the SCO has shifted from its border issues towards energy and security issues, particularly the so-called three evil forces of terrorism, separatism and religious extremism. These two focuses have been a result of different concepts about the SCO's role held by the organization's leaders: China advocates an economic-energy orientation, while Russia emphasizes security (Weitz, 2012). The different views on the SCO and internal conflicts have impeded the organization's effectiveness. The SCO's numerous bodies have worked more as platforms for communication between representatives of the member states, rather than as useful mechanisms in their fields. For instance, the SCO Business Council, set up in 2006, has up to date implemented only two joint projects, one on launching a high-speed data highway across the SCO space and the other on international telecommunications (www.bc-sco.org).

At the beginning, the SCO had little impact on the politics of its member states. In many fields cooperation has not gone beyond declarations. But events such as the killing of Osama bin Laden in 2011, the US forces' withdrawal from Afghanistan (and Central Asia) in 2014, the forthcoming power succession in Central Asia, problems with Iranian nuclear potential, and the consequences of the 2008–09 global financial crisis allow the organization to play a new role in the region. The SCO, due to its security mechanisms and legal provisions, as well as cooperative relations with Iran and Afghanistan, is increasingly seen as a potential security guarantor in the region. The organization will hardly engage militarily in Afghanistan, but it has already commenced programmes to advance the socio-economic development of this country. New challenges emanating from the SCO space and the SCO's rapid institutionalization suggest that the organization will invest more effort in its economic and energy institutions, especially the SCO Energy Club. The question remains how China will use this institution in its energy cooperation with the region and beyond.

Over the years, the importance of the SCO in Chinese diplomacy towards Central Asia has grown and the organization has become China's main channel for its relations with the region (Zhao, 2008, p. 39). First, the SCO allowed China to build cooperation with regional political elites with the consent from Russia, which sees Central Asia as its sphere of influence. Second, the SCO also provided another platform for China to further its dialogue with regional major powers, such as Russia and India. Third, China has used the SCO umbrella to foster a wider political and economic agenda in Central Asia, such as the USD 10 million loan for economic recovery of Central Asia in 2009 (Reuters, 06.12.2012).

2.2 China–Central Asia bilateral cooperation in energy sector

Along with the SCO multilateral mechanism, China has used a bilateral track to further its interests in Central Asia. In the energy field, China's Central Asian diplomacy resembles China's activities in energy-rich countries in Africa and Latin America. China first negotiates the energy deals with local governments bilaterally, without imposing conditions on domestic political reform. The financing of Chinese investments is secured through loans issued by Export Import Bank (Exim Bank) and China Development Bank. The loans guarantee feasibility of the project and that Chinese firms are the main constructors of the energy infrastructure. The acquisition and refining of energy resources is managed by China's largest NOCs – China National China National Offshore Oil Corporation (CNOOC), China National Petroleum Company (CNPC) and Sinopec (Bersager, 2012, p. 10; Seaman, 2010, pp. 12–13). In Central Asia, China's main NOC is CNPC and, to a lesser extent, Sinopec.

Central Asian energy imports secured a small share of China's current energy demand, estimated as 90 quadrillion British thermal units (Btu) in 2009 (EIA, 2012a, p. 1). Operating with a current capacity of 50 bcm, the Central Asian gas pipeline fulfils more than 30 per cent of China's gas consumption, estimated in 2011 as 130 bcm (IEA, 2012, p. 14). This accounts for about 1.4 per cent of China's energy portfolio, which relies on gas for only 4 per cent (EIA, 2012a, p. 1). The crude oil imports from Kazakhstan covered 4 per cent of China's total energy imports in 2011 (Zhang, 2011, p. 17). Although energy imports from Central Asia are still far from the expected ten per cent of total energy imports, China has nevertheless managed to reduce its dependence on the Middle East through forging Central Asian links (Zhang, 2011, p. 16).

China concluded its first energy agreement with Kazakhstan in 1997, when CNPC purchased 60.3 per cent of shares in AktobeMunaiGaz, Kazakhstan's fourth-largest oil company, which was on the verge of bankruptcy at that time. The CNPC almost tripled the crude oil output between 1997 and 2010, and it now owns over 85 per cent of the venture. In October 2005, the CNPC paid USD 4.18 billion for PetroKazakhstan, the owner of the second-largest oil field in Kazakhstan, only to re-sell in late 2005 33 per cent of China's shares to KazMunaiGaz (KMG), the state-run second-largest oil producer in Kazakhstan. Since then, the CNPC cooperated with the KMG on several deals, including the purchase of MagistauMunaiGaz, in 2009. In 2012, Chinese-owned operations accounted for 25–30 per cent of all oil production in Kazakhstan, having acquired access to several oil fields and shares in two out of three oil refineries in the country (Oil & Gas Eurasia, 23.09.2012). China's largest project in Kazakhstan has been 2228 km oil pipeline (Atyrau–Alashankou), owned by CNPC and KMG, which links Western Kazakhstan with Xinjiang. The pipeline started operating in October 2009 with a capacity of 240,000 barrels per day of crude oil. Although this is only a bit more than a half of the expected 400, 000 barrels per day, China has already become Kazakhstan's second-largest importer of liquid fuels, accounting for 16 per cent of Kazakhstan's total export (EIA, 2012b, p. 6).

The Atyrau–Alashankou pipeline is one of the two biggest Chinese investments in the energy sector in Central Asia. The other one is

China–Central Asia gas pipeline, which originates in North-East Turkmenistan and passes through Uzbekistan and Kazakhstan into Western China. The pipeline's construction was agreed bilaterally with regional governments and built by Chinese–local joint ventures.[2] The majority of gas transported to China through the pipeline comes from Turkmenistan, with which CNPC signed a preferential agreement for energy exploration in the eastern part of the country. Turkmenistan gas exports to China, estimated in 2012 to be 40 billion cubic meters (bcm) will increase to 65 bcm per year once the exploration in Turkmenistan expands (Balmforth, 2011). Since 2010, Kazakhstan has exported 10 bcm annually to China through the Central Asian pipeline (hydrocarbon-technology.com, undated). The pipeline's capacity will once again be improved in 2014 when Uzbekistan will start sending 10 bcm annually to China (EIA, 2012c, p. 6). In 2012, Kyrgyzstan also expressed its interest in joining the pipeline, as it would safeguard the country's energy security and allow Bishkek to benefit from transit fees (Oil & Gas Eurasia, 06.12.2012).

The cooperation on gas exports through the Central Asian pipeline has been a breakthrough in regional cooperation on energy. The threat of disagreements over customs, visas and transit regulations between conflicted transit states persists (Pannier, 2010), but the Central Asian gas pipeline has proved the feasibility of regional multi-party cooperation. While Central Asian states are able to secure their energy demand with domestic sources, due to the post-Soviet energy infrastructure in the region, they do not have the capability to do so. As a result, each one exports the energy to the neighbour only to import from another neighbour.[3] Ethnic and political conflicts, underdeveloped economies and widespread corruption affect the stability of domestic energy supply and lead to riots (Anceschi, 2009, p. 181; Ecoworld, 2009).

Apart from its oil and gas pipelines projects, China is involved in several hydro power projects in Kyrgyzstan and Tajikistan. The main contractor in both states is Tebian Electric Apparatus Stock Co. Ltd. (TBEA), a Chinese company quoted on the Shanghai stock market and the main producer of transmission and transformation equipment in China.[4] In Kyrgyzstan, TBEA has been involved in the construction of Datka–Kemin 500Kv transmission line. Beijing also placed bids on the renovation of the Bishkek thermal plant and the building of the Kara-Keche coal factory. In Tajikistan, TBEA invests in three other power transmission projects, receiving in exchange access to exploration of Tajikistan's natural mineral resources (Pannier, 2010). Although the energy projects in Kyrgyzstan and Tajikistan are of little significance for

China's overall energy security, they are important for Xinjiang, which borders both states (Xinhua, 06.09.2012). As indicated by Erica Marat, they also allow both states to break their dependence on the Central Asian "energy vicious circle" (Marat, 2010).

The cooperation on energy is an integral part of Beijing political and public diplomacy towards Central Asia. Chinese companies in Central Asia are responsible for their economic performance in Central Asia as well as building the Chinese image. As indicated by Chinese officials "Chinese enterprises should work hard in improving company image, safeguarding national reputation and lifting the credibility of Chinese companies, asking the Chinese employees to obey the Turkmen laws and respect local customs and traditions" (Malhotra, 2012, quoted after Chinese Daily). China's leadership has retained control over the NOC and has supported financially their endeavours in Central Asia and worldwide.

Security of energy demand is also a core interest of the Central Asian leadership, which is directly involved in the energy contracts. For instance, Kazakh president's son-in-law, Timur Kulibayev, for years led the wealth fund of Samruk-Kazyna, an owner of KazMunaiGaz. Kulibayev is also the chairman of the board of KazMunaiGaz and a board member at Russian Gazprom (Solovyov and Paxton, 2011). In Uzbekistan, the president's daughter Gulnara Karimova was deemed to own Zeromax, Switzerland-based company and the largest investor on the Uzbek energy market. The bankruptcy of Zeromax in 2010 raised speculation about whether it fell due to conflict at the top leadership in Uzbekistan or as a result of pressure from the Kremlin (Institute for War and Peace Reporting, 2010). The shares in the company were purchased by Russian Lukoil (49 per cent) and the Uzbek state-owned oil and gas company Uzbekneft (51 per cent).

Beijing had realized early that to secure energy contracts it required links with regional governments. Hence, mutual energy interests are an inseparable part of bilateral treaties with Central Asian[5] states as well as separate inter-governmental agreements preceding bilateral deals.[6] The agreements on energy cooperation are first concluded between Chinese and Central Asian leaders and then extended to commercial deals between national energy companies.[7] For instance, to monitor the Central Asian gas pipeline, China has set up the TurkmenChinese Cooperation Committee, co-chaired by vice-presidents of both countries (Oil & Gas Eurasia, 02.03.2011). The biggest projects in Central Asia have also been on the agenda of the PRC State Energy Small Leading Group (2005–08) and National Energy Commission (since

2010), supervised by the PRC Prime Minister Wen Jiabao until late 2012.

2.3 Central Asian energy market and Sino-Russian balancing

Although China's energy policy towards Central Asia resembles Beijing's approach to energy-rich African countries, in Central Asia, China is compelled to compete with Russia over energy resources. Russia has not only been a political partner for local governments, but it has long influenced local energy management and infrastructure. For Moscow, control over resources in the former Soviet Union is leveraged in negotiating energy contracts with its partners in the West. Thus China's energy cooperation with Central Asia has challenged Russian geopolitical interests in several ways. First, as mentioned earlier China reduced Turkmenistan's and Kazakhstan's dependency on Russia's energy imports. Second, it impedes Russian energy infrastructure plans, and bestows on Central Asia more bargaining power over energy prices. Central Asia is no longer subject to price discrimination emanating from its energy infrastructure, directed exclusively northward. The Kremlin's position in the Sino-Russian energy balance in Central Asia is challenged as Russia does not have the means to press Beijing, which is dependent on Russian sources for less than ten per cent of its oil and gas imports (IEA, 2012, p. 6).[8] In the mid-2000s, China's growing presence on Central Asian energy markets was still "ignored as the implied threat to Russian business" (Trenin, 2012, pp. 38–39). At that time, Russia was occupied with establishment of the Commonwealth of Independent States energy cartel that would allow Moscow to control the trade in energy in the former Soviet republics (Kassenova, 2009, p. 165). As China's stakes in Central Asia increased and Russia failed to attain its goals, Moscow realized that "China is prepared to counter Russia in Central Asia if the outcome is beneficial to its interests and the price is right, a trend that could have major future implications" (Blank, 2010). To avoid further consequences of its diminishing role in Central Asia, only a month after China started receiving Kazakh oil (Wishnick, 2006), Russia advocated the establishment of the multilateral SCO Energy Club in June 2006 (Ria Novosti, 2006).

3 The SCO energy institutions

The idea of multilateral energy cooperation was one of the SCO's aims from its inception in 2001. The Charter of the SCO encouraged regional cooperation in spheres as broad as trade and economy, energy, transport, credit and finance, among many others (www.sectsco.org). The SCO Business Council and the SCO Interbank Consortium, both founded in 2005 (www.bc-sco.org), were responsible for carrying on this regional cooperation. Nonetheless, these institutions have proved ineffective because they are too broad in focus and often seen as being of minor importance for the SCO states in their bilateral agreements. To increase its influence on regional energy contracts, Russia proposed establishment of an independent body – the SCO Energy Club.

3.1 The SCO Energy Club

The idea of an independent SCO Energy Club was first suggested by the Uzbek delegation during the international conference on Central Asian energy markets in Tashkent in December 2005. This proposal did not receive much attention until the SCO Annual Summit in June 2006, when Russian President Vladimir Putin proposed creation of the Club (Kassenova, 2009, p. 164). President Putin assured the summit that Russia's Gazprom was ready to "to take part and provide technological and, if necessary, financial assistance" in multilateral energy projects (Ria Novosti, 2006).[9] A year later, in June 2007 at the first meeting of the ministers of energy of the SCO countries, the statutes of the SCO Energy Club were signed.

The statutes define the SCO Energy Club as a non-governmental advisory mechanism, involving representatives of governments and business circles of the SCO six member states. SCO observer states and international organizations are allowed to attend, but not make decisions in, SCO Club meetings. The statutes describe the Club as a consultative platform, which aims at improving cooperation on energy. The decision-making body of the SCO Energy Club is the "High Level Group", where each SCO member state delegates 5 persons, including top officials from energy ministries, energy business circles and analytical centres. Observer states are eligible to send two representatives to the Group meetings. The High Level Group meets a minimum of once a year, decides on the SCO energy regulations and laws, sets the agenda for the ministers' meeting and establishes the SCO energy strategy (International Petroleum Economics, 2007, pp. 60–62).

The SCO Energy Club statutes were promptly signed only a year after Putin advocated the creation of the Club. This stirred debate in the West over the role and potential of this forum. Western concerns over the SCO Energy Club arose from the inaccessibility of SCO Energy Club statutes,[10] rapid institutionalization of the SCO between 2001 and 2007,[11] and the energy crisis in Europe when Russia cut gas supplies in

2006. Western countries perceived the potential creation of the club as an attempt to create a "gas OPEC" (Corn, 2007), that will ultimately control 50 per cent of global gas reserves and 20 per cent of oil reserves (Maksutov, 2006, p. 21). The SCO Energy Club was seen as a threat to European energy security (Rosner, 2010) and an obstacle to European interests in Middle East and Africa (Corn, 2007). The latter concern grew out of the proposals on expanding the Club into an Asian Energy Club, which would bring SCO observer states and Turkmenistan into the framework (Aris, 2009, p. 3).

3.2 The slowdown in the establishment of the SCO Energy Club – what went wrong?

Despite five-year efforts, existing legislative framework and permanent position at the SCO, little progress has been made on the implementation of the SCO Energy Club. This slow process has a triple rationale, involving the incompatibility of domestic energy institutions to act within the multilateral forum, different energy priorities of SCO member states, and the Sino-Russian debate over the club's functions.

Although energy security is a priority of the SCO member states, their energy agencies are not compatible with the multilateral cooperation agreed in the statutes. In China, the management of the energy sector is in hands of the state agency, National Development and Reform Commission (NDRC). Chinese NOCs also retain some decision-making power in the energy sector because they emerged in the 1980s from the Ministry of Petroleum Industry and Ministry of Chemical Industry. At the annual meetings of the SCO energy ministers, China is represented by Liu Tie'nan, vice-chairman of the NDRC. But the Commission deals primarily with economic issues, not energy, which might impede its performance at the SCO Energy Club forum.

In Kazakhstan, energy management underwent reform in 2010. Two new institutions were created: the Ministry Of Oil and Gas, and the Ministry of Industry and New Technologies. Since 2002, the role of Kazakhstan's leading NOC, KazMunaiGaz, has also grown in energy policy decision-making process (EIA, 2012b). In Uzbekistan and Russia, energy policy is similarly overseen by the president and trapped in presidential politics. Russia's Ministry of Energy was restructured in 2008, as a result of Medvedev taking over the presidential office, and was expected to change again following the return of Putin in 2012.[12] Tajikistan and Kyrgyzstan both have ministries of energy, but political instability in the latter results in frequent changes of the government structure and functioning of its bodies. In summary, Chinese, Russian and Central Asian political leadership is directly involved in the business and management of the energy sector, which makes energy security vulnerable to power succession and changes in central governments.

The second reason for the slowdown in the development of the Club is the different priorities of that SCO member states have sought through the Club. Russia is the largest global energy exporter, which historically dominated the energy trade in Eurasia. Moscow has sought to retain its control over the Eurasian energy market through several initiatives, including the Eurasian Economic Community, the International Alliance of Non-governmental Organisations from countries producing or transporting natural gas (Kassenova, 2009, p. 166), and the Customs Union. The SCO Energy Club can deliver benefits to Russia, such as external control over Chinese activities in the energy sector in Central Asia, but it is also a challenge to the Russian monopoly over the regional energy market.

Unlike Russia, China is a net importer of energy. The discrepancy between Chinese domestic energy deposits and its demand has been widening, making China increasingly dependent on external energy sources. Although energy imports still comprise a minority of the Chinese energy portfolio due to the country's dependence on coal, China's demand for crude oil, its main imported energy resource (Zhang, 2011, p. 8), grew three-fold over the decade 2001–10 in comparison to US oil imports (see Table 3.1). In 2008, China became a second-largest consumer (Zhang, 2011, p. 3) and in 2013–14 it is expected to become the largest net oil importer in the World (Reuters, 09.01.2012).

Table 3.1 Crude oil imports by the United States (US) and China (PRC) between 2000 and 2010 (measured in thousand barrels per day)

Year	China	United States
2000	1,400 542	9,070 536
2001	1,353 277	9,328 477
2002	1,394 782	9,140 205
2003	1, 805 8	9,664 921
2004	2,448 9	10,087 6
2005	2,598 9	10,125 95
2006	2,904 7	10,118 03
2007	3,264	10,031 24
2008	3,577 86	9,783 317
2009	4,081 893	9,012 808
2010	4,753 64	9,213 304

Source: U.S. Energy Information Administration International Energy Statistics, accessed 09.12.2012.

In this regard Central Asia seems to be an attractive destination for Chinese NOC operations, not only to meet China's energy needs, but also to reduce its dependence on the Middle East and diversify its energy sources. Kazakhstan and Uzbekistan, which seek to expand their energy exports, welcome China, with its huge investments in energy infrastructure.[13] Nonetheless, it is important to keep in mind that Kazakhstan is primarily focused on diversifying its energy importers, not switching towards China, which has already become Astana's second-largest energy importer. Kazakh energy policies are tailored to suit Western expectations and international oil companies, which suggests that Kazakhstan will aim at preserving its freedom of action within the SCO Energy Club (Kassenova, 2009, p. 172). Also, Kazakhstan is increasingly concerned about China's growing presence in its energy sector and the implications for Western investments (Oil & Gas Eurasia, 23.09.2012). Thus, on one hand, the SCO Energy Club might be seen as a forum for the SCO energy-producing countries to articulate a collective voice against China, but at the same time it will also likely accelerate Chinese investments and consolidate China's position in the region.

Kyrgyzstan and Tajikistan see the most possibilities for themselves in the SCO Energy Club. Both states seek to develop long-term energy policy and ensure energy security, largely based on their hydro power potential. However, the opportunity that Tajikistan and Kyrgyzstan see in the Energy Club, such as the loans and long-term investments in hydro power sector, may make for a crisis for Uzbekistan. Construction of hydro power stations and dams will potentially adversely affect Uzbek agriculture, which is watered by the Tajik and Kyrgyz rivers. This may lead to a crisis for the Uzbek economy that relies on cotton production, which consumes large quantities of water for around 20 to 30 per cent of total exports.

The third factor that has had a negative impact on the development of the SCO Energy Club is the Sino-Russian dispute over the role of the club. The Sino-Russian consensus is a decisive factor in making the SCO project feasible (Aris, 2008, p. 8; Swanstrom, 2007). Despite the outward agreement over the content of statutes signed in 2007, the Sino-Russian debate over the club's functions has persisted. Russian leadership circles advocated the SCO Energy Club as an external, advisory forum (Krans, 2009), but experts from country's top research institution saw it as "a sufficiently tough association of supranational nature, which supposes delegation of some sovereign power to it, [not a] discussion club" (Krans, 2009). China's energy interests within such a supranational, sovereign institution would be hampered. China lacks the geopolitical advantage of energy-producing countries and its energy agencies are not well prepared to negotiate at the multilateral forum. Hence, Chinese analysts see the Club as an auxiliary institution, with regional cooperation on energy primarily continued through bilateral means (Zhao, 2008, p. 407). Nonetheless, as noted by Chen Xiaoqin (2009, p. 60) from Renmin University, the SCO Energy Club will have an impact on "the cooperation in politics, economy, security and people-to-people relations [in the region]".

The SCO Energy Club is the SCO proposal with the longest implementation process. It illustrates a problem with SCO institutional inefficiency; signing of the document does not specify when it will be translated into domestic law. The SCO does not have any legislative tools to force its member states to adjust their domestic law to the SCO agreements.[14] The slowdown in the creation of the club is a result of internal institutional hindrances of the SCO within member states and frequent changes of those states' energy agencies. The problems also grow out of the different energy priorities of member states as well as the lack of Sino-Russian consensus over the club's functions. These two leaders of the SCO also represent the largest energy consumer of the World (China) and the largest global producer of energy (Russia). Not only do Russia and China have different energy strategies, but also their bilateral cooperation on energy lags behind. The global financial crisis of 2008–09 and their impact on regional economies, political unrest in Kyrgyzstan in 2010 and modest energy infrastructure linking all SCO member states further obstructed creation of the club.

4 China's stakes in the SCO energy multilateralism

The slow progress of the SCO Energy Club's development and China's preference to cooperate with Central Asia bilaterally suggest that the multilateral framework is marginalized in Beijing's foreign policy. Nonetheless, in September 2011, China concluded the Xi'an Proposal with Russia, Tajikistan and Kyrgyzstan calling for the prompt creation of the club. Unlike other SCO energy-related events, the Xi'an Proposal was assessed by Chinese analysts from Shanghai Academy of Social Sciences Center for SCO Studies as an important step towards creating an effective club.[15] In June 2012, during the SCO Annual Summit President Hu Jintao emphasized not only the need for cooperation on energy among the SCO member states, but specifically the establishment of the SCO Energy Club (durban.china-consulate.org, 2012).

Russia conformed to this view. In December 2012, during the annual SCO Meeting of Heads of Governments, Prime Minister Medvedev announced: "We are actively supporting the work of the SCO Energy Club, which should be a useful venue for a dialogue between representatives of our governments, academia and businesses" (government.ru, 2012). Medvedev's official statement suggests that Sino-Russian debate on the club has come to consensus.

China's supportive stance towards a multilateral institution grows out of geopolitical challenges to China's energy security after 2010. The Arab Spring revolutions in the Middle East and North Africa directly threatened China's energy imports, which accounted for over 50 per cent of China's total energy imports. Since 2011, the US and the EU imposed new sanctions on Iranian oil exports and on Iran's trading partners. Although China and Russia managed to halt the UN Security Council measures against Iran, China's involvement in the Iranian energy sector faces obstacles. China cannot increase its oil imports, because otherwise it will meet sanctions from the West. At the same time, Chinese energy demand is growing. In 2012, Beijing replaced one third of its Iranian imports with Sudanese oil and Middle Eastern oil, shipped via the Malacca Strait, but this route is vulnerable to piracy and terrorism and China's navy is unable to secure energy transports (Lanteigne, 2009, p. 105). Cooperation with Central Asia, through bilateral and multilateral channels, provides alternative energy resources and facilitates the access to more distant energy producers in the region via land routes.

The SCO Energy Club as an external, consultative body has two main advantages for China. First, it will allow China to further the dialogue with the leaderships of Central Asia and Russia as well as reduce the negative perceptions of China's appetite for Central Asian energy. In this regard, it will advance the political and diplomatic dimensions of China's energy security in the region. Second, the cooperation between the SCO members is not a direct threat to European energy security, which should soothe Western concerns over the club's potential as an "energy cartel".

4.1 SCO Energy Club as a potential political agency

SCO Energy Club as a potential political agency for inter-governmental dialogue corresponds with China's White Paper on Energy Strategy issued in 2012. According to the Paper, multilateral cooperation on energy has become an inherent part of China's energy strategy. Multilateralism does not replace bilateral commercial deals, but is necessary to secure China's interests and dialogue with its energy partners (Zhang, 2011, pp. 31–32). The White Paper stresses that Beijing has been a member of the energy working group of the SCO as well as other international organizations. The White Paper also calls for efforts in strengthening international dialogue and exchange on energy, carrying out effective energy cooperation, and collective efforts to maintain energy security (Xinhua, 24.10.2012).

The SCO Energy Club will play a critical role in advancing China's relations with its partner states at the leadership level. Analysis of the bilateral cooperation on energy between China and the Central Asian countries, presented in the first part of this chapter, and organization of the energy sectors in the SCO member states shows that the agreement between leaders is a precondition for trade in energy. The intergovernmental agreement defines the scope and potential of long-term commercial deals on energy. The SCO as a platform for multi-party political dialogue will facilitate regional cooperation, accelerate conclusion of multilateral projects, and provide an additional channel for bilateral agreements (Zhao, 2007, p. 156).

4.2 SCO Energy Club and the China threat theory in Central Asia

The SCO Energy Club will help to alleviate the so-called China threat in Central Asia. Although trade with China generates a significant share of GDP for the former Soviet republics, and China has invested USD 20 billion in Central Asia since 1991, Beijing is perceived as a threat to Central Asian integrity and identity. In Kazakhstan, China is accused of unequal treatment of Kazakh employees and of depleting the country's natural resources (Brauer, 2011). Chinese investments in Kazakhstan often meet strong resistance from the populace, which successfully forced Astana to cancel some deals agreed with Beijing.[16] In Tajikistan and Kyrgyzstan, China is blamed for the deteriorating local job market, because it does not employ local workers for its construction works. In Tajikistan, there is also a popular perception that China aims at eventually annexing Tajik territory that adjoins the PRC (Laruelle and Peyrouse, 2009, p. 115–16). In Uzbekistan, the only Central Asian SCO state that does not have borders with China, the China threat theory is less noticeable. Nonetheless, Uzbeks feel discriminated against and ignored by China, which commenced the talks on the Uzbek section of Central Asian Gas Pipeline construction only when Beijing had nearly completed negotiations with Turkmenistan and Kazakhstan. For Tashkent, this deprived Uzbekistan of geographic and diplomatic room for manoeuvre (Saipov, 2012).

China's involvement and initiatives channelled through the SCO are perceived as less threatening than bilateral ones. USD 10 billion in loans, which Beijing offered through the SCO framework and for Central Asian economic recovery in 2009, scored positive comments from regional politicians and populations. The loans were seen not as Beijing's gift to local leaderships, but as concrete assistance to their societies and economies. Beijing's bilateral initiatives can advance the SCO's multilateral level efforts to produce a more cooperative response from Central Asia.

4.3 The SCO Energy Club and Russian stakes in Central Asia

The SCO Energy Club will also bring Russia into the multilateral energy framework along with China and Central Asia. The Russian presence in the club will give Moscow the outward perception that it monitors and regulates China's engagement with Central Asia (Swanstrom, 2007). Over the 2000s, China threatened Russian energy security by channelling half of Turkmen gas exports to sustain China's economy. China's deals with Central Asia also gave the latter more bargaining power against Moscow, which influenced Russian–Central Asian agreements and energy prices (Blank, 2010). Moscow is not able to break Sino-Central Asian cooperation on energy, secured through long-term energy agreements and growing energy infrastructure, so it has to look for alternative means to contain China, which is a function the club can serve.

Wang Haiyun, director of energy diplomacy section at the China Foundation of International Studies in Beijing, has argued that the 2010s will be defined by Sino-Russian "quasi-alliance" (Yu, 2012, p. 2). Both states will forge an alliance bi- and multi-laterally to increase their benefits and influence in Asia. The SCO Energy Club will become a channel, which Russia will use as a counter-measure against Chinese energy strategies in Central Asia (Clarke, 2008, p. 108).

4.4 China's risks in the SCO Energy Club

The club fits well in China's official energy strategy and benefits China's overall energy security. It presents an alternative means to consolidate China's presence in Central Asia and a platform to foster political cooperation with Central Asia and Russia. Nonetheless, its creation can jeopardize China's interests in the region in two ways.

Firstly, China's positive experience with advancing its bilateral initiatives at SCO level, such as the loans, indicates that China will use the SCO Energy Club as a main means to promote its regional energy policy. Nonetheless, the existence of the club will give Central Asia and Russia a collective voice, and institutional and political tools to influence

China's energy policy. Despite Central Asian internal conflicts and its countries' inability to cooperate with each other,[17] the region remains united in its perception of China's energy thirst. Although Beijing has already secured its position in the region through bilateral long-term agreements and energy infrastructure, China's SCO partners may use the club to threaten China's interests in the region. This potential should not be underestimated by China.

The SCO Energy Club will tie China closer to Central Asian security. China successfully avoided involvement in political turmoil in Kyrgyzstan in 2005 and 2010. Since 2001, China has also advocated using the SCO as more of an economic- and energy-oriented organization rather than a security one. The SCO Energy Club is a step forward in this direction. However, China's growing dependence on Central Asian energy and a growing network of energy infrastructure in the region ties Beijing to regional security. Security of energy supply is a core interest for Beijing, so any threat to the energy infrastructure in the region, will require Beijing to respond militarily to protect its interests, nationals and investments.[18] Such a scenario will have major implications for China's relations with Central Asia, Russia and the West.

5 Concluding note

The findings of this chapter are that Sino-Central Asian multilateral energy cooperation will not replace bilateral agreements, but it will become a part of China's broader policy towards the region and beyond. The SCO Energy Club will play a role as an additional political platform to support bilateral deals in the energy sector. Formation of the SCO Energy Club will grow out of the common interest among regional ruling elites and a Sino-Russian consensus on the creation of the club. The club is unlikely to be an "energy cartel" due to the different energy security priorities of the member states and the incompatibility of their respective energy institutions. But the importance of energy security in the SCO region, problems with energy imports from Africa and the Middle East, and the United Nations Security Council (UNSC) sanctions imposed in 2012 on Iranian oil exports, do all suggest that the SCO Energy Club will exceed the scope of a consultative forum.

For China, the SCO Energy Club will become a means for diplomacy in Central Asia. The club will serve as a platform for political dialogue on energy between the SCO member states. It will also permit China to promote its projects in Central Asia. The club will work to reduce the perception of China as a threat in the region, and give Moscow an outward perception of assuming some control over Beijing. Despite these advantages, China's growing stakes in Central Asia through the SCO and its institutions will make China more vulnerable to regional insecurity from political unrest and internal conflicts in Central Asia. Any instability within Central Asia in the future will become a serious obstacle for securing the energy infrastructure, in which China has invested.

The multilateral forum of the SCO Energy Club will become an inherent part of China's energy policy in Central Asia and beyond. It will allow China to "test" its energy multilateralism, build political compromises and develop energy cooperation with multiple partners. This pattern might be copied in China's diplomacy towards Africa, and Central and South America.

Appendix 1 China–Central Asia bilateral agreements on energy cooperation

Date	Countries involved	Agreement
September 1997	China, Kazakhstan	"The agreement between the governments of the PRC and Kazakhstan on the cooperation in oil and gas sectors" (Huaxia, 2007)
June 2002	China, Kyrgyzstan	"The agreement between the governments of the PRC and Kyrgyzstan on the development of framework for cooperation in energy sector" (PRC Central Government, 2004)
May 2004	China, Kazakhstan	"The agreement between the governments of the PRC and Kazakhstan on the development of the comprehensive cooperation in oil and gas sectors" (Huaxia, 2007) "The Agreement between China's National Petroleum Group and KazMunaiGaz on the construction of Atasu – Alashankou oil pipeline" (Huaxia, 2007)
September 2004	China, Kyrgyzstan	"The Framework for the cooperation between PRC and Kyrgyzstan for years 2004–2014", section 4 of the treaty (PRC Ministry of Commerce, 2004)
August 2005	China, Kazakhstan	Agreement between China and Kazakhstan on the development of gas pipeline
December 2012	China, Kazakhstan	"The Agreement between the governments of PRC and the Kazakhstan on customs regulation of transportation of energy in border regions"
August 2007	China, Kazakhstan	The testimony China Oil and Gas Group and Kazakh Gas and Oil Group before the PRC and Kazakhstan presidents on "The agreement on the construction of the second phase of the crude oil pipeline"
June 2009	China, Uzbekistan	"The agreement between China's National Petroleum Company and Uzbekistan State Oil Company (Uzbekneft) on expanding cooperation in gas and oil sectors" "The amendment to the agreement between China's National Petroleum Company and Uzbekistan State Oil Company (Uzbekneft) on joint exploration of Mingbulak oil field" (Energy Resources Website, 2009)
April 2011	China, Uzbekistan	The agreement reached during the Uzbekistan President visit to Beijing on the 5 million USD loans towards the modernization of the energy infrastructure
September 2011	China, Kazakhstan, Uzbekistan	A series of agreements on energy cooperation between China and Kazakhstan, and China and Uzbekistan during the trip of Liu Tie'nan, the Head of the PRC National Energy Administration (Cutler, 2012)
June 2012	China, Uzbekistan	Both countries signed an agreement to sell 10 bcm to China through Central Asian pipeline once it will be fully operating.

Notes

1. The author's interviews with Central Asian scholars between December 2011 and January 2012 revealed that China's Central Asian policy is seen as driven by realism and oriented towards maximizing China's energy, security and economic interests. To attain this goal, China is deemed to have built its political and business lobbies.
2. The construction of the pipeline proceeded in three phases. The main constructor of the first phase, initiated in August 2007 in Turkmenistan, was Stroytransgaz, a subsidiary of Russian Gazprom. The other companies working on the Turkmen phase were China Petroleum Pipeline Bureau, China Petroleum Engineering and Construction Corporation, and Zeromax. The second phase of the construction started in June 2008 in Uzbekistan. The main contractor was Asia Trans Gas, a joint venture of Uzbekneftegaz and CNPC. The third phase started in July 2008 in Kazakhstan. The main contractor was Asian Gas Pipeline Company, a joint venture between CNPC and KazMunaiGaz, while other contractors included KazStroyService and China Petroleum Engineering and Construction Corporation. Russian Vyksa Steel Works, a subsidiary of United Metallurgical Company, was a producer of pipes for Uzbekistan and Kazakhstan sections of the project (hydrocarbons-technology.com).
3. Turkmenistan managed to secure its energy demand due to its abundant gas sources, but the remaining four Central Asian states are dependent on each other energy exports. Tajikistan energy imports, mainly from Russia and Kazakhstan, account for 40 per cent of its total consumption (Bukarica et al., 2011, p. 11). Kyrgyzstan energy imports reach 60 per cent, largely secured by Uzbekistan, which suffers from the energy shortages during winter due to mismanagement of the country's energy assets.
4. The CNPC made only one investment in Kyrgyzstan, in 2011, in the project of oil refinery in Kara-Balta near Bishkek (Central Asia Economy Newswire, 2012).
5. China was among the first countries, which recognized independent Central Asian republics. In the early 2000s China signed bilateral treaties on Good Neighbourhood Relations with all Central Asian states (with the exception of Turkmenistan). With Kazakhstan and Uzbekistan China also concluded strategic partnerships in 2005 and 2011 respectively.
6. For the list of China's bilateral agreements on cooperation in energy, see Appendix 1 in this chapter.
7. They include CNPC on the Chinese side and KazMunaiGaz and Uzbekneft from Kazakhstan and Uzbekistan. Another Chinese NOC, Sinopec, concluded only two deals in Central Asia – in 2004, when it bought the US First International Oil Corporation for USD 153 billion, and in 2009 when its subsidiary, Sinopec Engineering, became the main constructor of Atyrau refinery modernization (Sinopec Annual Report, 2011, p. 29).
8. China has aimed at increasing energy imports from Russia since the early 1990s, but Moscow disrupted these plans. The construction of Skovorodino–Daqing pipeline was ceased in 2003, following the arrest of Mikhail Khodorkovsky, and the break-up of Yukos which was leading the project. The pipeline was overtaken by Russian NOCs Rozneft and Transneft and instead of reaching China, it ends in Russian Eastern Siberia, which allows for oil exports to both China and Japan (Trenin, 2012, p. 38).

9. Putin specifically aimed at Gazprom participation in the construction of Iran–Pakistan–India gas pipeline.
10. There is only a Chinese-language version of statutes available for the general public. This document cannot be found on the SCO official website, but was reprinted by the Petroleum Economics International journal (国际石油经济) in 2007.
11. Until 2007 the SCO set up two permanent institutions – the SCO Secretariat in Beijing in late 2003 and the Regional Anti-Terrorist Structure in Tashkent in 2004. Formation of both took two years from the agreement of their establishment.
12. Vladimir Putin, upon re-taking presidential office in 2012, announced privatisation of Russian energy giants, what raised multiple concerns in Russian energy agencies (Daly, 2012b). However, due to the Russian-Ukraine crisis that commenced in December 2013, the privatisation was delayed.
13. Up to June 2012, China invested USD 20 billion USD in Central Asian republics, much of which went into the construction of energy projects and energy infrastructure (Shustov, 2012).
14. For instance, it took nearly a year for Russia to ratify the "SCO Charter" signed in June 2002, the most important document of the organization, by Duma. President Putin ordered the translation of the Charter into Russian domestic law only in June 2003 (Compilation of Materials & Documents of Shanghai Five-Shanghai Cooperation Organisation 1996.4–2008.8, 2003, p. 97).
15. Personal interview with China-based scholar (September 2011).
16. This was a case of Kazakh land lease to China in 2009–10 for agricultural purposes (Brauer, 2011).
17. Central Asian states proposed institutions to regulate regional economic, energy, political, social and especially ecological issues, but they never succeeded. For instance, the Central Asian Union, proposed in 2004 by Kazakhstan, never developed into an effective body, due to disagreements and mistrust between its members (Akhmadov, 2008).
18. A precedent was Chinese intervention during the 2011 domestic conflict in Libya, when the People's Liberation Army (PLA) evacuated over 30,000 citizens. This was a challenge for the Chinese pledge of non-intervention in the domestic affairs of other states. It also questioned the role of the PLA in China, formally responsible for domestic stability and protection of the ruling regime in China.

4

The Institutional Setting of China's Energy Policy

Karolina Wysoczanska

1 Energy institutions 1949–2003

People's Republic of China (PRC), was founded in 1949 with ambitions of rapid industrialization and economic growth but with insufficient oil and gas resources. Due to the rapid development of the Daqing and Shengli oilfields in north-east China in the early 1960s, the country reached self-sufficiency in oil production with surplus for export (Lee, 2005). Taking advantage of the first international oil crisis in 1973, China began to sell crude oil to Thailand, the Philippines and Japan in exchange for necessary equipment and technology (Zha, 2006). Despite these initial developments, China was never able to find a proper institutional setting to oversee its energy sector.

Between 1949 and 1980, despite two short periods during which a single ministry was in charge of China's energy policy, the country had no central administrative body responsible for coherent strategy. Instead, the power was assigned to individual ministries which were in charge of energy policies within their specific sectors. Moreover, in the oil sector, petroleum administration bureaux under local governments, acted as independent units responsible for their own production and investment plans. In the absence of a central ministry governing the country's energy industry, the State Planning Commission (SPC) and the State Economic Commission (SEC) became the lead agencies responsible for formulation and implementation of mid- and long-term energy plans, such as construction projects, production and conservation.

Consequently, from the very beginning of PRC, there were a number of competing ministries and government agencies in charge of the sector, resulting in an overlap of functions and an inefficient use of resources. For example, both the Ministry of Textile and the Ministry of Petroleum

Table 4.1 Responsibilities of energy institutions between 1949 and 1982

The Ministry of Petroleum Industry (1955–70 and 1978–88)	Minister: Yu Qiuli (previous commissar of the People's Liberation Army Logistic Department)	- advanced from the Ministry of Fuel Industry's General Bureau of Petroleum Management - drew heavily from the Logistic Department of the People's Liberation Party - supervised oil and natural gas exploration and development as well as production - based upon the SPC's national plan, supervised and integrated the marketing, production and transportation of oil and oil products
The State Energy Commission (1980–1982)	Chairman: Yu Qiuli (vice-premier, former minister of the Ministry of Petroleum Industry) Chairman- Gao Gang (former vice-chairman of the Central People's Government of the PRC);	- agency with supra-ministerial authority, but lacking meaningful control over the petroleum, electric power and coal ministries because the three were not officially subject to it - lacked authority over money for developing the energy sector, thus adding to its absence of control over policy-making partners in the energy sector - directed the creation and implementation of energy regulations and laws as well as clarifying the discharge of policy - State Energy Commission responsibility conflicted with that of the State Planning Commission
The State Planning Commission(1952–98) In 1998 changed into the State Development and Planning Commission	Chairman: Gao Gang (former vice-chairman of the Central People's Government of the PRC)	- crucial agency in charge of producing the Five-Year Plan - in charge of producing and distributing major commodities - created mid-range and long-range energy plans that included construction projects, energy production and energy conservation - authorized significant construction projects in the energy sector, supervised feasibility studies, decided the size and development rate of projects; frequently consulted external experts - orchestrated project construction - decided the yearly level of refined product imports

Continued

Table 4.1 Continued

The State Economic Commission (1978–88)	- created in 1956, it was consolidated in 1970 with the State Planning Commission, and then recreated in 1978 - directed the application of production strategies developed by the State Planning Commission by integrating the efforts of various ministries - ensured sufficient energy and raw materials were ready to achieve project goals - provided state-of-the-art execution for energy projects - significant contribution in updating technology for energy plants as well as energy conservation - in charge of directing energy production while facing energy shortages - The Energy Research Institute shared in long-range energy forecasting and planning - The Production Management Bureau coordinated the overall energy production operation based upon daily status reports - The Energy Bureau concentrated on policy issues and provided guidance on developing annual plans

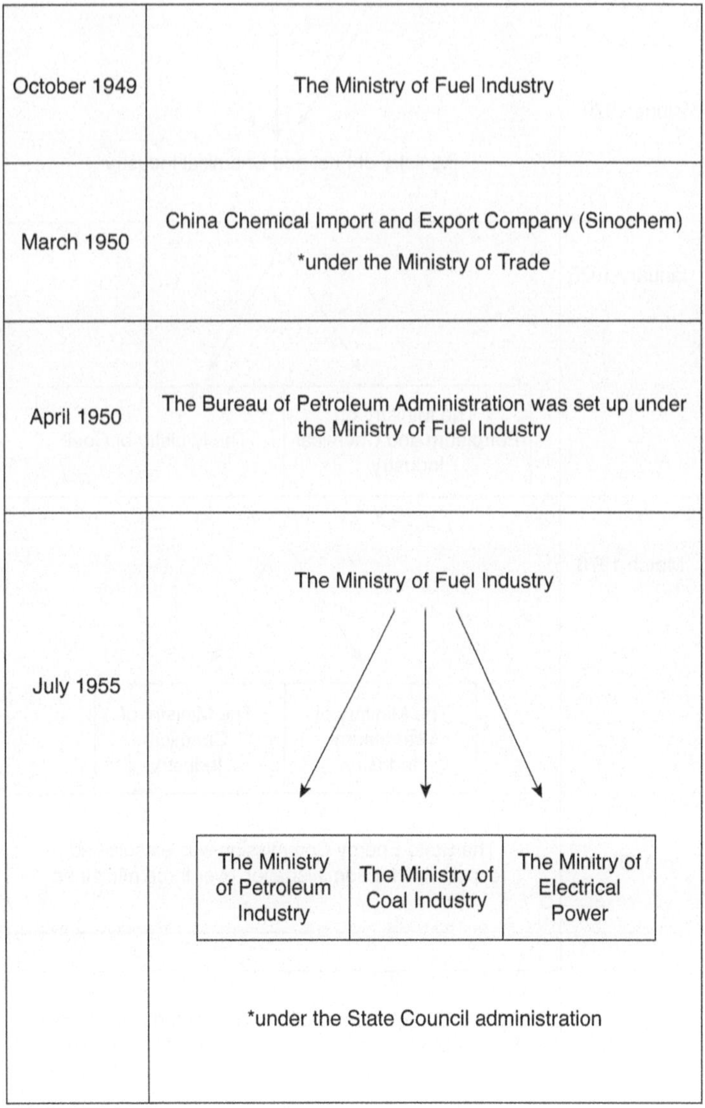

Figure 4.1 Continued

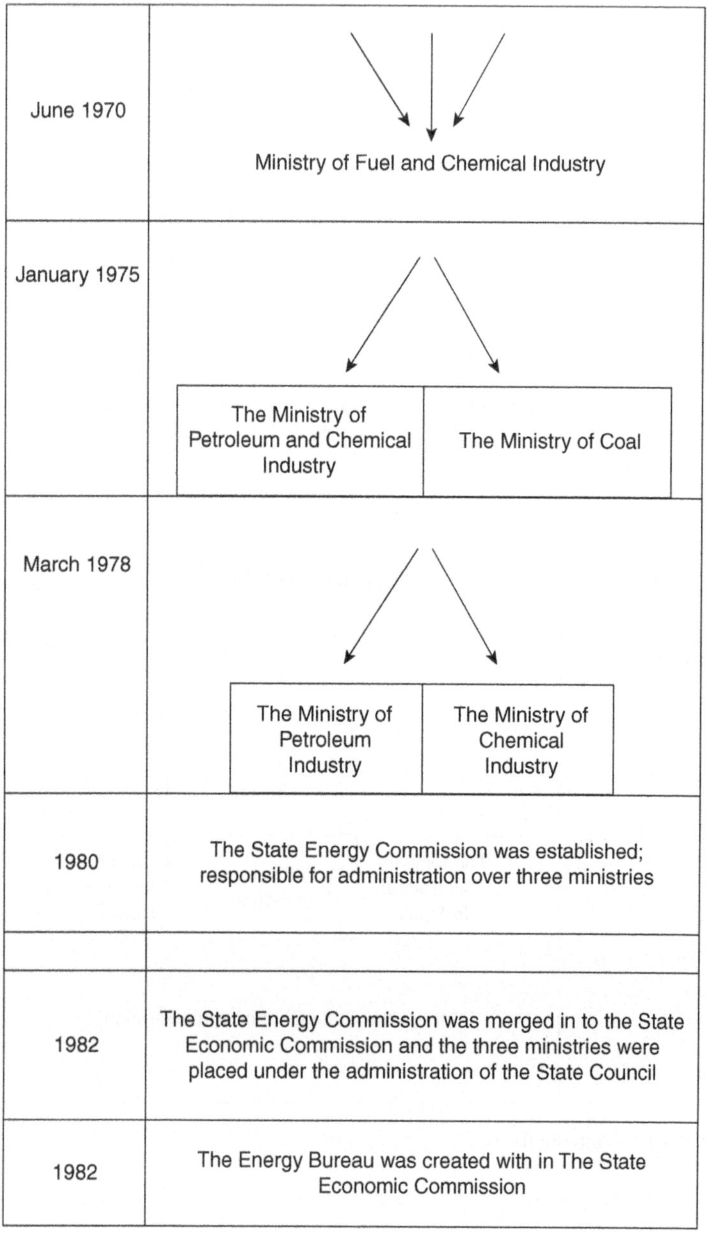

Figure 4.1 Evolution of energy institutions between 1949 and 1982

Industry shared the administrative power over the largest refineries in China (Tobin, 2008). Due to weak coordination between ministries and transportation bottlenecks, China was forced to begin importing crude oil from Oman in 1983 (Zha, 2006).

1.1 1983 restructuring

In the early 1980s, the Chinese government started restructuring of the whole energy industry by adopting the contract system and creating state-owned energy companies (Zhang, 2004). Although by doing so the Chinese government withdrew itself from direct control over the sector, the restructuring was not entirely driven by the need to modernize the institutional framework. It also served as a response to increased demand for petroleum products and fuel shortage in the early 1980s (Tobin, 2008). The oil industry was divided into upstream (exploration and production) and downstream (refining) businesses. The first national oil company (NOC), The China National Offshore Oil Corporation (CNOOC) was established from the offshore assets of the MPI in 1982. It was responsible for exploration, development and production of China's offshore oil and gas fields (China Business Review, 2005). China National Petrochemical Corporation (Sinopec) was set up in 1983 from the downstream assets of the Ministry of Petroleum Industry, the Ministry of Chemical Industry and the Ministry of Textile Industry. The company, as the ministry-level corporation under the direct control of the State Council, was in charge of China's petrochemical refineries, specifically to coordinate the smaller production units (Zhang, 2004). Responsibility for the upstream business was given to the China National Petroleum Corporation (CNPC), which replaced the Ministry of Petroleum Industry in 1988. In the same time, the State Economic Commission was abolished.

While the three state-owned oil companies took over the business functions of the Ministry of Petroleum Industry, the governmental functions were assigned to the newly established Ministry of Energy (Downs, 2006). The government set up the ministry in 1988, by merging the Ministry of Coal Industry, the Ministry of Nuclear Industry, the Ministry of Hydro and Electrical Power, and the Ministry of Petroleum Industry (ibid.).

The ministry, headed by Huang Yicheng, the previous vice-chairman of the SPC, was not very successful since its authority had overlapped with the SPC and NOCs. Moreover, it lacked the ability to create one, coherent strategy among all energy sectors. In fact, the electricity sector was the only one that recognized the ministry's authority over the energy industry (Downs, 2006). Since the majority of China's energy consumption has always been dominated by coal, the officials from the former Ministry of Coal had strong bargaining power to influence the central government to have their ministry reconstituted. As a result, the Ministry of Energy was abolished in 1993, and two ministries took over its functions: The Ministry of Coal Industry and the Ministry of Electric Power Industry. From 1993 to 1998, the SPC was the only significant agency in the State Council supervising the oil industry, leaving the NOCs responsible for both government and business functions. In reality however, the companies' administrative power was very weak. The headquarters did not have autonomy in product pricing or capital investment (Zhang, 2004). Although both companies could formulate their own production plans, the final production scheme was decided by the SPC. It was also the SPC's task to specify the list of key investment projects in each five-year plan and the amount of import quotas on refined products (Zhang, 2004). NOCs also failed to manage and control individual enterprises at the level of production unit. Oilfields and refineries tended to stay committed to local governments and their own production plans which in turn did not resolve the previous coordination problems (Lin, 2006). Also, because separate companies were responsible for different parts of the oil sector, administration and management of oil resources was fragmented, creating problems of allocation of funds and information flows (Smyth et al., 2001). For instance, CNPC was responsible for oil and gas exploration whereas downstream industries were under the control of Sinopec. This created distortions in investment because downstream industries are more profitable than upstream industries: while there was excessive duplication in downstream industries, upstream industries were starved of capital investment (Zhang, 2004). This resulted in CNPC's failure to provide stable deliveries of oil to Sinopec's refineries (Yan, 1998). Even though Sinopec could buy cheaper oil from international markets and ensure stable oil supplies to its refineries, the company was obligated to buy oil from CNPC (Zhang, 2004). Thus, from the very beginning it was difficult to find a smooth line for cooperation between Sinopec and CNPC as well as between both NOCs and government objectives.

1.2 Government reshuffle in 1998

Given the strategic importance of the oil sector and the growing dependence on oil imports, in the middle of 1990s, Beijing initiated the reconstruction of the domestic energy industry. The purpose was to separate companies' business and administrative functions and to create

State Economic and Trade Commission (1998–2003)

↓

State Bureau of Petroleum and Chemical Industry

↓	↓	↓	↓	↓
Offices	Dep. of Planning and Development	Dep. of Policy and Legislation	Dep. of Reform and Finance	Dep. of Personnel
1. General Sec.	1. General Sec.	1. Policy Studies Sec.	1. Industry Reform Sec.	1. General Sec.
2. Secretary Sec.	2. Statistics and Information Sec.	2. Economic Legislation Sec.	2. Subordinate Units Reform Sec.	2. Enterprise Cadre Sec.
3. Foreign Affairs Sec.	3. Oil Sec.	3. Technological Standard Sec.	3. Enterprise Finance Sec.	3. Administration Personnel Sec.
4. Research Sec.	4. Petrochemical Sec.	4. General Business Sec.	4. Administration Finance Sec.	4. Party and People Sec.
	5. Chemical Sec.			

Figure 4.2 Organizational structure of the State Bureau of petroleum and chemical industry
Source: Zhang, 2004.

modern, vertically integrated businesses covering the whole production chain (Guo, 2007; Smyth and Qingguo, 2001).

In 1998, China's two largest petrochemical companies, Sinopec Group and CNPC, were geographically divided, with CNPC controlling northern China and Sinopec the south. Additionally, from 1999 to 2001, all three companies set up subsidiaries listed on Hong Kong, New York and Shanghai stock exchanges.

As part of the reform, there was also a major reorganization of the central government bodies. The Ministry of Coal Industry, the Ministry of Power Industry and the Ministry of Chemical Industry were abolished. The State Bureau of Petroleum and Chemical

Industry (SBPCI) was established under the administration of the State Economic and Trade Commission (SETC). The SETC became the most powerful institution within the State Council. At macro-level it was responsible for the formulation of industrial policies and supervision of their enforcement. It also organized the drafting of comprehensive economic laws, regulations and policies governing industry, commerce and trade. At enterprise-level, the SETC designed the guidelines and restructuring programs for reform of the country's state-owned enterprises, as well as formulating the policies, laws and regulations governing the supervision and management of state assets in the enterprises. At international level it was in charge of coordination of the country's domestic and foreign trade policies as well as import and export policies, and in conjunction with the State Development Planning Commission.

The Bureau took over the governmental functions of the former ministries and that of oil companies, namely the supervision of both upstream and downstream businesses, implementation of reforms in management systems and the most important function – reorganization of the 7,500 subordinate enterprises of CNPC and Sinopec. The Bureau was also responsible for formulation of re-employment programs for laid off workers from these two companies (Zhang, 2004).

The State Development and Planning Commission (SDPC – former SPC) retained authority for planning, investment approval and pricing (Meidan et al., 2009). The newly established Ministry of Land and Natural Resources (MLNR) was given the responsibility for planning, administration, protection and utilization natural resources as well as issuing exploration and production licenses.

On the one hand the establishment of the SETC as the main agency responsible for the operation of the economy, and the creation of the SBPCI reflect Beijing's recognition of a need for more effective institutional setting to govern the sector. Dependence on international audit firms – KPMG and Pricewaterhouse – to oversee the industrial restructuring program, showed the State Council's scepticism towards its own agents (Lin, 2006). On the other hand, with the growing concern over the security of China's oil supply and the impact of the Asian financial crisis, the central government allowed the oil industry to increase its influence. The newly appointed President of SETC, Sheng Huaren – former President of Sinopec, and the Minister of MLNR, and Zhou Yongkang – former President of CNPC, enhanced NOCs' presence among the bureaucratic elite in Beijing (Meidan et al., 2009).

1.3 The energy bureau under the National Development and Reform Commission

The reorganization of government and industry in 1998 still did not bring an adequate solution to manage and balance interests between all parties involved. The next attempt to streamline supervision of the energy sector and the whole economy took place just a few years later. After the session of the National People's Congress in March 2003, the SDPC merged with the State Council Office for Restructuring the Economic System and part of the SETC and was restructured into the National Development and Reform Commission (NDRC). The SBPCI was abolished along with other bureaux of industrial administration.

The NDRC became the most important government agency involved in energy policy with a broad mandate, which includes managing the country's energy industries, drafting energy plans and policies, examining and approving major construction projects, managing national oil reserves, setting energy prices, negotiating with international energy agencies and approving foreign energy investments. The Energy Bureau, a newly established body under NDRC supervision, was responsible for managing the energy sector and for policy implementation (Meidan et al., 2009).

However, the Energy Bureau, the institution that was meant to coordinate the energy sector, was only one of over 30 departments and bureaus under the NDRC and was initially composed of just 30 people, a number later upgraded to 57 (Downs, 2006). The small staff had been overwhelmed with daily issues and had no time for formulating broader energy development strategies and policies (Kong, 2006). In many cases the bureau had to rely on other departments within NDRC and needed cooperation from other government bodies. For example, the Energy Bureau had to cooperate with the Ministry of Commerce (MOFCOM) in areas such as supervision of refined products distribution or implementation of import and export quota plan of raw materials. Moreover, as an agency under NDRC, it lacked the political power to coordinate energy policy among other government organizations or the NOCs, which hold ministry-level rank (Downs, 2006).

1.4 The State Energy Leading Group (SELG)

The Energy Bureau's lack of authority, and power shortages across the country which contributed to increase oil imports, caused further changes in China's energy governance (Pop, 2010). In June 2003, Premier Wen Jiabao created the State Energy Leading Group (SELG) composed of 13

Table 4.2 Portfolios of departments related to energy policy within NDRC

Department of National Economy	- supply and demand of crucial goods, - examining and developing policy proposals regarding national economic security and overall industry security approach presenting yearly cumulative goals and polices to stabilize the operation
The Bureau of Economic Operations Adjustment	- coordinating the development of distribution of gas, oil, electricity, coal and other key commodities - organizing their transportation
The Department of Fixed Asset Investment	- developing laws and regulations regarding management of fixed asset investments - reviewing and authorizing large construction projects
The Department of Foreign Capital and Overseas Investment	- presenting goals and guidelines concerning approaches, methods and structural optimization of investing overseas and using foreign capital - accepting crucial overseas-invested projects as well as ones consuming significant supplies of foreign currency
The Department of Basic Industries	- organizing the transportation and energy development strategies with national economic projects - evaluating the work of the transportation and energy industries
The Department of Resource Conservation and Environmental Protection	- coordinating creation and application of strategies and actions regarding the preservation and overall use of energy and resources, - planning and directing crucial pilot programs for emission reduction and energy conservation
The Department of Trade	- creating and applying strategies for the total of imports and exports of significant industrial products, raw materials and agricultural products
The Department of Price	- developing price and fee-charging guidelines and rules - determining and modifying prices and fees overseen by the central government
The Office of Key Project Inspectors	- reviewing and tracking application of crucial national infrastructure projects - following and reviewing the application of national investment rules and strategies in pertinent industries and by local governments
Energy Bureau	- overseeing power, coal, natural gas, oil and other segments of the energy sector and the national oil reserve - proposing energy development programs and major guidelines - responsible for evaluating the use and development of energy at home and overseas - creating policy guidelines for renewable energy and energy conservation

Source: NDRC website.

Table 4.3 Members of the State Energy Leading Group

The State Energy Leading Group	
Name	**Function**
Wen Jiabao	Premier
Huang Ju	Vice Premier
Zeng Peiyan	Vice Premier
Ma Kai	Minister, National Development and Reform Commission
Li Zhaoxing	Minister of Foreign Affairs
Xu Guanhua	Minister of Science and Technology
Zhang Yunchuan	Minister, Commission of Science, Technology and Industry for National Defence
Jin Renqing	Minister of Finance
Sun Wensheng	Minister of Land and Resources
Du Qinlin	Minister of Agriculture
Bo Xilai	Minister of Commerce
Li Rongrong	Minister, State-owned Assets Supervision and Administration Commission
XieZhenhua	Director, State Environmental Protection Administration
Li Yizhong	Director, State Administration of Work Safety
Chai Songyue	Chairman, State Electricity Regulatory Commission
GeZhenfeng	Deputy Chief of the General Staff of the People's Liberation Army

Source: Downs, 2006.

members, from the NDRC and other key ministries. The SELG, headed by the premier, was set up as an ad hoc supra-ministerial body to coordinate and steer the country's energy sector and make recommendations to the State Council (Meidan et al., 2009). It did not formulate concrete policies but rather it provided the general framework for the development of the energy sector (Downs, 2006). The State Energy Office (SEO) provided administrative support to the Leading Group and managed day-to-day operations and research. It also prepared policies concerning energy development and conservation, monitoring the country's energy security condition, predicting and providing early warnings about energy problems.

The SELG, which includes some of China's most powerful officials, has power and authority to streamline the operations of the energy sector and build the necessary consensus among involved agencies. However, its lack of expertise and involvement in the daily management of the sector prevented it from solving discrete issues. The SEO, with its vice-ministerial, neither had authority over NOCs or the political muscles to influence energy policy-making (Downs, 2006). Its mandate overlapped with the Energy Bureau which still retained its function of policy implementation (Meidan et al., 2009). Moreover, the SEO's cadres indicate the importance of NDRC in the energy policy-making process and the growing influence of NOCs. The office was headed by Ma Kai, minister of the NDRC, Xu Dingming, the former director of Energy Bureau and Ma Fucai, the former head of CNPC (Downs, 2006). These close connections between the SEO's leadership prevented conflicts of interest between NDRC, oil companies and SEO (ibid.). They also show the leadership's intention to utilize the vast experience and knowledge of experts on China's energy sector (Tobin, 2008).

2 New institutional setting of China's energy policy

The latest changes to China's energy policy-making apparatus took place in March 2008 when the ELG and the SEO were abolished and the National Energy Administration (NEA) replaced the Energy Bureau under NDRC. The NEA incorporated the functions of the State Energy Office and those of the Commission of Science, Technology and Industry for National Defence (abolished in 2008) over the nuclear power sector. It is responsible for administering all energy sectors, formulating and implementing energy development plans and industrial policies as well as promoting institutional reform in the sector. Headed by Zhang Guobao, the vice-minister of the NDRC, NEA was upgraded to the vice-ministerial level rank and reports directly to the State Council. However, this new institutional arrangement still struggles to fulfil its mandate. First, in many aspects NEA resembles its predecessor, the Energy Bureau. It is divided into a number of departments with overlapped functions, blurred division of work and, often, conflicting interests. The lack of a single authoritative department to shape the board's energy policy impedes the formulation of a uniform strategy.

Second, the NEA has not been given sufficient authority and autonomy to coordinate the interests of all ministries, commissions and NOCs. Although NEA reports directly to the State Council, NDRC retains for

Table 4.4 Departments within National Energy Administration

General Administration	Oversees the government's day-to-day activities, including financial and asset management, press affairs, personnel, and Chinese Communist Party affairs
Energy Conservation and Scientific Equipment	Supervises comprehensive resource use and energy conservation, creates requirements, and advocates energy-conserving equipment and technologies.
Oil and Natural Gas	Directs the oil and natural gas industry, organizes development of oil and natural gas, advocates industry reforms, and oversees commercial and national oil reserves.
Policy and Legislation	Reviews significant energy challenges, coordinates creation of energy laws, and directs administrative investigations and inspections.
Power	Prepares development of thermal and nuclear power coordinates the nation's power network, and manages nuclear power station crisis management.
New and Renewable Energy	Controls and organizes energy development in rural areas and prepares for using new energy sources, including renewable energy.
Development and Planning	Investigates and presents proposals for energy development strategies; coordinates the creation of macro-level programs for energy development, annual plans, and industrial policies; and begins reforms of the energy industry
Coal	Coordinates the coal industry, creates coal mining plans, launches reforms of the system, and creates advanced technologies for decreasing coal-burning pollution
International Cooperation	Launches international energy cooperation, creates programs, laws, and guidelines for increasing access to China's energy sector and organizes the use and development and of foreign energy.

Source: Downs 2008.

NEA's logistics and it still approves major projects and controls important pricing bureaux (Downs, 2008). Moreover, Zhang Guobao's "dual role" raises further questions about NEA's autonomy (Downs, 2008). Finally, the same as the Energy Bureau, the NEA does not have enough personnel. The administration's staff of 112 people makes it unlikely that the governance over the sector will be improved (ibid.). For instance, the US Department of Energy has about 4,000 people, half of whom work on policy strategy (Kong, 2006).

Similar to the institutional reshuffle in 2003, when the Energy Bureau was established, the government restructuring in 2008, did not bring any substantial improvement in the management of the energy sector. Despite the leadership's recognition of the need for a high-level coordination body, the same as last time, the establishment of the Ministry of Energy was not possible due to strong opposition from both the NDRC and NOCs (Downs, 2008). The NDRC fears that creation of such a ministry would undermine its dominant position; and NOCs are reluctant to have an influential supervisory agency. Thus, the establishment of the National Energy Commission (NEC) became the compromise. The NEC, similar to the SELG, is like "cabinet within the Cabinet": Premier Wen Jiabao and Vice Premier Li Keqiang hold chairman and vice-chairman positions respectively, and the leaders of most important government bodies are members (Bo, 2010). Similar to SELG, the Commission is not responsible for specific policies but rather it is a high-level discussion body to map out the country's domestic and international energy policies. NEA handles the NEC's daily affairs. The energy bureaucracy does not look very different from the previous incarnation, and few changes have occurred. First, unlike SELG, the NEC is housed in the State Council, not within the Central Committee of the Party, what might be seen as government's effort to boost its power (ibid.). Second, with the growing public concern over environmental issues in China, the establishment of SELG reflects the top leadership's recognition of the problem and the need to respond to it (Bo, 2010). Indeed, the 12th Five-Year Plan, unveiled in March 2011, focuses on how to control China's energy demand and emphasizes energy conservation, renewable energy sources and reduction of greenhouse gas emissions (Kennedy, 2010; Szamosszegi and Kyle, 2011). Third, the members of the Commission represent not only key ministries but also various commissions and the military. This clearly reflects the growing number of political actors that can impact both policy-making and implementation. For

Table 4.5 National Energy Commission members (as of January 2013)

Name	National Energy Commission	Current position
Wen Jiabao	Director	Premier
Li Keqiang	Deputy Director	Executive Vice Premier
Zhang Ping	General Office Director	Minister of the NDRC
Liu Tienan	General office Deputy Director	Director of the NEA
You Quan	Member	Deputy Secretary General of the State Council
Zhu Zhixin	Member	Director of Central Finance General Office
Yang Jiechi	Member	Minister of Foreign Affairs
Wan Gang	Member	Minister of Science and Technology
Miao Wei	Member	Minister of Industry and Information Technology
GengHuichang	Member	Minister of State Security
XieXuren	Member	Minister of Finance
Xu Shaoshi	Member	Minister of Land and Resources
Zhou Shengxian	Member	Minister of Environmental Protection
Li Shenglin	Member	Minister of Communication and Transport
Chen Lei	Member	Minister of Water Resources
Chen Deming	Member	Minister of Commerce
Zhou Xiaochuan	Member	Governor of People's Bank of China
Wang Yong	Member	Director of State-Owned Assets Supervision and Administration Commission
Xiao Jie	Member	Chief of State Administration of Taxation
Luo Lin	Member	State Administration of Work Safety
Liu Mingkang	Member	Chairman of China Banking Regulatory Commission
Wu Xinxiong	Member	Chairman of National Electricity Regulatory Commission
Zhang Qinsheng	Member	Deputy Chief of the General Staff Department

Source: China Directory 2012.

example, the appointment of Lieutenant General Zhang Qinsheng, current deputy chief of the General Staff Department of the People's Liberation Army might indicate the government's growing concern over energy transportation routes and, in this regard, the leadership's reliance on the military.

2.1 Other actors

The energy sector, by its nature, always attracts much attention from various political actors and institutions involved in the decision-making process. In China, the bureaucratic matrix is the result of central government inability to establish one central institution responsible for the industry. The fragmentation of governmental structure was further exacerbated by economic decentralization and the leadership's reliance on market forces. And the energy sector, by its nature, is shaped by both internal and external influences and therefore its development depends to a large extent on interactions between different players who seek to maximize their own interest.

Historically, the Ministry of Foreign Affairs was one of the most influential bodies in policy-making. However, due to implementation of economic reforms and the growing role of international economic issues, the ministry lost its political clout (Jakobson and Knox, 2010). The MOFCOM, the Ministry of Finance, the NDRC as well as state-owned banks became the new players involved in foreign trade and economic policies. In the case of China's energy sector, authority is divided among a number of other ministries and commissions: the MLNR, the Ministry of Transportation, State Asset Supervisory and Administration Commission (SASAC) as well as Export Import Bank of China, China Development Bank and local governments.

Although the bargaining power of these institutions is largely determined by their own political clout, they can still take advantage of the decision-making process of the decision-making process and influence or modify any policy (Liberthal and Oksenberg, 1988). Proposals are passed through different agencies for authorization which means that approval times are often long and messy. Moreover, ministries frequently promote projects according to their own interests thereby making energy policy very additive. Although the NDRC and NEA are in charge of China's overall energy policy, they have to coordinate with other governmental bodies, therefore, all decision-making power has to be divided or shared. For example, regarding project financing they have to collaborate with the Ministry of Finance and China Development Bank, regarding transportation with the Ministry of Railways, regarding overseas investment with the MOFCOM etc. More importantly, the central government did not clearly define the division of labour between agencies; therefore no one can clarify who is responsible for making and implementing energy policy in China.

Another barrier to implementing coherent energy strategy comes from local governments. Due to economic decentralization in the 1980s, provincial authorities were granted fiscal authority and become responsible for local economic growth. Additionally, central government implemented the cadre evaluation system, which shaped local officials' behaviour by linking the remuneration of local leaders to economic performance and industrial development (Whiting, 2000). Therefore, local leaders will simply refuse to follow any central policies that might slow down local economic development and hinder their own career paths. For instance, the NDRC efforts to rise energy prices and reduce consumption are held back by provincial leaders' concerns of providing high GDP statistics (Rosen and Houser, 2007). Increased autonomy in terms of economic decision-making also allowed provinces to become independent actors and pursue policies in their own economic interests often beyond the extent of central policies (Liu, 2008). The government of Anhui, for example, through its state-owned construction companies, has direct links with provincial governments in Angola, the main exporter of oil to China. Furthermore, since joining the World Trade Organisation (WTO) in 2001, the Chinese government made commitments to gradually open the economy to foreign firms. In 2007, new guidelines regarding foreign participation in downstream businesses were set to increase foreign access to China's oil sector. Many local provinces however, again have demonstrated their independence and refused to implement the new regulations to protect local petrol stations.

2.2 Powerful oil companies

China's national oil companies have power and influence over energy policy mainly due to their origins as government ministries (Downs, 2006). Based on the current direction of economic policy-making, NOCs in China will continue to play an important role, even if the relationship between state and business has changed. There are several factors underlying this conclusion. First, there are institutional reasons why China's NOCs are likely to remain important political players. Second, the government relies on oil companies as part of broader political agenda. Third, Sinopec, CNPC and CNOOC have become powerful and autonomous economic entities.

2.2.1 Institutional reasons

China's three major NOCs' get their influence from the fact they began as government agencies and the influence they held over the policy-making process. The power of these firms increased further, when China had to face increasing reliance on oil imports and the impact of the Asian financial crisis. In the second half of the 1990s, China's NOCs were given more administrative and financial autonomy by Zhu Rongji for the express purpose of making them more productive prior to their subsidiaries being listed internationally (ibid.). Moreover, the NOCs' power and autonomy have advanced as the government's authority over the sector has weakened (Downs, 2010). Holding ministerial-level rank, the NOCs were always able to bypass lower-ranking government departments such as the Energy Bureau or NEA. The general managers of NOCs can also reach China's seniors leaders directly which further enables them to advance their own interests. Wang Yilin, chairman of CNOOC and Jiang Jiemin, chairman of CNPC are members of CCP Central Committee. Other senior managers whose corporate functions overlap with the energy bureaucracy are: Su Shulin (member of CCP Central Committee, former general manager of Sinopec Corp), Fu Chengyu (chairman and party secretary of Sinopec, former member of CCP Central Committee and former CEO of CNOOC). This kind of relationship between political leadership and oil industry has endured since the PRC was founded. For example, Yu Qiuli, who started his career in the Minister of Petroleum Industry (1958–64), became a vice premier (1975–82), and member of the Politburo (1976–87) (Downs and Meidan, 2011). All three major NOCs also have many opportunities to interact and present proposals to the top leadership. For instance, from 2005 to 2010 more than half of Hu Jintao's overseas trips were to oil-rich countries where Hu has signed contracts for supply, joint exploration and asset transfer on behalf of NOCs (Jakobson and Knox, 2010).

The power and profitability of NOCs has also ironically increased with the formation of another governmental agency – the State-owned Assets and Administration Commission (SASAC) (Naughton, 2008). After all three firms went public in 2000 and 2001, they took on dual identities as state-owned energy companies, responsible for political goals, and publicly listed companies, with the aim of protecting commercial interests. Since that time, there has been a growing tendency for Sinopec, CNPC and CNOOC to behave in ways consistent with their commercial rather than political objectives which has often led to tensions between them and governmental authorities. SASAC was established to act on behalf of the central state as the dominant shareholder of state-owned enterprises (SOEs), including NOCs, so its role is to protect the state's economic interests rather than its political ones. Its three main functions and responsibilities are: (1) supervision and evaluation of state-owned enterprises; (2) oversight of state-owned assets; (3) drafting of laws, administrative rules and regulations that promote increased development of corporate law in China. SASAC also appoints and removes the top executives of the supervised enterprises, and evaluates their performances. With SASAC advocating the merger of corporate control and the related corporate near-term reward system, NOCs managers get more financial independence and their investments are primarily based upon economics as opposed to politics (Liou, 2009). Thus SASAC supports the NOCs' pursuit of profits in that it wants to upgrade the companies' management skills and technical proficiency and make state-owned assets worth more (Naughton, 2008).

2.2.2 Political and financial reasons

Developing the NOCs underscores the government's overreaching political objective aimed at energy security, competitiveness and geopolitics. The Chinese "going out policy", proposed in 2000 at the 5th plenary session of the 15th Central Committee (Lee, 2009) was meant to create national champions, companies which can compete with the world's leading competitors, both domestically and abroad. According to Peter Nolan (2001), the creation of such world-class companies is a matter of national prestige and big state-owned enterprises seem to be a crucial part of the government's strategy to foster domestic innovation; build globally recognized brands and improve national security. This might be seen in China's latest Five-Year Plan which emphasizes the importance of pillar industries and encourages internationalization of large enterprises (NDRC, 2011). The challenge posed by China's growing energy demand have forced Beijing to list oil as the major strategic resource that impacts growth of China's society and economy (Kong, 2005). To enhance the reliability of oil imports, the government relies primarily on the power of its oil companies. Perceiving oil as a scarce commodity and the oil market as manipulated by major international monopoly capital, the Chinese government believes oil that comes from foreign state-run enterprises is a more reliable energy supply than oil bought on the overseas markets (Kennedy, 2010). Operating on that principle, the Chinese government has received significant scrutiny for advocating the international development of the NOCs. Companies and their subsidiaries benefit from preferred access to capital, below-market interest rates on loans from state-owned banks, favourable tax treatment, policies that create a favourable competitive environment for them, and large capital injections when needed. For example, Sinopec's weighted average interest rate on short-term loans (loans with duration of one year or less) was 2.7 per cent in 2010 (Szamosszegi and Kyle, 2011). The government also has vigorously pursued "energy diplomacy" by building numerous political and economic relationships with oil exporters and supplying a number of monetary enticements for providing investments to China's oil companies. For example, in a series of "loans for oil" deals, Beijing facilitated long-term supply agreements with Russia, Kazakhstan and Angola.

Besides China's reliance on NOCs in enhancing oil security, the Chinese government also depends on NOCs in other areas such as specialized expertise, revenues and employment. As already discussed, the most crucial energy policy decisions are made in the NEC. However, since the commission is more like a high-level coordination body, most of their members are not well versed in the detail of complex energy policy issues and must therefore rely on the expertise of NOCs' specialists. For example, the CNPC runs an office for policy research and collaborates with many government agencies on numerous policy reports (Jakobson and Knox, 2010). Although NOCs are not policy-makers per se, the output of their research does have considerable impact on the Chinese leadership (Meidan et al., 2009) and in certain cases they can exert influence on energy policy.

Profit-making and financial independence offer another way to assess the weight of NOCs in the Chinese political economy landscape. Sinopec Group, CNPC and CNOOC Corp accounted for 45 per cent of revenues in China's petroleum and petrochemical industry in 2010 (CPCIF, 2010). These companies were already significant interest groups throughout the reform period. Yet, the companies' profits since 1998 have grown significantly due in large part to their subsidiaries being listed internationally and to increasing oil prices, from USD 12 a barrel in 1998 to USD 111 in 2011 (BP, 2012). For example, Sinopec Group, the largest refiner in Asia by capacity, said its net profit in 2010 reached Yuan 72.124 billion (USD 11.6), up from Yuan 19.546 billion (USD 3.07) in 2008 (Sinopec, 2010). Greater profitability has brought NOCs greater autonomy from the Chinese government and greater influence. The Chinese government also depends on successful NOCs in terms of employment. At the end of 2011, CNPC had 1,668,072 employees and Sinopec had 1,021,979 employees (Fortune Global 500, 2012). Since the political leadership places social welfare and balanced development on the top of its agenda, it will need NOCs and other state-owned companies to facilitate structural change in the Chinese economy.

Chinese oil companies have benefited from their close connections to the state, nonetheless, their status and government intervention have also hindered further development. These firms, created from government ministries in the early 1980s, helped to extend the influence of self-preserving bureaucratic players and showed little muscle in coordinating subsidiaries. The policy, aimed to increase autonomy of subordinate enterprises at the level of production unit, enhanced the sense of independence and the lack of corporate identity in Sinopec and CNPC's constituent enterprises (Nolan, 2003). NOCs also enjoyed several favourable government policies before WTO accession such as restriction on foreign companies' entry to the sector to protect state-owned firms or high tariffs and to limit imports of petrochemical products (Chen, 2000). In that sense, Chinese oil companies are young firms with little international experience. They have only a little background in competition and dealing with the political aspects of entering foreign markets. The foreign energy markets also have not been receptive to the new Chinese companies. This was illustrated in 2003, when Sinopec and CNOOC were excluded from participation in a Caspian Sea oil field project when the original partners opted to increase their own shares in it (Zha, 2006). At a corporate level, all three NOCs seek to see themselves as equals to foreign oil. In fact, government policy seeks to represent them as competitive on the international stage (Nolan, 2001). However, they still have many challenges to overcome: small scale of production, surplus of labour, weak technical know-how and continuing state intervention (Tobin, 2008).

Although their political clout and financial muscles have increased in recent years, NOCs are not fully independent actors and they are still subject to government control. The state exercises control over China's largest SOEs in two ways: (1) appointing and terminating top company officials and (2) approving any significant projects or investments. Top leaders of NOCs, having ministry-level standing, are powerful players inside the Communist Party structure so their appointment lies with the CCP Organisation Department. Decisions are ratified by the Politburo Standing Committee and implemented by the Ministry of Personnel (Downs and Meidan, 2011). The SASAC appoints the rest of the top ranking positions (vice presidents, deputy party secretary and similar posts) in deliberation with party's Organisation Department (Szamosszegi and Kyle, 2011). Thus, under the CCP and SASAC's influence, NOCs' managers are strongly intertwined with the comprehensive personal

The State Development and Planning Commission + The State Economic and Trade Commission		The State Council Office for Restructuring the Economic System
↙	↘	↙
The Ministry of Commerce	The National Development and Reform Commission (NDRC)	
	↓	
	The Energy Bureau	

Figure 4.3 Institutional reshuffling in 2003

patronage and bureaucratic systems that are at the core of institutional life in China. NOCs' managers have to juggle two sets of incentives. First, the companies the managers oversee are expected to make profit, and those managers are now compensated on the basis of the company's financial achievements. Second, the managers' long-term career prospects are decided by the CCP's Organisation Department (Szamosszegi and Kyle, 2011). Thus, NOCs executives must learn to balance corporate and state interests. SASAC's role, as a main shareholder, is to reinforce NOCs' competitive advantage and increase their profitability. In that case, SASAC indirectly forces managers to follow economic objectives. However, their careers and financial success depends on how well they adhere to CCP priorities and government orders since the country's leaders judge those company officials on not just how well they operate their businesses but also to what extent they work for the party's interest (Deng et al., 2011).

The government also exercises control over NOCs through the investment approval system. Chinese outward investments remained highly regulated during the first two decades of economic reform.

Table 4.6 Government institutions in energy sector

Ministry of Commerce	- set issues licenses for energy imports and exports - provide regulations for investments by foreign firms in China's energy markets and by Chinese firms in foreign energy markets
Ministry of Finance	- formulates tax and fiscal policies to promote the central government's energy objectives
Ministry of Foreign Affairs	- provides support to Chinese firms in foreign markets - promotes commercial relations with other countries - ensures that the deals pursued by the Chinese companies do not run counter to other foreign policy objectives
Ministry of Land and Natural Resources	- oversees the surveying of natural resources - administers the registration and assignment of exploration and production licenses
Ministry of Water Resources	- responsible for hydro reserve management and other areas relevant to hydroelectric power - in charge of reviewing and approving dam projects.
Ministry of Transportation	- supervises and coordinates energy transportation by road and water
Ministry of Railways	- responsible for the transport of coal by railway
Ministry of Agriculture	- supervises the utilization of energy in rural areas.
Ministry of Human Resources and Social Security	- regulates the income distribution and pension plans of the employees of state-owned energy companies.
Ministry of Personnel	- determines the personnel structure and managerial appointment of state-owned energy companies
Ministry of Science and Technology	- responsible for research and development in the energy sector and promotes new energy technology development
Ministry of Environmental Protection	- responsible for environment issues
Ministry of Housing and Urban-Rural Development	- responsible for urban planning, relevant to issues such as energy efficiency
State-owned Assets Supervision and Administration Commission of the State Council	- supervises the state-owned assets of centrally owned energy companies - appoints corporate executives of major state-owned energy companies
State Administration of Taxation	- responsible for collection and administration of the enterprise income tax
State Administration for Industry and Commerce	- in charge of market supervision/regulation and related law enforcement through administrative means
State Electricity Regulatory Commission	- responsible for administration and regulation the electricity and power industry - regulates the development of electricity markets - advices the NDRC on the setting tariffs
Export Import Bank of China	- allocates Chinese foreign aid - promotes Chinese trade
China Development Bank	- provides funds for economic and infrastructure development

Even though many government agencies were included in the review and approval process, the Ministry of Foreign Trade and Economic Cooperation was the primary one accountable for promoting, approving and supervising NOCs' investments (Liou, 2009). The implementation of the going out strategy, which aimed to push for the development of national champions, as well leadership efforts to meet the requirements of WTO membership forced the government to simplify overseas investment regulation. The State Council increased the minimum for foreign energy resource projects in 2004, so the NDRC had to approve anything from USD 1 million to 30 million (Downs, 2006). The limit was further raised in China's most recent Five-Year Plan passed by the National People's Congress in March 2011, and now NDRC approval is needed only for investments exceeding USD 300 million in the resources sector (Szamosszegi and Kyle, 2011). However, any major investment that exceed USD 300 million still need the explicit approval of at least four government agencies: the NRDC, MOFCOM, State Administration of Foreign Exchange (SAFE) and the SASAC. The NDRC releases recommendations for locating the NOCs' foreign investments based upon national security considerations. SASAC controls the state's economic interest, MOFCOM checks whether the project conforms to the economic and political environment in the targeted country. SAFE is accountable for investigating the origin of any investment funding and authorizing conversion of Chinese currency into foreign currency (Liou, 2009; Szamosszegi and Kyle, 2011).

3 Bureaucratic matrix and national oil companies

The ineffectiveness of China's energy institutions and the strength of the energy companies have impacted its energy sector management in several ways. First, the current institutional setting and the way it is structured results in an inconsistent and ad hoc management approach. Second, they prevent China from effective planning since the government gives up its control over the sector by transferring it to ministries and commissions, NOCs and local governments (Kong, 2006). Third, by dividing authority over energy policy among twenty governmental organizations, the leadership has produced a bureaucratic network in which no single agency has authority. This leads to disintegration of China's energy policy-making with a result of constant trade-offs (ibid.). All these produce further opportunities for

NOCs corporate autonomy and affect their operations which in turn can undermine government interests. For example, CNPC investments in Sudan provoked accusations by Western governments that China supports the Sudanese government. NDRC had to remove Sudan from the list of countries for oil investments in 2007. However, even after the NDRC's decision, CNPC purchased new Sudanese assets (Kennedy, 2010). Similarly, in 2004 CNOOC began work at the East China Sea Chunxiao field without consulting Japanese authorities, thereby triggering a diplomatic crisis until Hu Jintao and the Japanese Prime Minister Yasuo Fukuda officially agreed on 'cooperative development' (Jakobson and Knox, 2010).

3.1 Price mechanism

The example of oil price regulation reveals how compartmentalizing bargaining and policy-making among government and the national oil companies creates inconsistent policies and unclear regulations.

The prices of gasoline and diesel are directly controlled and fixed by NDRC. The government's objective is to keep domestic prices below international prices to not trigger social instability, sustain economic growth and prevent inflation. The problem is, that approach leads to increased domestic oil and diesel consumption, which requires increased import of foreign supplies, straining China's downstream sector (Kong, 2006). NOCs refine this imported oil at a loss when the domestic prices are lower than those on global market. The crude oil is imported at international market prices but then the refined diesel and gasoline is sold at the cheaper domestic prices. Therefore, when international prices increase, Chinese refineries are hesitant to sell their products in the domestic market (Kong, 2006). To meet the WTO requirements the Chinese government integrated domestic prices with international prices in 1998 (Lin, 2008). At the same time the government organized competition among the NOCs to create better productivity and create market incentives as autonomous drivers for their operations. It also awarded monopolies to China National Petroleum Corporation and Sinopec for the wholesale refined-oil market (Liou, 2009). Yet, the outcome was a price war as the national oil companies, no longer under government control, exploited the free (or freer) market. CNPC and Sinopec both pared diesel and gasoline prices trying to control central and eastern China's market. This competition between the two companies compelled the Chinese government to begin setting domestic diesel and gasoline prices again (Tobin, 2008; Liou, 2009).

In 2000, the government began to reform its pricing system. The prices of petrochemical products were updated monthly on the basis of Singapore prices. This lead to four price increases for domestic oil within six months and encouraged NOCs' to increase imports (Zha, 2006).

Then in 2001, the NDRC established new recommended prices for refined-oil products based upon the weighted monthly average on the New York, Rotterdam and Singapore markets. The mechanism also permitted retail prices to rise and fall within eight per cent of that price (Downs, 2006). Although the government kept its control over prices, the new arrangement was elastic enough to permit companies to set prices based upon input costs (Tobin, 2008). This was generally seen by domestic and foreign analysts as unfairly favouring the NOCs (Lin, 2006). Yet, the government usually did not change domestic prices unless the international prices changed substantially. Consequently, Chinese fuel prices usually remain lower than international ones (Downs, 2006). Indeed, the international market experienced repeated increases from 2003 to 2006, totalling 107 per cent (IEA, 2005). The NOCs reacted by cutting down their supplies to domestic gasoline stations and exporting their oil products for better returns. This behaviour contributed to wide oil shortages throughout Guangdong Province, the country's manufacturing heartland (Liou, 2009). On the one hand, from the government's perspective, NOCs, as state firms, were supposed to shield the Chinese economy from wild swings in international oil prices (ibid.). On the other hand, the companies' behaviour might be seen as the effect of the aforementioned inconsistent policies and unclear regulations. The government's price controls required the NOCs to lose money when domestic regulated prices fell below international market prices. Therefore, the NDRC was forced to increase domestic diesel and gasoline prices and subsidize the NOCs to make up some of their losses. In 2008, the NDRC released a blueprint for improving the oil pricing structure. It proposed that domestic crude oil prices should be based upon international prices but that connection should be regulated. Under the reform scheme, "pricing of domestic refined oil prices should not only reflect fluctuations of international oil prices and production cost, but also take into account domestic oil supply and demand" (Xinhua, 2008). Even though the present oil price structure helps keep wild price swings in check, the NDRC concedes that it isn't transparent. Professor Dong Xiucheng, a professor with the China University of Petroleum, said the present pricing structure only deals with international market and domestic inflation without considering demand in the domestic market. Creating a true market-oriented system is imperative and should include greater consideration of domestic consumers (Xinhua, 2011). As a matter of fact, the existing structure fails to encourage the NOCs to reduce their prices because they do not experience competitive pressure. Although the Chinese government has opened the retail market for petroleum products to foreign oil companies, the NOCs have taken measures to reinforce their monopoly. Particularly, they have "snapped up" the country's fuel retail stations before its retail oil market opened up. Numerous international companies, including BP, Exxon-Mobil and Shell had no choice, but to open joint fuel retail stations along with Sinopec and CNPC (Chen, 2009).

4 Conclusion

Energy has been deemed strategically important since the establishment of PRC. Nonetheless, so far the country has not been able to establish a proper institutional structure to effectively operate and oversee the energy sector. Although there is on-going debate about re-establishing the Ministry of Energy, such an agency would not "magically transform China, energy industry" (Zha, 2006) and there are several reasons for this. First, there have always been a number of competing ministries and government agencies in charge of the sector, resulting in an overlap of functions and an inefficient use of resources. The number of official actors ranges widely from issue to issue and can include institutions as varied as NDRC, oil companies, SASAC, MOFCOM as well as local government. Second, the role of oil companies in the policy-making process is increasing simultaneously with their financial power. Based on the current direction of economic policy-making, in China this trend will continue even if the relationship between state and business keeps fluctuating. The top management of NOCs and the Chinese leadership have maintained a close relationship and thus it is not always obvious who the key decision-maker is. On the one hand, NOCs are subordinate to political authority because they must seek government approval for large projects. On the other hand, Beijing still depends on NOCs in many respects. Third, Beijing's efforts to create one central institution supervising the energy sector is still partial and inconsistent due to the problems of balancing the interests of several of actors and the importance of consensus-building in decision-making. This considers not only political players but also Chinese society. As the case of pricing regulation showed, the Chinese government faced a severe dilemma in coping with fuel price-setting.

On the one hand, the top leadership had to confront pressure from oil companies to further raise petrol prices to off-set their losses triggered by the record high international crude. On the other hand, Beijing wanted to keep prices low to retain social stability and to control inflation. Therefore, the government commitment to sustainable stability will result on continuing fragmentation of the political landscape and inconclusive policy decisions.

5

Energy Security in China: An Analysis of Various Energy Sources

Dan Luo and Shujie Yao

1 Introduction

After more than 30 years of fast expansion, China has become the world's second-largest economy and the largest energy consumer and CO_2 emitter. In 2010, China consumed 3.2 billion tons of coal equivalents (TCE) and 4.2 trillion kWh of electricity, up by 6 per cent and 13.7 per cent respectively from a year earlier. It is estimated that from 2010 to 2035, global energy demand may increase by 30 per cent, in which China and India will contribute 50 per cent of the growth (Figure 5.1, IEA, 2011). Facing such a rapid increase in demand, how to meet the country's energy needs and avoid environmental damage on a massive scale will become huge challenges on China's future economic development and prosperity.

Energy has long been considered by the Chinese government as one of the most important national strategic issues. To ensure a sustained energy supply, which keeps pace with production and residential consumption needs, the government has to improve energy efficiency and develop alternative energy sources other than fossil fuels. Since the late 1990s, several laws and regulations have been issued targeting the energy industry and environmental protection. However, as economic growth was the most important policy objective and energy shortage was not really serious before 2006, little progress was made regarding energy efficiency and environmental protection. Not until 2006 did the Chinese government for the first time combine the targets of energy efficiency improvement with economic growth in the 11th Five-Year Plan (FYP).

Despite facing rocketing energy demands, the Chinese government remains confident about solving the energy issue through adjusting

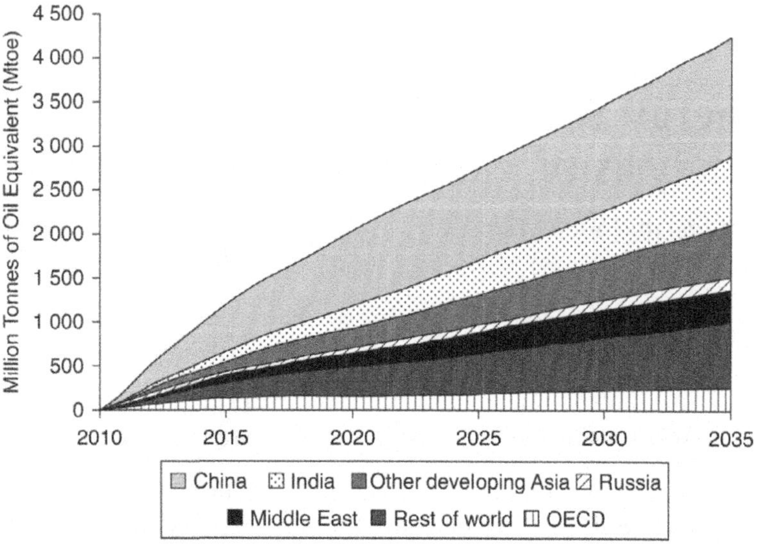

Figure 5.1 Growth in primary energy demand in the new policies scenario, 2010–35

Source: IEA, World Energy Outlook, 2011.

internal supply and consumption. It was stated explicitly in the long-term energy policy that China would like to meet 90 per cent of its energy demand with domestic resources and generating capacity (Zhou, 2010).

To tackle the energy issue, China launched three big projects at the beginning of the 20th century: The Three Gorges Dam, The South–North Water Diversion Project and West–East Gas Transmission Project. It is expected that once the three projects are completed, the coastal region will largely resolve the energy shortage problem and northern China, especially Beijing and Tianjin, will not be short of water. However, apart from the huge costs and potential impact on the environment, unexpected rising demand for energy was not adequately considered when the projects were planned. Consequently, even with the help of these projects, the whole country continues to suffer from a severe energy shortage, particularly in the most developed eastern areas during the peak seasons.

Hence, China has to re-consider its energy strategy more carefully, taking into account economic structure, technological change and, more importantly, the development of alternative energy sources. It is therefore important to develop all kinds of renewable resources. A sustainable energy policy in China should consider energy supply, resource mix and environmental protection together. Sufficient energy must be supplied from a balanced resource mix to satisfy the demand for social and economic development while restricting harm to the natural environment (Wang and Lu, 2002).

This becomes the focus of this chapter, which aims to review the development of different energy resources in China over the past decades. In particular, our focus is on investigating the key obstacles faced by each of the energy resources and the factors that may influence their deployment in China in the future.

The rest of the chapter is organized as follows. Section 2 will review the main challenges on China's energy consumption. This is followed by a review of China's reliance on fossil fuels in Section 3. Section 4 discusses the development of and constraints on renewable resources and nuclear power in China in recent years. Section 5 makes some conclusions and policy recommendations.

2 China's energy supply challenges

2.1 Rising energy demand

Rapid economic expansion in China has driven energy demand up enormously in the last two decades. Total electricity production rocketed in China from 650 billion kWh in 1990 to 4.14 trillion kWh in 2010, with its share of the world total rising from 5.5 per cent to 19.4 per cent over the same period (Figure 5.2). By the end of 2011, China had installed an electricity generation capacity of 1.06 billion kW, increasing by over 90 million kW each year for six consecutive years. Total electricity production reached 4.7 trillion kWh in 2011, an 11.9 per cent rise on its 2010 level. Ironically, despite the massive increase in electricity supply, severe electricity shortages prevailed across the country, creating the so-called "electricity panic" phenomenon in some fast-growing provinces during the peak season. This gives rise to the following question: has China made any real progress in improving the efficiency of energy/electricity consumption? If not, what will be the implications on China's sustainable economic growth and its impact on the environment?

Over the period 2000–09, China's electricity output rose by 11.4 per cent per year, significantly higher than the average annual GDP growth of 10.2 per cent. The situation was just the opposite during the previous

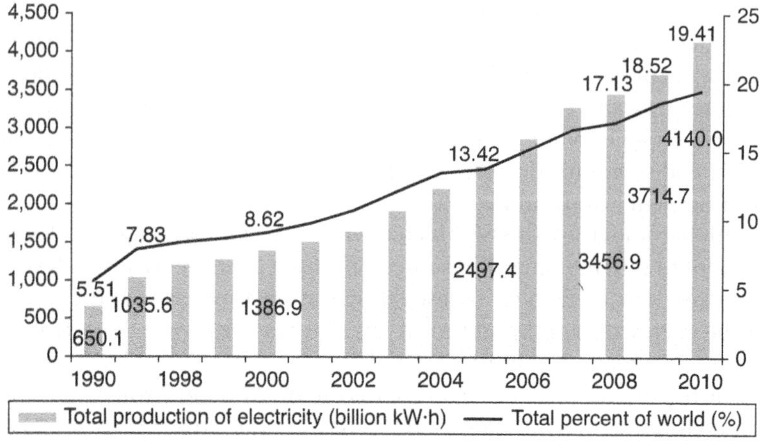

Figure 5.2 Total electricity production in China and its share to the world total
Source: China Energy Statistical Yearbook, 2011.

decades of 1990–2000 and 1980–90. This suggests that, as measured by the elasticity of electricity consumption with respect to GDP growth, China's electricity, and hence its energy efficiency, experienced a rapid deterioration rather than an improvement in the latest decade compared to the previous decades, thus contradicting the government's policy on sustainable growth and environmental protection.

Electricity shortage can be partially explained by the rising demand of residential consumption, but most of it will have been caused by the industrial structure which has been increasingly dominated by industries, or industrial products, which are energy and electricity intensive.

Rising residential demand is shown in Figure 5.3. By the end of 2009, per capita residential electricity consumption was 2,631 kWh, rising almost ten-fold in a decade.

However, residential electricity consumption is still low in China compared to the level in developed countries (Table 5.1). For example, per capita electricity consumption in China in 2009 was 93 per cent of the world average and only one-third and one-fifth of the respective levels in Japan and the USA. As China has overtaken Japan as the world's second- largest economy and is quickly catching up with the USA, electricity demand in China is expected to continue to rise rapidly in the coming decades. The real question is how to meet China's demand for energy and electricity?

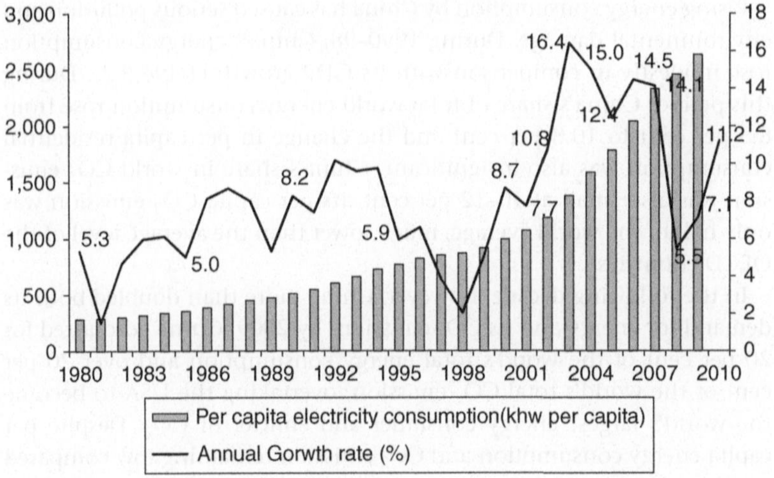

Figure 5.3 Per capita electricity consumption in China and annual growth rate, 1980–2009

Source: The World Bank 2011,http://data.worldbank.org/indicator/EG.USE.ELEC.KH.PC/countries?display=default.

Table 5.1 Per capita electricity consumption in China and other countries (kWh per capita)

	1980	1990	1995	2000	2005	2006	2007	2008	2009
World	***1,586***	***2,123***	***2,200***	***2,392***	***2,675***	***2,756***	***2,851***	***2,877***	***2,826***
Euro area	4,205	5,340	5,637	6,321	6,839	6,930	6,930	6,934	6,592
High income	4,203	5,185	5,329	5,855	6,305	6,385	6,391	6,387	6,066
Middle income	375	945	959	1,067	1,387	1,498	1,612	1660	1,693
Low income	135	221	181	174	214	224	224	228	230
OECD	5,361	6,669	7,213	7,957	8,308	8,315	8,397	8,368	7,984
BRICs									
China	**282**	**511**	**770**	**993**	**1783**	**2,041**	**2,329**	**2,457**	**2,631**
China/World (%)	17.8	24.1	35	41.5	66.7	74.1	81.7	85.4	93.1
China/Japan (%)	6	7.9	10.5	12.5	21.7	24.7	27.4	30.4	33.7
China/USA (%)	2.9	4.4	6.1	7.3	13	15	17.1	18	20.4
Brazil	1,008	1,454	1,636	1,891	2,020	2,078	2,175	2,237	2,206
India	142	276	365	401	475	516	563	589	597
Russia	–	6,673	5,110	5,209	5,785	6,122	6,317	6,435	6,136
France	4,426	5,974	6,631	7,255	7,677	7,558	7,541	7,683	7,488
Germany	5,796	6,640	6,331	6,636	7,113	7,174	7,184	7,149	6,779
Japan	4,718	6,486	7,365	7,974	8,213	8,253	8,490	8,091	7,819
UK	4,684	5,357	5,576	6,115	6,289	6,226	6,152	6,055	5,692
USA	9,862	11,713	12,660	13,671	13,694	13,574	13,642	13,651	12,904

Source: The World Bank 2011, http://data.worldbank.org/indicator/EG.USE.ELEC.KH.PC/countries?display=default.

Rising energy consumption by China has caused serious pollution and environmental damage. During 1990–98, China's energy consumption rose modestly in comparison with its GDP growth (Table 5.2). During this period, China's share of total world energy consumption rose from 8.3 per cent to 10.8 per cent and the change in per capita residential consumption was also insignificant. China's share in world CO_2 emission was also small at 10–12 per cent. Its per capita CO_2 emission was only half of the world average, much lower than the average level of the OECD countries.

In the following decade, however, China more than doubled both its demand for energy and its CO_2 emission. By 2009, China accounted for 20 per cent of the world's total energy consumption and over 20 per cent of the world's total CO_2 emission, overtaking the USA to become the world's largest energy consumer and emitter of CO_2. Despite per capita energy consumption and CO_2 emission remaining low compared with the developed countries, the massive increases in energy consumption and CO_2 emission have made China the most sensitive nation in the world in terms of climate change, pollution and sustainable growth. All the OECD countries, including the USA, have been able to reduce

Table 5.2 China's energy consumption and CO_2 emissions

	Energy consumption			CO_2 emissions		
	Consumption (Mtoe)	**Proportion (%)**	**Per capita consumption (t per person)**	**Emissions (Mt)**	**Proportion (%)**	**Per capita emission (t per person)**
	1990			1990		
World	8,350	100	1.58	21,452.50	100	4.1
OECD	4,084.70	48.9	4.77	10,099.40	47.1	11.8
USA	1,920.60	23	7.69	4,869.40	22.7	19.5
China	***690.9***	***8.3***	***0.6***	***2,053.30***	***9.6***	***1.8***
1998				1998		
World	9,689.60	100	1.66	22,524.80	100	3.9
OECD countries	3,790.30	39.1	4.63	12,076.60	53.3	10.9
USA	2,181.80	22.5	8.11	5,409.80	24	20.1
China	***1,048***	***10.8***	***0.84***	***2,893.20***	***12.8***	***2.3***
2009				2008		
World	11,787.10	100	1.8	32,082.60	100	4.8
OECD	5,237.70	44.4	4.26	12,845.70	40	10.5
USA	2,162.90	18.3	7.05	5,461.00	17	17.9
China	***2,257.10***	***19.1***	***1.7***	***7,031.90***	***21.9***	***5.3***

Source: The World Bank 2011, http://www.worldbank.org/.

CO_2 emissions. Per capita CO_2 emission levels of the OCED countries as a group and the USA were reduced from 10.9t and 20.1t respectively in 1998 to 10.5t and 17.9t respectively by 2009. While all the developed countries are committed to cutting greenhouse gas (GHG) emissions, China has now become the focus of concern and criticism as it continues to consume more energy and emit more GHG at a rate that is alarming to every country in the world, including China itself. Therefore it appears that controlling energy consumption and CO_2 emission has become an imminent challenge for China's policymakers.

Let us just compare the energy consumption levels of the world's two largest economies today, the USA and China, to demonstrate the pressing need for China to pay serious attention to energy efficiency. As shown in Figure 5.4, the Chinese economy has grown much faster than that of the USA for more than three decades. However, the difference in the growth of energy consumption between the two countries was not large in the 1990s, with China growing about 2.5 percentage points more than the USA. Not until the 2000s did the gap in the growth of energy consumption become far more substantive.

Over the period 2000–10, China achieved an annual GDP growth of 10.3 per cent, 1.2 times higher than the average annual growth of its energy consumption of 8.4 per cent. In the same period, the USA's GDP

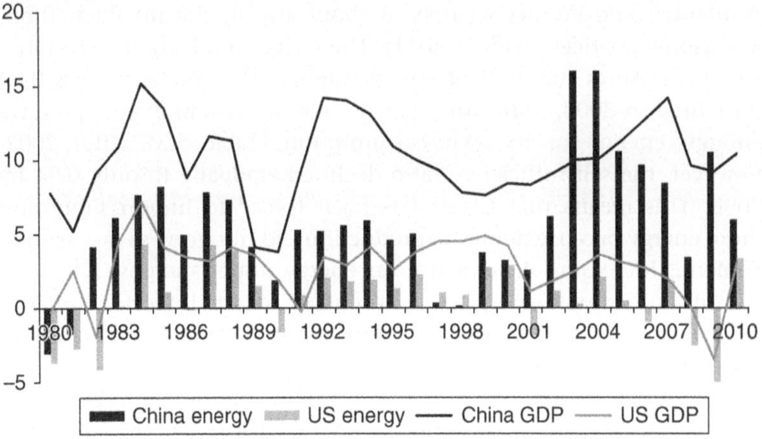

Figure 5.4 Energy consumption and GDP growth rates of China and the USA (per cent)

Source: The World Bank, http://data.worldbank.org/indicator/EG.USE.COMM.KT.OE/countries; China Statistical Yearbook, 2011.

growth was 1.85 per cent per year but energy consumption growth was only 0.13 per cent per year, implying a GDP/energy growth ratio of 14.5. This comparison suggests that for each extra unit of GDP created, the USA requires only a tiny fraction of the energy that is required by China. China is rapidly catching up with the USA to become the world's largest economy. By the time China's economy is as large as the USA's, its energy consumption and CO_2 emissions may be two to three times as large as those of the USA. This will create massive destruction of the global environment and constraints on energy resources if China does not introduce a dramatic change in its growth pattern from now on.

3 Energy security

China's fast-growing demand for energy has put the country under a severe energy security risk. At the aggregate level, China's reserves of coal, oil and natural gas rank 3rd, 13th and 17th in the world respectively. Measured on a per capita basis, coal, oil and gas reserves in China are only about 79 per cent, 6.5 per cent and 6.1 per cent of the world's average levels respectively (Jiang, 2008). The extremely low levels of per capita reserves, particularly oil and gas, mean that China is highly vulnerable to external supplies of such energy resources.

Broadly defined, energy security measures whether a nation's energy demands could be met securely, without any significant fluctuation, at reasonable prices (Winzer, 2011). The energy production/TPES ratio, which measures the level of energy supply self-sufficiency, was 0.99 for China in 2002, indicating that the country could almost produce enough energy for its own consumption (Table 5.3). After 2002, however, the self-sufficiency ratio declined gradually to only 0.94 by 2008. This means that China has been forced to import more and more energy because domestic production did not grow as fast as total demand. Increasing dependence on energy imports expose China to risks in both supply and prices, particularly for the imports of oil and natural gas, which have to come from the most troublesome areas in Africa and the Middle East.

A similar situation has also happened in another fast-developing BRICs country, India. For resource-affluent countries, such as Russia and Australia, however, the ratio has been kept well above one with few fluctuations. For the USA, its energy production/TPES ratio was relatively stable over 2002–07 and recovered substantially after the financial crisis broke out.

Table 5.3 Energy Production/Total Primary Energy Supply (TPES) (Self sufficiency)

Country or Area	2002	2003	2004	2005	2006	2007	2008
World	1.01	1	1	1	1	1	1.01
OECD Total	0.72	0.7	0.7	0.69	0.7	0.7	0.71
NON-OECD Total	1.32	1.34	1.33	1.35	1.33	1.31	1.31
BRICs							
China	0.99	0.98	0.95	0.96	0.93	0.93	0.94
Brazil	0.85	0.89	0.87	0.91	0.93	0.92	0.92
Russia	1.67	1.73	1.8	1.82	1.83	1.84	1.83
India	0.82	0.8	0.78	0.79	0.78	0.76	0.75
Selected Developed Countries							
United States	0.73	0.72	0.71	0.7	0.71	0.71	0.75
Canada	1.54	1.47	1.48	1.47	1.53	1.53	1.53
United Kingdom	1.13	1.06	0.97	0.87	0.81	0.84	0.8
France	0.51	0.5	0.5	0.5	0.5	0.51	0.51
Germany	0.39	0.39	0.39	0.39	0.39	0.4	0.4
Japan	0.19	0.16	0.18	0.19	0.19	0.18	0.18
Australia	2.27	2.25	2.28	2.22	2.19	2.4	2.32

Source: China Energy Statistical Yearbook 2011. *Notes*: If the ratio of Energy Production/TPES equals 1, it means that the energy supplied could just meet the energy production needs. In other words, the country would just be able to fully rely on itself to supply the energy needed. For a ratio of less than 1, the country is a net energy importer, while for a ratio higher than 1, the country is a net energy exporter.

Another indicator for energy security is the ratio of energy imports to total energy use. Energy import is calculated as energy use minus energy production and energy use refers to use of primary energy before transformation into other end-use fuels, all measured as TOE. A negative value indicates that the country is a net energy exporter and vice versa. Figure 5.5 portrays the changes in China's energy imports since 1978. Before 1998, China was a net energy exporter, being able to produce sufficient energy for its domestic demand. However, the situation changed significantly afterwards. Since 2003, China's reliance on external supplies of energy has been increasing rapidly. The discrepancy between energy production and energy usage reached 7.6 per cent in 2009.

The Chinese government has set the target of quadrupling the country's GDP by 2020 as compared to the level in 2000. This ambitious growth target will lead to a much bigger deficit between energy production and demand, forcing the country to import more and more energy from other countries. At the time the mid- to long-term energy plan was

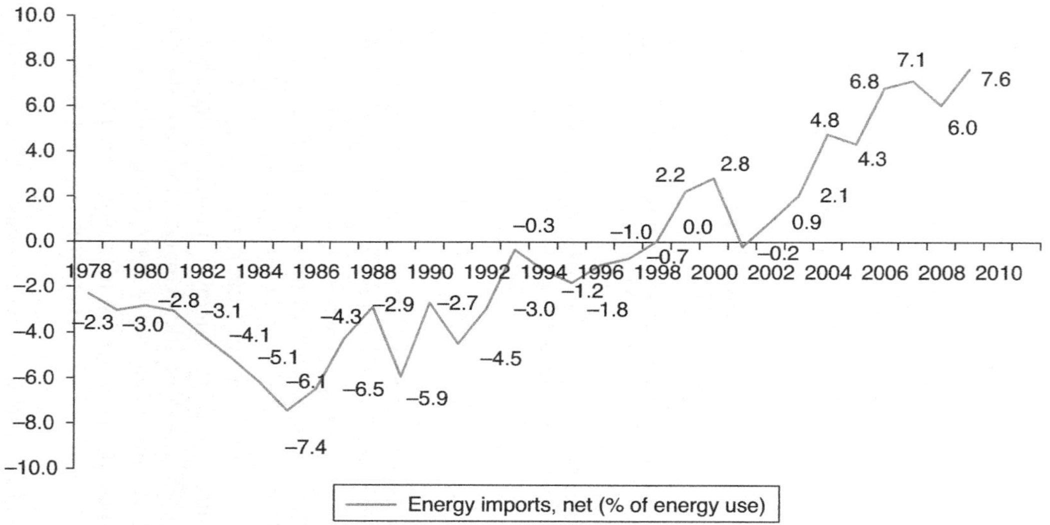

Figure 5.5 Percentage of energy imports to total energy use, China, 1978–2009

Source: The World Bank 2011, http://data.worldbank.org/indicator/EG.IMP.CONS.ZS/countries?display=default.*Notes*: Net energy imports are estimated as energy use minus production, both measured in oil equivalents. A negative value indicates that the country is a net exporter. Energy use refers to use of primary energy before transformation into other end-use fuels, which is equal to indigenous production plus imports and stock changes, minus exports and fuels supplied to ships and aircraft engaged in international transport.

drafted in 2004, it was predicted that total energy needs would be 3–3.2 billion TCE by 2020. However, the unanticipated rocketing demand in recent years has rendered this prediction totally invalid. If China maintains its current GDP growth rate and an energy elasticity ratio above one, the energy demand of the country could reach 5 billion TCE by 2020 – far beyond the target. Even under the best scenario when substantial efforts have been undertaken with regard to energy conservation and economic restructuring and have proved to be effective, China will still need to consume over 3.6 billion TCE by 2020 (Zhang et al., 2010). By that time, the country will need to consume about 3 billion (Zhang et al., 2010) tons of coal and 0.64 billion tons of oil each year, leaving a huge gap between supply and demand.

As of 2009, over 50 per cent of the oil supply in China has relied on imports and even for its most abundant reserve, coal, the country has become a net coal importer since the first half of 2007 (Wang, 2010). In 2011, China imported 260 million tons of oil, accounting for 56.5 per cent of total oil consumption, compared to 53 per cent in 2010. If such a trend continues, China would expose itself to serious energy security problems. Therefore, in addition to implementing effective energy conservation plans and enhancing energy intensity at a faster speed, diversifying the supply of energy would become an enviable choice for China. The country's fast economic expansion and huge population determine that its energy needs will be enormous. To provide sufficient energy for manufacturing production and residential consumption calls for a dramatic expansion of the use of renewable energies.

4 China's reliance on traditional energy resources

4.1 Coal

China has diverse energy resources and is especially rich in coal. By the end of 2010, the proven coal reserves of the country were about 114 billion tons, placing it third in the world, just after the USA and Russia (BP, 2011). In terms of the production and consumption of coal, China has constantly ranked first among all other countries. In 2010, China produced 3.2 billion tons of coal, accounting for 48 per cent of the world's total. Meanwhile, it consumed even more coal for energy production. Up by 10.1 per cent year-on-year, total coal consumption of China was about 3.3 billion tons in 2010, accounting for 48.2 per cent of the world's total (BP, 2011).

China's primary energy consumption in 2010 was 3.25 billion TCE, of which coal, oil, natural gas and other energy resources account for 68 per cent, 19 per cent, 4.4 per cent and 8.6 per cent respectively (China Statistical Yearbook, 2011). Despite declining slightly from its near peak of 71.1 per cent in 2006, coal remains the predominant source of energy in China (Figure 5.6).

Coal is also the most dominant source of power for electricity generation in China, accounting for more than two-thirds of the country's newly added capacity for generation for many decades (Xu, 2008). Figure 5.7 depicts the electricity generated from different resources in China during 1980–2011. Thermal power constantly produces about 80 per cent of total electricity output whereas nuclear power accounts for only 2–3 per cent. Although China has set the target of reducing the amount of coal used in its total primary energy consumption to 40 per cent by 2050, the dominant role played by coal-fired power generation is unlikely to be changed dramatically in the next decade.

Coal-fired power generation is preferred to other energy generation methods, as its cost of investment is relatively lower with shorter construction periods. The related technologies are mature and coal is more readily available. However, with just over 13 per cent of the world's reserves but contributing almost 50 per cent of the world's total production, the threat of coal depletion is imminent, especially when China has turned into a net coal importer since 2007 (Xu, 2008). The heavy

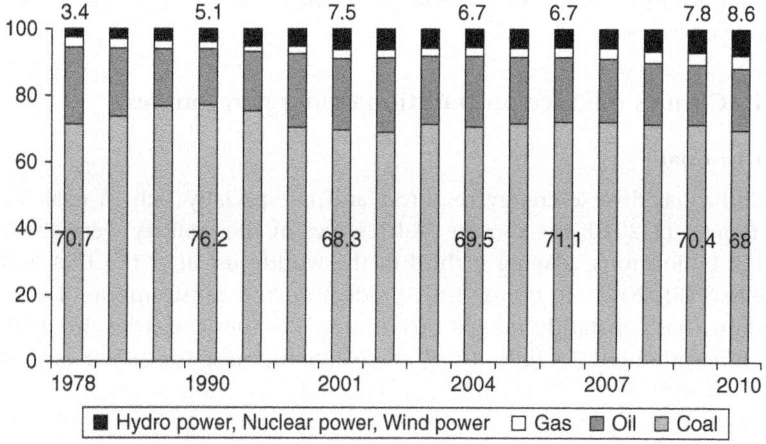

Figure 5.6 Composition of China's energy consumption, 1978–2010
Source: NBS, China Statistical Yearbook, 2011.

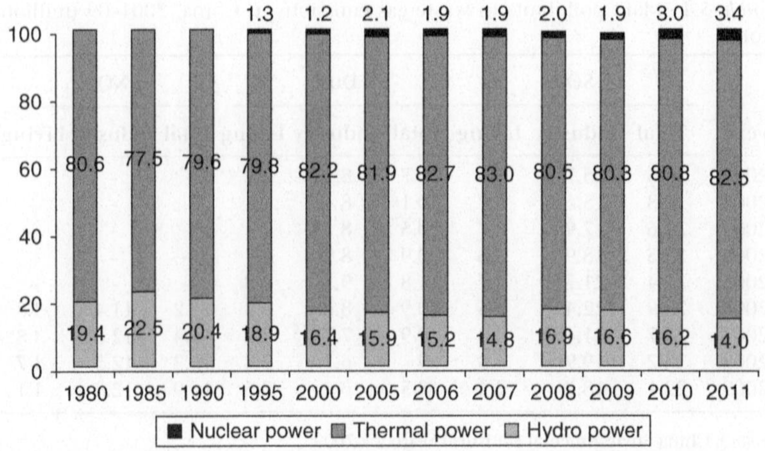

Figure 5.7 Electricity generation from different resources in China, 1980–2011

Source: China Statistical Yearbook, 2011.

reliance on coal has led to various problems including environmental, transportation and safety issues.

The severe environmental pollution caused by burning coal is irreversible and devastating. Coal use is responsible for about 90 per cent of total sulphur dioxide (SO_2) emissions, 50 per cent of particulate emissions, 70 per cent of the total dust, nitrogen dioxide (NO_2) and carbon dioxide (CO_2) emissions (Xu, 2008; Zhou, 2010). Table 5.4 lists the amounts of the main pollutants in waste gas emissions in China over the period 2001–09.

At the peak level, China produced almost 26 million tons of SO_2 in the year 2006 alone, representing an increase of 34 per cent in five years. The country has now become the world's largest SO_2 emitter. According to China's Environmental Protection Agency, over 70 per cent of the country's river systems are badly polluted. More than 300 million people do not have access to clean water and about 400 million urban residents are unable to get access to clean air (Xu, 2008). The coal consumption-related air pollution has led to a sharp rise in the number of people suffering from respiratory illnesses caused by particulates. China now hosts 16 of the world's most polluted cities. A survey conducted in 2005 concluded that about one-third of the country's territory was affected by acid rain, posing a great threat for its soil and food safety (Xu, 2008; Reuters, 2006; Zhou and Zhang, 2010). Due to the effects of pollution

Table 5.4 Main pollutants in waste gas emissions in China, 2001–09 (million tons)

	SO_2			Dust			NO_2		
year	Total	Industry	Living	Total	Industry	Living	Total	Industry	Living
2001	19.5	15.7	3.8	10.7	8.5	2.2	–	–	–
2002	19.3	15.6	3.7	10.1	8	2.1	–	–	–
2003	21.6	17.9	3.7	10.5	8.5	2	–	–	–
2004	22.5	18.9	3.6	10.9	8.9	2	–	–	–
2005	25.4	21.7	3.7	11.8	9.5	2.3	–	–	–
2006	25.9	22.4	3.5	10.9	8.6	2.3	15.2	11.4	3.8
2007	24.7	21.4	3.3	9.9	7.7	2.2	16.4	12.6	3.8
2008	23.2	19.9	3.3	9	6.7	2.3	16.2	12.5	3.7
2009	22.1	18.7	3.4	8.5	6	2.5	16.9	12.8	4.1

Source: China Environmental Statistical Yearbook 2009.

being carried by winds and rivers, acid rain has already grown into a regional problem, seriously affecting China's neighbouring countries, such as South Korea and Southwest Japan (Streets et al., 1997).

On the other hand, China's heavy use of coal has had a bad impact on the global climate. While the developed countries endeavour to cut CO_2 emissions, emissions from China alone more than doubled during the past decade. Figure 5.8 captures the changes in CO_2 emission in both China and the USA during the period 1980–2010. In 1980, China's annual CO_2 emission was just about 1.5 billion tons, less than one-third of the US level, and only accounted for 7.5 per cent of the world's total. However, the country's fast economic development, unbalanced industrial structure and relatively low efficiency in energy production and consumption caused a sharp increase in its demand for energy and, accordingly, much greater CO_2 emission. In 2005, China surpassed the USA to become the world's largest CO_2 emitter for the first time (The Word Bank, 2011). Since then, the country constantly contributes around 20 per cent of the world's total CO_2 emissions, peaking at almost 25 per cent in 2010. It has been projected that if China's carbon intensity keeps pace with a GDP growth of 7 per cent, by 2030 the country will emit as much as the total world emission today (Wang, 2010).

As a developing country, although China has no enforceable obligation to cut emission under the Kyoto Protocol, the country has ratified the treaty and set a voluntary target to cut carbon emission intensity, or emission per unit of GDP, by 40–50 per cent below the 2005 levels by 2020 (Liu and Wang, 2009). In doing so, China not only proves to the

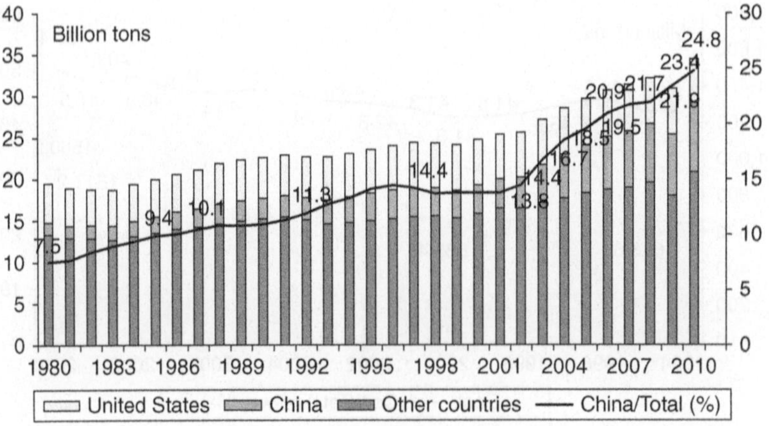

Figure 5.8 CO_2 emissions of China, the USA and the rest of the world, 1980–2010
Source: The World Bank,http://data.worldbank.org/indicator/EN.ATM.CO2E.KT/countries?display=default.

rest of the world that it acts responsibly as a big nation and cares about the living conditions of its people, but more importantly it may push the country to accelerate the process of economic restructuring.

Apart from the severe damage caused to the environment, the uneven distribution of China's coal reserves has imposed heavy burdens on the transportation system. Over 80 per cent of coal reserves are located in the mountainous regions of the north-western provinces, including Shaanxi, Shanxi and Inner Mongolia, far away from the economic centres and highly populated coastal areas (Zhou, 2010; Zhang et al., 2011). Even in good weather conditions, coal transportation has already imposed serious challenges on China's road and railway systems, not to say under severe winter snows. The worst winter snowstorm in 2008 interrupted the transport of coal to the coastal regions, forcing some places to cut the power supply to factories to secure the residential electricity supply (Zhou, 2010).

Figure 5.9 shows the amount of coal transported as a percentage of total national railway freight traffic over the period 1994–2011. During 1994–2011, coal transportation consistently accounted for over 40 per cent of the total national railway freight traffic and it rose to more than 50 per cent in 2010 (Figure 5.9). During 2000–10, the annual growth rate of coal freight carried by the national railway system was 8.4 per cent,

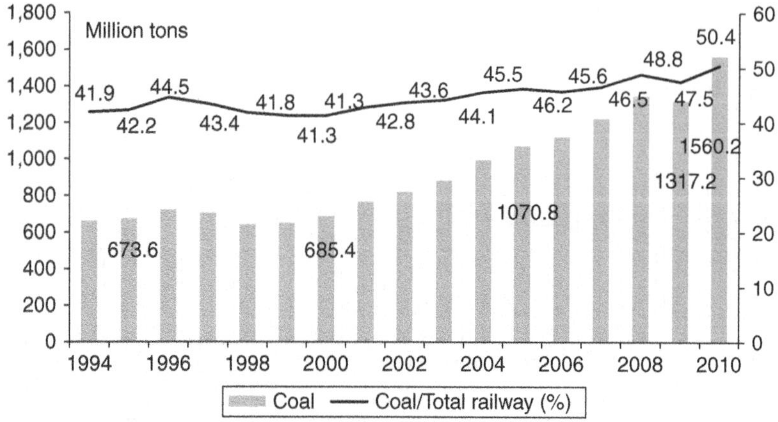

Figure 5.9 Amount of coal transported as a percentage of total national railway freight traffic

Source: China Statistical Yearbook, 1996–2011.

much less than the 13.7 per cent growth rate of coal production over the same period (China Statistical Yearbook, 2001–11). The development of China's railway networks is unable to keep pace with its demand for coal transportation. It is estimated by the Ministry of Railways that the demand for rail transport of coal could reach 2,000–2,200 million tons per year by 2020, significantly larger than the expected expansion of the railway capacity in the coming decade (Zhou, 2010). Therefore, China's continuing overdependence on hard coal could inevitably face another bottleneck in the near future – limited transportation capacity.

Lastly, the issue of coal safety has also caused serious concerns. Regulations related to safe coal-mining are not well established in China and the existence of thousands of small coal mines has made it even harder to supervise and monitor. Statistics show that in 2005 alone, 5,938 coal miners were killed in accidents due to inefficient safety measures and poor management (Oster, 2006). Despite being urged to shut down thousands of small coal mines by the central government, lucrative profit potential has spurred the emergence of even more of them. Some are said to be under the protection of the local authorities since many coal-rich provinces relying on coal-mining to boost local economic growth (Oster, 2006). The shortfall caused by the closure of small coal mines is estimated to be 250 million metric tons (NDRC). Unless the large state-owned mining companies can raise their output to fully compensate for the deficit, it will be impossible for the central government to crack down on illegal coal-mining and to implement effective energy policies.

The discussions set out above summarize the major challenges that China would face by relying on coal as its primary energy supply. Although it seems unlikely that China can reduce its reliance on fossil fuels significantly in the near future, it could devote more efforts to developing clean coal technologies (CCT), such as carbon capture and sequestration (CCS). Nevertheless in the long-term, the devastating environmental pollution, saturated transportation system and unsafe coal mines all suggest that China will have to diversify its energy mix to sustain its economic growth.

4.2 Gas

Apart from coal, another fossil energy that is widely used by China is natural gas, which has contributed about 3 per cent of the country's total energy needs over the past three decades. By the end of 2010, the proven reserves of natural gas in China were about 3.8 trillion cubic metres, just about 1.3 per cent of the world's total. Nevertheless, the overall resources are estimated to be much larger and have continued to rise over the past decades (Zhang et al., 2011). Similar to coal, the distribution of gas resources is spatially uneven. Four Western provinces, Xinjiang, Sichuan, Shaanxi and Inner Mongolia account for three-quarters of the country's total gas reserves. This explains why China has devoted substantial efforts to developing the 4,200 km "West-to-East Gas Transmission Pipe Line Project" in its 10th FYP.

On the other hand, China has also built several large-scale liquefied natural gas (LNG) power plants in the southern and eastern regions. LNG power plants are superior as they emit only 42 per cent of the CO_2, 21 per cent of the NO_2 and a small part of the SO_2 that a coal-fired power station of a comparable size would otherwise release (Zhou, 2010). The construction costs of LNG plants are just about two-thirds of the costs for similar-sized coal-fired plants. In addition, LNG power plants have far lower requirements in terms of operational inputs, including labour, land and water.

Fuel costs are found to contribute about 60 per cent of the total generation costs of LNG plants, hence making the cost and profitability of electricity generation highly sensitive to gas prices. In recent years, the price of natural gas has increased, while the price of coal is under tight control, making it difficult for LNG power plants to compete with coal-fired power stations (Yang et al., 2007).

On the other hand, limited domestic production of natural gas means that LNG power plants have to rely on increasing imports of natural gas, which presents other problems such as supply and price risks. Figure 5.10 tracks China's production and consumption of natural gas as a percentage of the world's total. The country's consumption of gas has almost quadrupled over the past decade, reaching 81.3 billion cubic metres in 2008. The supply and consumption of natural gas in China seems relatively balanced over 2002–08, both accounting for an average of 1.8 per cent of the world's total. However, it should be noted that, as of 2007, China has officially become a net importer of gas. Despite remaining small in terms of the absolute amount, it does underline the problem of China's severe energy shortage.

4.3 Oil

China's recent surging demand for energy has put the country in a very dangerous situation. China's proven and exploitable oil reserves were about 3.2 billion tons by the end of 2010, accounting for 1.2 per cent of the world's total. The per capita oil reserve is just 6.5 per cent of the world's average (Wang, 2010). Similarly, the distribution of oil reserves is also uneven, being mainly concentrated in the northeast (e.g., Heilongjiang), eastern (e.g., Jiangsu) and northwest (e.g., Xinjiang) regions.

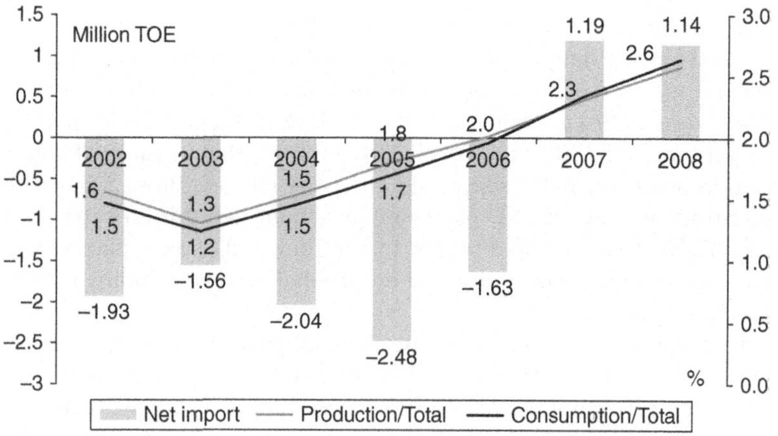

Figure 5.10 China's production and consumption of natural gas
Source: China Energy Statistical Yearbook, 2011.

Before the 1990s, the growth of China's oil consumption was moderate, up by just 30 per cent during 1980–90. China remained a net oil exporter until 1993 but since then the situation has been completely reversed. In recent years, China's oil production has been kept at about 0.2 billion tons, far from being enough to meet domestic demand. This has made China increasingly dependent on oil imports. In 2010 China consumed 0.45 billion tons of oil, of which 53 per cent was imported (Figure 5.11). Total oil demand rose to 0.48 billion tons in 2011 and the dependency ratio rose to 56.6 per cent. Rising demand for oil has been propelled by a rapid growth in car ownership. In 2010 and 2011, vehicle sales were more than 18 million units per year, an enormous rise over the previous year, and surpassing car sales in the USA by over 50 per cent. If current trends in oil demand, production and imports continue, China will need to consume over 0.6 billion tons of oil by 2020 and, by 2030, over 80 per cent of the country's oil supply will have to be imported (Zhang et al., 2010).

Although China may develop more advanced oil exploitation and drilling technologies in the future to increase oil production, it will still be impossible to meet the country's soaring demand. China has already diversified its oil supply towards more secure sources, like Brazil, Russia and Australia. Nevertheless, such a high dependency on external supply inevitably exposes the country to serious energy security problems. Oil has become one of China's most costly import items in recent years. As

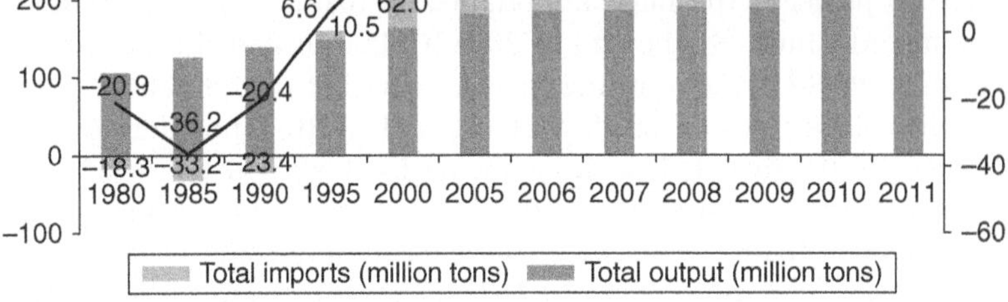

Figure 5.11 China's consumption of crude oil, 1980–2010

Source: China Energy Statistical Yearbook, 2010.

the amount of oil imports rises and the price of oil remains stubbornly high, China's future economic growth could easily be jeopardized by oil imports alone.

Energy shortage is a serious challenge but it also brings opportunities for the development and utilization of non-fossil energy sources. However, significant challenges, including technological, financial and institutional risks, are huge. To what extent can clean and renewable energy be used to help solve China's energy problem? What are the main risks and constraints on the development and utilization of such energy sources? What policies are needed to facilitate the development of alternative energies? Answering all these questions requires a thorough analysis of each of the potential energy sources, to which we now turn in the next section.

5 Development of renewable energy resources

5.1 Renewable resources

To cope with its growing energy demand and international pressure on GHG emissions, China has accelerated its research and deployment of renewable resources. In February 2005, the People's Congress passed *China's Renewable Energy Law* to take effect from 1st January 2006. The *Law* recognizes the strategic importance of renewable energies in "optimizing the country's energy supply mix, mitigating environmental pollution, improving energy supply security and promoting rural social development" (Zhang et al., 2010, pp. 4392). Following this law, the Mid- and Long-Term Development Plan for Renewable Energy specifies that China will accelerate the use of non-fossil energies and increase their share in the country's total primary energy consumption to 10 per cent, 15 per cent and 30 per cent by 2010, 2020 and 2050, respectively (Zhao et al., 2011).

Hydro power is the most important and mature renewable energy resource in China. By the end of 2008, China's installed capacity had reached 196.8 GW, accounting for 22.5 per cent of the nation's total installed electric power capacity (Zhang et al., 2010). The intention was to increase the installed capacity further to about 300 GW, or 25 per cent of the total power capacity by 2020. China is in the leading position in small hydro technology and it has built a series of large-scale hydro power stations, such as the Three Gorges Dam and Nu River Dam projects. However, despite being rich in hydro power, the distribution of hydro power resources is extremely unbalanced across the country. They are mainly located in southwest China, far away from the electricity consumption centres, making electricity transmission the most difficult issue in the development of hydro power.

In addition, the construction of large hydro power projects has caused controversy and opposition as such projects may lead to unforeseen environmental, social and ecological disasters. Opponents argue that it would damage the local environment and biodiversity, affect water quality and destroy cultural heritage. For instance, altering the route of the Yangtze River may cause all kinds of problems mentioned above (Zhou, 2010). A large number of local residents, about 2 million people, have been forced to leave their homes due to the construction of dams. Strong public opposition has already slowed down several other large-scale hydro power projects. If the Chinese government is unable to manage concerns about the environmental and social impact appropriately, it will make future development of hydro power projects highly unpopular.

Another rapidly developing renewable energy in China is wind power. Since the implementation of the *Renewable Energy Law* in 2006, China has increased its wind power capacity by over 100 per cent per year, making the country one of the world's leading nations in wind power (Zhang et al., 2010). By the end of 2008, the total installed capacity reached 12.2 GW (Wang, 2010). However, effective utilization of wind power has encountered a series of challenges.

Most wind resources are located in the northern and western parts of the country. Provinces like Xinjiang, Inner Mongolia and Gansu are rich in wind power but have limited electricity grid connections (Brennand, 2001). It is estimated that only 60 per cent of the wind power capacity is connected to grids (Forbes, 2009). Although the government has set a favourable price for electricity generated by wind power and allowed priority access for wind power to grids, the recommendation has not been well followed due to the physical constraints of the grid capacity (Wang, 2010; Zhou, 2010). Moreover, wind power is regarded as an "intermittent" source whose output level is dependent on the resource and is unable to be fully controlled. Consequently, lack of financial motivation and instability of the power supply have made grid companies unwilling to agree to additional investments to accommodate electricity generated by wind power plants. Furthermore, China's wind power technology still lags behind Europe. So far, over 75 per cent of the wind turbines in China are imported, especially the 1–2 MW scale turbines. If China were able to manufacture major parts like blades, gearboxes and engines domestically, the costs of wind turbines could be reduced by 20–30 per cent. This would make wind energy more competitive compared with other energy resources.

As for solar energy, China is blessed with abundant resources. More than two-thirds of the country's territorial areas could receive an annual radiation of over $5.02*10^6$ KJ/m^2 and an average of more than 2000 hours' sunshine each year (Zhang et al., 2009). The distribution of solar radiation in China is also widespread. Regions or provinces including Tibet, Qinghai, Xinjiang, southern Inner Mongolia, Shanxi, northern Shaanxi, Shandong, Liaoning, south-eastern Guangdong, south-eastern Fujian and eastern and western Hainan Island all receive large amounts of radiation (Zhang et al., 2009). However, the development of China's solar power industry is still in its infancy.

Over the period 2001–08, the newly installed capacity of solar PV was growing at 25 per cent annually (Jiang et al., 2010). The grid-connected PV, nevertheless, remains marginal and mainly in the demonstration stage due to the high cost of solar photovoltaic technology. In 2008, China produced about 2000 MW of solar panels, nearly half of the world's total. However, over 90 per cent of them were exported rather than installed domestically due to the under-developed grid connection network and the high cost of electricity generated from the PV system in China (Wang, 2010). The country has set a target of increasing the capacity of solar power to 0.3 GW and 1.8 GW by 2010 and 2020, respectively. Meanwhile, there are also plans to increase the area of solar water heater installations to 150 and 300 million m^2 respectively over the same period (Zhang et al., 2010).

5.2 Nuclear energy

Given the growing cost and limited reserves of fossil fuels, oil supply security, uneven resource distribution, inadequate and inefficient power transmission network, environment pollution and immature technologies of renewable energies, nuclear energy is considered an inevitable strategic option for China (Wang and Lu, 2002; Zhou, 2010). Although, to date, the country's dependence on nuclear power is limited, it has built an extensive infrastructural base and grasped key technical capabilities that have the potential for large-scale expansion.

As early as 1972, the Chinese government approved a nuclear project, known as the 728 project. In 1985, the first indigenously designed nuclear power plant (NPP) was constructed in Qinshan, Zhejiang province. However, little progress was made in the following decade. As a result, nuclear energy contributed only 2 per cent of China's total electricity supply during 2005–10, much lower than the world average level of 13 per cent (China Energy Statistical Yearbook, 2011). By December 2007, the total number of constructed nuclear power units (NPUs) was 439 in 30 different counties and regions, with a total installed capacity of about 372 GW (Zhou and Zhang, 2010). The USA and Japan possess 103 and 55 NPUs respectively, contributing 19 per cent and 30 per cent of their total electricity supplies.

The slow development of nuclear energy in China was not hindered by finance or technology constraints. Instead, it was due to the belief that the country had abundant coal reserves and hence there was no need to invest in expensive alternative energy resources (Xu, 2008). The harsh reality of energy shortage has now forced China to realize the strategic importance of nuclear energy. Consequently, an ambitious plan has been designed to support the expansion of the nuclear power industry despite the disastrous Fukushima Nuclear Power Plant accidents in Japan, caused by the Tohoku earthquake and tsunami in Sendai on 11 March 2011. China has set a medium-term target of building a 40 GW nuclear power generation capacity by 2020. Three scenarios have been discussed to build 360 GW (30%), 240 GW (20%) and 120 GW (10%) nuclear power generation capacities respectively by 2050 (Xu, 2008).

China is well on its way to meeting the highest scenario. Now the country has three nuclear power bases, the Zhejiang Qinshan Nuclear Power Base with five reactor units, the Guangdong Daya Bay Nuclear Power Plant base with four reactor units and Jiangsu Tianwan Nuclear Power Plant Base with two reactor units. Table 5.5 lists the 11 Nuclear Power Units (NPUs) in operation, together with the other NPUs that are currently under construction. The installed capacity of the 11 existing NPUs is 8,587 MW and by 2012, when another seven NPUs are completed, the total installed capacity will reach 15 GW. If the proposed NPUs still to be built are taken into account, by 2020 the installed capacity of all the units will be 26 GW, which will be the largest capacity in the world.

According to the International Energy Agency (IEA), nuclear energy is particularly suitable for countries that have established nuclear energy programmes, with rapid growth in demand for energy but are unable to find economically viable alternative resources (Xu, 2008). This explains why China has made substantial efforts on developing its NPPs in recent years. Compared with other energy sources, nuclear power has the following advantages.

First of all, nuclear fuel, predominantly consisting of uranium, has the advantage of being a highly concentrated energy resource that can be stored or transported easily. Uranium resources are considered to be

Table 5.5 China's nuclear power projects

Name	Commenced	Capacity (MW)	Reactor Supplier	Operation	Operator
Qinshan 1	1985	300	PWR, CNNC	1991	CNNC
Daya Bay 1	1987	2 x 984	PWR, Framatome, France	1993, 1994	CGNPC
Qinshan 2	1996	2 x 600	PWR, CNNC	2002, 2004	CNNC
Ling'ao	1997	2 x 990	PWR, Framatome, France	2002	CGNPC
Qinshan 3	1998	2 x 728	PHWR, Candu-6, Canada	2003	CNNC
Tianwan	1999	2 x 1000	PWR, Russia	2007	CNNC
Hongyanhe 1	2007	2 x 1000	PWR, CPR1000, CGNPC	2012, 2014	CGNPC
Haiyang 1	2008	2 x 1250	PWR, AP1000, Westinghouse, USA	2015	CPI
Sanmen	2009	2 x 1250	PWR, AP1000, Westinghouse, USA	2013, 2014	CNNC
Shidao Bay	2011	2 x 1250	PWR, AP1000, Westinghouse, USA	2016	CNNC
Fangjiashan	2008	2 x 1000	PWR, CPR1000, CGNPC	2013, 2014	CNNC
Ningde 1	2008	4 x 1000	PWR, CPR1000, CGNPC	2012	CNNC
Fuqing	2008	2 x 1000	PWR, CPR1000, CGNPC	2013, 2014	CNNC
Ling'ao 2	2005	2 x 1000	PWR, CPR1000, CGNPC	2010, 2011	CNNC
Yangjiang	2007	2 x 1000	PWR, CPR1000, CGNPC	2012	CNNC
Taishan 1	2009	2 x 1750	PWR, EPR, EDF, France	2014	CNNC
Changjiang 1	2010	2 x 650	PWR, CNP650	2015	CNNC

Source: Official website of China National Nuclear Corporation, http://www.cnnc.com.cn/Default.aspx; Official website of China Guangdong Nuclear Power Corporation, http://www.cgnpc.com.cn/n2881959/index.html.*Notes*: PWR – pressurized water reactor; PHWR – pressurized heavy water reactor; CNNC – China National Nuclear Corporation; CGNPC – China Guangdong Nuclear Power Corporation; CPI – China Power Investment Corporation.

more evenly distributed geographically, although a few countries, like Australia (23%), Canada (8%) and Russia (8%), hold a larger percentage of the most economical, high-grade uranium ores (Zhou, 2010; Zhou and Zhang, 2010). Given such widespread distribution, the risk of supply disruption will be significantly reduced compared with oil and natural gas (EIA, 2009). In China, despite limited reserves, uranium is regarded as a quasi-domestic resource (Wang and Lu, 2002). The current market price of uranium is relatively low, both domestically and internationally. Therefore, China can purchase a large amount of natural uranium when the international market condition is favourable and keep it as strategic reserves. In fact, countries like France and Germany rely heavily on the importation of uranium for their NPPs. It is estimated that even when the installed capacity of China's NPPs reaches the target of 40 GW in 2020, it is expected to import less than 3,000 tons of uranium each year, which is only 5 per cent of the world's total supply (Zhou and Zhang, 2010).

Secondly, the generating cost of a nuclear power plant is much lower than coal-fired or LNG power plants. Fuel costs account for about 40–60 per cent of the total cost for the latter two types of plant, whereas this figure is only 5 per cent for nuclear power plants (NPPs). Although the construction of nuclear power reactors may incur high initial costs, nuclear energy is more cost-effective in the long run, particularly when the cost of fossil fuels is continuously increasing due to severe supply shortages and rising demand.

In addition, acceptance by the people will determine the extent to which nuclear power can be developed as an important alternative to fossil fuels. In the West, public opposition is a key impediment to nuclear power development, especially after the serious nuclear power accidents in Chernobyl and Fukushima. In March 2011, the Fukushima disaster caused by the Tohoku earthquake and tsunami made Germany decide to close down all its nuclear power plants by 2022. However, the Chinese public seems more willing to accept and embrace nuclear technologies. They generally believed that this clean energy has the potential to play a key role in the country's future energy mix (Zhou, 2010). Local governments are also found to act positively in terms of cooperation with nuclear investment corporations, as they believe that nuclear plants may assist the development of local economies by mitigating the problem of electricity shortfalls, increasing local tax revenue and also creating more employment opportunities.

Last but not least, the location of a nuclear power plant is also believed to be less weather and resource sensitive. They can work under extreme weather conditions and could also be constructed everywhere across the country. This is particularly important for China as it may help the country to solve its serious energy shortage issue along the coastal regions.

Despite all the advantages and potential of nuclear energy, the development of nuclear power in China also faces tough challenges.

The biggest challenge is the lack of nuclear technology. So far, China has only mastered the generation II technologies and is trying hard to import and absorb the generation III technology (Zhou and Zhang, 2010). Through collaboration with foreign partners, China aims to develop and upgrade its technology and achieve localization through the introduction, digestion and demonstration of advanced international technologies. However, due to collaboration with partners from different countries, the types of imported reactor technology are too diverse (Zhou and Zhang, 2010). This would affect the efficiency of technology digestion and domestic production and may consequently influence independent R&D of China's nuclear power industry and its nuclear power security (Zhou and Zhang, 2010).

The second challenge comes from the treatment of nuclear waste. Due to the limited use of nuclear energy for electricity generation in China, nuclear waste remains small in quantity. However, with greater installed nuclear power capacity in the coming years, nuclear waste will increase dramatically, to about 1000 metric tons per year. Therefore, how to deal with this waste safely and economically would become a big challenge. Lastly, with such aggressive expansion, whether China could maintain its safety culture and be able to employ enough qualified human resources to operate and manage the NPPs remains questionable. Today, only a few Chinese universities have nuclear engineering programmes and it has been expected by the Commission on Science, Technology and Industry for National Defence that China will need over 13,000 new university graduates in the next 15 years (Zhou, 2010). Therefore, how to recruit enough people with the right skills will become another serious challenge for China in the coming decades.

Nevertheless, with the great potential for reducing fossil fuel consumption and alleviating pressure on environmental pollution, nuclear energy has become an inevitable choice for China. It may help the country to achieve the goal of meeting growing energy demands while keeping environmental issues under control.

6 Conclusions

China's rapid economic expansion has stimulated its soaring demand for energy. In this paper, we have summarized the key challenges faced by the nation regarding its energy supply and consumption. This is then followed by a detailed analysis of the advantages and limitations of each of the energy resources. The country has become fully aware of the potential problems that might come about if it continues to require as much energy to support each unit of its GDP growth. To direct its economic development towards a healthier and sustained growth path, the central government has set specific "energy targets" in the 11th and 12th FYPs, as summarized in Table 5.6 below. And it is trying to incorporate new policies on energy consumption and conservation into the overall economic development blueprint to achieve a total transformation of China's economic structure and a reduction in environmental pollution.

Table 5.6 Energy targets in China's 11th and 12th Five-Year Plans (FYP)

Target	**11th FYP Proposed (end 2005–end 2010)**	**11th Achieved (end 2005–end 2010)**	**12th FYP Proposed (end 2010–end 2015)**
Energy intensity reduction	0.2	0.191	0.16
Carbon intensity reduction	n/a	0.162	0.17
Sulphur dioxide emissions reduction	0.1	0.1429	0.08
Chemical Oxygen Demand (COD) reduction	0.1	0.1245	0.08
Ammonium nitrate reduction (new)	n/a	n/a	0.1
Nitrogen oxide reduction (new)	n/a	n/a	0.1
Five heavy metals reduction – lead, mercury, chromium, cadmium and arsenic (new)	n/a	n/a	15% from 2007
Water intensity (water consumed per unit of value-added industrial output) reduction	0.3	0.37	0.3
Non-fossil fuels proportion of primary energy mix	(15% renewable energy by 2020)	0.083	0.114

Source: http://chinawaterrisk.org/regulations/water-policy/12th-five-year-plan/.

However, for a country like China, there is hardly any single approach capable of meeting rising energy demand and protecting the environment at the same time. The projected electricity demand of China by 2020 is in the range of 2,254 to 5,200 tWh depending on different assumptions imposed on the relationship between electricity demand and GDP growth (Zhou, 2010). Since China has always insisted on relying mainly on domestic supply for primary energy resources, it calls for a more rapid development of the country's non-fossil energies. Table 5.7 summarizes the projected contribution of each of the energy resources in China over the next decade.

It is apparent that renewable resources are expected to play a much more important role in the coming decade. Nevertheless, due to grid constraints, insufficient long-distance transmission infrastructure and immature technology, China's large-scale implementation of a renewable energy strategy remains challenging. Currently, the average on-grid electricity price of wind power, hydro power, PV power and nuclear power are about 0.617 Yuan/kWh, 0.244 Yuan/kWh, 0.4 Yuan/kWh and 0.436 Yuan/kWh, respectively (Wang, 2010). Compared with a price of 0.346 Yuan/kWh for coal-fired plants, despite their relative cleanness, it seems that coal will continue to be the primary energy resource in China in the foreseeable future.

Table 5.7 Power generation from different resources in China

	2005	2010	2020
Proposed energy consumption (Billion TCE)	2.25	3.2	4.5
Electricity installed capacity (GW)	500	800	1000
Oil (Million tons)	225	384	600
Nuclear Power (GW)		20	40
Power generation			
Solar energy			
Photovoltaic power generation (kW)	$7x10^4$	$3x10^5$	$1.8x10^6$
Installed area of solar water heater (m^2)	$7x10^7$	$1.5x10^8$	$3x10^8$
Hydro power (kW)	$1.17x10^{11}$	$1.9x10^{11}$	$3x10^{11}$
Wind energy (kW)	$1.26x10^6$	$5x10^6$	$3x10^7$
Biomass power (kW)	$2x10^9$	$5.5x10^9$	$3x10^{10}$
Percentage of non-fossil energy to total primary energy (%)	7.5	10	15

Source: Zhou 2010.

Therefore, in the short to medium terms, to mitigate effectively the serious environmental issues caused by coal consumption, China should encourage the deployment of advanced coal technologies, such as coal gasification, liquefaction and carbon capture and storage. To help the price of electricity generated by renewable engines compete with those from traditional fossil resources, extensive policy support and law enforcement are needed, such as adopting suitable fiscal and tax measures and increasing public R&D and information support (Zhang et al., 2010). In addition, market entry barriers should also be removed to allow free competition among companies.

6
Oil and China

David C. Broadstock

1 Introduction

China is an oil-dependent nation, consuming large amounts of oil to help power the economy. This is a fact that is true of many if not all of the developed nations around the world, and so by itself is not unique. What, however, does make China unique is that it consumes more oil than it produces by itself (as depicted in Figure 6.1); hence, to sustain consumption levels, it must import oil from other countries or regions. More specifically, Figure 6.1 plots data on the consumption (demand) and production (domestic supply) of oil in China. From 1970 through to 1994 the domestic supply of crude oil was sufficiently large to meet all domestic consumption needs, and China retained the potential to export the remaining balance. Between 1994 and 1995 this position changed; domestic production levels continued to rise, but the growth in demand was faster, and China no longer produced enough oil to meet domestic consumption needs, thus causing the energy supply gap (i.e., the shortfall of supply relative to domestic demand). As a result, to sustain a growing demand for oil, China was forced to become an oil importing nation – more importantly, a *major* importing nation. As such, China can therefore be considered as "import-dependent" in terms of meeting its energy needs. This supply gap, which continues to get larger, creates a concern regarding the domestic security of energy supply, and as noted by Wu et al. (2007, 2009) for instance, creates exposure to undesirable risks due to a reliance on international oil prices, geo-political issues and other issues besides.

China is not the only major importer of oil; accordingly, some of the concerns regarding oil-dependency are reasonably well documented. When looking into the issue of energy policy under oil-dependency,

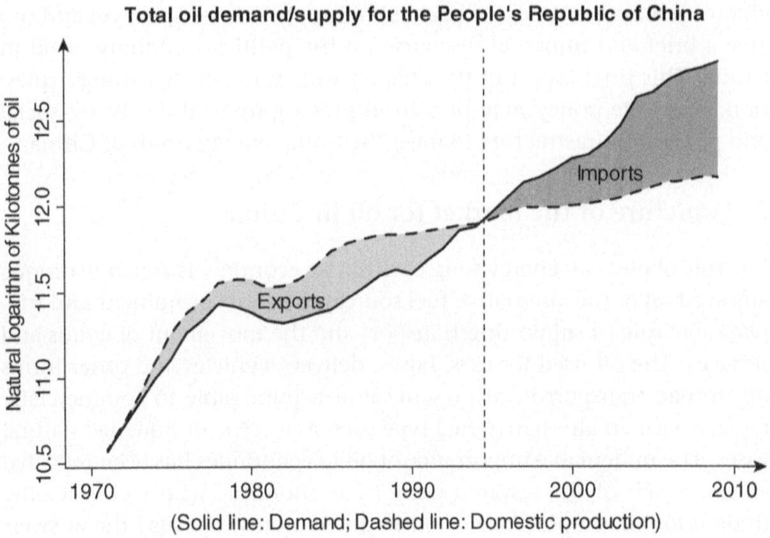

Figure 6.1 Domestic consumption and production of oil products and balance of oil trade

Source: International Energy Agency databanks, accessed July 2012.

Vivoda (2009) highlighted that in addition to the Chinese, the US and Japan are also major importers of oil, noting also that Japan and the US are far more advanced in terms of their economic development. As a result of the discrepancy in levels of economic development, it should not be assumed that the lessons learned from Japan and the US are directly transferable to the Chinese context. There are a number of reasons that can help to substantiate this reasoning, including cultural differences, natural resource endowments, skill availability (e.g., China having a larger but generally less educated labour force) and also the notable difference in the populations. The difference in populations is of quite some importance, as although the growth trends in China have been witnessed in other countries before, never have they occurred on such a large scale.

The aim of this chapter is then to explore this issue of oil-dependency and the supply gap for the Chinese context. In so doing the chapter will (i) broadly outline the market for oil in China, and the ways in which it helps to support economic activity (a demand side perspective) (ii) offer some remarks/projections of the future trends of oil consumption (iii) review some of the issues facing the current and future global oil supply chain such as the notion of peak oil (a supply side perspective) and (iv) give a brief and impartial discourse on the political economy of oil in China. This final aspect of the chapter will, among other things, question what role policy may play in improving upon the existing social and physical infrastructure to meet the future energy needs of China.

2 A picture of the market for oil in China

The role of oil as an energy source within an economy is arguably unique amongst all of the alternative fuel sources due to its prominent and irreplaceable role in supporting transport and the movement of goods and services. The oil used for cars, buses, delivery vehicles and other forms of on-road transport is, at present, almost impossible to commercially replace with an alternative fuel type such as electric or liquefied natural gases. The undeniable importance of oil to economies has been reflected within much of the research done by economists, who seek not only to describe the importance of oil to an economy, but also the answers to more specific questions such as what consequence do shocks to oil supply chains have on an economy, for example Kilian (2009) and Kilian and Park (2009). Such matters will also be considered to some degree later in the chapter. In what follows the focus will first turn towards characterizing the manner in which oil is used in China in terms of its share of total energy and then the sectors which consume it.

As mentioned in the introduction, the growth in demand for oil in China is virtually unprecedented by international standards. However, whilst the nation has been witnessing increases in the overall demand for oil products, the relative demand for oil is being dominated by other fuel sources (for instance by coal which an important energy source for China). This is illustrated by Figure 6.2, which plots the monthly share of oil-based energy in the total amount of energy consumed in China taken from the Chinese National Bureau of Statistics.

The trend over the period January 2000 through to September 2009 is clearly decreasing over time, albeit subject to some monthly variation, showing that the share has fallen from around 17.5 per cent to well below 10 per cent in recent years. The seasonal behaviour in the data, which has clear peaks in demand generally occurring around December/January, roughly coincides with both the international and Chinese New Year festivals. In December it might be expected that there would be increased freight deliveries including deliveries to shipping freight terminals to support increased global consumption during the Christmas and New Year festivities (and subsequent January sales). At

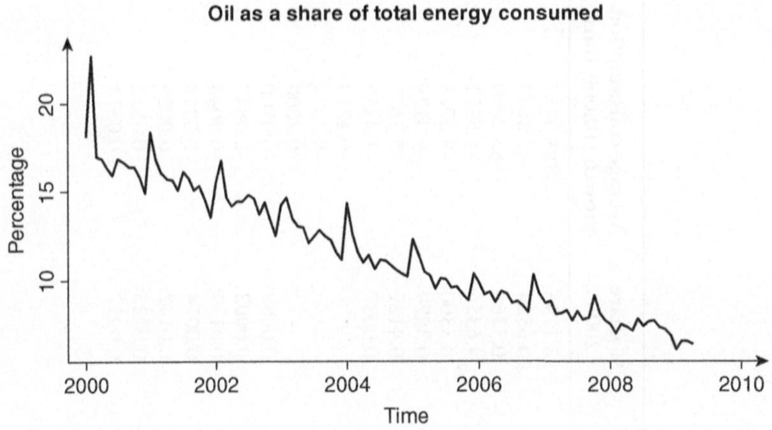

Figure 6.2 Monthly oil consumption in China and its declining share of total energy consumption
Source: National Bureau of Statistics of China, accessed July 2012.

the same time there will be increased domestic deliveries as well as massive demand for transport as many residents travel between cities from where they currently live and work to their home town, to spend time with their friends and family. This places an almost unmanageable burden on parts of the transport network, and of course a huge spike in the demand for oil. This peaking effect is decreasing over time, raising some questions as to the nature of seasonality in China and the management of peak oil demands during certain periods of the year, however there is not scope to discuss this further here.

2.1 Sectoral demand for oil

With a view to better understanding how oil is used internally within China, Table 6.1 gives details of industry-/sector- specific consumption of oil over the period 2000–06.[1] The demand for oil across the various sectors of the Chinese economy is rapidly changing. In 2000, the main consumer of oil was the "Mining and Processing of Ferrous Metal Ores" sector, but by 2006 this sector had been demoted to second place, making way for the "Manufacture of Raw Chemical Materials and Chemical Products" sector. Four of the industries stopped using oil in their production process, while an additional six industries started using oil. The last column of the table gives the average change in actual oil consumption over the seven-year period, and highlights that

Table 6.1 Oil using industries in China, 2000–06

Industry	**% share 2000**	**% share 2006**	**Average consumption growth (10,000 Tons)**
Mining and processing of Ferrous metal ores	53.2092	33.1796	–288.9457
Manufacture of raw chemical materials and chemical products	30.1492	60.6524	47.3643
Manufacture of chemical fibres	9.9072	0.3368	–83.2600
Transport, storage and post	2.9161	4.6356	–1.6271
Production and supply of electricity, gas and water	1.2759	0.3300	–9.2771
Production and supply of electric power and heat power	1.2759	0.3229	–9.3129
Manufacture of non-metallic mineral products	0.8919	0.4127	–5.5671
Smelting and pressing of Ferrous metals	0.1708	0.0037	–1.4457
Construction	0.0550	–	–0.4714
Extraction of petroleum and natural gas	0.0386	–	–0.3314
Others	0.0233	–	–0.2000
Smelting and pressing of non-Ferrous metals	0.0133	0.0088	–0.0700
Manufacture of artwork, other manufacture	0.0100	0.0003	–0.0843
Manufacture of beverages	0.0087	0.0139	–0.0043
Manufacture of electrical machinery and equipment	0.0083	0.0074	–0.0343
Manufacture of paper and paper products	0.0080	0.0142	0.0029
Manufacture of foods	0.0080	0.0025	–0.0557
Processing of food from agricultural products	0.0070	0.0017	–0.0514

Manufacture of plastics	0.0067	0.0023	–0.0457
Manufacture of special purpose machinery	0.0045	0.0031	–0.0229
Wholesale, retail trade and hotel, catering services	0.0030	–	–0.0257
Manufacture of textile wearing apparel, footwear and caps	0.0027	0.0065	0.0100
Manufacture of general purpose machinery	0.0018	0.0042	0.0057
Manufacture of articles for culture, education and sport activities	0.0017	0.0023	–0.0029
Manufacture of transport equipment	0.0010	0.0042	0.0129
Manufacture of textile	0.0008	0.0054	0.0200
Manufacture of rubber	0.0008	0.0229	0.1086
Manufacture of metal products	0.0005	0.0017	0.0043
Production and supply of gas	–	0.0071	0.0357
Processing of timbers, manufacture of wood, bamboo, rattan, palm and straw products	–	0.0031	0.0157
Manufacture of measuring instrument and machinery for cultural activity & office work	–	0.0014	0.0071
Manufacture of leather, fur, feather and its products	–	0.0011	0.0057
Manufacture of furniture	–	0.0008	0.0043
Manufacture of communication equipment, computer and other electronic equipment	–	0.0113	0.0571

Source: National Bureau of Statistics of China, accessed July 2012.

the majority of industries (20 out of 34) had decreased their levels of oil consumption, even though the economy continues to boom (and hence places an increased pressure on the consumption of all energy types).

The latter point discussed in the previous paragraph regarding the widespread reduction in the use of oil is of some interest. The implication is that the continued economic growth of China, which is benefiting all sectors of the economy, is being coupled with substantial changes in the way oil is used in the economy. A measure used by energy economists to describe the connection between energy consumption and economic activity (or output) is "energy intensity" which can be generally defined as:

$$\text{energy intensity} = \frac{\text{Output}}{\text{Oil consumption}}$$

Given this relationship and holding output constant, as the oil consumption of an industry decreases, the value of energy intensity will become larger, meaning that fewer units of energy (or barrels of oil) will be needed to maintain the same level of industrial production. There are two main channels by which such improvements can occur, namely efficiency improvements (using the currents resources with less wastage or energy loss) and technological advances (developing new ways to use resources). China is currently benefiting from both, with important advances in domestic technology being met with an increased presence of international technologies. At the same time continued improvements in the education sector are helping to ensure a higher skill base, and eliminate work-based inefficiencies from the labour force, and produce leaders of industry who better understand the importance of efficiency.

Turning back to the numbers given in Table 6.2, the final column shows that few of the sectors increased oil consumption, and most actually decreased oil consumption. Broadly speaking the sectors of the economy are growing in size, and the implication of this is therefore that the energy intensity of the sectors is generally improving (decreasing in size). Detailed discussion on energy and the intensity of its use across sectors in China can be found in Ma (2010). In recent years there have been widely documented improvements in energy intensity and energy efficiency in China, which is a positive sign for the future. Being able to sustain and even increase economic output without substantially increasing energy demand will be critical to the future development of China although, as discussed further on, the near future will be met with some inevitable increases in energy consumption.

Table 6.2 Freight shipping rates from Africa to various destinations, 2010–12

Destination	Dead weight tonnage	Approximate Distance (km)	USD per barrel (Oct. 2010)	USD per barrel (Oct. 2012)	Normalized price (2010)	Normalized price (2012)	Growth rate
China	260	10500	1.75	1.87	1.00	1.07	7%
US Gulf	260	9100	1.05	1.36	0.69	0.90	26%
Mediterranean	130	3110	1.28	1.54	2.47	2.97	18%
UK/Continent	130	4650	1.2	1.59	1.55	2.05	28%
US Atlantic	130	4250	1.34	1.63	1.89	2.30	20%
US Gulf	130	9100	1.44	1.76	0.95	1.16	20%

Source: Bloomberg financial database, accessed October 2012.*Notes*: Price normalization is defined here as the price per barrel per km relative to China 2010=1. It therefore reveals price variation due to shipping distance and can be immediately interpreted as being a higher (>1) or lower (<1) relative price to that offered to China in 2010. The normalized prices for 2012 therefore represent the adjustment towards (e.g. US Gulf 2012 is closer to 1 than US Gulf 2010) or away from (e.g., US Gulf 2012 is further from 1 in absolute terms than US Gulf 2010) to the price for China in 2010.

2.2 A note on the future demand for oil

A common topic of discussion when considering energy and China is the nature of future demand. While it is universally accepted that economic development is positive, it inevitably comes with an increased consumption of energy, and given the sheer scale of the Chinese populous, it is unsurprising that there are some concerns regarding the sustainability of future energy demand. The type of growth that is exemplified by Figure 6.1, has in particular generated some concerns regarding the seemingly exponential nature of growth in energy demand, see for example Martenson (2011).

It is however almost inconceivable that the demand for energy in China, or indeed any rapidly developing economy, would continue to grow in the same manner as seen in Figure 6.1 ad infinitum. In forming plausible expectations as to how oil is going to be consumed in China over the coming decades it is interesting to consider the "energy ladder", originally suggested by Romani et al. (2006). The ladder, an example of which is depicted in Figure 6.3, illustrates the connection between economic activity/development and energy consumption in per capita terms.

The importance of the figure comes in the S-shape pattern of energy consumption with respect to income levels. Income per capita is measured for different countries over time, and is adjusted to reflect the relative cost of living in different countries, which is done by using a purchasing power parity (PPP) adjusted measure of income. The combination of per capita and purchasing power parity adjustments ensure that the patterns in the figure for any given country can be compared with any other country. Hence the lines offer the ability to spot directly comparable trends in energy consumption in relation to economic activity. In Figure 6.3 only a select few countries are presented to ease clarity, although the general trend remains for almost all countries, see for example Romani et al. (2006).

The S-shape trend depicted in Figure 6.3 highlights some distinctly important features, which strongly suggest that energy consumption growth in China will not be exponential and that it will plateau after incomes rise further. In 2009, the income per capita in China was moving close to the USD 10,000 mark. From the graph it can be seen that incomes in the USD 5,000–15,000 range are predominantly associated with a high rate of growth in energy demand, with the per capita consumption increasing five-fold. This is due for instance to the transition from a basic way of living that sustains life, through to a standard

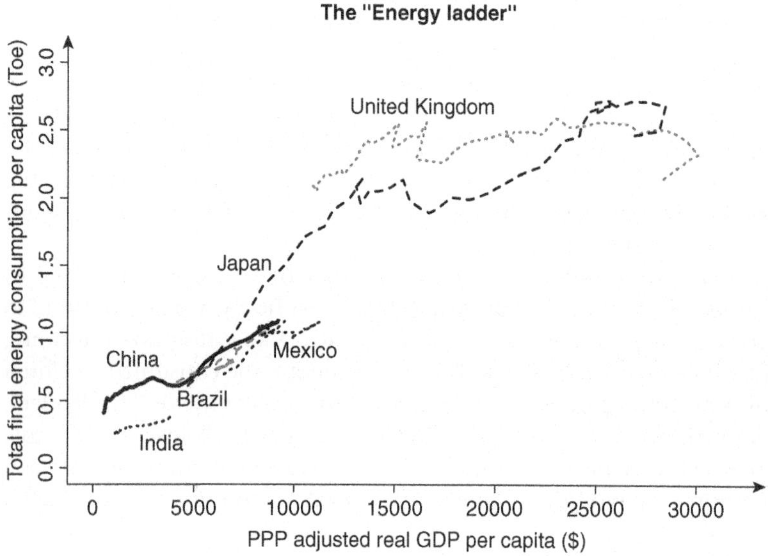

Figure 6.3 China and the "energy ladder": energy consumption per capita versus income per capita, 1971–2009

Source: International Energy Agency databanks, accessed July 2012.

of living that offers more desirable levels of quality of life. Households increase consumption of all goods and services, and perhaps most importantly, seek to acquire high energy-consuming goods such as a car. Hence over the coming years, China will surely witness continued rapid growth in energy (and implicitly oil) consumption as domestic economic growth continues to raise per capita incomes. However, when the per capita incomes get to be around USD 15,000, it can be seen that energy consumption patterns generally stabilize.

The energy ladder therefore offers some important insights into the nature of energy demand in China at least over the foreseeable future and the knowledge that it should not be naively considered to grow exponentially into the future, and growth in income will eventually become detached from growth in energy consumption. Although, in the short run the sort of trends seen in Figure 6.1, of increasing demand for oil, will most likely persist as overall energy demand continues to rise, and could easily rise to be double or more than the current levels. Recent estimates and media reports have suggested that economic growth in China is slowing down, the underlying feature is nonetheless of positive growth, the implication is that per capita income will continue to rise and hence per capita energy consumption will also rise, for related discussions see for example Adams and Shachmurove (2008) or Crompton and Wu (2005).

3 Global oil supply and the peak oil issue

So far a general picture of the demand for oil in China has been established, both demonstrating the present position as well as providing some reasonable expectations as to the future trends in energy consumption. While the demand side aspects are undeniably important, a matter of equal if not greater importance is the supply side of oil and what can be expected of that leading into the future.

The issue of oil supply needs to be tackled from two perspectives to provide a complete picture. The first aspect relates to relatively simple geo-physical features of oil supply, which have tangible/measurable economic implications, specifically the fact that (i) oil is not necessarily located where it is consumed and (ii) oil is a finite energy supply that is visibly declining in its abundance. Secondly, there are much more complicated matters relating to the political economy of oil and what can and should be done to alleviate domestic oil dependencies. Both will be considered, as they are deeply interconnected.

Considering firstly the geo-physical aspects of oil supply. The supply of oil can be considered as being constrained by resource abundance. The geographical constraint comes from the fact that oil reserves do not exist everywhere. China does have oil reserves, but these reserves are not large, and the extraction of oil from these sources is not able to be done at a rate which fulfils domestic consumption needs, thus leading to the oil supply gap demonstrated in the introduction. In terms of the physical constraint, oil is not a renewable form of energy (in the sense that it is not reproducible/replenished over any desirable time-span) and is hence finite in supply. Consumption of oil reduces the availability of oil not only for the current generation but also for future generations.

In 1958, Marion King Hubbert developed a theory to predict future production (based on a bell-shaped curve), which although mathematically/technically quite simple, managed to provide an accurate prediction for when rates of domestic production (for the US) may begin to decline.[2] The purpose of the method was to try and understand the urgency in needing to identify alternative energy sources to oil, based upon reasonable projections of how long existing reserves could last. These reserves, known as the ultimate recoverable resource (or URR) are one of the key pieces of information used in determining how long production for an oil field or group of oil fields can continue to produce oil in an economically feasible way (i.e., when the costs of extracting the oil do not exceed the revenues from selling it to the market).

Using methods derived from the work of Hubbert, and information on the URR of different countries, Bezdek (2007) projected when peaks in domestic oil production may occur in a selection of countries. It is worth highlighting that the peak is not the date when production will cease; rather it is the point when production is at its largest, after this point supply to market will start to decrease. China was predicted by Bezdek (2007) to peak at around 2012, however at about the same time Tao and Li (2007) also studied the problem of peak oil for China, and under alternative scenarios estimated the most likely peak of domestic oil production to be somewhere between 2019 and 2022. The difference in these estimates is most likely due to the different knowledge/expectations regarding the ultimate rate of recoverable oil reserves, but nonetheless the difference also demonstrates the amount of uncertainty amongst oil professionals, heightening concern regarding the pending peak.

As discussed, the concept of peak oil is not so much to describe when oil becomes unavailable, but rather to suggest when its supply goes into

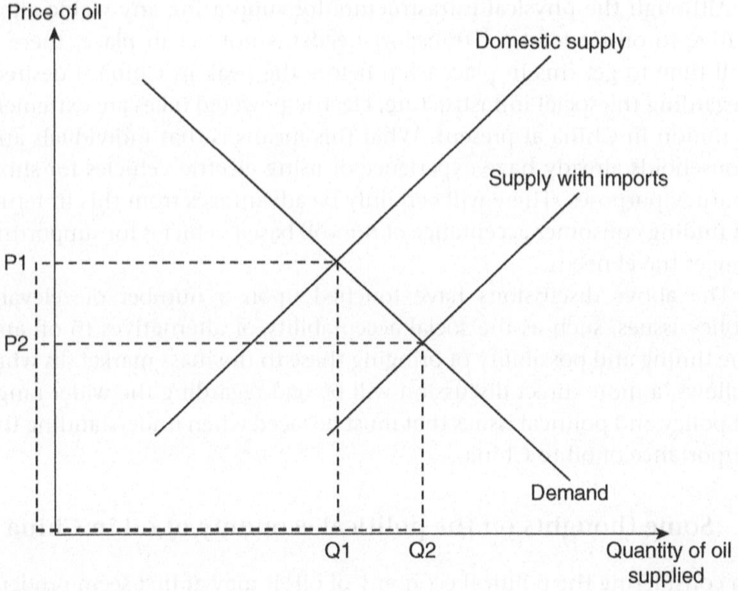

Figure 6.4 The market for oil and the consequences of imports on domestic price possibilities
Source: Author generated.

unstoppable decline. This is important information as it helps give an indication of when the social and perhaps more importantly physical energy infrastructure needs to be prepared for a post-oil era. Assuming the peak suggested by Tao and Li (2007) is approximately accurate, production rates in China will start to decline sometime around 2020. Oil will continue to be produced, but at a lower rate of supply than before, and year-on-year, the production rates would in the absence of market control, continue to decline. Consumers will be forced into finding alternative fuel sources, especially for transport needs. For the automotive industry current trends in alternative fuel designs would suggest an important future role for electric vehicles. However, at present the physical infrastructure in China is not well enough suited towards electric vehicles, although in some ways it may be better positioned than other more developed countries. For example, while existing fuel stations offer no current services to charge electric vehicles, there are suggestions that policy will change to require electric charging points at all fuel stations in the future.

Although the physical infrastructure for supporting any viable alternative to oil (at least for transport needs) is not yet in place, there is still time to get this in place even before the peak in China if desired. Regarding the social infrastructure, electric-powered bikes are extremely common in China at present. What this means is that individuals and households already have experience of using electric vehicles for short journey purposes. There will certainly be advantages from this in terms of finding consumer acceptance of non-oil based vehicles for supporting longer travel needs.

The above discussions have touched upon a number of relevant policy issues, such as the social acceptability of alternatives to oil and the timing and possibility of bringing these to the mass market. In what follows, a more direct discussion will be had regarding the wider range of policy and political issues that must be faced when understanding the importance of oil to China.

4 Some thoughts on the political economy of oil in China

In considering the political economy of oil[3] it may at first seem prudent to proceed by discussing the structure of the underlying domestic political system, that is communism. The nature of political systems has been hotly debated over many decades, often coming to the conclusion that communist regimes are counterproductive to an economy. It would however be remiss to say that it is an incorrect structure for the political system; furthermore the nature of the political system in China is clearly going through a gradual stage of transition following the market reforms of 1979. Nonetheless the nature of the politics does still have ramifications upon markets. This part of the chapter is less interested in the specific features of the communist political model as much as it is in outlining the issues in the political economy of oil that would remain true in any alternative political regime.

The importance of oil to economies is well documented, see for example Kilian (2009) and Kilian and Park (2009) for two good recent examples. While there is ongoing debate as to the specific role of oil, the general mechanisms by which it contributes to the economy are reasonably straightforward. Consider a rise in the price of oil. It is widely accepted that oil is needed to support most economic activities, underpinning the energy requirements of transport that is needed to move both goods and the individuals who provide services. Bhattacharyya (2011) for example provides a succinct review of these mechanisms, highlighting that a rise in the price of oil, effectively increases the costs of all consumption, thereby reducing consumer demand for all goods and services. At the same time, an increase in energy prices makes energy a less desirable factor of production for firms, causing firms to substitute energy for other factor inputs such as labour. In a textbook example of a statistical model of the macro-economy, Pindyck and Rubinfeld (1997) go further in specifying these effects as leading to price inflation, and in turn wage inflation.

There are further ways in which oil is vital to an economy as highlighted by the following quote:

> no efficient and economical substitutes exist for diesel, gasoline and jet fuel (aviation kerosene) for transport and the military, oil is a necessity to the economy and military (Downs, 2006). Thus, a reliable and adequate supply of oil at reasonable prices is crucial to national values and objectives and underpins, in part, the CPC's governance. (Leung 2010, p. 934)

This quote reminds us that oil, crucial to underlying economic activity, is also of great importance to the military, which protects the assets and resources of an economy. Moreover, that there is a need to ensure that oil policy is effective, so as to ensure that it underpins the long-term vitality of the political party. Although not the main focus of their paper, Ma et al. (2008) went further to highlight that the security of energy supply in China and the dependence of oil from overseas countries has resulted in some domestic "political tensions", thus implying that current policy towards oil is not yet right. Such tensions are economically rational if it is considered that the risk of oil dependence has the consequence of a supply chain disruption to China. This would suddenly and forcibly reduce oil supply and would then in turn impose upon the economy a necessary shift away from the use of energy towards, for example, more labour-intensive processes that is to reduce the number of machines used in low-skilled production, replacing them instead with low-skilled labour. The implication is thus that the supply gap introduced at the start of the chapter then poses a plausible economic risk.

Turning attention back to the geo-physical issues introduced at the start of this section, in 2007 just short of 40 per cent of all imported oil was from the Middle East, Vivoda (2009, Table 6.2), which therefore means that the oil supply chain is heavily dependent on a region which is fraught with frequent social and political unrest. The political economy of oil is then made infinitely more complicated by the fact that the security of oil supply in China will be influenced by politics that China has very limited influence over.

So far the discussion has concentrated on the generally negative aspects of oil-dependency, but it should however be noted that not all aspects of importing are to be considered negative. A simple review of the economic concepts of supply and demand in the presence of imports can serve to illustrate this point:

This depiction of the market for oil in China, although highly simplistic demonstrates the value of imported oil-to-oil consumers. The figure shows the supply and demand for oil, with two supply curves given, one reflecting the level of supply available from domestic sources and another if imports are included. This second supply curve is farther to the right indicating that at the same price (and assuming the world price is lower than the domestic price) there will be an increased number of firms willing to supply oil. If there are no imports of oil from external sources, then the market would choose to consume some quantity of oil Q1, at an equilibrium price P1. However, by introducing imported oil to the market the market is able to consume a larger quantity of oil, and at a lower market price as a result of the increased number of firms selling oil. Therefore, the market outcome within China is seemingly improved by enabling oil imports.

In further considering the issue of imports and also how they are related to prices, Table 6.2 contains information regarding the liquid freight shipping rates from Africa to China as well as Africa to other destinations such as the US, UK and the Mediterranean. Perhaps the most important feature of the table is to illustrate the relative growth in freight rates between 2010 and 2012. Although the absolute dollar rate per barrel for China is the highest of all the rates in the table, both in 2010 and in 2012. It is seemingly clear that there is a form of price discrimination occurring, and that of all the rates considered, China clearly is subject to a much lower rate of growth in shipping rates than other routes. The shipping distance for China is longer than any of the other distances, and so it is useful to consider the relative prices adjusted for distance travelled and scale economies (e.g., from shipping oil in larger container vessels). The calculated normalized prices in the table do this, and show that in 2010 China pays the third-lowest price while in 2012 it is the second-lowest. Political/trade relationships, coupled with the magnitude of trade required by China are likely reasons for this possible positive price discrimination that is lower growth in prices than any other region. Destabilization of relationships for any reason may result in such advantages being eroded.

In addition to shipping costs, oil import dependency exposes China to more general oil price risk. Not all oil prices are the same. While global oil markets illustrate trends of generally similar prices there are notable differences. Consider for example Figure 6.5 that plots the difference in nominal USD between the Chinese Daqing oil price and the West Texas Intermediate oil price (WTI). On this figure, a value close to zero indicates that the two prices are about the same, while values going below zero occur when WTI>Daqing, and values above zero when WTI<Daqing. From the early 1990s through to around 2005, there was little difference between the two alternative prices, highlighting no additional price risk exposure to the Chinese economy. Over the period 2005[4]–08 however there would seem to be a divergence emerging between the two, with Daqing oil seemingly becoming cheaper than WTI. In 2005 there was a sudden fall in prices, as there was again later in the series at around 2008, but markets responded differently to each shock owing to the 2008 global financial crisis.

Following a sudden shock to the global markets, the difference between the two oil price series has clearly diverged in a significant fashion. In particular in recent months the difference between the two prices has moved to being around USD 20–30, whereas in the preceding years this had remained much closer to zero. Admittedly, the WTI oil price may not

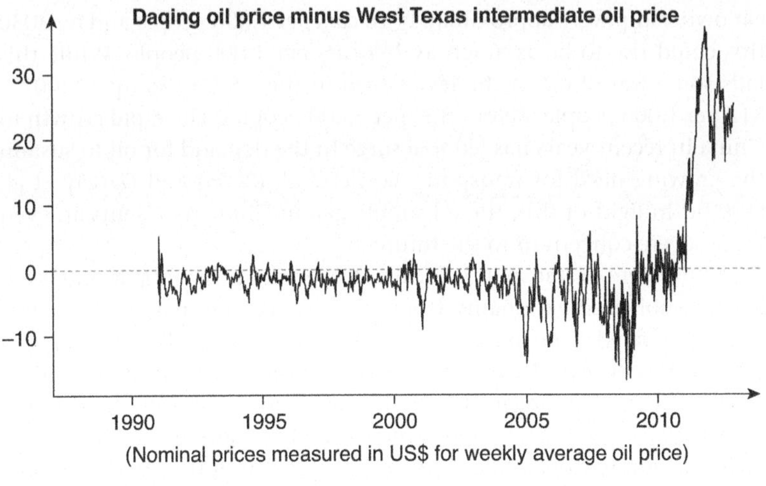

Figure 6.5 International oil price differences, and their divergence following the 2008 "financial tsunami"

Source: Bloomberg Financial Database, accessed October 2012.

be the most relevant to Chinese oil imports, but the example nonetheless illustrates the potential severity of oil price risk exposure, especially given the quantity of oil that China imports. While the current position of the Daqing in reference to the WTI is in the Chinese favour, it demonstrates that the oil markets are not currently integrated as much as they were before. As countries further try to ensure domestic oil supply security, price divergence may get stronger, which could in turn increase the likelihood of price-based risk exposure so long as imports continue.

Moving away now from financial matters and international political issues, focus is turned towards the unique nature of transport and the transport sector in general, as a major consumer of oil. Arguably the main problem of transport in China at the moment can be summarized thus:

> China's vehicle stock will increase nearly twenty-fold, to 390 million in 2030. This fast speed of vehicle ownership expansion implies rapid growth in oil demand. (Dargay et al., 1999, p. 143)

The problem of transport and expectations of its future growth in consumption in China are exacerbated by expectations of car ownership in the coming years. Dargay et al. (1999) analyse historic patterns of car ownership and future predictions for many different countries, and highlight among other things that for China in 2002 the levels of car ownership were approximately 16 cars per 1,000 people and by 2030 this could rise to be as much as 269 cars per 1,000 people. While this falls some way short of the levels seen in the US for example (2002 = 812 per 1,000 people, 2030 = 829 per 1,000 people). The rapid growth in China in recent years has led to a surge in the demand for oil to sustain the growing need for transport, see He et al. (2005) and Dargay et al. (1999).[5] In light of this, the oil supply gap in China represents an even more severe concern in to the future.

The problem of transport is further deepened by the notable and often highly publicized externality from oil consumption, namely the emissions generated from oil consumption. Ou et al. (2010) for example discuss the context of emissions resulting from transport use in China, and its expected trends leading in to the future under different growth scenarios. They conclude that, even in the best-case future scenario by 2050 the amount of carbon dioxide emissions from transport would be 3.87 times greater than the levels of emissions in 2007.

Fisher-Vanden et al. (2006) discuss the problem of emissions in China more generally, and the alternative sources of emissions in terms of sectors of the economy. They demonstrate variation among the sectors, which by itself is not surprising, and additionally consider how improved technology, specifically from foreign direct investment, affects emissions in China. The connection between foreign investment/consumption and emissions levels in China has been a subject of debate in recent years. There is huge international pressure on China to curb emissions, but at the same time sustain high production levels of goods for exports. The two are incompatible, as production of goods generates emissions, but the goods are often not for consumption in China.

It is worth noting that the problem of emissions from energy is a "hot-potato" in China. Ma et al. (2008) in a recent paper discuss an already changing public attitude towards the use of coal, owing to the emissions it generates, which has caused a preference for alternative energy sources. Their work implies that some firms had considered oil a feasible alternative to coal in their production processes, but oil does not present a solution in terms of emissions, simply a less severe problem.

In summary, oil represents a problem for economies, a problem that manifests through a range of issues that are in many cases political in nature. Oil is needed to support certain activities, such as transport, but it generates emissions, and more importantly has a supply chain dependency that offers the potential to negatively affect the strength of the Chinese economy if it is disrupted. Disruptions in the physical supply may emanate from broken down political relations in the future, but more likely political instability in the regions from which the oil is supplied and which China has no ability to control. Price disruptions, which may be independent of physical supply shocks, are again determined outwith China's sphere of influence and are a potential risk to domestic inflation. Additionally the domestic policies that might be needed in the not-so-far future as a result of domestic peaking oil supply may not be desirable to the general public. All in all, the political economy of oil is a complicated landscape.

On a closing note, another feature of possible interest is the role of state ownership in energy-related firms, and the manner in which political motivations may impact upon domestic oil market outcomes. Wang (1995, p. 634) in discussing oil policy in China noted that "Reforms in the oil industry are far from complete, and the legacy of central control remains", which still remains true even today. This diminishes the efficiency of oil markets in China by reducing the competition among firms, leading to potentially negative welfare outcomes for society. This issue is far from straightforward to discuss given, among other things, the ongoing change in the domestic political structure which currently mixes communistic principles, which tend to favour equity, with market principles that tend to favour efficiency. Without seeking to draw conclusions on whether such state ownership is good or bad, and keeping in mind that energy provision does benefit from scale economies that only arise at a very large scale (which governments often need to support), it does have potentially distorting effects upon market prices for energy products and also the market capitalization of firms.

5 Chapter summary

This chapter has presented a brief but encompassing view of the nature of oil markets in China. Beyond characterizing some of the key features of current and future demand, the chapter further outlined the complicated nature of oil supply, and in particular the issues in the political economy of oil in China emanating from a domestic oil supply gap.

It has been suggested that there is a range of "risks" to which the Chinese economy is exposed as a result of the existing, and growing, supply gap. Political instability, in terms of both the relations that China is directly involved with and those that it is not, has the ability to disrupt physical supply chains. Any unanticipated but prolonged disruption to the oil supply chain could result in severe disruptions of the internal operations of the Chinese economy. General market activity and international oil price determination directly impact upon the relative cost of importing oil. Peak oil concerns give rise to an unstable/uncertain future of when and how oil may need to be replaced as a fuel source, but with no obvious market-ready alternative. Notwithstanding these issues, the irreplaceable nature of oil as a source of energy cannot be ignored. Oil is a unique source of energy that has been a major driving factor behind the economic development of many of the world's leading economies.

There are natural policy responses to some of the issues discussed; Ma et al. (2012) concluded for instance that due to energy security concerns and the inevitable and substantial growth in transport consumption over the coming years, increased investment is necessary to identify new domestic oil reserves and to reduce future import dependency, and in addition to also reduce existing oil-dependency, especially for transport. However, it is probably not right, given available technology, to discourage growth in the consumption of oil. This is surely a necessary component of sustaining economic growth targets in the near future. But in the short term perhaps some of the possible existing opportunities in China can be further exploited before oil-dependency becomes too locked in to the economy. For example, the extremely low rates of car ownership mean that drivers have not yet become locked into oil-based technologies for personal transport needs, implicitly suggesting that there is an opportunity to encourage other solutions, for example non-car based, and/or non-oil based technologies.

To summarize the relationship between oil and China is complicated, although there is some solace in the knowledge that the complications faced by China are shared by many other nations too. There are deep and highly consequential issues relating to the political economy of oil that cannot go unabated and China must prepare for a non-oil future at some point, but so must every nation. The uniqueness of the Chinese situation is dominated by its scale and the timing of its rapid economic development at a time when the importance of emissions are better understood. Nations such as the US, Japan, and UK etc. all experienced the main part of their economic development prior to emissions becoming a major international concern. China is met with a different set of concerns in meeting its future development targets/needs, and oil is no longer the problem-free "black-gold" that it maybe was in the past.

Notes

1. No distinction is made regarding the source of the oil, from the consumer's side, there is generally no way of knowing the source of the oil, that is, whether the oil is produced domestically or imported.
2. For further discussion on the techniques and history of the methodology see for example Deffeyes (2005) and Laherrère (2001).
3. Political economy can be broadly defined as economics that intersects directly with politics and how the two may relate to or interact with each other.
4. No adjustment is made for API fuel gravity.
5. The phenomenon of rapid growth in car ownership (and use) in low-income and developing economies has for instance been documented by Button et al. (1993), who stylized the unavoidable growth in personal transport as well as commercial travel.

7
China's Alternative Energy Sources

María J. García

1 Introduction

China's sustained industrialization since Deng Xiaoping's reforms has turned the country into the world's largest user of energy resources. To date, manufacturing processes and the country's modernization have relied mostly on energy and electricity derived from burning fossil fuels. Coal, found in abundance in China, still accounts for seventy per cent of all energy consumed in the country. Oil dependence has also been on the rise. It accounts for 23 per cent of the energy mix, which has turned China into a net importer of this crucial commodity and a net importer of energy since 1997 (Liu et al., 2011, p. 518). Estimates suggest that China's dependence rate on imports of oil is expected to increase to over 70 per cent by 2020 (Brookings Institute 2006, p. 6).

The current energy structure presents the Chinese leadership with three major challenges for the future. Firstly, environmental degradation, particularly in terms of air pollution, derives from industrial processes and from the burning of fossil fuels at the massive scale required to sustain China's energy demands. Increasingly, the social side effects of decades of rapid industrialization are being felt in the form of health problems and greater citizen activism in the sphere of environmental protection (Ecoworld 2007). To retain its control and the citizenry's support, the government is increasingly aware of the need to resolve the environmental problems in the country, as reflected in its policies (see NDRC 2007).[1]

Secondly, greater reliance on external energy sources like oil pose a strategic challenge in terms of securing future supply and averting over-reliance on foreign suppliers. China's state-owned enterprises (SOE) in the oil sector, Sinopec and China National Offshore Oil Corp (CNOOC), have secured investments and oil field exploitation rights abroad. Although their current aims appear more aligned with creating global oil companies to compete on a par with Western companies such as ExxonMobil, BP or Shell (Philips 2012), these investments could help secure oil supplies for China in the future. China's increased expenditure on military and blue water naval capabilities could aid in securing sea lanes for trade and oil supplies. These endeavours are expensive and do not necessarily guarantee the safe passage of oil through some of the world's volatile regions (e.g., Straits of Hormuz and Malacca). A first oil pipeline linking the world's largest energy producer Russia to China's north-eastern city of Daqing began operations in January 2011, there are also plans for future natural gas pipelines linking both countries (BBC 2011). However, whilst this supports diversification of energy sources it still relies on purchases from abroad. Like many other countries concerned with energy security, China is increasingly focusing on the development of internal solutions to its energy needs, seeking alternative energy sources within its borders including renewable, nuclear and gas resources.

Thirdly, reliance on burning fossil fuels for energy has turned China into one of world's largest sources of greenhouse gas emissions, maybe even the first one (Weber et al., 2008). Consequently, the Chinese leadership is under intensifying pressure from foreign counterparts to actively reduce emissions and engage in global climate change actions. Unlike the United States, China signed the Kyoto Protocol on climate change and has set for itself ambitious targets for emissions reduction. Although, as it is categorized as a developing country, its targets are not in absolute terms but refer instead to a reduction of emissions intensity (emissions per unit of GDP). The Chinese government has committed to a 40 to 45 per cent reduction in emissions intensity by 2020 from 2005 levels and increased share of non-fossil fuels to 15 per cent by 2020 under the Copenhagen Accord of 2010 (Climate Action Tracker 2013).

Fostering the development and uptake of renewable energy sources, "green" energy, and technology simultaneously addresses these three major challenges. Since the 1990s, successive Chinese leaders have promulgated various policies on renewable energy sources, and these are summarized in Section 2. These policies have placed an emphasis on technology transfers and the development of domestic industrial capacity to further reduce external dependence. As a consequence, the policies have succeeded in promoting industrial and manufacturing growth in the green technology sector, to the extent that in 2013 China is the world's top manufacturer of photovoltaic panels (Algieri et al.,

2011). Subsequent sections highlight the progress that has been achieved in the sectors that have received more attention from the government's policies (hydro-electricity, wind and solar power).

As exemplified in the National Development and Reform Commission (NDRC)'s 2007 Energy Policy, and the 2012 Energy Policy (Information Office 2012), China is seeking solutions to these challenges through renewable and other alternative resources. Emphasis has been placed on: energy savings, reliance on domestic resources, reliance on technological solutions, encouraging diverse patterns of development (development of coal resources, accelerating oil and natural gas exploration, boosting hydro-electric and other renewable power, promoting nuclear power, and developing substitute energy resources in a scientific way to guarantee a steady energy supply), protecting the environment, and cooperating with international bodies for mutual benefit. Thus, the last sections of this chapter review the current state of play of some of these scientifically advanced searches for secure alternative domestic energy sources (e.g., non-conventional gas and coal fuels).

2 Policy background

China's policies for renewable energy date back to the outline of New Energy and Renewable Energy Development of 1996. This was followed by the 10th Five-Year Plan of New Energy and Renewable Energy Development (2001), the 11th Five-Year Plan of Renewable Energy Development (2006), and the Medium- and Long-Term Plan for Renewable Energy Development (2003) (Shi 2010). As the literature highlights, the initial renewable energy policy revolved around reducing energy poverty in rural areas (Shi 2010; Zhang et al., 2009), and thus extended the use of micro- and small-scale hydro-electric plants which have brought electricity to China's countryside. Policies in the 2000s have placed greater emphasis on the environmental aspects, the substitution of fossil energy, and the development of the renewable energy industry with independent design capacity (Shi 2010, p. 204).

Renewable energy requires higher initial investments than fossil-based energy production, hence the emergence of government support systems throughout the world to foster its development and adoption. In China, the Renewable Energy Law of 2006 was crucial in establishing targets for renewable energy, mandating compulsory on-grid systems, tariff prices, distribution and a special funding system (Shi 2010, p. 208). Economic incentives for the development and use of renewable energy include tax reduction and exemptions on the import of equipment, halving value added tax on renewable energy companies, discounted-interest loans (mostly for wind power promotion, solar energy and large- and medium-sized marsh gas projects) (Zhang et al., 2009). Prices for renewable electricity are set by the government based on the principle of "rate of return", that is cost plus a reasonable return on capital. Thus, these prices remain higher than those for fossil-fuel generated electricity (Cherni and Kentish 2007). The purpose of guaranteed grid access and government set prices is to ensure a market for renewable electricity, which may not otherwise emerge (Wang et al., 2010, p. 1874). In addition, there is a fiscal subsidy policy in place for renewable energy development, demonstration projects and bidding prices of renewable energy power, as well as direct investment funds from the Ministry of Finance. As Evan Hills and Zhengxu Wang highlight in their contribution to this volume (Chapter 12), there remain numerous institutional barriers to the fruitful implementation of China's renewable energy policies derived from the fragmented nature of authority between central and local governments, different agencies and SOEs. Further obstacles arise from high production costs, inadequate grid facilities unable to support the more irregular flow of solar and wind-generated electricity, rapid growth in installation but incomplete usage, and competition amongst SOEs and smaller private companies (Shi 2010, p. 212).

3 Hydro-electric power generation

Hydro-electric power generation in China was initially established as a mechanism to alleviate the absence of electricity in remote rural areas through the installation of micro- and small-scale hydro-electric plants (those with installed capacity below or equal to 5,000 kW). Small-scale hydro projects still account for 35 per cent of all electricity generated in China from hydro resources (Zhang et al., 2009, p. 441). Including the power generated by more recent large-scale hydro-electric plants such as the Three Gorges Project, hydro-electricity represents the majority of power generated from renewable sources in China, and six per cent of China's energy mix (Larson, 2012). According to the Government's 2012 energy policy, the country's exploitable hydro power resources stand at 542 million kW, and less than 30 per cent are being exploited. The Government plans to increase non-fossil energy consumption to represent 15 per cent of all energy by 2020, and it expects over half of this to come from hydro power development (Information Office of the State Council, 2012). Whilst there is still further potential for the development of hydro-electric resources in China, this type of energy presents several drawbacks. Firstly, investment costs in large-scale plants are high. Secondly, the social and economic costs of relocation of populations flooded by associated reservoirs are increasing. Thirdly, associated environmental costs of river diversion, enhanced risks of flash floods, water use in times of drought are also garnering more attention. The government's proposals for greater exploitation of hydro resources do stress the need to take these issues into account and to perfect benefit sharing schemes with the affected populations (Information Office of the State Council, 2012). Finally, seventy-eight per cent of hydropower resources are located in the Western part of the country, where development still lags behind the rest of China. Further exploitation of China's renewable resources will require increased investment in infrastructure to transport the electricity to the areas where it is most needed. This has been recognized and prioritized in the 2012 Energy Policy (Information Office, 2012). Moreover, as large hydro power is able to compete in price with conventional power, it is not included in preferential policies for renewable energy, although small hydro power stations are (Shi, 2010, p. 202). Much of the impetus of recent Chinese legislation to incentivize renewable energies has, therefore, focused on other types of renewable resources – a tendency that is reflected in the literature on the matter (Wang 2010), however the 2012 policy, with a clear focus on energy self-sufficiency, indicates that the number of hydro-electric plants will increase in the short term.

4 Wind power generation

Wind power is considered China's renewable energy success story. The industry dates back to 1986 when the first pilot wind farm was established in Rongcheng City in eastern China. Qiang Wang (2010) distinguishes three phases in the development of China's wind power market. In the first stage grants from foreign donor countries and loans were used to create small demonstration projects, with very low prices paid for the electricity generated. During the second stage (1994–2003) development was still slow due to high costs and unclear policy support, despite a series of government plans to promote the industry. The final phase commenced in 2003 with the implementation of the "Wind Power Concession Programme". The aims of the programme were to improve domestic manufacturing capacity for parts and to reduce electricity generation costs. Within the programme, the government offers concessions for wind farms through a public tendering process, where low costs offered and high local content in terms of the parts and equipment are significant factors in winning the bid (Wang, 2010, p. 705).[2] To allay some of the problems that have beset the wind and solar power generators with regards to inability to connect with the electric grid, the programme determines that the provincial grid company must sign a power purchase agreement with the wind farm owners and purchase all the electricity generated by the plant. It further lays the responsibility for investment in transmission lines and connection of the wind farm to the nearest electricity network with the grid company. To neutralize some of the higher electricity costs of wind-generated power, the programme demanded that the price difference be shared across all the provincial grid users, and since 2006, across the entire national grid (Wang, 2010, p. 706).

The bid system has facilitated the dual objectives of cost reduction and domestic manufacturing capacity. Local content requirements in the bids have encouraged the growth of a domestic wind power equipment industry. Sponsorship of domestic wind turbine and parts manufacturing has been furthered through the "Notices on the Requirements of Local Content in Wind Power Construction" implemented in 2005, which raised the 50 per cent local content requirement of 2003 to 70 per cent (Wang, 2010, p. 706). In 2007, China became the world's fourth-largest producer of wind power equipment behind the United States, Germany and Spain. Awarding concessions to the bids offering lowest costs has also lowered wind power costs. An effect of this has been fierce price competition, with many concessions being granted to large SOEs which can offer the lowest prices as they can withstand short-term losses, which are tempered by their profits in coal or nuclear electricity generation and their financial support networks, to enable them to control the resources and realize profits from them in years to come (Wang, 2010, p. 707). This has resulted in rapid growth of installed capacity. In 2008 four provinces (Inner Mongolia, Liaoning, Hebei and Jilin) had an installed capacity in excess of 1 GW each.

Government support measures have been further scaled up since 2009 when, in the aftermath of the global financial crisis, the government regarded the development of wind energy as one of the key areas for economic growth. The government has tripled its target for wind power capacity to 100 GW by 2020, after reaching its original target of 30 GW a decade early, making China the world's largest market for wind energy technology (Wang 2010, p. 708). Despite impressive advances in capacity building, challenges still remain for China's wind power generation. China's electricity grid has been described by Qiang Wang (2010, p. 709) as backward. Rather than creating a "smart grid" able to withstand the irregular inputs of electricity from renewable sources, which by their very nature are volatile, the State Grid Corp of China, the largest grid operator, is instead investing in ultra-high-voltage transmission lines (Wang, 2010, p. 709).

5 Solar power

Solar power energy in China presents a paradox. On the one hand, China has become one of the world's top manufacturers of photovoltaic (PV) panels and equipment. On the other hand, uptake of the technology has lagged far behind manufacturing capabilities. China has overtaken early leaders in PV production (United States, Germany and Japan) and by 2009 accounted for 41.2 per cent of the global PV exports market (Algieri et al., 2011, p. 7277). In recent years a comprehensive production chain has emerged including polysilicon feedstock, silicon slices, silicon carbide, solar panels and modules, solar power systems and PV power stations (Hu, 2012, p. 2). Chinese companies have now mastered some of the processes for which they previously relied on imports like polysilicon production. By 2011, China was responsible for 38 per cent of the world's production of the latter. In the same year, PV batteries production increased 100 per cent with respect to the previous year in China with a manufacturing cost 30 per cent below international levels given economies of scale, technology and cheaper labour (Hu, 2012, p. 3).

PV power generation on a large-scale began in 2009 with the launch of large-scale projects such as "PV Building", "Golden Sun Demonstration Project" and the "Dunhuang Desert PV Station Tendering". In 2011, to stimulate the growth of the PV power generation market, the government initiated a PV feed-in tariff. That year 2.2 million kW PV power generating capacity was installed bringing the total up to 3 million kW (Hu, 2012, p. 3).

Solar thermal power in China is mostly confined to household hot water production, with an operating capacity in 2011 of 217.4 million square metres, and where the direct-plug compact solar water heater dominates the market (Hu, 2012, p. 3). More industrial and large-scale solar thermal power generation is still at the experimentation and demonstration phase. The Ministry of Science and Technology has supported research and development in the field by launching the "Tower Solar Thermal Power Technology Research and System Demonstration Project" in the 11th Five-Year Plan (2006–10), and furthering its promotion in the 12th Five-Year Plan period (2011–15) (Hu, 2012, p. 3).

6 Biomass

China's potential biomass resources are vast. Crop stalks, foul wastes, domestic garbage, industrial organic waste residue and waste water are currently used for energy production. About 60 per cent of crop stalks are used for energy production, but little waste is used. It is estimated that up to 80 per cent of industrial organic waste residue and domestic waste could be employed as biomass resources. (Zhang et al., 2009, p. 441). Biomass energy in China comprises biological chemical transition (marsh gas and fuel alcohol), biomass gasification (power generation or thermal power co-production), biomass liquefaction (biodiesel) and direct burning (boiler burning, dense burning and garbage burning). Government targets aim to increase biological solid fuel to 5 x 10^7 tonnes by 2020 (Zhang et al., 2009, p. 441). The respective targets for fuel alcohol and biomass energy generation are 2 x 10^6 tonnes (5.5 x 10^6 kW) and 1 x 10^7 tonnes (3 x 10^7 kW). Biomass development offers China a potential source of energy, and a way of disposing of large quantities of waste. In rural households 75.8 per cent of energy consumed derived from biomass (firewood, crop stalks and biogas) (Ma et al., 2010, p. 439). However, as most of this was directly combusted this adds to pollution and emissions problems. Furthermore, as Ma et al. (2010) have remarked little attention has been paid to the link between grain-based bio-energy and its impact on food production, despite a few studies that discovered that bio-fuel production had increased grain prices (wheat, maize, soybean) between 25 and 45 per cent in the 2005–08 period (Yang et al., 2008; Huang et al., 2009 cited in Ma et al., 2010). Expanding bio-fuel production has turned China into a net grain importer, thus the Chinese leadership has begun to review its bio-fuel policy and to dampen domestic production (Yang et al., 2008).

7 Other renewable resources

Other renewable sources of energy with zero emissions include geothermal energy and ocean energy, both of which could be abundant given China's vast landmass and long coastline. Over 3,200 geothermal spots have been found, of which over 1,300 are exploited for energy production. These are distributed mainly in Beijing, Tianjin, Hebei, Jiangsu, Jiangxi, Shaanxi, and Guangxi, and are mostly employed to provide heat, and also in the planting and breeding industries. Fifty per cent of the Lhasa power grid's electricity comes from the Tibet Yangbajing geothermal plant. Providing the energy equivalent of 0.65 metric tonnes of coal, geothermal energy provides the least usable power to China's current energy mix (Zhang et al., 2009, p. 441), and does not feature explicitly in the Government's 2012 Energy Policy.

Only recently has the Chinese government focused attention on the potential for ocean power, as technologies in this field advance worldwide. The New Energy group has estimated a theoretical tidal energy reserve of up to 1.9 x 10 kW, 90 per cent of which is located in the shores of Zhejiang and Fujian. Small projects have been exploiting tidal energy, the most developed of ocean resources, for over a decade now (see Charlier, 2001). Wave energy resources are estimated at 1.29 x 10 kW, of which one-third is located in Taiwan. Theoretical ocean temperature energy resources are located mainly in the South China Seas. Unresolved sovereignty disputes in the region could hamper the development of these resources. Currently, these resources remain at experimental levels, and do not feature explicitly in the 2012 Energy Policy.

8 Non-renewable alternative energy sources: natural and unconventional gas

To achieve the priorities of saving energy, relying on Chinese energy sources, protecting nature and improving livelihoods as set out in the 12th Five-Year Plan (2011–15), the Chinese government's 2012 Energy Policy has encouraged efficiency (decrease by 16 per cent the energy consumption per point of GDP), and increased usage of renewable energy sources, including the development of safe nuclear power, which at present accounts for 1.8 per cent of China's electricity well below the global average of 14 per cent (Information Office 2012, see Figure 7.1).

To further self-reliance, the government is also focusing on the expansion of the use of domestic gas resources. According to Hu Zheng, counsellor on China's State Council and former Vice-President of China National Petroleum Corporation, "natural gas is abundant, economic, produces low emissions and represents the bridge to the low carbon economy", and, thus, is a key priority of the Chinese government. In 2012 China's natural gas consumption totalled 1,300 million cubic metres. To further encourage its usage, China is investing in two new major natural gas pipelines (Shaan–Jing and West-to-East) to deliver gas to the broadest possible area.[3]

The development of natural gas as an energy source in China has been hampered until recently by various factors. Firstly, only the three SOE energy giants, Sinopec, CNOOC, China National Petroleum Corporation (CNPC) were bidding on gas drilling projects until recently, when other

Self-Reliance
Further develop renewable energy sources
Further develop hydroelectricity capacity
Increase wind power generation and grid connection
Increase solar panel use
Ameliorate electric power in rural areas
Demonstration Increase projects:
By 2015 200 green-energy counties and 1000 villages using solar power
Build new small hydropower stations and rebuild old ones to reduce use of wood
Promote use of solar heaters
Electrification of border regions
Develop safe nuclear power
Upgrade urban grids and natural gas networks
Accelerate natural gas development
Accelerate energy technology
Improve efficiency
Institutional reform
International cooperation

Figure 7.1 Key objectives of China's energy policy, 2012
Source: Information Office, 2012.

power and mining companies have entered the bids. Secondly, difficulties for smaller players are compounded by the fact that 90 per cent of all pipelines are owned by CNPC, which is under no obligation to link its system to rivals. Thirdly, gas prices are regulated by the government, and this makes it difficult for companies to pass exploration and production costs to the customers, thus limiting their interest in investing in the sector (Larson 2013).

Much attention has been paid recently to the United States' dash towards energy self-reliance through the exploitation of controversial shale gas resources. China's shale gas reserves have been estimated at 1,275 trillion cubic feet, double those of the United States, but whilst the United States has 200,000 fracking wells in operation China has 60 (Larson, 2013). China, too, is exploring its shale gas options, and Beijing has set ambitious plans for shale gas production of 6.5 billion cubic metres by 2015 and 60 to 100 billion cubic metres by 2020 (Information Office, 2012). To gain expertise in this field China is engaging in foreign collaborations, as it has done in the past in the wind and solar power industries. Within its energy cooperation partnership with the European Union joint development of shale gas technology is one of the intentions expressed in the 2012 EU–China High Level Meeting, alongside facilitating large-scale European investments in China to meet natural gas demand, facilitating third-party access to natural gas development, and a pilot pricing scheme based on EU practices for natural gas (Europe China Clean Energy Centre 2012). Large Chinese energy companies are also actively seeking investment opportunities abroad, particularly in the world's shale gas leader, the United States. CNOOC and Sinopec have secured a minority stake in the Devon and Chesapeake exploitations, which could help them secure access to technology and know-how to be applied later in China for the exploitation of Chinese resources (Philips, 2012).

Shale gas exploitation poses extra challenges for China. Whilst the United States industry uses horizontal drills in flat areas, China's major shale gas deposits are found in the deserts of Xinjiang and the rugged mountains of Sichuan, thus extraction in many cases will be more complex than it has been in the United States. Furthermore, in a country already beset by environmental degradation problems, shale gas exploitation could result in greater problems. The process whereby rock beds are cracked so as to reach the gas reserves requires large amounts of water, and China's water resources are already under severe pressure. Moreover, various studies have established a link between hydraulic fracking practices to break rocks, and oil and gas extraction more generally, and greater seismic activity (Holland 2011),[4] which in parts of China that already lie on seismic fault-lines, could result in tragic consequences. Despite these obstacles, most analysts think it's only a question of time before large-scale commercial shale gas production starts in China. Research firm IHS Cera's China energy team predicts the industry must travel a "long and winding road" well into the 2020s before China's shale gas is an important domestic energy source. On the other hand, Martin Stauble, who runs Shell's exploration and production in China, where the company is investing USD 1 billion annually in gas exploration in joint projects with CNCP in Sichuan and Shaanxi, reckons commercial shale gas development "is likely to be in a three- to five-year time frame" (Larson, 2013). Government enthusiasm for shale gas will, in either case, have to be tempered with stringent regulation and oversight to avoid some of the problems that have arisen in the United States as a result of leakage from poorly constructed wells and to avoid the potential hazards of shale gas.

9 Non-renewable alternative resources: coal-to-gas and coal-to-liquid technologies

China holds some of the world's largest coal reserves, with an estimated remaining 96.5 billion tonnes of bituminous, subbituminous coal and lignite, approximately forty years- worth of consumption at current levels (Source Watch 2013). Coal accounts for 70 per cent of China's current energy mix.[5] Massive energy consumption for industry and its enormous population, mostly derived from burning coal, has propelled China to the top spots in the world rankings of greenhouse gas emitting states, and has forced China to turn to importing coal in the late 2000s. In 2007 it imported more coal than it exported contributing to a sharp rise in global coal prices. By 2011 given high coal prices and the effects on global demand from the financial crisis, Chinese coal imports fell, resulting in lower prices (Source Watch 2013). Increased reliance on oil imports for transport fuel[6] and industrial processes (currently 17 per cent of the energy mix), increases China's energy insecurity and exposure to volatile external prices. In recent years oil prices have risen sharply, making states, not least China, eager to find alternatives.

Coal-to-liquid technologies offer the appealing possibility of using domestic coal resources to produce fuel for transport without external reliance, and at cheaper prices. China has been developing this resource for some time. Initial experiences date back to the 1980s, but since China became a net oil importer in the mid-1990s they have gained in significance (Asia Times, 2006). In 2006, China signed an agreement with South African company Sasol to jointly build two coal-to-liquid plants with a combined cost of USD 6 billion and output of 60 mm tons of liquid fuel per year at a projected cost of USD 15 per barrel, which is cost effective as long as oil prices stay above USD 30 per barrel (Beyond Fossil Fuel, 2006). In 2007, the Shenhua Group Corp, one of China's largest coal producers, initiated the construction of its first coal-to-liquid plant in Inner Mongolia, which marks the world's first direct liquefaction plant.[7] In its first two years of operation the Shenhua plant realized profits of USD 15.38 million, and it is expected to reach annual production capacity of one million tonnes (Institute for Energy Research, 2011). Other major coal producers have also gained approval for projects: the Lu'an Group for a project in Shanxi province and the

Yankuang Group for another project in Shanxi province projected to yield 10 million tonnes of oil products per year by 2020 (Asia Times, 2006).

The liquification of coal involves applying high temperatures and pressure to the coal. Sulphur released as a by-product can be sold, but the process does also release carbon dioxide, which the various plants expect to bury or treat in diverse ways. The Shenhua Group worked with West Virginia University on carbon limitation systems for example, and the Yankuang Group has partnered a Houston-based company (Accelergy Corp) to use its algae-based terrestrial sequestration system in Yankuang's future facility in Erdos, Inner Mongolia (Geiver, 2011). However, the water intensity of the process is even greater than that required for oil extraction (8 tonnes of water for coal liquification, compared with 6 tonnes of water for oil extraction, per tonne of fuel) (Ecoworld 2007). Whilst this provides relief from energy insecurity it does little to resolve the environmental externalities of large-scale energy production and consumption. So as to allay some of the potential ecological damage caused by an over-exploitation of coal-to-liquid resources, in 2006 the National Development and Reform Commission (NDRC), the top economic planning body, decided that only coal-to-liquid projects with an annual capacity above 3 million tonnes would be granted permits, in view of a growing number of smaller projects that were being sponsored by investors and local and provincial governments (Asia Times, 2006).

In July 2012, SEO Datang Power launched the first coal-to-gas conversion plant in Inner Mongolia, which is expected to reach a full capacity of 4 billion cubic metres by 2014. Together with a further three approved projects in northern provinces, these plants are expected to produce 15 billion cubic metres of gas annually from 2015, almost 7 per cent of the country's demand, thus reducing reliance on imports of natural gas (Solid Ground Magazine 2013). These new projects are placing China at the forefront of coal conversion technologies and development, thus fulfilling the goal of domestic technology generation, and they represent further examples of the Chinese leadership's drive to secure domestic energy sources and further technological advancement as a solution to the country's energy needs.

10 The international factor

The development of alternative energy sources in China is inextricably linked to its relations with the rest of the world. Firstly, commitments undertaken under the Kyoto Protocol to lower greenhouse gas emissions have strengthened the government's resolve to promote renewable energies. Secondly, some of the mechanisms developed within the international climate regime spurred a series of initial renewable energy projects in China, which facilitated technology and know-how transfers. The United Nations Framework Convention on Climate Change established the Clean Development Mechanism (CDM) as a means for the developed and developing world to collaborate in greenhouse gas emissions reduction. In practice, it has become a system whereby developed world enterprises fund reforestation or renewable energy projects in the developing world, lowering emissions in the host country as a way of offsetting the emissions their industry produces elsewhere. Despite a slow initial uptake, once the Chinese government issued the 2005 "Measures for operation and management of CDM projects in China", which clarified the rules and legislation regarding these projects, CDM projects rose rapidly, to such an extent that China has become host to nearly 60 per cent of all certified emission reduction (CER) schemes registered under the CDM (Wang and Chen, 2010, p. 1992).

Of all CDM projects in China, 27.9 per cent relate to renewable energy production, almost 10 per cent to efficiency and energy conservation, nearly 9 per cent to methane use, and the largest share (33.5 per cent) relate to projects that capture industrial greenhouse gases and which generate the highest number of CERs to the investing party. Within the renewable energy CDM projects, 51.2 per cent are hydro power resources and 43.9 per cent have been invested in wind power plants. In this way external investment has contributed to the growth in installed capacity of these renewable energy sources and has also facilitated technology transfer, which was an initial barrier to the development of these industries. However, as Qiang Wang and Yong Chen (2010) have pointed out, the CDM's potential for enhancing the development of renewable energy in China is limited, as foreign project sponsors are interested in the projects that generate the maximum number of CERs, that is dealing with the consequences of fossil fuels rather than replacing them.[8]

Thirdly, Chinese energy demand has helped to drive coal and oil prices up in the international markets. In turn higher prices have encouraged the Chinese Government to seek energy self-reliance. Fourthly, the Government's insistence on developing domestic renewable power technology production capacity, and its desire to create jobs through its industrial policy, have turned China into the world's top manufacturer of wind turbines and PV components, so as to service demand for "green" energy elsewhere, particularly in Europe (Algieri et al., 2011). Demand has been rising in China, which is now the largest market for renewable technologies. Its market has encouraged Western market leaders to invest in manufacturing capacity in China and to transfer the required high-end technology and know-how, as Danish wind turbine manufacturer Vestas has done (*New York Times*, 2010). Chinese renewable equipment overcapacity has lowered global prices for these products, facilitating the assimilation of these technologies throughout the world, but has also placed great strain on Western manufacturers. American producer Solyndra went out of business, and European PV manufacturers grouped under their association umbrella have pressured the European Commission to investigate Chinese subsidies to the solar industry as a first step towards potential future anti-dumping measures being applied to Chinese imports at the European borders (European Commission, 2012). The Chinese leadership is fighting these European actions, and has also retaliated by presenting a case at the World Trade Organisation (WTO) against the subsidies to renewable power given by some European Union member states (WTO, 2013). Yet the same problem is also affecting Chinese manufacturers. Lower prices mean that China's USD 30 billion solar power industry, which is overbuilt and heavily in debt, despite continued government support to prevent job losses, is also under threat (Goossens, 2012).

In 2012 Suntech Power Holdings, the world's largest solar panel maker announced the reassignment of 1,500 workers in its photovoltaic cell factory in Wuxi. In the same year LDK solar, China's second-largest maker of solar wafers was forced to sell a 20 per cent stake to a renewable energy investor part-owned by the city of Xinyu where the company is located. In 2012 Chinese solar power manufacturers posted losses of USD 987 million, and although the Government intervened to support the largest manufacturers, it would prefer consolidation of companies (Goossens, 2012). Regional governments, on their part, are loath to allow their local solar industry to fail, again revealing the jurisdictional matters that have hampered renewable energy development in China.

China's wind turbine manufacturers, responsible for 40 per cent of the world's output, are also suffering a double squeeze, as demand has stalled both abroad and domestically, partly due to regional utilities' lack of capacity to absorb wind-generated power into their grids. China Datang Corporation, a SOE wind energy developer saw its profits fall by 76 per cent in the first half of 2012 due to these problems (Goossens, 2012). Lower global demand led Sinovel Wind Group, the world's largest wind turbine maker by market value, to post its largest loss since going public in January 2011 and an 82 per cent drop in sales (Goossens, 2012). The Chinese government's continued support for these industries, and expansion plans for the use of renewable power sources, should guarantee the long-term survival of these industries. However, lower international demand and the effects of potential sanctions and the ongoing financial crisis will undoubtedly severely affect the industry in the short-term.

11 Conclusion: challenges and difficult choices for the future

China possesses phenomenal potential domestic energy sources, and is well on its way to achieving energy self-reliance. As the 2012 Energy Policy highlights China already produces almost 90 per cent of the energy it consumes. Reliance on domestic coal sources has had grave consequences for the environment and population. Eager to lower greenhouse gas emissions, produce "cleaner" energy and achieve self-reliance, the Chinese government has embarked upon an ambitious energy policy to promote the use of renewable energy resources and technological advances in gas and coal technologies including carbon capture technologies to "clean" its coal industry.

Renewable energy sources (RES) in China could potentially support Chinese energy needs as the following figures of projected resource capacity reveal. Estimates suggest that by 2030, at least 40 per cent of Chinese energy consumption (at current rates) could be obtained from

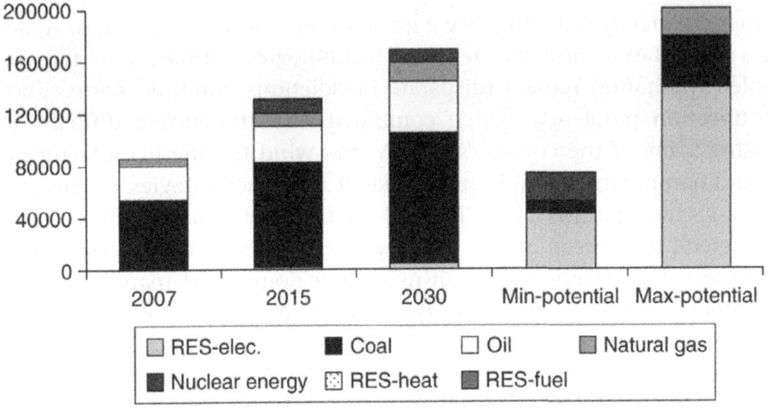

Figure 7.2 Potential of renewable energy sources in China compared to general energy consumption in PJ/year

Source: Liu et al. (2011, p. 522).

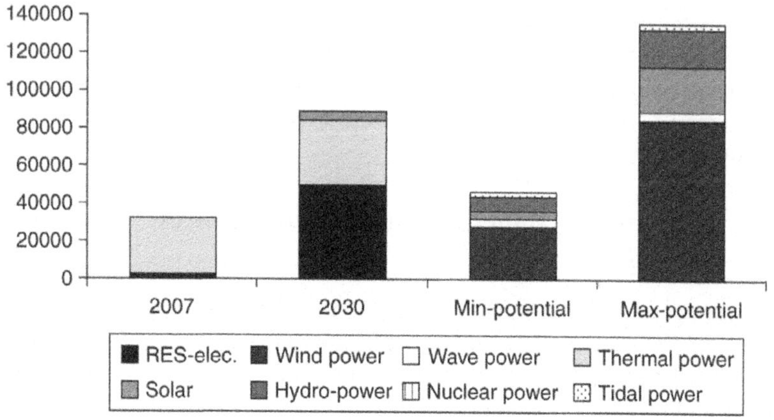

Figure 7.3 Potential of renewable energy sources electricity in China compared to the electricity consumption equivalent (fuel equivalent: electricity multiplied by 3) in PJ/year

Source: Liu et al. 2011, p. 522.

renewable sources. Making use of all estimated renewable capacity could fulfil the majority of China's energy needs. However, the uncertainties highlighted above lead some commentators to estimate that in 2050, coal will remain the major source of Chinese energy, but accounting for a much lower stake of around 39 per cent (Zhang et al., 2010).

Despite the vast potential of renewable energies in China, the 2012 Energy Policy appears to place a greater emphasis on natural gas, shale gas exploitation and cleaner coal technologies. Obstacles to renewable exploitation remain (disparate jurisdictions, multiple actors, grid connection problems), which combined with the current difficulties facing some of the country's top PV and wind turbine manufacturers could hamper more ambitious uptake of these technologies. Externally vis-à-vis trade partners, the Chinese leadership are taking a strong stance to defend their green energy manufacturers and secure their continued business. Facilitating and ensuring greater domestic demand for their products could be a solution to their current distress. The government's emphasis on gas, non-conventional gas and cleaner coal could pave the way to energy security, and reduced emissions. However, reductions will be less than through the development of renewable energy sources and will have to be carefully managed to prevent further environmental degradation. The road to energy self-sufficiency will be a difficult one requiring high investment, creativity and dedicated stewardship.

Nevertheless, it seems more than likely that China will reach that goal in the coming decades. It certainly has the potential resources, and the government appears to have the will to commit to this goal.

Notes

1. Following record-breaking pollution in January 2013, the Chinese government set new targets for the reduction of major pollutants by 2 per cent throughout 2013, will commence monitoring smaller particles in major cities and aims to reduce the latter by 6 per cent annually by 2015 in three key regions. Measures include banning older vehicles, limiting production of certain vehicles and improving gasoline and diesel quality (China Daily 2013).
2. Concessions are granted for 25 years and the bid price is guaranteed as a feed-in-tariff for the first 30,000 full load hours (depending on the site this equals 10 to 15 years), after which the owner receives the average local feed-in-tariff on the electricity market.
3. Hu Zheng's speech at the European Union and Emerging Powers Conference held in Brussels on 29–30 April 2013.
4. There has been much controversy in the United States and Europe about the shale gas industry. Some scientific reports have established seismic links and verified the damage caused to underground aquifers from chemical leakage and increased methane content in wells near fracking sites, whilst some scientists have defended the industry.
5. Source Watch (2013) has documented some of the pollution and health consequences of reliance on coal, as well as government actions to close down 1,298 illegal coal mines, and popular protests against the polluting effects of coal plants.
6. City planners have also fostered programmes for reduced reliance on oil by promoting the use of alternative fuels on city buses (including coal derived fuel). An analysis by Ou et al. (2010) revealed that only half of the vehicles running on alternative fuels were achieving the dual objectives of energy savings and greenhouse gas reductions.
7. South Africa's Sasol, and to a lesser extent Shell, have been the most significant of the few companies commercializing coal-to-liquid technology. They have always used indirect liquefaction – first gas is extracted from the coal and then it is liquefied (Andrews-Speed 2007).
8. They further stress that the "additionality [principle] would pose a perverse incentive for host countries not to implement ambitious policies for deployment of renewable energy" as it would be hard for a country with progressive policies to justify that the project would not have occurred without the CDM (Wang and Chen 2010, p. 1994).

8

Regional Electricity Consumption and Economic Growth in China

M.J. Herrerias and Roselyne Joyeux

1 Introduction

The success of economic reforms in China, initiated at the end of the 1970s, as measured by economic growth, was driven mainly by the promotion of capital accumulation and openness (Herrerias and Orts, 2011). In recent years, while the majority of Occidental economies were suffering the consequences of the global crisis, the Chinese economy grew 10.3 per cent in 2010 and, on average, 10.92 per cent from 2003 to 2010, making a significant and steady contribution to the dynamism of world economic activity (see Figure 8.1(a) and 8.1(b)). However, at the same time economists have questioned the sustainability of this fast economic growth, the growth model promoted by the government and the possible consequences. The strong dependence upon external demand, income inequalities, and environmental damage are almost ignored and left unresolved by the government. While it is true that some efforts have been made, with little success, in terms of the promotion of internal demand and inequality, energy and environmental policies were totally forgotten until the 11th Five-Year Plan (2006–10). In this plan, China, committed to achieve a green economy, aimed to increase consumption of renewable energy sources and prevent environmental pollution by increasing environmental investment by 1.33 per cent of GDP by 2009. These actions were working in parallel with reforming the environmental management institutions by granting the public open access to environmental information, establishing the National Leadership Committee on Climate Change, setting energy efficiency and pollution targets, encouraging the adoption of measures by local governments to pursue environmental excellence, and adopting market mechanisms for pollution reduction.

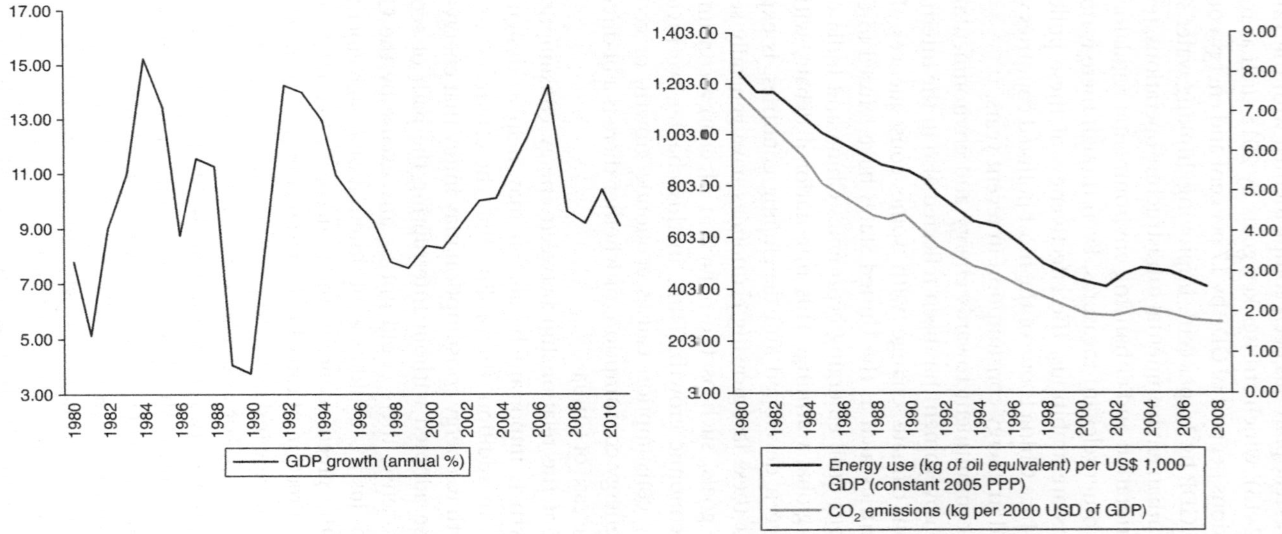

Figure 8.1 GDP growth rate, 1980–2011 (left), energy intensity and emissions (right), 1980–2008

Source: World Bank.*Note*: Energy Use right axis; CO_2 Emissions left axis.

This 11th Five-Year plan has been complemented with the 12th Five-Year Plan (2012–15), which stresses key goals by 2015 such as reducing pollutant emissions per unit of GDP by 17 per cent and energy consumption by unit of GDP by 16 per cent, improving drinking water sources, its quality, and urban environmental infrastructure operations, reversing ecological deterioration and enhancing environmental regulatory institutions among other relevant measures. Even though there is no doubt that these plans are ambitious, the effectiveness of these policies are rather modest since China is one of the most polluted countries with an increasing trend in energy consumption in recent years.

The modest commitment towards energy and environmental issues by the Chinese government has been reflected also in the international negotiations on climate change with some consequences. Indeed, developed countries such as the United States have refused to commit to any agreement until emerging economies China and India commit themselves on global warming. This international debate, with little consensus between developed and developing countries, is explained by the fact that these fast-growing economies have generally seen the environmental goals, such as the reduction of energy consumption, as threats to economic growth. Thus, in this chapter, we investigate whether energy consumption causes economic growth, or economic growth causes energy consumption, or whether there is a bi-directional causation in the case of China.

The analysis of the relationship between energy consumption and economic growth is important because it may help to design better energy policies. In addition, the finding that the causation runs from economic growth to energy consumption may imply that energy-saving measures can be adopted without interrupting the path of economic growth. In this sense, there could not be any excuse by the Chinese government to justify avoidance of international agreements and promotion of the green economy in its domestic economy. Finally, research on the direction of causality between energy consumption and growth can reveal new insights into the economic model that prevails in such a relationship. For example, if from the results it is found that energy consumption causes economic growth, this finding would imply that energy consumption should be seen as an input, and therefore, the production model would be supported by the data. On the other hand, if energy is considered as a good, this would imply that the demand model applies because economic growth causes energy consumption.

The Chinese economy is an interesting case study since China is the most populous country in the world, with an extraordinary economic performance. In addition, this country overtook the United States in the world ranking in terms of production and consumption of energy in 2009. So, China's policies on climate change not only affect China itself but, given its relevance and contribution to the world economy, should be considered in the international context, as the Copenhagen Conference highlighted in 2009.

China's successful economic experience, of course, is related to the change of the institutional setting from planned to a more market economy at the end of the 1970s and Deng Xiaoping's famous tour in the South of China. Market reforms focusing on openness to trade and foreign direct investment have been recognized in the empirical literature as the major forces driving the fast economic growth (Herrerias and Orts, 2010). However, this economic performance is distributed unequally among China's regions: eastern zones being more developed than the central and western ones due to the preferential policies adopted by the government through the application of the Special Economic Zones (Herrerias, 2011; Herrerias et al., 2011). These characteristics, as well as the high profile of the state sector, influence the development of the energy sector in China. Unlike the open-door policy initiated in 1979, reforms in the energy sector started in 1985. State-owned companies still dominate except in the coal industry that has recently liberalized. This delay is affecting the overall development of the energy sector.

In addition, energy resources are unequally distributed in the vast territory of China. First, coal, the most important source of energy, is only concentrated in Shaanxi and Inner Mongolia, while the generation of electricity from hydropower is located in Sichuan and its neighbours. Second, consumers of energy, not surprisingly, are located in coastal areas and their fast economic growth requires large amounts of energy. Finally, the transmission grid plays a key role in the efficient use of energy resources and the transportation of energy between provinces in China.

However, the six transmission grids all operate independently, therefore creating some inefficiency. The Chinese government has stressed that by 2020 they will have a unified system, but for now there are problems inherited from the past.

In the relevant energy-economics literature, the relationship between energy consumption and growth has been analysed in the majority of cases at country level. Few studies have tried to examine this relationship by exploring the regional component. Only a few papers have investigated this issue in the case of Chinese regions including: Li and Leung (2012) who found bi-directional causality between coal

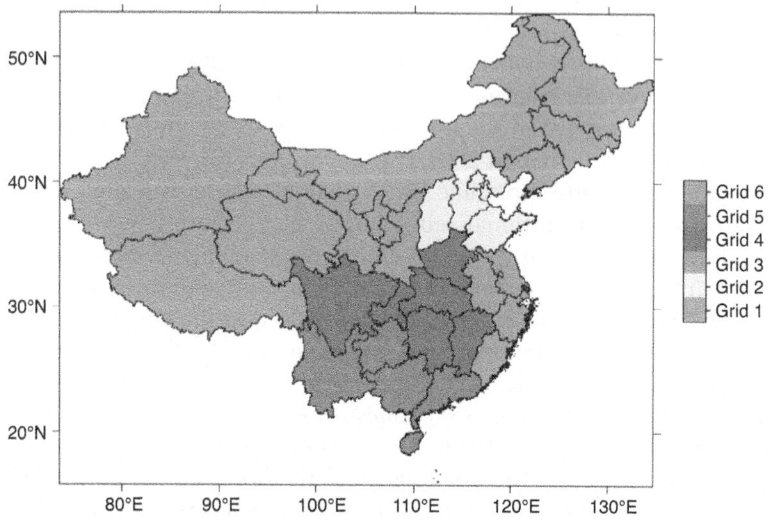

Figure 8.2 Map of the coal transmission grid

Source: Coal transmission grid. Authors own elaboration. Transmission Grids:

Grid 1: North-East: for Heilongjiang, Jilin, Liaoning and Inner Mongolia;

Grid 2: North: Beijing, Tianjin, Hebei, Shanxi and Shandong;

Grid 3: East: Shanghai, Zhejiang, Anhui, Jiangsu and Fujian;

Grid 4: Central: Jiangxi, Henan, Hubei, Hunan and Sichuan;

Grid 5: South: Guangdong, Guangxi, Yunnan and Guizhou;Grid 6: North-Western: Shaanxi, Gansu, Qinghai, Ningxia and Xinjiang;

consumption and GDP growth from 1985 to 2008; Wang et al. (2011a) who also found a bi-directional causality between energy consumption and economic growth over the period 1995–2007; and Herrerias et al. (2013) who found uni-directional causality from economic growth to different sources of energy consumption. However, while it is true that examining such a relationship at the provincial level provides greater detail than at national level, it ignores the large variation that exists between cities in the same province, the different degrees of urbanization and the industrialization process undertaken since the reforms began. Thus, this chapter contributes to the literature by filling the gap in existing knowledge by exploring this relationship at the city level. To the best of our knowledge, it is the first attempt to analyse empirically this relationship at this high level of detail from 1996 to 2010.

The investigation of this topic at city level is important because the industrialization process in China, as in other economies in transition, has been followed by an increase in the urbanization rate. In 1953 this rate was 13.26 per cent, and has sharply increased to 26.44 per cent in 1990 and to 49.68 per cent in 2010. This rapid increase has been reflected in an increasing trend in energy consumption, creating an imbalance between the demand and supply of energy.

Another interesting characteristic is the population in each city. For example, by the year 2010 there were 14 cities with a population of more than four million, 30 cities between two and four million, 81 cities between one and two million, 109 cities with 0.5 to one million, 49 cities between 0.2 and 0.5 million, and 4 cities under 0.2 million. This scenario is significantly different from the one applying in the year 1999: in that period there were 13 cities with two million of people and over, 24 cities with one to two million, 49 cities with 0.5 to one million, 216 with between 0.2 and 0.5 million and 365 under 0.2 million (National Bureau of Statistic of China, 2011, 2000). Not only is the concentration of population in few cities important, but also the varying sizes of cities in the provinces is significant. For example, if we consider electricity consumption, we can observe that Hangzhou in Zhejiang province consumed 423,202 kWh of electricity in 1996, whereas Zhoushan in the same province only 48,174 kWh. This behaviour can be observed in Guangzhou with 5,629,954 kWh and in Yunfu with 91,291 kWh consumed in 2010, as well as in other central and western areas of China. So the analysis at the prefectural level of the relationship between electricity consumption and growth will provide more precise information on the nature and source of causation between energy and economic growth.

We apply panel techniques to test for bi-variate causality at city level between per capita GDP and per capita electricity consumption. The use of panel data methodology in this context improves the power of non-causality tests applied to time series. It also allows us to consider a heterogeneous model to test the non-causality hypothesis; it is therefore possible to test the relationship between per capita GDP and per capita electricity consumption without considering the same dynamic model for all the cities in the sample.

The results indicate that in the short-run there is feedback between GDP and electricity consumption for the northern grid. There is also uni-directional causality from GDP to electricity for the north-western grid. There is however no short-run causality either way for the other grids. In the long-run there is very strong evidence that there is uni-directional causality from per capita GDP to per capita electricity consumption for all the grids except for the eastern grid where there is no causality either way.

This chapter is organized as follows. In Section 2, we present a short review of the literature. In Section 3 we discuss the results; while in Section 4 we report the conclusions and policy implications.

2 Overview on the relationship of energy and growth

The relationship between energy and economic growth is a topic of interest for economists and policy makers because of its implications in the design of economic and environmental policies. In the 1970s investigation of this relationship was prompted by very sharp increases in oil prices following the oil embargo to the United States in 1973. The motivation then, as it is now, was to establish whether energy conserving measures could be implemented without affecting economic growth. Kraft and Kraft (1978), using data for the United States from 1947 to 1974, found that there was uni-directional causation in the long-run from economic growth to energy consumption. Their research was then extended to both developed and developing countries. There is now a large number of empirical studies often presenting contradicting evidence.

This earlier line of research is still relevant although it is now motivated by policy proposals to reduce CO_2 emissions by reducing energy consumption. Evidence from this research can be categorized into four groups according to their findings: (1) uni-directional causality running from economic growth to energy consumption, (2) uni-directional causality running from energy consumption to economic growth, (3) bi-directional causality between energy consumption to economic growth, and (4) no causality.

If there is uni-directional causality running from economic growth to energy consumption conservation programs, including those aimed at reducing CO_2 emissions, are not expected to affect economic activity. In the case of China, Zhang and Chen (2009) utilize cointegration techniques on Chinese data at the national level from 1960 to 2007 to determine that economic growth causes energy consumption. There are numerous other studies reaching this conclusion for other countries or groups of countries: Yu and Choi (1985), Abosedra and Baghestani (1989), Gosh (2002), Fatai et al. (2004), Oh and Lee (2004), Thoma (2004) and Yoo (2006) use time series analysis; Al-Iriani (2006), Huang et al. (2008) and Ozturk (2010) apply panel cointegration.

Alternatively, if the conclusion is of uni-directional causality running from energy consumption to economic growth then policies aimed at reducing energy consumption might impact negatively on economic growth. In the case of China such a conclusion is reached by Shiu and Lam (2004), Wang and Yao (2007), Zhao and Fan (2007), Wang et al. (2011a) and Li et al. (2011), Zhou and Chau (2006) for oil consumption, Yuan et al. (2008) for electricity consumption. Bloch et al. (2012) find that China's coal consumption causes economic growth. They conclude that it is very difficult for China to reduce greenhouse gas emissions by reducing coal consumption. They recommend switching to greener energy sources in the long-run. For other countries Masih and Masih (1998), Chang et al. (2001), Altinay and Karagol (2005), Lee (2006) and Akinlo (2009) use time series analysis, whereas Lee (2005), Chen et al. (2007), Narayan and Singh (2007), Narayan and Smyth (2008), Lee and Chang (2008), Akinlo (2009), Apergis and Payne (2009a), and Apergis and Payne (2009a, 2009b) apply panel cointegration techniques.

The presence of bi-directional causality between energy consumption and economic growth indicates that conserving energy might have an adverse effect on economic growth. For China at the national level Han and Wei (2004) find bi-directional causality, whereas Wang et al. (2011b) reach the same conclusion with data on Chinese regions between 1995 and 2007. They conclude that China should weigh up the impact of energy supply constraints on economic growth. For other countries Stern (1993, 2000), Yang (2000), Soytas and Sari (2003), Ghali and Et-Sakka (2004), Oh and Lee (2004), Jumbe (2004), Paul and Bhattacharya (2004), Lee (2006), Soytas and Sari (2006), Lise and Monfort (2007), Zamani (2007) and Chontanawat et al. (2008) utilize time series data, Apergis and Payne (2009b), Mishra et al. (2009), Apergis and Payne (2009a) and Ozturk (2010) use panel cointegration.

Finally, a result of no causality in either direction is still consistent with the overall conclusion that energy conservation programs would not be expected to negatively affect economic activity. For China, Yuan et al. (2008) derive evidence supporting the same conclusion. Akarca and Long (1980), Yu and Hwang (1984), Erol and Yu (1987), Yu and Jin (1992), Cheng (1995), Asafu-Adjaye (2000), Yu and Choi (1985), Altinay and Karagol (2004), Huang et al. (2008), and Acaravci and Ozturk (2010) present evidence which supports this view for other countries.

The variety of the results on the causal relationship between energy consumption and economic growth often depends on the variables included, the methods applied, the sample of countries or regions and the period considered. Thus, in this chapter we attempt to provide fresh empirical evidence on this relationship by using recent econometric methods such as panel cointegration allowing for cross-sectional dependence in the case of Chinese cities from 1996 to 2010.

3 Empirical evidence

Data have been collected from the National Bureau of Statistics of China. They cover 216 cities for electricity consumption and real income (per capita basis) from 1996 to 2010. Cities where we do not have information for all the years have not been considered in the study since a balanced panel is required for our econometric study.

The sample period average log electricity consumption per capita is plotted against the average log GDP per capita in Figure 8.3. The data is in logs since the relationship between GDP and electricity consumption is not linear but log-linear. From this graph we can conclude that there is a positive relationship between GDP and electricity consumption. There are two cities that appear to have high electricity consumption relative to their income.

Figures 8.4–8.6 give us a closer look at the relationship between per capita income and electricity. These figures show such a relationship in the three main areas in China that is, eastern, centre and western, using the official administrative division of regions in China. From these we

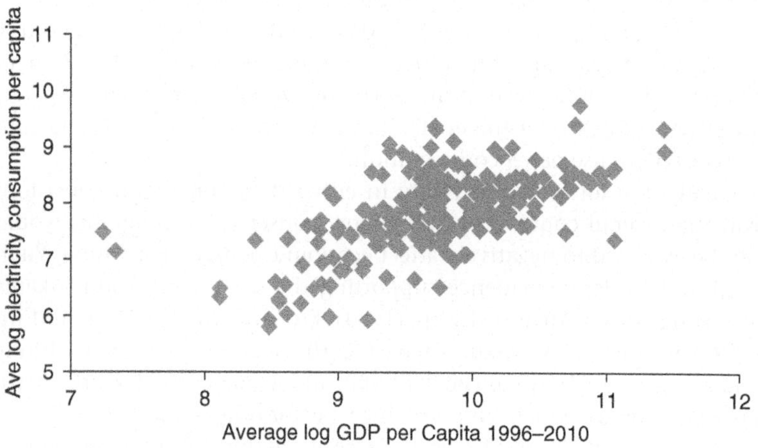

Figure 8.3 Relationship between log GDP (X) and log electricity consumption (Y), per capita basis. All cities, average of the logs, 1996–2010

Source: National Bureau of Statistics of China.

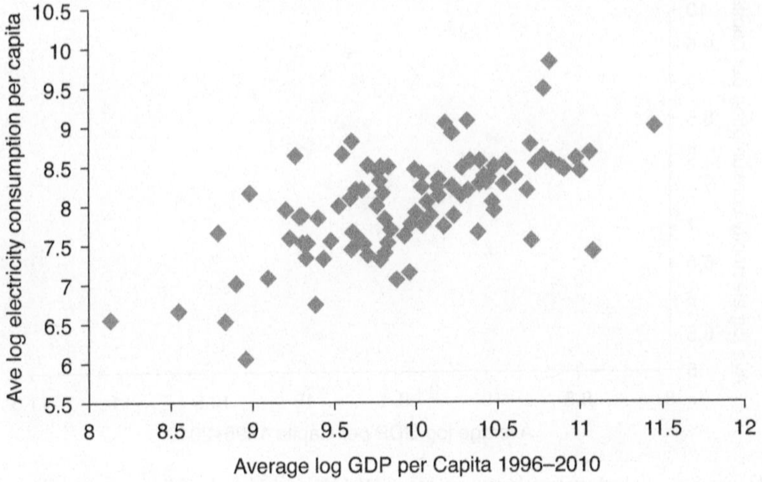

Figure 8.4 Relationship between log GDP (X) and log electricity consumption (Y), per capita basis. East region, average of the logs, 1996–2010

Source: National Bureau of Statistics of China.

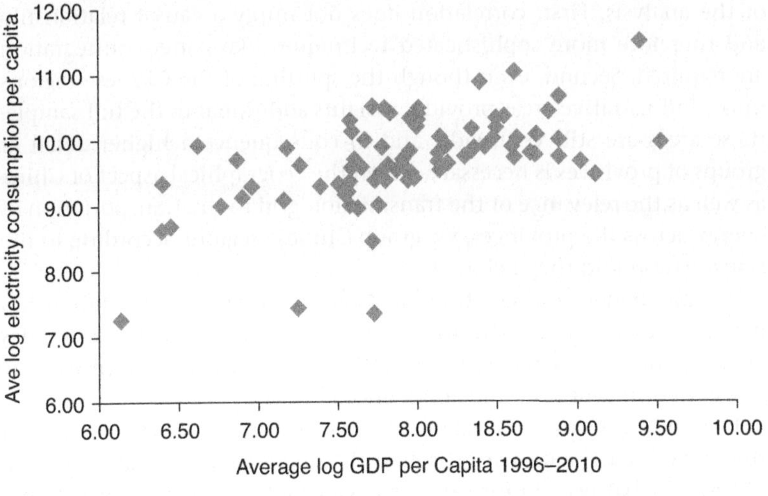

Figure 8.5 Relationship between log GDP (X) and log electricity consumption (Y), per capita basis. Centre region, average of the logs, 1996–2010

Source: National Bureau of Statistics of China.

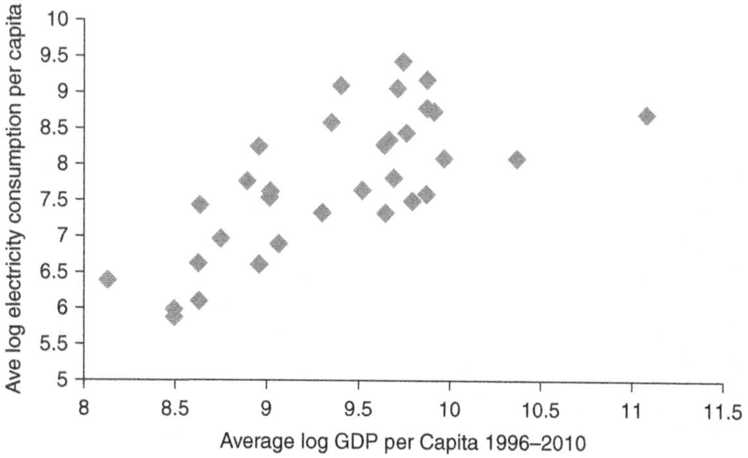

Figure 8.6 Relationship between log GDP (Y) and log electricity consumption (X), per capita basis. Western regions, average, 1996–2010

Source: National Bureau of Statistics of China.

can see that in all areas there is a positive relationship between electricity consumption and per capita income.

From these plots, we can draw two main conclusions for the next stages of the analysis. First, correlation does not imply a causal relationship and therefore more sophisticated techniques like panel cointegration are required. Second, even though the splitting of the Chinese regions into administrative areas provides insights additional to the full sample, these areas are still very wide, and in consequence a higher detail of groups of provinces is necessary. Given the geographical aspect of China as well as the relevance of the transmission grid to the transportation of energy across the provinces, we group Chinese regions according to the transmission grid they belong to.

We use panel cointegration methods to analyse the relationship between economic growth and electricity consumption for 216 cities grouped into 6 transmission grids. The use of panel data improves the power of unit root tests and cointegration tests.

The empirical analysis begins by investigating whether the logs of the variables are stationary through the application of unit root tests. Among the battery of unit root tests available in panel data, we choose the one developed by Pesaran (2007) that takes into account cross-sectional dependence (CIPS*). We also use the Im et al. (2003) (IPS) test which assumes cross-sectional independence. Results from this analysis appear in Table 8.1 for the variables, in levels and first differences, for the six transmission grids used in the coal industry in China. Results show that by using the Pesaran (2007) test, the log of per capita GDP is stationary in first differences only in the north-east, north and central grids. However, when we apply the IPS test, we find that per capita GDP is stationary in first differences for all grids. We can also conclude that the log of per capita electricity consumption is stationary in first differences for all grids.

Having established that both the log of GDP per capita and the log of electricity consumption per capita are difference stationary, the next step in the analysis is to test for cointegration among these two variables, or, in other words, if there is a long-run relationship between them. Results appear in Table 8.2, where we present the results of two panel cointegration tests: first, the Pedroni (1999) test – Group ADF Test – which

Table 8.1 Panel unit root tests

	GDP				Electricity			
	CIPS*(1)		IPS(2)		CIPS*(1)		IPS(2)	
GRID	Level, c, t	1st diff, c	Level, c, t	1st diff, c	Level, c, t	1st diff, c	Level, c, t	1st diff, c
North East	−1.89	−2.12*	−0.07	−4.49***	−2.08	−2.69***	0.24	−9.17***
North	−1.69	−2.12*	0.15	−4.67***	−2.37	−2.80***	1.38	−10.99***
East	−1.78	−2.05	1.86	−6.87***	−1.97	−2.84***	0.82	−11.31***
Central	−2.26	−2.25**	1.65	−10.09***	−1.87	−2.76***	0.01	−13.35***
South	−1.54	−1.79	−2.21	−6.74***	−1.47	−2.24**	0.83	−14.25***
North West	−1.35	−1.83	2.00	−4.42***	−2.11	−2.90***	0.70	−7.85***
All	−1.70	−1.91	−0.52	−14.63***	−2.36	−2.94***	1.75	−25.94***

Notes:(1) *, ** and *** indicate rejection of the null of a unit root at 10 per cent, 5 per cent and 1 per cent respectively. All tests are one-sided tests, thus values of the test statistic to the left tail of the critical values are evidence for rejection of the null of a unit root. Exact 1 per cent, 5 per cent and 10 per cent critical values for the CIPS* tests obtained from tables IIb-IIc in Pesaran (2007) are used. For this test, there is no unit root if the test statistic is less than the critical value.

(2) *, ** and *** indicate rejection of the null of a unit root at 10 per cent, 5 per cent and 1 per cent respectively. All tests statistics are asymptotically distributed as N(0,1). All tests are one-sided tests, thus values of the test statistic in the left tail of the standard normal distribution are evidence for rejection of the null of a unit root. Exact critical values for the IPS tests obtained from IPS (2003) are used. Common time dummies were included to take into account cross-section dependence.

assumes cross-sectional independence, and second, the Westerlund LM test which allows for cross-sectional dependence.

From Table 8.2, with either test we can conclude that, when the dependent variable is per capita electricity consumption, there is a long-run relationship between both variables, except in the case of the north-west grid (cointegration is found with the Westerlund test but not the group ADF test) and the east grid (cointegration is found with the group ADF test but not the Westerlund test). Given that such a relationship exists, the next question to answer is what the source of causation both in the short- and long-run is, to recommend appropriate energy policies. Results from those analyses are reported in Tables 8.3 to 8.5.

Tables 8.3 and 8.4 present the formal short-run statistical tests developed by Dumitrescu and Hurlin (2012) and a summary of them respectively. Given the results from our unit root tests, we need to look at the results for first differences in Tables 8.3 and 8.4; we find that only for the transmission grid located in the north there is bi-directional causality between per capita GDP and per capita electricity consumption. Regions in the north grid include Beijing, Tianjin, Hebei, Shanxi and Shandong, which are characterized by their industrial activity and high dynamism. The north grid also includes one of the most important provinces for the production of coal, Shanxi. The finding of no causality in the short-run for the remaining grids probably is explained by the fact that energy and

Table 8.2 Panel cointegration tests

	Dependent variable: Electricity	
GRID	**Group ADF Test(1)**	**Westerlund LM test(2) (Bootstrap *p*-value)**
North East	−2.23**	0.89
North	−1.73**	0.76
East	−4.41***	0.02
Central	−2.17**	0.90
South	−3.89***	0.14
North West	−0.24	0.91
All	−6.07***	0.54

Notes:(1) All tests statistics are asymptotically distributed as N(0,1). All tests are one-sided tests: reject the null hypothesis of no cointegration if the test statistic value is less than the negative of the normal critical value. *, ** and *** indicate rejection of the null hypothesis of no cointegration at the 10%, 5% and 1% respectively. An intercept, a trend and common time dummies were included in the cointegrating regression.

(2) For the Westerlund and Edgerton (2007) test the null hypothesis is cointegration. A constant was included in the cointegrating regression.

Table 8.3 Panel short-run causality tests (p-values)[(1)]

	Levels		First Differences	
Causality from	**GDP**	**Electricity**	**GDP**	**Electricity**
To	**Electricity**	**GDP**	**Electricity**	**GDP**
North East	0.00	0.02	0.81	0.50
North	0.00	0.00	0.00	0.06
East	0.00	0.00	0.54	0.38
Central	0.00	0.00	0.27	0.72
South	0.00	0.10	0.24	0.39
North West	0.00	0.00	0.04	0.76
All	0.00	0.00	0.15	0.75

Note:[(1)] For all tests one lag or two lags were used. All tests statistics are asymptotically distributed as N(0,1). The Z test is a two-sided test. A p-value below 0.05 indicates rejection of the null of homogeneous non-causality at 5 per cent level.

Table 8.4 Summary of panel short-run causality tests[(1)]

	Levels		First Differences(2)	
Causality from	**GDP**	**Electricity**	**GDP**	**Electricity**
To	**Electricity**	**GDP**	**Electricity**	**GDP**
North East	Yes	Yes	No	No
North	Yes	Yes	Yes	Yes
East	Yes	Yes	No	No
Central	Yes	Yes	No	No
South	Yes	Yes	No	No
North West	Yes	Yes	Yes	No
All	Yes	Yes	No	No

Notes:[(1)] Yes indicates that the null of no causality was rejected at 10 per cent significance level or less.
[(2)] Applying the causality tests to the first differences we find no causality in either direction on the sub-period. For the full sample period, we find causality going from total energy, electricity and coal to PC-GDP, and from PC-GDP to electricity and coke.

economic activity policies are not yet linked with each other, and also for the fact that each transmission grid is operating in an independent way, creating some inefficiencies in the system. The Chinese government has stressed that by 2020, all the transmission grids will be unified into a single one, and this is expected to improve the efficiency of transportation and use of energy resources across cities in China.

Table 8.5 Panel long-run causality tests (p-values)[(1)]

Causality from	GDP	Electricity
To	Electricity	GDP
	Long-run Causality group mean *t* test	Long-run Causality group mean *t* test
North East	0.016	0.935
North	0.021	0.947
East	0.253	0.453
Central	0.041	0.843
South	0.043	0.819
North West	0.069	0.699
All	0.053	0.852

Note:[(1)] For all tests one lag was used.

Table 8.6 Panel DOLS estimates of elasticities of electricity with respect to GDP

Grid	Elasticity
North East	0.66
North	3.50
East	0.38
Central	0.64
South	1.34
North West	0.16
All	0.55

Knowing the direction of causation in the short-run provides interesting insights for the design of energy policies due the power cuts that appear each summer in the Chinese regions. However, to adopt energy-saving measures to mitigate climate change, the causality in the long-run has to be investigated.

Table 8.5 reports the results of the long-run causality tests when per capita electricity consumption is the dependent variable and when it is the independent variable. From such an analysis, we learn that there is uni-directional long-run causation from per capita GDP to per capita electricity consumption for all transmission grids, except for the east grid where no causality is present. This interesting finding implies that the Chinese government can adopt policies to curb electricity consumption in the long-run as well as commit to international agreements on climate change without impact on economic growth. However, one of the possible explanations in the east grid, which covers regions like Shanghai, Zhejiang, Anhui, Jiangsu and Fujian, can be that in all these regions there is a high presence of non-state sector and more specifically foreign companies. It is acknowledged in the relevant literature that these investments are deemed to be more efficient than the ones coming from the state sector for the use of advanced technology. New innovations and technology favour lower electricity use without reducing the level of output. In other words, they are more productive than in other regions such as the northern or western areas, where heavy and rural industries dominate regional economic activity (Herrerias et al., 2013).

Finally, elasticities of electricity with respect to income are shown in Table 8.6 for each of the transmission grids analysed. From there, we can observe that there are large variations in elasticity. For example, we can see that in the north, grid elasticity is 3.50, which is probably explained by the presence of heavy industry in this area of China; in the south it reaches 1.34, this includes Guangdong province and has a high presence of foreign investment. In contrast, at the bottom appears the north-west with a value of 0.16, where rural activity predominates, or the east grid with an elasticity of 0.38. The elasticity for the full sample is 0.55, which is lower than that found in Herrerias et al. (2013) in the case of Chinese provinces. In that analysis, it was found that elasticity is 0.87, which suggests that we should analyse this relationship at city level given the significant variation within the same province as well as between provinces in the vast territory of China.

4 Conclusions and policy discussion

One of the most active debates in the empirical literature on energy-economics is the relationship between energy consumption and economic growth since the seminal paper by Kraft and Kraft in 1978. This interest among researchers corresponds to the need to reduce the level of emissions to protect the environment. While there is general agreement among developed countries, apparently little consensus exists among developing and emerging economies in adopting energy and environmental policies. This is because often these countries have the dilemma of promoting energy-saving measures at the expense of economic growth. However, if the source of causation runs from economic growth to energy consumption, then implementing energy conservation policies should not hinder economic growth. Thus, given the substantial policy implications for the debate on climate change, an essential area of research consists in investigating the direction of the causality between energy consumption and economic growth. This is the goal of this chapter.

Among emerging economies, China is probably one of the most interesting countries for investigating such a relationship due its vast territory as well as the size of its population. However, the significant heterogeneity across regions and also within provinces requires investigation of the relationship between electricity consumption and economic growth at city level. In doing so, we use a rich annual dataset, which covers 216 cities from 1996 to 2010 in China. To the best of our knowledge there is no work that makes use of such detail in analysing this relationship. In addition, to detect the source of causation between both macro-magnitudes, we use cointegrated panel data techniques, allowing for cross-sectional dependence. The results indicate that in the short-run there is feedback between GDP and electricity consumption for the northern grid. There is also uni-directional causality from GDP to electricity for the north-western grid. There is however no short-run causality either way for the other grids. In the long-run there is very strong evidence that there is uni-directional causality from per capita GDP to per capita electricity consumption for all the grids except for the eastern grid where there is no causality either way.

The finding that per capita GDP influences per capita electricity consumption in the long-run allows us to conclude that energy-saving measures can be adopted without interrupting the path of growth. However, in the eastern grid we didn't find such relation. One possible explanation of this phenomenon is that in the eastern grids belong to those provinces with a higher presence of foreign direct investment, which is a well-known source of technological transfer, creating in turn spillovers in the goal of reduction of electricity consumption across cities. Our results are related with previous literature on the same issue such as Herrerias et al. (2013), who found that both foreign direct investments as well as non-state investments are useful mechanisms to reduce energy intensity across provinces from 1985 to 2008. Thus, from a policy perspective, a recommendation would be to liberalize the energy sector since increasing efficiency allows for new technology, innovations and better managerial skills to be introduced and therefore ultimately reduce the upward trend in the consumption of energy in China. Our results suggest that such reduction in energy consumption would not restrict economic growth in the long-run.

9
Regional Energy Intensity and Productivity in China

M.J. Herrerias

1 Introduction

At the end of the 1970s, the Chinese economy started a process of industrialization and modernization of its domestic economy based mainly on the promotion of openness and capital accumulation (Herrerias and Orts, 2011). As a result of such process, China experienced a boom in trade and foreign direct investment that in turn was transmitted into a high growth rate. This exceptional performance was quite steady with an average around 9–10 per cent in the last decades, achieving a new position in international markets, and therefore changing the scenario worldwide. The performance of the economy overall, however, is explained by the dynamism of the coastal areas that received preferential policies by the government at the expense of central and western ones, creating unbalanced growth (Herrerias et al., 2011).

Fast economic growth led in turn to increases in energy consumption, especially in coal, due to the characteristics of production processes in China. This growing demand for energy allowed China to overtake the United States as the most important consumer in the world in 2009. However, similarly to the unbalanced growth mentioned earlier, the consumption of energy resources is unequal across regions. The most important regions that consume energy resources, not surprisingly, are located in the east of China, while it is the production of such resources that appear in less developed regions like Shaanxi and Inner Mongolia in the case of coal, western areas in the case of gas and oil, and the central and south of China in the case of the generation of electricity. This singular distribution of energy resources in terms of consumption and production of energy makes the China an interesting country to be investigated because of its vast territory and the implications for the welfare of the whole population.

The policy of the Chinese government in the last forty years without any doubt has been focused on promoting economic growth. Energy and environmental policies were totally ignored until early 2000s. The reason for this attitude is that in the case of developing or emerging economies, energy and environmental policies are seen as a constraint to promoting economic growth. A good example of this attitude is the refusal of China to accept any international agreement on climate change for reducing carbon dioxide emissions and cutting energy consumption. From a more domestic perspective, probably, China is one of the most polluted countries in terms of the degree of particulate emissions in the atmosphere, the treatment of the water, etc., but at the same time it is the industrial sector, which drives the overall GDP in this economy, and consumes a large amount of coal that is the most polluting source of energy. So, from the Chinese government perspective there has been little incentive to promote any energy-saving measure in the past. However, with the energy crisis in 2000, the growing trend in energy consumption, the scarce alternative energies and the recurrent electricity shortages every summer in the majority of regions, the Chinese government became concerned about the relevance of energy and environmental policies. This concern was expressed in its Five-Year Plan in 2006, the government's stance being that such energy and environmental situation can damage the sustainability of economic growth. This change has opened the door for new stricter policies to prevent global warming and to inspire new developments to improve the *quality* of growth in China.

One of the key policy variables to implement energy-saving measures is energy intensity that is the ratio of energy consumption per unit of output. Thus, this interest has created a growing body of research that investigates the trends and determinants of energy intensity in the case of developed and developing countries (Herrerias et al., 2012a). In the singular case of China, energy intensity has gone through different stages. First, a decrease in energy intensity has been found up until the early 2000s, due the implementation of strong energy policies to reduce energy consumption; and second, from 2000 onwards, when some deterioration of energy intensity is observed due to the relaxation such policies and the consequent increase in energy consumption. These two distinct trends have been investigated in, for example, Zhang (2003), Ma and Stern (2008), Ma et al. (2009), Zhao et al. (2010) and Herrerias and Liu (2013). On the other hand, active research has been carried out on the drivers of these changes in the trend of energy intensity. Fisher-

Vanden et al. (2004) argued that the observed decline in energy intensity in China can be attributed to two factors. First, changes in sectorial composition and second in technological progress. Moving away from the heavy industry that consumes a large amount of energy in favour of light industry may explain this phenomenon. In addition, innovations and the adoption of new technology can lead to energy savings, increasing the productivity of firms. However, while there is a general consensus about the key role played by technological progress, little agreement appears about structural changes as driver of such changes (Zhang, 2003; Fisher-Vanden et al., 2004; Liao et al., 2007 and Ma and Stern, 2008). Knowing that these two factors have played a key role on energy intensity, the key question to analyse is what specific mechanisms can lead to reductions in energy intensity. This chapter argues that productivity efficiency may operate through technological progress and sectorial composition allowing energy savings. However, this aspect has not yet ben fully analysed in the empirical literature and such analysis constitutes the goal of this chapter.

More specifically, the aim of this chapter is to examine the linkages between productivity and energy intensity across Chinese regions over the period 1995–2008. The unbalanced growth and the uneven distribution of energy resources across regions justify the need to investigate this relationship at provincial level. Moreover, as the linkage between energy intensity and productivity is expected to be industry specific, we also evaluate this relationship at sectorial level from 2004 to 2009. Additionally, to provide a complete picture of such relation, we consider electricity intensity as well as coal and crude oil intensities, which may provide new insights on the nature of the relationship between different types of energy intensity and productivity. Thus, this chapter contributes to the relevant energy-economics literature in the following aspects:

First, we investigate the evolution of electricity, coal and oil intensity as well as productivity efficiency over the period 1995 to 2008 at regional level and for 2004 to 2009 at sectorial level. To the best of the author's knowledge, there is no work that describes the evolution of both macro-magnitudes in the case of regions and sectors in China.

Second, we analyse whether the observed decline in energy intensity can be attributed to improvements in productivity efficiency, or by contrast there are other factors behind this process. Even though in Herrerias et al. (2012a) is found that non-state investment is one of the factors that may explain this phenomenon, the author does not consider explicitly the role played by productivity efficiency. Thus, examining the latter may provide new insights for the design of energy policies in China.

Third, we make use of non-parametrics techniques to get productivity efficiency through the application of Data Envelopment Analysis, which is rarely adopted in the energy-economics literature, and we use a rich dataset at regional and industry level that allow us to determine the role played by technological progress that may operate through productivity efficiency and sectorial composition, by investigating its variation across sectors over the most recent period available. It is found that these two mechanisms may improve energy intensity. Therefore, results from this analysis are of enormous relevance to implementing energy-saving measures and to preventing electricity shortages and environmental damage in China.

Finally, the results indicate that the relationship between productive efficiency and energy intensity is complex. On the one hand side, it seems that this phenomenon appears for some regions that display a high level of productivity efficiency and they are clustered in a group; on the other hand, regions with low productivity efficiency show higher energy intensity. However, even though it seems that at least at regional level such a relationship exists with some exceptions, this is not clear-cut in the case of eight sectors investigated. We find, for example, that production and supply electricity gas and water, is perfectly efficient, however it has the highest energy intensity ratio. So it seems that productive efficiency does not capture all the explanation of the decline of energy intensity across sectors at all and further research is needed on this matter.

The chapter is organized as follows. Section 2 presents an overview of the literature review. Section 3 covers the description of the data and provides a policy discussion of the evolution of energy intensity and productivity over time as well as its relationship at regional and sectorial level. Conclusions are drawn in Section 4.

2 Literature review

Energy issues have been receiving considerable interest among economists in the recent decade for their implications on the debate on climate change and the sustainability of economic growth. Traditionally, the core of the debate has focused only in developed countries due to the fact that these economies have experienced moderate economic growth but this phenomenon has moved in parallel with an increasing trend in energy consumption and carbon dioxide emissions. Energy and environmental policies in developed countries in some cases have stimulated the decoupling between growth and energy consumption/emissions in some of the European countries. However, the emergence of developing countries such as India, China or Brazil has re-opened the discussion because of the fast industrialization process and the increasing trend in the consumption of energy resources and environmental damage in recent years. Given the size of the population of these economies, energy and environmental measures have considerable interest for the welfare of the wider world. Thus, a detailed analysis of an emerging country such as China can give relevant insights for the design of energy policies and can act as an example for other economies in transition, which face similar characteristics.

In energy-economics literature, one of the most vigorous debates has been focused on energy intensity, which reflects the degree of efficiency of energy resources per unit of output and is often used as an energy target across developed and developing economies. Probably one of the most popular lines of research across these economies, including China, has been the evolution of energy intensity and its convergence behaviour (Herrerias and Liu, 2013). The finding of convergence in energy intensity can imply that technological differences diminish over time across countries or regions and receive considerable interest among economist and policy makers. However, in the energy-economics literature relatively few efforts have been made on identifying the drivers for a reduction of the energy intensity ratio.

Probably one of the first attempts to analyse the drivers of energy intensity came from Sam Schurr et al. (1960). They suggested that improvements in the use of energy resources per unit of output could come through an increase of productivity in the case of the American economy. He observed that from 1920 to 1955 the energy intensity of production had fallen, while both labour and total factor productivity (TFP) were rising. However, the simultaneous decline in energy intensity and labour intensity of production ruled out the possibility of explaining the productivity performance through a substitution effect between energy and capital accumulation (Jorgenson, 1984). Schurr et al. (1960) noted that the quantity of both energy and labour inputs required for a given level of output decreased, and therefore he argued that technological progress is also an important factor that accounts for the decline in energy intensity.

Technology diffusion is a well-known topic of research in international economics literature. Researchers have attempted to disentangle the specific mechanisms through which technological progress may operate in an economy. In the case of an open economy, openness and more specifically imports receive considerable interest as a channel to diffuse new knowledge across countries. The existence of embodied technological progress in capital goods imports and spillovers in the adaptation and absorption of technology have been considered essential mechanisms for technology transfer in international trade literature (Keller, 2004; Caselli and Wilson, 2004; Eaton and Kortum, 2001; Herrerias and Orts, 2011).

In addition, empirical evidence has suggested that foreign direct investment (FDI) is also a suitable channel for technology transfer. Since it is commonly assumed that the technology used by multinationals is superior to the one used for the host economy, it is expected that the presence of multinationals in a domestic economy facilitates the transfer of knowledge through labour training, better skills acquisition and managerial skills (Blalock and Gertler, 2008). In the specific case of China, not only FDI has played an important role in the economy, but also the reform of state-owned enterprises, which stimulated the emergence of non-state enterprises – domestic and foreign – allowing the market mechanisms to work in the economy and more specifically in the energy sector helping to reduce energy intensity (Herrerias et al., 2012a).

Fisher-Vanden et al. (2004) argued that it is not only technological progress that can explain the observed improvements in energy intensity in China, but also sectorial composition. One can expect that as far a particular economy focuses its main activity in less energy-using sectors, energy intensity decreases. However, at the same time it is also feasible that the change from agriculture to industry has led to higher energy intensity ratio. In the singular case of China, Fisher-Vanden et al. (2004) argued that sectorial change can be an additional factor accounting for the decline of energy intensity. However, other works like Garbaccio et al. (1999), Liao et al. (2007), and Ma and Stern (2008) find that sectorial composition contributes in a small amount in the decline of energy intensity in China.

It is argued in this chapter that both technological progress and sectorial composition can lead to productivity improvements which, in turn, may affect energy intensity. To the best of the author's knowledge, there is no empirical evidence on the relationship between productivity and energy intensity in the case of Chinese provinces and sectors. However, we can find empirical evidence based on other countries. Schurr (1982) extended the previous analysis until 1981, and he concluded that although the inverse relationship between total factor productivity and energy intensity virtually disappeared during the 1953–69 period, it is still noteworthy that high rates of improvement in TFP were not correlated with improvements in energy intensity. Jorgenson (1984) following Schurr's work arrived to similar conclusions. He found that over the period 1920–53, energy intensity of production was falling while productivity was rising. He argued that one of the possible explanations was the substitution of energy inputs for other inputs, especially for labour input. In the subsequent sub-period 1953–73, energy intensity was stable and TFP increased, but during this sub-period the growth rate of real energy prices was slower than the previous sub-period. As a result, there was again a substitution effect between inputs but in this period this effect was offset by the growth in output per unit of energy input, leaving energy intensity of production unchanged. The following period until 1979 with the oil shock in early 1970, there were a substitution of capital, labour, and material inputs for inputs of electricity and non-electrical energy, which accounts for the reduction in energy intensity of production in the United States.

Previous evidence on the role played by technological progress on energy intensity has been investigated in Hübler (2009) and Hübler (2011). However, few efforts have been made on the mechanisms that operate through technological progress. We can find works like Cole (2006), Peterson (2008), Mielnik and Goldember (2002), Hübler and Keller (2010) and Herrerias et al. (2012a) who argue that trade and FDI have been useful channels to reduce the energy intensity ratio through productivity improvements. In addition, Herrerias et al. (2012a) find that also in the case of China, the increasing role of non-state investment has been relevant to reducing energy intensity. The reform of state-owned enterprises into non-state ones has led to significant improvements in productivity of these firms since decisions are more oriented to the market. However, as Kounetas et al. (2012) stated, technological progress and the resulting productivity gains, are all heavily dependent on a firm's absorptive capacity and strategic orientation as well as the existence and intensity of knowledge spillovers.

Thus, knowing that improvements in productivity can come from technological progress and sectorial composition, a novel aspect in the relevant literature is to investigate the relationship between productivity efficiency and energy intensity across provinces and sectors.

3 The Chinese experience

We investigate the evolution and relationship between energy intensity and productivity efficiency across 28 Chinese provinces from 1995 to 2008 and also at industry level in the case of 8 key sectors in China from 2004 to 2009. In doing so, first we use coal intensity as well as electricity and oil (also expressed into intensities) and second, we get productive efficiency indices following Data Envelopment Analysis (DEA) proposed by Farrell (1957) and later on by Shephard (1970). This measure comes from an optimization of inputs – stock of physical capital and labour force – that are used to get output under constant returns to scale. In other words, it usually means its success in producing as large an output as possible from a given set of inputs. Productive efficiency ranges between the value of zero and one [0,1], where one indicates a perfectly efficient region, and will become indefinitely small if the amounts of input per unit output become indefinitely large. By contrast, values lower than one represent lower technical efficiency. In all cases data comes from the National Bureau of Statistics of China.

We start the analysis by reporting the box plots for the productive efficiency indices for selected years across regions. From there, we can observe two characteristics, first there is a slight increase in efficiency of Chinese regions from 1995 to 2008, but this increase is not homogeneous among regions since a large variation is also observed between

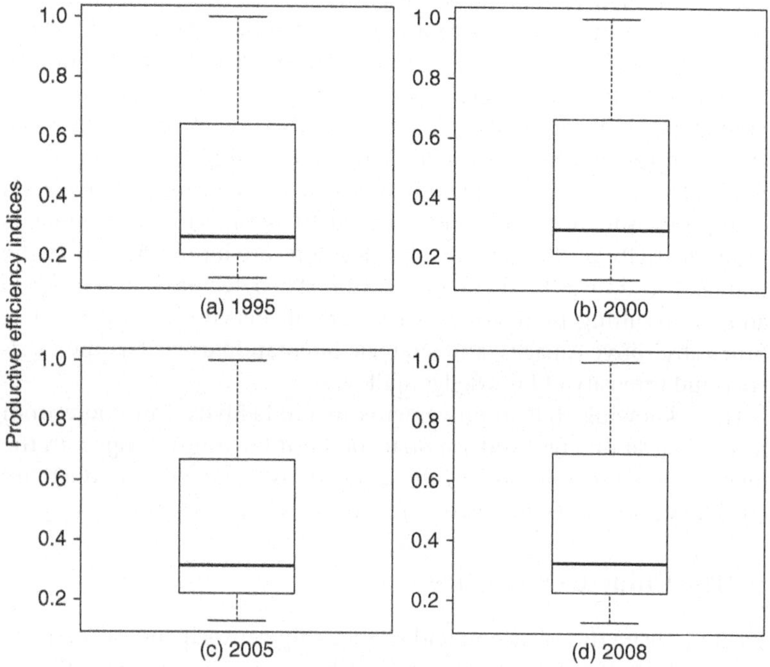

Figure 9.1 Box plots, productive efficiency indices, Chinese regions

them; and second, it is also worth mentioning that the average of the productive efficiency still remains at low values, due to the massive accumulation of capital that in many cases was assigned due to the state intervention without considering market forces.

Figure 9.2 shows the other key variable in our analysis, that is, coal, electricity and oil intensity in 1995, 2000 and 2008 respectively. From there, we can see two different trends. On the one hand, coal and electricity intensity has decreased from 1995 to 2000, but has remained steady up to 2008. By contrast, oil intensity has improved over the period analysed. These two trends can be explained by the energy policies encouraged by the Chinese government up to the early 2000s. However, after that these policies were relaxed to promote economic

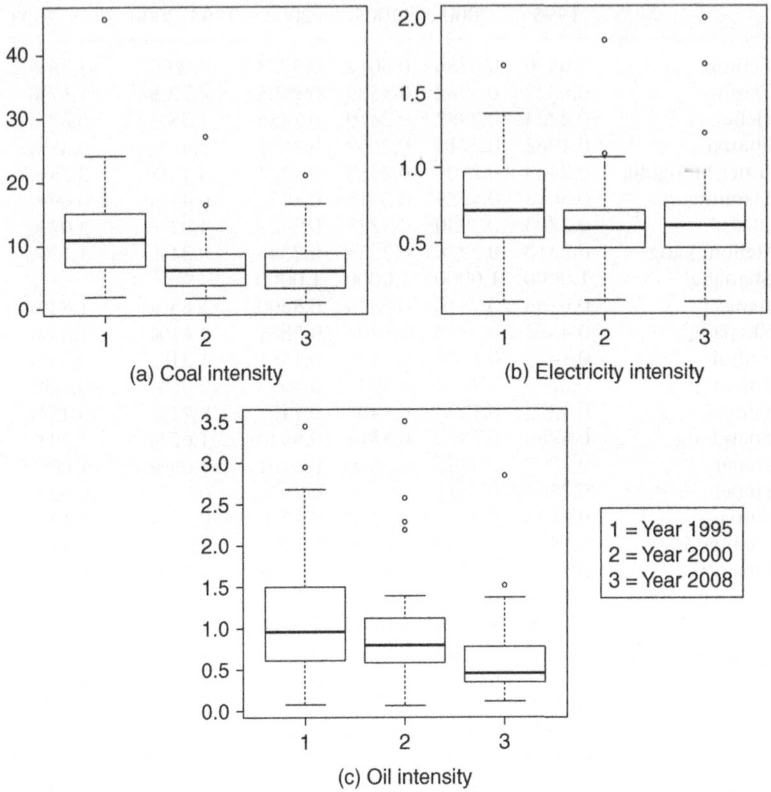

Figure 9.2 Box plots, coal, electricity and oil intensity, 1995, 2000, 2008, Chinese regions

growth. Knowing the different trends in energy intensity as well as the ones in productive efficiency, interesting issues to investigate are (1) the evolution of productive efficiency across the large heterogeneity of Chinese regions and sectors, and (2) what is the relationship between energy intensity and efficiency.

3.1 A regional perspective

Table 9.1 reports productive efficiency indices in the case of 28 Chinese regions from 1995 to 2008, while Table 9.2 shows coal, electricity and oil intensities for the same period. The relationship between both magnitudes is presented in Figures 9.3–9.5.

Table 9.1 Productive efficiency index, Chinese regions

	1995	2000	2005	2008	1995–2000	2005–2008
Beijing	0.6490	0.6786	0.6019	0.5773	0.90%	−1.38%
Tianjin	0.6322	0.7982	0.9539	0.9995	4.77%	1.57%
Hebei	0.2224	0.2382	0.2410	0.2456	1.38%	0.63%
Shanxi	0.1962	0.2214	0.2669	0.2697	2.45%	0.35%
Inner Mongolia	0.2483	0.2900	0.3783	0.4224	3.15%	3.74%
Liaoning	0.5613	0.5729	0.5918	0.6077	0.41%	0.89%
Jilin	0.2303	0.2930	0.3225	0.3424	4.93%	2.02%
Heilongjiang	0.2312	0.2276	0.2655	0.2746	−0.31%	1.13%
Shanghai	**1.0000**	**1.0000**	**1.0000**	**1.0000**	–	–
Jiangsu	0.6766	0.7416	0.8333	0.8800	1.85%	1.83%
Zhejiang	0.4572	0.4952	0.5702	0.5881	1.61%	1.04%
Anhui	0.1433	0.1522	0.1545	0.1561	1.21%	0.34%
Fujian	0.2778	0.3074	0.3075	0.3053	2.05%	−0.24%
Jiangxi	0.1277	0.1323	0.1408	0.1427	0.71%	0.45%
Shandong	0.6786	0.7371	0.8314	0.8640	1.67%	1.29%
Henan	0.3207	0.3385	0.3529	0.3701	1.09%	1.60%
Hubei	0.2504	0.2611	0.2606	0.2655	0.84%	0.62%
Hunan	0.2133	0.2220	0.2238	0.2250	0.80%	0.18%
Guangdong	0.5571	0.6003	0.6940	0.7266	1.50%	1.54%
Guangxi	0.1533	0.1522	0.1535	0.1585	−0.14%	1.07%
Sichuan	0.2095	0.2137	0.2215	0.2270	0.40%	0.82%
Guizhou	**1.0000**	**1.0000**	**1.0000**	**1.0000**	–	–
Yunnan	0.1332	0.1344	0.1290	0.1264	0.18%	−0.68%
Shaanxi	0.1670	0.1821	0.1989	0.2071	1.75%	1.36%
Gansu	0.1980	0.2150	0.2153	0.2175	1.66%	0.34%
Qinghai	**1.0000**	**1.0000**	**1.0000**	**1.0000**	–	–
Ningxia	0.8010	0.6509	0.6410	0.6601	−4.07%	0.98%
Xinjiang	0.3110	0.3042	0.2950	0.2880	−0.44%	−0.80%
Mean	0.4160	0.4343	0.4588	0.4695	0.87%	0.78%
Standard dev.	29%	29%	30%	31%	0.09%	0.69%

Table 9.2 Energy intensity across regions

	Coal Intensity						Electricity Intensity						Oil Intensity					
	1995	2000	2005	2008	1995–2000	2005–2008	1995	2000	2005	2008	1995–2000	2005–2008	1995	2000	2005	2008	1995–2000	2005–2008
Beijing	4.30	2.67	1.71	1.10	−9.11%	−13.70%	0.42	0.38	0.32	0.28	−2.05%	−3.58%	1.05	0.74	0.44	0.45	−6.68%	0.09%
Tianjin	7.20	4.30	3.43	2.34	−9.81%	−12.05%	0.53	0.41	0.36	0.31	−4.99%	−4.21%	1.45	1.23	0.78	0.46	−3.17%	−15.85%
Hebei	24.18	16.35	16.74	14.37	−7.53%	−4.96%	1.33	1.09	1.22	1.23	−3.82%	0.24%	1.10	1.01	0.82	0.80	−1.68%	−0.77%
Shanxi	45.74	27.08	26.51	20.99	−9.96%	−7.49%	1.22	0.96	0.97	0.97	−4.60%	0.07%	NA	NA	NA	NA	NA	NA
Inner Mongolia	16.09	12.73	13.64	13.09	−4.58%	−1.37%	0.68	0.55	0.65	0.72	−4.10%	3.23%	0.32	0.27	0.13	0.11	−3.06%	−4.75%
Liaoning	8.17	5.54	4.33	3.55	−7.48%	−6.43%	0.54	0.46	0.38	0.33	−3.26%	−4.80%	2.20	2.28	1.84	1.37	0.73%	−9.32%
Jilin	15.16	8.31	7.67	6.43	−11.32%	−5.72%	0.84	0.59	0.45	0.38	−6.77%	−5.36%	1.55	1.39	1.15	0.70	−2.24%	−15.16%
Heilongjiang	15.14	9.32	8.26	7.73	−9.25%	−2.17%	1.00	0.64	0.55	0.48	−8.66%	−4.45%	2.95	2.57	1.73	1.20	−2.73%	−11.51%
Shanghai	2.76	1.83	1.23	0.90	−7.94%	−9.82%	0.28	0.23	0.21	0.19	−4.26%	−4.20%	0.68	0.53	0.46	0.32	−4.89%	−10.94%
Jiangsu	6.47	3.74	3.98	3.25	−10.38%	−6.57%	0.50	0.41	0.51	0.49	−3.52%	−1.37%	0.73	0.59	0.53	0.36	−4.32%	−11.67%
Zhejiang	4.53	3.42	3.33	3.12	−5.46%	−2.16%	0.47	0.47	0.57	0.56	0.06%	−0.56%	0.62	0.71	0.73	0.55	2.80%	−9.04%
Anhui	16.96	12.53	10.69	10.09	−5.87%	−1.90%	0.99	0.72	0.75	0.76	−6.15%	0.66%	0.95	0.73	0.53	0.38	−5.01%	−10.77%
Fujian	3.40	2.55	3.34	3.13	−5.62%	−2.19%	0.53	0.48	0.54	0.55	−2.15%	0.56%	0.46	0.42	0.25	0.15	−1.52%	−15.78%
Jiangxi	11.65	6.05	5.99	5.21	−12.28%	−4.58%	0.69	0.51	0.58	0.54	−5.87%	−2.59%	0.88	0.81	0.52	0.41	−1.69%	−7.89%
Shandong	7.04	3.73	6.15	5.52	−11.93%	−3.53%	0.53	0.43	0.47	0.44	−4.30%	−2.10%	0.97	0.76	0.78	0.74	−4.82%	−1.57%
Henan	12.15	8.22	10.15	8.92	−7.51%	−4.19%	0.87	0.68	0.76	0.78	−4.96%	0.87%	0.61	0.58	0.37	0.26	−1.27%	−10.52%
Hubei	10.57	7.46	6.72	5.26	−6.73%	−7.88%	0.81	0.62	0.66	0.55	−5.24%	−5.49%	1.00	0.83	0.62	0.46	−3.76%	−9.89%
Hunan	12.83	4.82	7.75	6.22	−17.80%	−7.05%	0.86	0.59	0.70	0.69	−7.37%	−0.36%	0.80	0.78	0.59	0.38	−0.49%	−13.77%
Guangdong	4.34	3.08	2.76	2.58	−6.66%	−2.27%	0.69	0.70	0.78	0.68	0.14%	−4.62%	1.08	1.02	0.67	0.59	−1.07%	−4.10%
Guangxi	7.44	4.74	4.61	4.04	−8.62%	−4.31%	0.70	0.69	0.65	0.66	−0.56%	0.37%	0.14	0.13	0.12	0.12	−0.72%	−2.56%
Sichuan	20.82	7.33	7.55	6.72	−18.85%	−3.84%	1.36	0.70	0.84	0.76	−12.55%	−3.16%	0.07	0.06	0.12	0.18	−3.90%	12.68%
Guizhou	1.93	1.66	1.57	1.38	−3.00%	−4.22%	0.10	0.11	0.10	0.10	1.59%	−0.09%	NA	NA	NA	NA	NA	NA
Yunnan	10.16	7.40	10.51	8.91	−6.13%	−5.36%	0.82	0.77	0.88	0.93	−1.37%	2.13%	NA	NA	NA	NA	NA	NA
Shaanxi	11.34	4.97	6.27	6.21	−15.19%	−0.36%	0.72	0.57	0.54	0.49	−4.70%	−2.80%	0.46	0.94	1.29	1.22	15.22%	−1.68%
Gansu	10.15	6.16	5.60	5.07	−9.49%	−3.27%	0.96	0.73	0.73	0.73	−5.23%	0.13%	2.68	2.19	1.83	1.51	−3.98%	−6.31%
Qinghai	11.23	8.34	8.60	8.38	−5.77%	−0.85%	1.68	1.85	1.88	2.00	2.01%	1.95%	2.04	0.99	0.86	0.70	−13.41%	−6.87%
Ningxia	15.63	9.65	18.00	16.52	−9.19%	−2.81%	1.34	1.07	1.69	1.69	−4.41%	0.16%	NA	NA	NA	NA	NA	NA
Xinjiang	11.58	8.82	7.79	8.35	−5.30%	2.33%	0.57	0.60	0.63	0.70	1.08%	3.79%	3.44	3.50	3.29	2.84	0.32%	−4.84%
Average	11.75	7.24	7.68	6.76	−9.22%	−4.13%	0.79	0.64	0.69	0.68	−3.98%	−0.60%	1.18	1.04	0.85	0.68	−2.36%	−7.38%
Standard dev.	860%	524%	559%	480%	−9.42%	−4.99%	36%	32%	39%	41%	−2.01%	2.15%	89%	82%	72%	61%	−1.60%	−5.68%

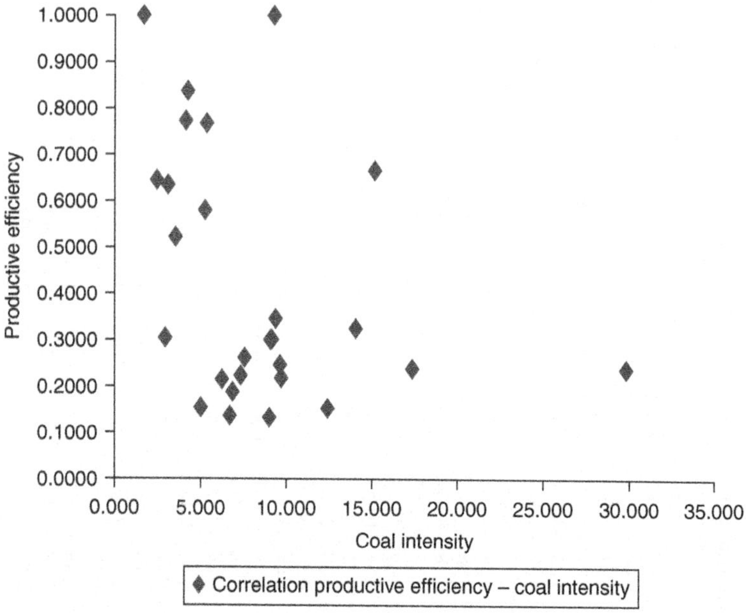

Figure 9.3 Relationship productive efficiency – coal intensity

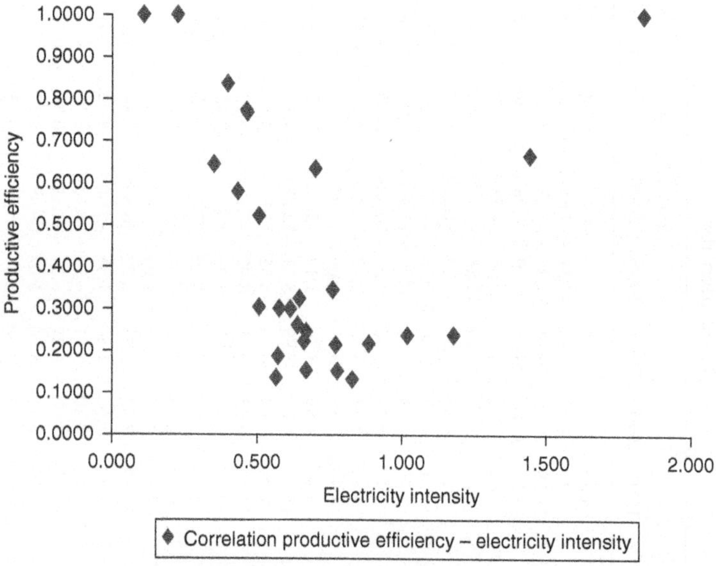

Figure 9.4 Relationship productive efficiency – electricity intensity

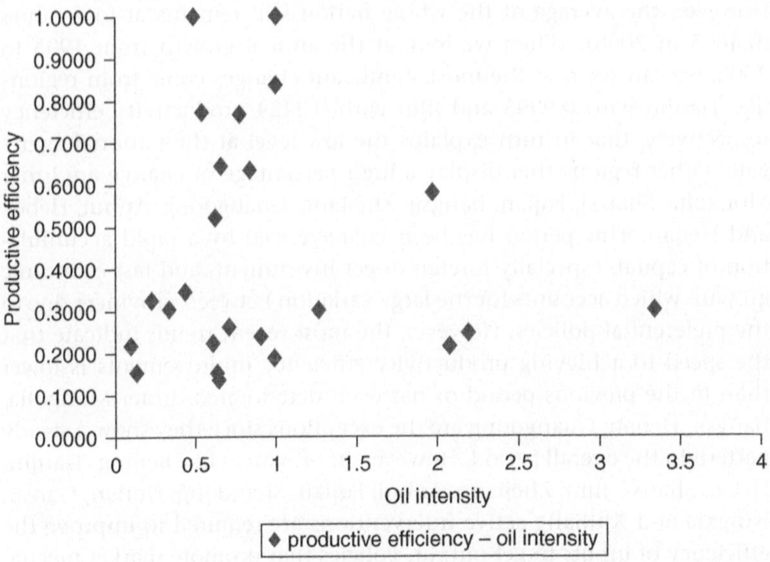

Figure 9.5 Relationship productive efficiency – oil intensity

From Table 9.1, we can observe the productivity efficiency index in 1995, 2000, 2005 and 2008 as well as the growth rate from 1995 to 2000 and from 2005 to 2008. Recall that productivity efficiency ranges from zero up to the unity, the later indicating perfect efficiency. Knowing this, we get that Shanghai, Guizhou and Qinghai are perfectly efficient in the use of inputs – labour and capital – to produce output. The findings in the case of Shanghai are expected because it is one of the most dynamics regions in China with a high presence of non-state sector, which in turn allows improvement in the efficiency of resources. However, there is no prior evidence on this matter in the case of Guizhou and Qinghai. These regions are characterized by the predominance of agriculture and high presence of the state sector, but surprisingly they are perfectly efficient. In general, we find that those regions that are located in the west and centre of China such as Anhui, Gansu, Guangxi, Henan, Hubei, Hunan, Jiangxi, Shaanxi, Sichuan, Yunnan, and Xinjiang display the lowest productivity efficiency index. In northern regions like Hebei, Shanxi, Inner Mongolia, Jilin, and Heilongjiang it is also possible to observe this phenomenon, and surprisingly the efficiency of the capital of China – Beijing – is quite modest with only 0.5773. By contrast, regions like Tianjin, Jiangsu, Shandong, Ningxia, and Zhejiang show the highest levels of productivity efficiency in the most recent period.

However, the average of the whole nation still remains at low values (0.4695 in 2008). When we look at the annual growth from 1995 to 2000, we can see that the most significant changes come from regions like Tianjin with 0.9995 and Jilin with 0.3424 productivity efficiency respectively, that in turn explains the low level at the national aggregate. Other regions that display a high percentage of change are Inner Mongolia, Shanxi, Fujian, Jiangsu, Zhejiang, Guangdong, Anhui, Hebei, and Henan. This period has been characterized by a rapid accumulation of capital, especially foreign direct investment, and fast economic growth, which accounts for the large variation between provinces due to the preferential policies. However, the most recent trends indicate that the speed to achieving productivity efficiency improvements is lower than in the previous period or has even deteriorated. Inner Mongolia, Jiangsu, Henan, Guangdong are the exceptions since they show a steady pattern in the overall period. However, in provinces like Beijing, Tianjin, Hebei, Shanxi, Jilin, Zhejiang, Anhui, Fujian, Shandong, Hunan, Gansu, Ningxia and Xinjiang active interventions are required to improve the efficiency of inputs to get output. Policies that promote market mechanisms as well as technological progress are needed to sustain and increase the gains from productivity improvements.

Table 9.2 presents the evolution of coal, electricity and oil intensity in 1995, 2000, 2005 and 2008, and the corresponding growth rates from 1995 to 2000 and from 2005 to 2008. From this table, it is possible to observe the following stylized facts:

First, coal intensity, coal being the most important source of energy in China, not surprisingly displays a higher ratio than electricity and oil. However, at the same time it is the source of energy that shows the highest improvements from 1995 to 2000 due the policies adopted by the government such as the shutdown of small and inefficient coal mining plants, and after that period a significant relaxation of energy-saving policies. The exception to this behaviour is oil intensity that reduced its ratio up 2.36 per cent from 1995 to 2000 and from 2005 to 2008 a 7.38 per cent.

Second, northern regions like Hebei, Shanxi, Inner Mongolia Jilin and Heilongjiang and centre regions such as Sichuan, Anhui and Ningxia displayed the highest coal intensity ratio in 1995, and except Inner Mongolia all of them experienced reduction over 9 per cent of coal intensity from 1995 to 2000. However, improvements of coal intensity were lower than 5 per cent from 2000 to 2008. These provinces are specialized in heavy industry such as northern regions, or in the industrial sector that consumes 70 per cent of coal. Thus, reductions in coal intensity in these regions improve the energy efficiency of the overall economy. By contrast, the best performance on this matter relies in regions like Beijing, Shanghai, Fujian, Guangdong, Guizhou, and Zhejiang that show coal intensity ratios below 5. The high presence of a non-state sector that favours the implementation of new technology and a better use of energy resources may explain this phenomenon (Herrerias et al., 2013).

Third, hydropower electricity generation is mainly located in the south of China and Sichuan and its neighbours. Knowing this fact, we can see from Table 9.2 that Sichuan has decreased to 12.55 per cent its electricity intensity from 1995 to 2000, followed by Heilongjiang (8.66%), Hunan (7.37%), Jilin (6.77%), Anhui (6.15%), Jiangxi (5.87%), Hubei (5.24%), and Gansu (5.23%). However, as mentioned before, also in electricity industry the pace of reduction of electricity intensity was much slower from 2000 to 2008 or even increased such as in Gansu or Anhui. Provinces located in the east of and south of China displayed the best performance in general. These include regions like Beijing, Tianjin, Liaoning, Jiangsu, Zhejiang, Fujian, Shandong, and Guizhou. By contrast, regions like Qinghai and Ningxia present the highest levels of electricity intensity.

Finally, oil intensity has shown a distinctive behaviour. We find higher reductions of oil intensity ratio from 2005 to 2008 with a percentage of 7.38 than from 1995 to 2000 with a value of 2.36 on average of the whole economy. However, the significant heterogeneity found earlier is also present in the oil industry. Regions showing the most important oil-savings with a percentage over 10 per cent are: Tianjin, Jilin, Heilongjiang, Shanghai, Jiangsu, Anhui, Fujian, Henan and Hunan. By contrast, the worse performance appears in Sichuan province with an increase of 12.68 per cent from 2005 to 2008 followed to a lesser extent by Beijing with a value of 0.09 per cent. This source of energy is growing in importance in recent years due the industrialization process, and regulators therefore should pay specific attention to this sector to address energy policies.

Once we have described the evolution of the productivity efficiency index and energy intensity, the next question to ask is whether both magnitudes maintain any relationship. We present in Figures 9.3–9.5 the relationship between these two key variables as a starting point to analyse the nature of the linkage.

One of the common features that we can observe is that the relationship between productivity efficiency and energy intensity is heterogeneous across regions and appears clustered, regardless of the source of energy considered. This phenomenon makes it difficult to implement a common energy policy for all regions and local actions are required to improve the use of energy resources per unit of output.

Second, we found that those regions that display the highest productivity efficiency show a better performance in the use of energy intensity. This is especially true in the case of coal and oil. However, in the case of electricity, we found some regions that in spite of being perfectly efficient, show high values of electricity intensity. In this latter case, there is no clear picture of the relationship between electricity intensity and productivity efficiency.

Finally, we observe that those regions that are clustered at low values of productivity efficiency, display in general low values of energy intensity but with some exceptions. So, it seems that the relationship between productivity efficiency and energy intensity across regions is a complex phenomenon that needs further research for a better understanding of the adoption of energy intensity measures. According with our figures, the relationship between productivity efficiency and energy intensity is more evident only when provinces present high values of productivity efficiency, but still remain unclear for other regions that show lower values of energy intensity and productivity efficiency. In this case, other factors may account for this relationship like for example a substitution effect between capital/labour and energy consumption across regions.

3.2 A sectoral perspective

Similar to the previous analysis, Table 9.3 reports the evolution of coal, electricity and oil intensity for 8 sectors in China, while productive efficiency is presented in Table 9.4. The relationship between both variables is shown in Figures 9.6–9.8.

Table 9.3 Sectoral energy intensity

	Coal Intensity			Electricity Intensity			Oil Intensity		
	2004	**2009**	**Change**	**2004**	**2009**	**Change**	**2004**	**2009**	**Change**
Total	1.39	0.86	−9.18%	0.147	0.108	−6.08%	0.19	0.11	−10.48%
Farming	0.07	0.04	−9.01%	0.039	0.026	−7.23%	1.43	1.07	−5.70%
Mining and quarrying	1.81	1.29	−6.55%	0.195	0.104	−11.74%	0.18	0.06	−19.11%
Manufacturing	1.71	1.01	−10.06%	0.237	0.177	−5.64%	0.57	0.33	−10.11%
Production and supply elec.	17.71	17.26	−0.51%	0.663	0.639	−0.74%	–	–	–
Construction	0.07	0.03	−16.78%	0.025	0.019	−5.62%	–	–	–
Transport and storage	0.07	0.03	−17.20%	0.036	0.025	−7.15%	0.01	0.01	−9.03%
Wholesale and retail	0.10	0.05	−11.12%	0.047	0.031	−7.83%	–	–	–

Table 9.4 Productive efficiency index, sectoral

	2004	2009	Change
Total	1.0000	1.0000	–
Farming, forestry, animal husbandry and fishery	1.0000	1.0000	–
Mining and quarrying	0.3488	0.4230	3.93%
Manufacturing	0.9396	0.9714	0.67%
Production and supply electricity, gas and water	1.0000	1.0000	–
Construction	1.0000	1.0000	–
Transport, storage, post and telecommunications services	0.5744	0.5960	0.74%
Wholesale and retail trade and catering services.	0.7812	0.9885	4.82%

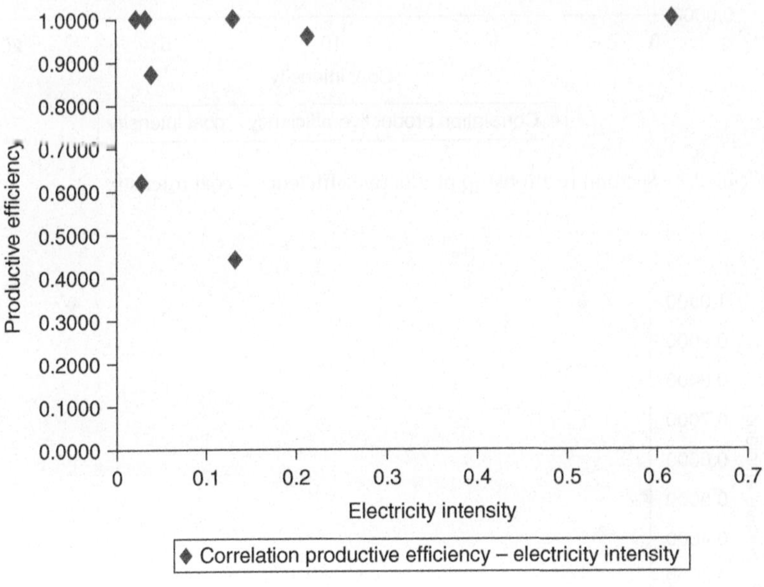

Figure 9.6 Sectoral relationship productive efficiency – electricity intensity

Table 9.3 and 9.4 present the evolution of coal, electricity and oil intensity as well as productivity efficiency across industries respectively in 2004 and 2009. From there, we can see that production and supply of electricity, gas and water show the highest coal intensity ratio and the one that has experienced lower improvements from 2004 and 2009. However, at the same time, this sector is perfectly efficient according

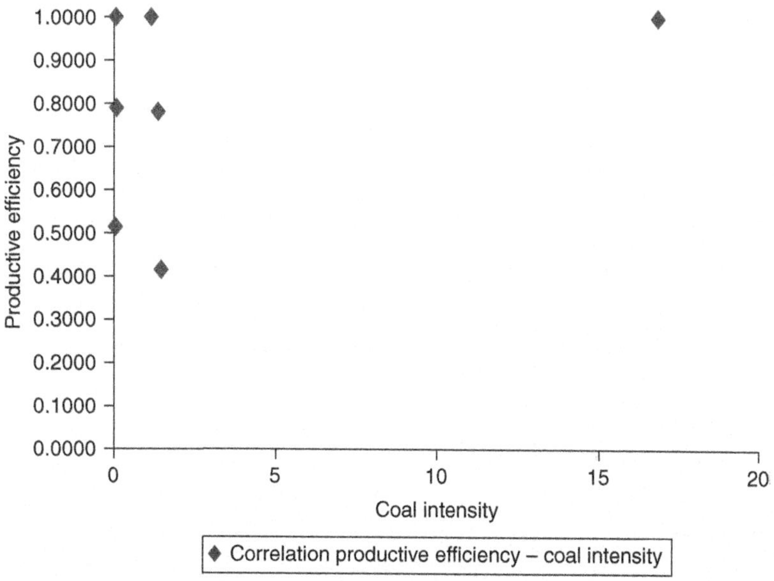

Figure 9.7 Sectoral relationship productive efficiency – coal intensity

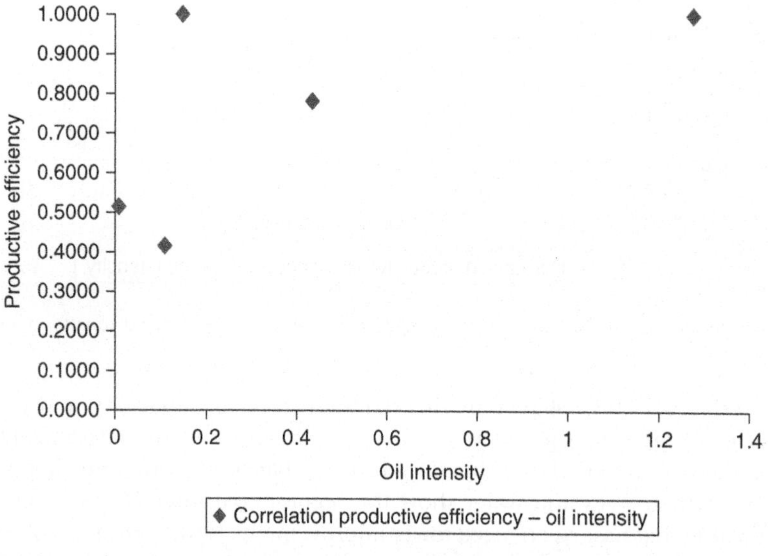

Figure 9.8 Sectoral relationship productive efficiency – oil intensity

to our estimates. These apparent contradictions allow us to conclude that productivity efficiency and coal intensity in this sector do not have a clear relationship, and thus reduction of coal intensity is explained by other factors different from productivity efficiency. On the other hand, mining and quarrying and manufacturing also display a high coal intensity ratio compared with other sectors in China. These sectors have shown a decrease of the growth rate of coal intensity of 6.55 per cent and 10.06 per cent over the considered period respectively. Even though the mining and quarrying sector is quite inefficient since its productivity efficiency is very low, from 2004 to 2009, this sector improved its productivity by 3.93 per cent. On the other hand, the manufacturing sector is almost perfectly efficient with a value of 0.9714 in 2009. In these two sectors, it seems that improvements in both productivity and coal intensity are related to each other. Finally, in the case of farming, construction, transportation, and wholesale and retail, coal intensity is very low, because it is an unusual source of energy in their production processes, yet improvements in such ratio were over 9 per cent. Looking at their productivity efficiency, we can see that the most important improvements in coal intensity come from sectors that are perfectly efficient like farming and construction, or a relatively high productivity like in case of wholesale. The only exception is the transportation industry, the improvements in which do not come from productivity efficiency since it still shows a modest index.

The evolution and relationship between electricity intensity and productivity efficiency is more obvious than in the case of coal intensity. In all sectors there are significant observed reductions (improvements) of electricity intensity (productivity efficiency) from 2004 to 2009, except in the case of production and supply of electricity, gas and water. In this latter case, it is detected that even though it is perfectly efficient, the improvements in the use of electricity per unit output are modest. Finally, for those sectors for which we have data on oil intensity and productivity efficiency, we detect that from 2004 to 2009 there were significant improvements in oil intensity in mining and quarrying (–19.11%) and manufacturing (–10.11%), which were working together with a better performance of productivity efficiency, especially in the former.

To conclude our comprehensive overview of the relationship between productivity efficiency and energy intensity, we report the relationship between both macro-magnitudes in Figures 9.6–9.8. From there, we can confirm our previous findings: First, reductions in electricity intensity are associated with high productivity efficiency. Second, even though we can see this phenomenon in coal and oil intensities too, the relationship is less clear since we find sectors with relatively low values of productivity efficiency and energy intensity, which in turn implies that productivity efficiency can be an important explanation of energy-saving measures, but other factors play a key role too. Finally, we observe some sectors displaying high values of productivity efficiency as well as high values of energy intensity, which require further active policies to improve the use of energy per unit of output.

4 Conclusions and policy implications

The Chinese economy has achieved exceptional performance over the last forty years, changing the structure of the international market. This fast growth has been followed by an intensive use of energy resources and serious environmental damage. In 2009, China overtook the United States as the most important consumer and producer of energy in the world, especially coal, and all seems to indicate that the current trend is heading towards intensive energy consumption. The emergence of China on energy issues has raised the concern to ensure inclusion of developing countries in international agreements on climate change. However, until recent years, the Chinese government refused to be part of any agreement which might have consequences for the country's economic growth. Butin the mid-2000s, due to electricity shortages and the increasing level of pollution, the government recognized the need to adopt a set of energy policies to cut energy consumption. This chapter attempts to give some policy insights into adopting energy-saving measures across Chinese regions and to prevent global warming.

More specifically, this chapter gives a comprehensive overview of the evolution of energy intensity in terms of coal, electricity and oil as the most important sources of energy across the Chinese provinces from 1995 to 2008 and across key sectors. Then, we get the productivity efficiency estimates through the application of data envelopment analysis and we analyse its trends. Finally, we investigate the type of relationship that prevails between energy intensity and productivity efficiency. This relationship is an important one to be investigated because the observed decline in energy intensity can be attributed to changes in sectorial composition and technological progress. On the one hand, the gradual moving away from heavy industry that consumes significant amount of energy resources towards light industry can led to improvements in the use of energy resources per unit of output. However, a sectorial change from agriculture to industry can lead to the opposite effect. On the other hand, the transfer of technology from abroad through foreign direct investment and imports along with domestic innovation facilitate energy savings through improvements in productivity, therefore showing a decrease in energy intensity. Since both sectorial composition and technological progress can led to improvements in the use of energy consumption per unit of output, an interesting question to be analysed is what type of the relationship exists between both macro-magnitudes.

Graphical analysis reveals that the relationship between coal, electricity and oil intensity and productivity efficiency is a complex issue and needs further research. We find that in some of the Chinese provinces higher/lower levels of productivity efficiency are associated with low/high values of energy intensity. In this situation it seems that productivity explains the performance of energy intensity. However, for other regions we find co-movements between higher values of productivity efficiency as well as higher values of energy intensity or low values of productivity efficiency and low values of energy intensity. In consequence, in this situation, productivity improvements do not account for increases/decreases of energy intensity and other factors may explain this phenomenon. Analysis at sectorial level provides similar insights on the relationship between energy consumption and productivity efficiency. Our results suggest that improvements in productivity are correlated with an decrease in energy intensity, except in production and supply of electricity, gas and water where we find that is perfectly efficient, but at the same time displays the highest levels of energy intensity (coal, electricity and oil).

From our results it seems that at least for some regions and sectors productivity improvements influence the performance of energy intensity. So that, what type of measures can policy makers adopt to stimulate productivity and therefore to decrease energy intensity?

- The Chinese economy is coal-dependent, which it is expensive and highly polluting, so that to move gradually away from such dependence in favour of clean energies can lead to productivity improvements and to lower energy consumption.
- The energy sector is still one of the latest bastions of the Chinese government, with energy prices being fixed without considering the market forces. A liberalization of the sector allowing market mechanisms to work is essential to improving productivity.
- Previous evidence highlighted that foreign direct investment, non-state investment, and imports are feasible mechanisms for technology

transfer, which in turn improves the performance of energy intensity (Herrerias et al., 2012a). So, economic incentives to promote such investments in the energy sector as well as the importation of advanced technology can be useful to reduce energy consumption.

- The industry sector in China accounts for around 70 per cent of total energy consumption and is the driver of the whole economy. However, as other economies have done in the past when industrialization has achieved its mature stage, switching to development of the service sector can also lead also to reductions in energy consumption.
- Given the regional heterogeneity in the Chinese economy, active interventions should be made at national level and in coordination with local governments to achieve energy and environmental goals.

10
Energy Intensity and Its Policy Implications in China

Ana Cuadros and Vicente Orts

1 Background facts on the energy situation in China

The Copenhagen Conference on climate change in 2009 stressed the need to support developing countries in employing energy-saving technologies. According to International Energy Agency (IEA, 2007) projections, developing countries whose economies and populations are growing fastest contribute 74 per cent of the increase in global primary energy use in the Reference Scenario between 2005 and 2030.[1] China and India alone account for 45 per cent of this increase. More recently, the US Energy Information Administration (EIA, 2011) forecasts that energy demand in the OECD economies will grow at an average annual rate of 0.6 per cent over the projection period (2008–35), whereas energy consumption in the non-OECD emerging economies will expand by an average of 2.3 per cent per year. Energy use in non-OECD Asia (led by China and India) shows the most robust growth of all the non-OECD regions. Thus, as you can see in Figure 10.1, China will play a major role in driving energy consumption growth in the medium to long term.

Economic growth is among the most important factors to be considered when projecting changes in world energy consumption. The emerging markets, particularly the economies of Asia (led by China and India) appear to be recovering quickly and driving current world economic growth (EIA, 2011). Since 1996, rising demand has turned China from a net energy exporter to a net energy importer, with consumption more than 10 per cent above production since 2005. This switch is even more marked for petroleum products. China's import share of petroleum dramatically increased from less than 8 per cent in 1995 to 53 per cent in 2008 (Ma et al., 2010). This scenario clearly shows that the evolution of the energy situation in China has important implications for

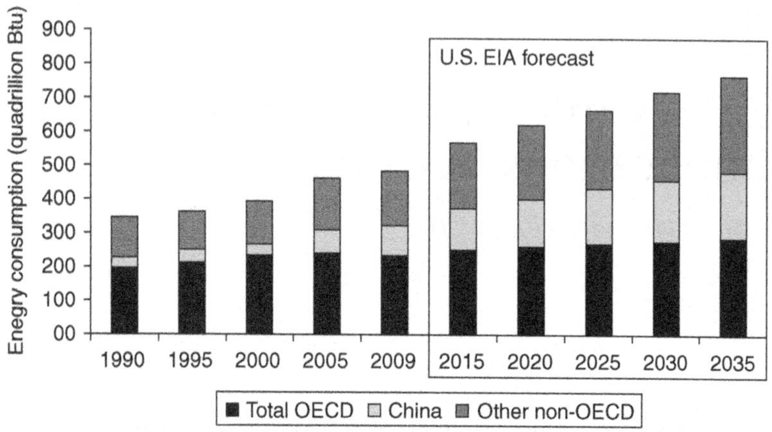

Figure 10.1 Total primary energy consumption, 1990–2009 and forecast
Source: U.S. Energy Information Administration. International Energy Statistics and International Energy Outlook 2011.

energy demand. Moreover, its impressive growth is associated with deteriorating environmental conditions. China is now the world's largest energy consumer as well as CO_2 emitter. Thus, activities undertaken in China will have a significant influence on the global effort to reduce greenhouse emissions (Zhou, 2010 and Wu, 2012).

Chai et al. (2009) argue that energy intensity[2] reflects the energy usage efficiency of an economy. When China initiated its economic reform program in the late 1970s, its energy intensity was double that of the United States and triple that of Japan (Hang and Tu, 2007). Figure 10.2 shows the evolution of this variable. As can be seen, energy intensity declined substantially in China during the post-reform period. The sequence of economic and institutional reforms initiated by the country in 1978 and accelerated in the early 1990s with openness to foreign direct investment inflows (FDI), the transformation of the state-sector and the emergence of new forms of investment ownership have accompanied its decline in energy intensity.

The above figure illustrates that the decreasing trend has not been constant during the analysed period. Energy intensity declined steadily between 1980 and 2002. Since China accelerated its economic reform at the end of 1992, its energy intensity declined substantially. During 1997–2002, the energy efficiency of China improved continuously (Fan et al., 2007). However, the period 2002–05 saw a dramatic reversal of

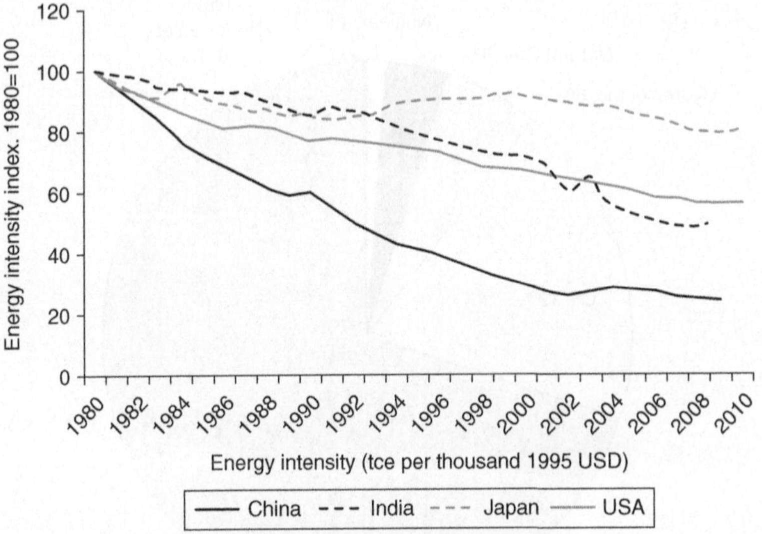

Figure 10.2 Energy intensity: primary energy consumption per unit GDP, 1980–2010

Source: China Energy Databook, October 2008 (period 1980–2005). Authors estimations from the World Development Indicators for the period 2005–10.

the above tendency with an energy use per unit of GDP increasing at an average of 3.8 per cent per year (Zhou et al., 2010). As we will try to set out in the next section, this behaviour can be explained by changes in sector composition and industrial structure as well as by technical effects.

China's lower energy efficiency is largely attributed to its coal-dominated energy structure (see Figure 10.3). A large share of coal-based energy in China's total energy consumption has not only resulted in low energy efficiency and high energy intensity, but has also caused serious environmental pollution. Compared with the average world energy structure, the proportion of coal in total consumption is 70 per cent (high above the world average which is around 30 per cent).[3] Oil's share in total primary energy consumption is 19 per cent, nearly 16 percentage points lower than the world average. The proportion of natural gas consumption is 4 per cent, far below the world average (23 per cent). Thus, it would be desirable to increase the proportion of other sources of energy (different from coal) in the total energy consumption to save energy and reduce energy intensity.[4]

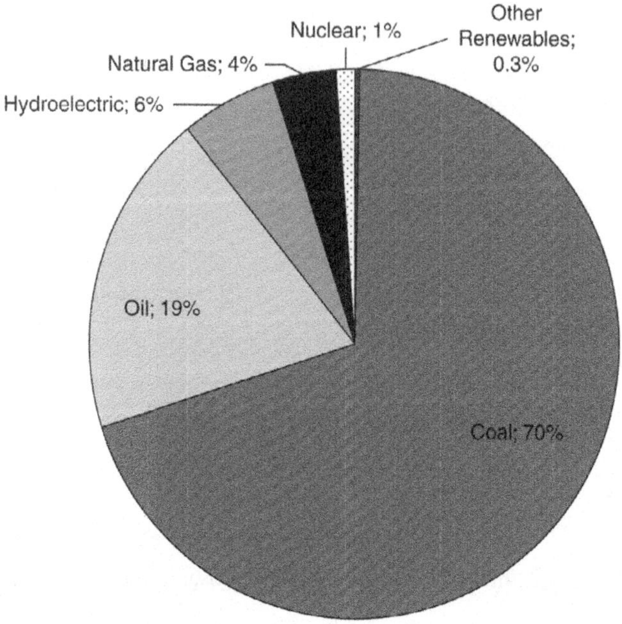

Figure 10.3 Total energy consumption in China by type, 2009

Source: U.S. Energy Information Administration. International Statistics. China Report, September 2012.

In spite of the improvements in energy efficiency during the eighties and most of the nineties, China's overall energy efficiency in 1990 continued to lag behind that of other countries with similar levels of per capita income (Fisher-Vanden et al., 2004). The 10th Five-Year Plan set a target of 15–17 per cent reduction in energy use between 2000 and 2005. It completely failed in achieving this goal. In fact, energy intensity increased during this period, for the first time since 1980. As a result, the Chinese government recognized that success in pursuing energy intensity improvements would require the deep involvement of the Chinese Communist Party and the government. The 11th Five-Year Plan established the target of reducing energy intensity by about 20 per cent by 2010 compared to 2005 values. Zhou et al. (2010) provides a review and initial assessment of the policies and programs that China instituted to achieve this goal. In less than three years, beginning in 2006, a policy apparatus to implement energy efficiency has been created. While still in progress, according with these authors, China is making a significant new beginning in its pursuit of greater levels of energy efficiency.

Finally, in the analysis of the energy situation in China, we cannot ignore the regional dimension. This country is the largest in the world by population and the 4th by area; it is divided into twenty-two provinces, five autonomous regions and four direct-controlled municipalities, all with different degrees of autonomy. Each of the provinces[5] is in a different stage of economic development, leading to a high diversity in the energy situation among regions. Therefore, any strategy to improve energy efficiency needs to account for regional heterogeneity.

Summing up, the energy issue has become strategic for China's future development. Section 2 tries a descriptive picture of the most relevant drivers behind energy improvements in this country, focusing especially on the role played by openness to both trade and foreign direct investment as well as on the reforms in investment ownership. Section 3 incorporates the regional perspective in the analysis of energy efficiency. Section 4 concludes.

2 Drivers of energy-saving

China's economic development has been greatly enhanced since the reform and opening up policy adopted at the end of the 1970s, with the aim of increasing the importance of foreign inflows and achieving a change from a planned to a market-oriented economy. The process of marketization, including ownership and prices reforms, and the improvement of the legal system was accelerated at the end of 1992. Consistent with this progress, energy intensity has declined substantially in China. However, as has been highlighted in the previous section, there have been temporary disruptions in this declining trend and there's still a lot of room for improvement in the energy situation.

Broadly speaking, explanations for China's decline in energy intensity fall into three categories. The first focuses on the role played by energy prices. The second explanation relies on the structural and technical changes associated with the openness process. The third explanation centres on the influence of the reforms in the structure of investment ownership and on the incorporation of energy-saving technologies.

Energy prices in China have been significantly lower than international ones. The price of energy was fully state-controlled until the beginning of reforms in late 1978. With the initiation of China's "two-tiered pricing system" in 1982, prices set by the central plan have been gradually replaced with market-mediated prices. In the early 1990s, for almost all goods, the market replaced the plan as the primary means of allocation. However, price reform in energy sectors (e.g., coal, electricity and crude oil), which had long been heavily subsidized, lagged behind. After years of suspension, energy price reform regained its momentum in 1996. By 1999, plan allocations of energy had been largely eliminated (Hang and Tu, 2007). By 2006, subsidies for energy had been dramatically reduced and energy prices in China increasingly reflected actual costs (Zhou et al., 2010). Ma et al. (2009) highlight that the market appears to be playing an increasing role in determining energy prices in China.

In spite of the improvements, there is still a long way to go. Energy prices in China have not fully reflected environmental externalities, scarcity of energy resources and imbalances in domestic demand and supply. Moreover, low energy prices contribute directly to rapid growth in energy consumption, favour the development of energy-intensive industries and contribute indirectly to the structural shift from light to energy-intensive industries (Chai et al., 2009 and Zhao et al., 2010). The findings by Hang and Tu (2007) show that the own-price elasticity of coal, oil and aggregate energy were negative in the periods before and after 1995, which implies that an increase in relative prices of different energy types leads to a decrease in coal, oil and aggregate energy intensity. Thus, rising energy prices is considered an effective policy tool to improve energy efficiency (see also Fan et al., 2007 and Wu, 2012).

An additional and important question to consider is the role played by subsidies in the government policy for energy price-setting. Different authors and institutions (e.g., International Energy Agency) highlight that energy subsidies in China have distorted market price signals, resulting in higher energy consumption and production. For example, a recent work by Lin and Jiang (2011) states that China's residential electricity tariffs are much lower than their supply costs, leading to low energy efficiency. Similarly, productions subsidies to the state-owned oil companies promote oil consumption. And the government interventions to maintain lower price for coal used to produce electricity lead to substantial rapid increase in coal-fired power capacities. Results obtained by these authors indicate that China needs to reform its energy subsidies to improve energy efficiency and reduce emissions.[6] Some actions by the Chinese government indicate its understanding about the negative impact of energy subsides. Recently, the oil-pricing mechanism has been reformed, while maintaining universal subsidy on electricity, which is considered to be more important in household budgets. According to International Energy Agency estimations, the total consumption subsidies (net of taxes) in China, which amounted about USD 26 billion in 2005, dropped sharply in 2006 to USD 11 billion.[7] In spite of these improvements, the price-setting mechanism remains a sensitive issue in China. Besides, whereas price guidelines are set by a national planning agency (the National Development Research Council), energy policy making is largely decentralized. Thus, actual costs and subsidies vary across China as prices are influenced by local regulators.[8]

Moreover, energy price deregulation differs substantially for different types of energy. The price of coal has been market-mediated since 1996, whereas the price of electricity has remained under state control due to its high political and social sensitivity. Compared to coal prices, crude oil prices have become comparable to those of the world markets (Hang and Tu, 2007). The unreasonable price structure of energy has not been conducive to the optimization of the composition of energy sources. Specifically, low coal price easily leads to the high consumption of coal in relation to other types of energy (see Chai et al., 2009).

Although changes in relative prices of energy have undoubtedly played an important role in explaining the evolution of energy intensity in China, we believe that both transnational linkages (particularly those through imports and inward foreign direct investment) and changes in ownership structure have accelerated the transfer and diffusion of environmentally superior technologies. Therefore, in the next two sections, we focus on the role played by both openness and the reforms in the structure of investment ownership in China.

2.1 Openness, structural and technical effects

Improvements in domestic environment-efficient technologies in the context of developing countries such as China are likely to depend on technology transfer from more environment-efficient economies (Perkins and Neumayer, 2009). Openness to trade and FDI can affect energy use in an economy by a composition and a technique effect (see Fisher-Vanden et al., 2006 and Hübler and Keller, 2010). On the one hand, opening up to international trade can alter the relative profitability of certain industries – particularly heavy industry – which would explain the gradual move away from energy-intensive heavy industries. This composition effect will reduce a country's energy use if the economy specializes in sectors with lower energy intensity. But, at the same time, as countries develop, the sectorial change shifts economic activity from the agricultural to the industrial sector. Since the latter is more energy-intensive, this implies a positive composition effect. Thus, signs of the composition effect can be either positive or negative. On the other hand, the technique effect covers the impact of openness on the implementation of less energy-intensive technologies or the adoption of ecologically beneficial management practices with an energy-reducing effect.

As we will try to highlight, there seems to be general agreement in the relevant literature about the key role played by technological progress in explaining China's declining energy intensity, although the role played by structural change (composition effect) remains a controversial issue. Most previous studies have found sectorial shift from more energy-intensive to less energy-intensive industries to be a relatively small contributor to the decline in China's energy intensity (Zhang, 2003; Fisher-Vanden et al., 2004; Liao et al., 2007; Ma and Stern, 2008; Zhao et al., 2010; Wu, 2012 and Herrerias et al., 2013). In China, industry accounts for approximately 70 per cent of the total energy consumption, being the largest energy-consuming and end-use sector (Liao et al., 2007). This reality has promoted some empirical works about the role that both structural change across sectors (agriculture, services and industry) and the above mentioned composition effect within the industrial sector may have played in the evolution of energy intensity. As you can see in Figure 10.4, over the period 1980–2010, the service sector has been steadily gaining share in the GDP (from 22 to 43%), while agriculture shows a decreasing trend (from 30 to 10%). In contrast, the evolution of industry has been more stable (from 48 to 47%), albeit with some significant variations along the period. As has been highlighted by several authors (see, for example, Ma and Stern, 2008), the actual changes in industrial structure were very different between the 1980s and the period following 1990. From 1980 to 1990, structural change occurred mainly from primary industry to services and the share of industry in GDP decreased from 48.22 per cent to 41.3 per cent (see Figure 10.4). However, from 1990 to 1997, a shift in output from primary to secondary industry and services dominated, and the share of secondary industry reached a new peak in 1997 (47.5%). In these years, the expansion of industry was dominated by light industry at the expense of heavy industry (see Figure 10.5). Yet, from the late 90s onwards, there is a significant change in this pattern, and heavy industry systematically grew faster than light industry,[9] while the total share of the industry sector, experienced very small fluctuations.

The above behaviour is consistent with the evolution of energy intensity described in Section 1. Thus, while from 1997 to 2002 energy intensity in China continued its falling tendency, the period 2002–05 showed a dramatic reversal in this tendency. Probably, the reduction in the weight of the industry sector between 1997 and 2002, and the fact that China was experiencing a downturn due to Asia's financial

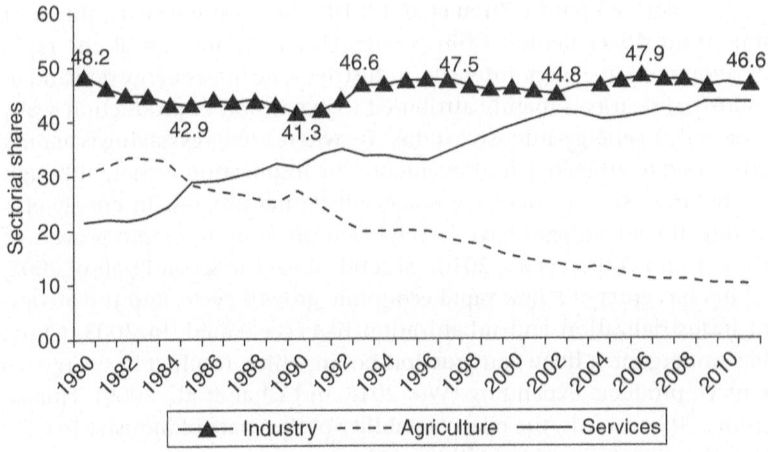

Figure 10.4 Sectorial shares of GDP in China, 1980–2011
Source: The World Bank. World Development Indicators.

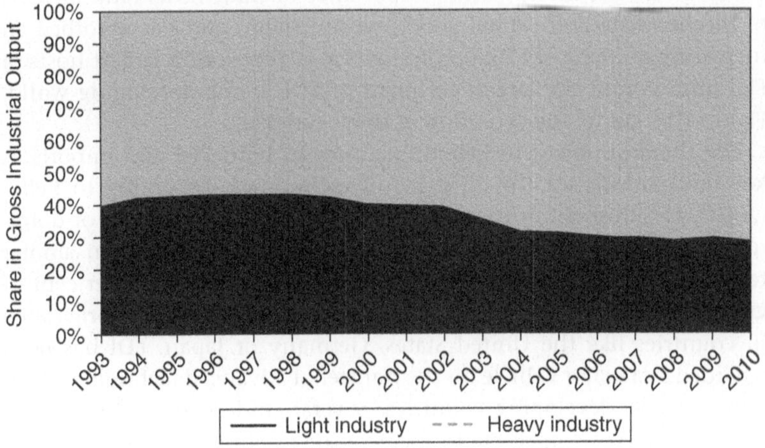

Figure 10.5 Share of light and heavy industry in gross industrial output
Source: National Bureau of Statistics in China.

crisis (with the subsequent insufficient domestic demand), contributed to China's declining energy intensity during these years (Liao et al., 2007). However, between 2002 and 2005 the concurrence of two distinct facts reversed the previous decreasing trend in energy intensity.

First, as pointed out by Zhou et al. (2010), during these years, the most important driver behind China's energyintensity increase is the rapid development in energy-intensive industries. The high energy demand in industrial sectors is mainly attributed to expansion of production scale, especially in energy-intensive industries whereas energy-saving is mainly attributed to efficiency improvement. The implication is that, although energy-intensive sectors have made substantial progress in energy efficiency, the advantages have largely been offset by the rapid growth in these sectors (Zhao et al., 2010). Second, since the second half of 2002, China has entered a new rapid economic growth cycle, and the process of industrialization and urbanization has accelerated. In 2003, China has undergone a huge construction boom which resulted in energy-intensive products expanding (Wu, 2012 and Chai et al., 2009). Finally, from 2005 onwards, the relative stability of the share of industry in GDP and the change in composition of the secondary sector, from light to heavy industry, made technical change the main factor responsible for explaining the improvement in energy efficiency.

Turning to the technique effect, since opening up its economy in 1978, China has increased the importance of trade flows (and imports of intermediate and capital goods, within them) and has absorbed an increasing amount of FDI, becoming one of the world's largest hosts of FDI inflows and the largest recipient of FDI in the developing world. Figure 10.6 shows the evolution of these variables.

The literature has considered openness to both FDI and imports as key mechanisms for the diffusion of technology. According to Keller (2004), for most countries, foreign sources of technology are of dominant importance (90% or more) for productivity growth. In similar terms, Eaton and Kortum (1996) stated that more than 50 per cent of growth in some countries can be attributed to innovation originated in countries like the United States, Germany or Japan. FDI has been regarded as a major vehicle for the transfer of advanced technology from developed to developing countries. Several studies highlight the fact that FDI inflows contribute to increase the existing level of knowledge through labour training, skills acquisition, and the introduction of alternative management practices as well as new inputs and technologies (see Cuadros et al., 2004; Kemeny, 2010 and Alguacil et al., 2011; among others). Imports of machinery and equipment are another important channel for improving the efficiency of domestic production due to the technology embodied in these goods. These imports create productivity spillovers via imitation of the imported goods and via improved application methods adopted together with the imported goods (Hübler, 2011;

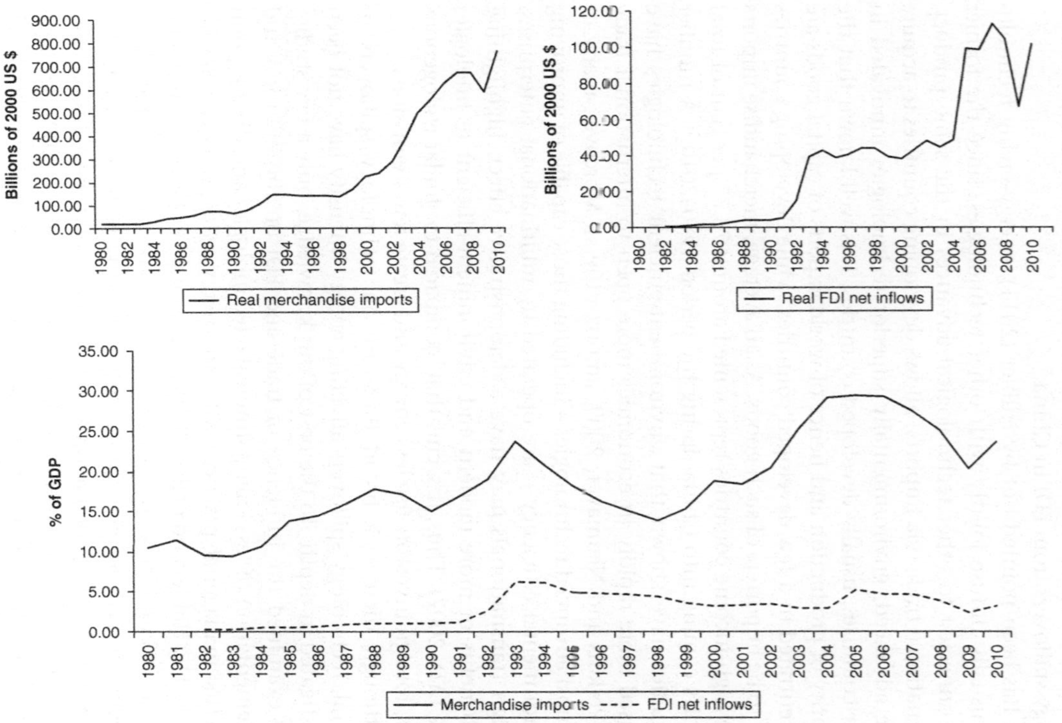

Figure 10.6 Real merchandise imports and real FDI

Source: The World Bank. World Development Indicators.

Herrerias and Orts, 2011). For China, Lai et al. (2006) highlight that technology spillovers coming from FDI seem to be more significant than those of imports. Liu (2008), Luo (2007), Girma and Gong (2008) and Abraham et al. (2010) (among others) confirm the existence of technology spillovers from FDI in China.

As has been pointed out by Hübler (2011), energy-saving technologies usually diffuse jointly with other technologies, since the former are connected to other technological advances in the same product. International trade (via imports) allows developing countries to acquire more advanced, environmentally superior technologies innovated in other countries, usually developed countries. It is well known that the majority of production and hence of world exports of capital goods are concentrated in a few developed countries, while developing countries tend to be importers of such goods. As an average, merchandise imports from high-income countries represented around 78.77 per cent of total imports coming into China during the period 1980–2010.[10] A number of studies have shown that environment-efficient technologies have diffused more rapidly in economies more open to international trade (see Perkins and Neumayer, 2009, among others). Moreover, many of the most advanced technologies – including those capable of improving environmental efficiency – are operated by multinational enterprises. Foreign transnationals may have a demonstrative effect, highlighting the benefits of more modern and environment-efficient technologies (UNCTAD, 2007). Thus, it seems that, compared to similar endogenous firms, foreign investors use less energy and create fewer emissions.

Although there is a broad literature on technology spillovers in general, technology spillovers affecting energy intensity have not been investigated in depth. To the best of our knowledge, only a few studies have examined the influence of trade and FDI on the diffusion and implementation of less energy-intensive technologies and the adoption of better managerial practices with an energy-reducing effect. Results obtained by Hübler and Keller (2010) for a sample of 60 developing countries (including China) do not find evidence for a general or uniform influence of FDI on energy intensity. According to these authors, the effects of FDI inflows on energy use depend on country-specific characteristics. On the other hand, Mielnik and Goldemberg (2002) confirm the negative effect of FDI on energy intensity for a sample of 20 developing countries. Hübler (2011) confirms these findings for China. More recently, Herrerias et al. (2013) confirm that openness to FDI and imports has been a significant driving force in the reduction of energy intensity in China. According to these authors, regulatory pressures in their developed parent-countries probably explain the use of cleaner technologies by multinational firms investing in China. Moreover, the fact that exports to developed countries represent a significant share of the sales of these companies forces their affiliates to meet the stringent environmental standards of export markets for their Chinese-manufactured products.

2.2 Reforms to investment ownership

The ownership structure of Chinese enterprises has changed dramatically over the past two decades (Jefferson and Su, 2006). Without any doubt, the transformation of the state-sector and consequent emergence of new forms of investment ownership has been one of the fundamental keys to understanding China's process of transition from planned to market economy. Reforms to investment ownership within China have included a rapid expansion of various ownership classifications outside the state-sector, both through new entry and through the conversion of state-owned enterprises (Fisher-Vanden et al., 2004). As we will try to show through this section, the emergence of new forms of investment ownership is an additional question to explain the evolution of energy efficiency in China.

In 1985, around of 95.5 per cent of enterprises in China were classified as state-owned enterprises (SOEs). This singular structure changed dramatically with the reform of the non-state sector in the mid-1990s. In 1993, the Chinese government initiated the share holding program, which became the principal vehicle for implementing ownership reform for the SOEs (Jefferson et al., 2003). While until 1993, state-owned enterprises still dominated the scenario, in 2005 they represented less than 5 per cent of the total number of firms operating in China, while private firms represented 73.53 per cent, collective firms 6.33 per cent and foreign firms 15.38 per cent (Guariglia et al., 2008) (see the Appendix for a detailed description of ownership classification in China). Although the proportion of the state-owned economy has decreased over time, state ownership is still the main driving force in total fixed investment to date. State ownership still represents the major share in physical capital (see Luo, 2007 and Li, 2009). However, as you can see in Figure 10.7, the private sector that already accounted for slightly more than half of industrial output in 1996, reached more than 70 per cent in 2010. As has been pointed out by Dougherty et al. (2007), the private sector that has emerged in China operates much more efficiently than the public sector. Over the considered period, the share in industrial output by enterprises fully owned by the state has been decreasing from 43.5 per cent in the mid-1990s to 8.2 per cent in 2010. This decline has been accompanied by a gain in the weight of the aforementioned non-state enterprises as well as in state-holding enterprises, that is, enterprises where the percentage of state assets is larger than any other single shareholder (see Appendix and Figure 10.7).

Also, the Chinese government favoured international joint ventures between foreign and Chinese firms (over wholly owned foreign corporations) to avoid concerns about the benefits related to the presence of multinationals. Most firms are joint ventures between local (frequently state-owned) and foreign enterprises (Harrison and Rodriguez-Clare, 2010). The promotion of joint ventures has been the core of China's policy to benefit from inward investment. The goal has been to create linkages between foreign and local firms (see Fu et al., 2011). Greenaway et al. (2013) confirm that joint ventures perform better than wholly foreign-owned and purely domestic firms. These authors argue that some domestic ownership is necessary to ensure optimal performance. According to them, multinational firms seem to have played a significant role in restructuring state-owned firms by introducing new technology and better managerial skills into the domestic economy through the

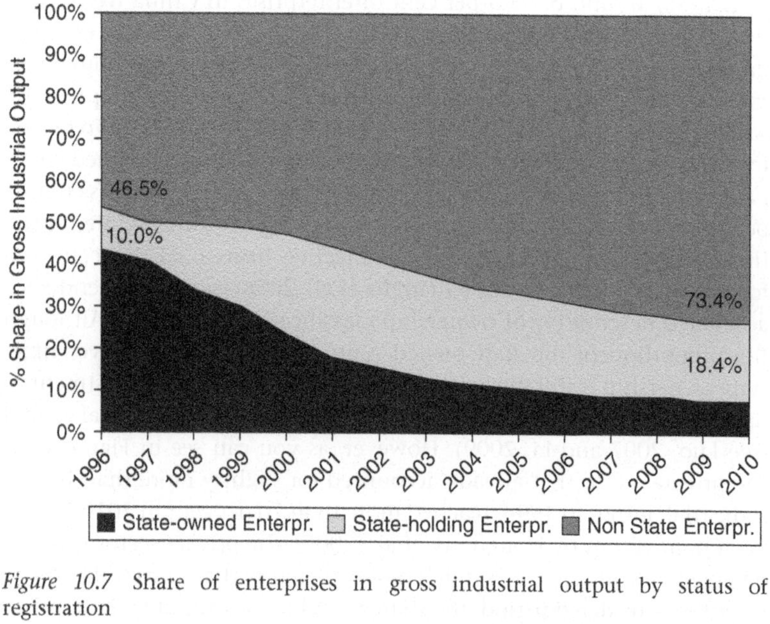

Figure 10.7 Share of enterprises in gross industrial output by status of registration

Source: National Bureau of Statistics in China.

joint ventures and indirectly through the synergies that are generated to the benefit of Chinese domestic firms. Girma et al. (2009) highlight the fact that foreign capital participation in state-owned enterprises is associated with higher innovation activity.

The hypothesis that foreign companies are more efficient in their use of energy than their domestic counterparts has been confirmed by several studies. Kumar (2003) and Sahu and Narayama (2009) confirm this hypothesis for India. According to these authors, foreign ownership in this country is associated with lower energy intensity while state ownership is found to be associated with higher energy intensity. Eskeland and Harrison (2003) found a negative effect of FDI on energy intensity for manufacturing plants in Côte d'Ivoire, Mexico and Venezuela. For China, Fisher-Vanden et al. (2004, 2006) found that foreign-invested firms in China are consistently more energy-efficient than their state-owned counterparts. Sinton and Fridley (2000) conclude that the shift from state-owned to collective, private and foreign-invested ownership plays an important role in improving energy efficiency since 1996 in China.

Results obtained by Herrerias et al. (2013) indicate that both foreign and non-state investment play a leading role in the decline of energy intensity across 28 Chinese regions. According to these authors, these findings could be reflecting the specific nature of state-investment in China, which mainly focuses on infrastructure construction such as railways, and energy-intensive industries of which energy intensity is relatively higher. In fact, state-investment has been mainly located in some energy-intensive industries that non-state owned firms find hard to access.

We can conclude that reforms carried out by China since the end of the 1970s, especially those focused on openness and changes in the patterns of investment ownership seem to be relevant drivers of energy-saving measures in China. Therefore, it seems that China should continue the policy of reform and opening up, seeking to achieve a more balanced structure of ownership that may contribute to a more efficient allocation of resources into the energy sector.

3 Regional heterogeneity and energy efficiency

An additional and important question to address in the analysis of the energy situation in China is the high level of regional heterogeneity. Since the opening and reform policy of 1978, China's modernization strategies have been focused on the development of the coastal areas.

Thus, regardless of whether the issue is economic performance or energy consumption, eastern China is always the leading area, with central and western China falling substantially behind. This unbalanced regional growth has been translated into differences in the need for energy resources (Huang and Todd, 2010 and Herrerias et al., 2013). As we can observe in Table 10.1, East provinces require more energy, compared to central and western ones. Regarding energy intensity, there is also a substantial variation across regions; eastern provinces being those that register lower values for the energy intensity index: 42 versus 65.9 for central provinces and 88.9 for western provinces in 2009. These differences are amplified when we compare provinces bilaterally. The highest energy intensity of some provinces is six times higher than the lowest one.

A feature common to almost all provinces is the declining trend in energy intensity through the considered period, although with temporary disruptions in several years and provinces, particularly in western ones. Nevertheless, as the coefficients of variation in the above table clearly show, the decline in average energy intensity does not indicate a process of convergence in energy intensity across provinces in recent decades. Considering the 28 provinces into which China is divided, this coefficient increased from 0.36 to 0.49 between 1985 and 1995, remaining almost constant and around a 0.5 value from 1995 to 2009. These values imply that there has been no convergence in energy intensity across provinces within China. Furthermore, whereas the pattern of intra-regional convergence in the central and western provinces is similar to the whole of China, the eastern provinces present a pattern of increasing divergence, with increasing values for the coefficient of variation between 1990 (0.53) and 2009 (0.67). The same conclusions are reached by Huang and Todd (2010) and Wu (2012), which show that western regions recorded with the highest average energy intensity, followed in turn by the central and coastal regions, with no evidence of convergence in regional energy intensity.

These facts show that the effective reduction of energy intensity in the Western provinces and the narrowing of the regional gap are of great practical importance for reducing China's overall energy intensity. Therefore, as has been pointed out by several authors, Chinese authorities should incorporate a regional perspective while formulating and implementing energy policies.[11] Instead, some local officials only pursue GDP growth, without concern for energy-saving and environmental protection (Liao et al., 2007). According to Herrerias and Liu (2013), divergence in energy

Table 10.1 Energy consumption and energy intensity across Chinese regions, 1985–2009

	Total energy consumption (10,000 tce)						Energy intensity (Index, Total China 1985 = 100)					
	1985	1990	1995	2000	2005	2009	1985	1990	1995	2000	2005	2009
East provinces												
Beijing	2,249	2,709	3,518	4,144	5,522	6,570	77.4	63.6	47.2	34.1	25.8	21.8
Tianjin	1,677	2,071	2,569	2,794	4,085	5,874	94.0	90.0	64.0	40.8	31.0	29.0
Hebei	4,715	6,124	8,990	11,196	19,836	25,419	221.8	213.8	166.2	126.9	135.8	125.8
Liaoning	6,342	7,856	9,671	10,656	13,611	19,112	108.6	93.7	70.9	51.7	39.0	37.2
Shanghai	2,362	3,175	4,466	5,499	8,225	10,367	33.9	34.6	26.3	18.8	16.0	14.6
Jiangsu		5,509	8,047	8,612	17,167	23,709		73.3	48.9	30.8	33.5	31.3
Zhejiang	1,711	2,580	4,580	6,560	12,032	15,567	53.1	55.6	41.2	35.0	34.8	31.6
Fujian	942	1,451	2,280	3,463	6,142	8,916	59.3	57.5	38.9	34.3	36.6	35.7
Shandong	4,640	6,830	8,780	11,362	24,162	32,420	90.9	89.8	53.2	40.9	47.9	43.7
Guangdong	2,529	4,065	7,345	9,448	17,921	24,654	85.2	73.4	54.2	41.4	42.2	40.4
Guangxi	1,015	1,309	2,384	2,669	4,869	7,075	74.1	71.0	63.9	47.7	52.1	50.8
Hainan		121	303	480	822	1,233						
Total East Prov.	28,182	43,800	62,933	76,883	134,394	180,916	89.8	83.3	61.4	45.7	45.0	42.0
CV East Prov.							0.54	0.53	0.58	0.59	0.67	0.67
Central provinces												
Shanxi	3,619	4,710	8,413	6,728	12,750	15,576	202.3	197.4	215.3	107.3	109.8	99.7
Jilin	2,637	3,523	4,109	3,766	5,315	7,698	167.5	150.1	108.6	62.4	53.1	50.7
Inner Mongolia	1,835	2,424	2,632	3,549	9,666	15,344	128.1	120.9	80.5	64.2	79.4	76.5
Heilongjiang	3,822	5,285	5,935	6,166	8,050	10,467	155.6	156.7	122.0	83.0	65.5	60.9
Anhui	2,037	2,761	4,194	4,879	6,506	8,896	139.5	142.3	120.3	86.9	70.2	66.1
Jiangxi	1,339	1,732	2,392	2,505	4,286	5,813	101.0	91.5	77.0	51.6	50.9	48.3
Henan	4,066	5,206	6,473	7,919	14,625	19,751	141.6	122.7	83.0	62.7	67.5	62.7
Hubei	2,996	3,997	5,655	6,269	10,082	13,708	117.9	116.2	92.9	64.9	64.2	59.3
Hunan	2,938	3,821	5,426	4,071	9,709	13,331	128.3	121.1	104.6	49.4	72.3	68.6
Total Central Prov.	25,289	33,459	45,229	45,852	80,989	110,584	142.4	135.4	111.6	70.3	70.3	65.9
CV Central Prov.							0.20	0.21	0.36	0.25	0.23	0.22

Continued

Table 10.1 Continued

	Total Energy Consumption (10,000 tce)						Energy intensity (Index, Total China 1985 = 100)					
	1985	1990	1995	2000	2005	2009	1985	1990	1995	2000	2005	2009
Western provinces												
Sichuan	4,749	6,353	9,525	8,946	16,759	23,352	136.1	130.9	111.1	67.1	74.4	69.7
Guizhou	1,202	2,133	3,183	4,279	5,641	7,566	154.6	198.1	194.6	172.2	139.8	133.9
Yunnan	1,296	1,954	2,641	3,468	6,024	8,032	102.9	99.3	81.5	70.4	79.6	75.0
Shaanxi	1,698	2,239	3,134	2,731	5,571	8,044	103.2	88.0	79.0	41.3	48.5	48.1
Gansu	1,735	2,172	2,738	3,012	4,368	5,482	146.4	116.1	91.6	62.9	54.8	49.7
Qinghai	322	507	688	897	1,670	2,348	122.2	149.0	140.5	120.4	127.1	129.6
Ningxia	370	707	759	1,179	2,536	3,388	97.5	127.2	92.4	91.7	117.0	110.4
Xinjiang	1,340	2,063	2,830	3,328	5,506	7,526	148.2	142.9	112.4	91.3	93.5	95.0
Total Western Prov.	12,712	18,128	25,498	27,840	48,075	65,738	126.4	131.4	112.9	89.7	91.8	88.9
CV Western Prov.							0.17	0.24	0.32	0.43	0.34	0.35
CV All Chinese Prov.							0.36	0.39	0.49	0.52	0.51	0.52

Notes: i) We have excluded Tibet and Hainan Island (for energy intensity) due missing data.
ii) Chongqing is included as part of Sichuan province, given that it was part of Sichuan until 1997.
iii) CV: Coefficient of Variation.

Source: National Bureau of Statistics of China and China Energy Databook.

intensity could imply a lack of diffusion of energy-related technologies across regions. These authors provide empirical evidence in favour of convergence in the majority of the Chinese regions in terms of electricity intensity over the period 2003–09. Their findings indicate that this convergence occurs within clubs, although some regions still show divergence. They conclude that a common energy policy for all regions may fail, with it being necessary to design specific energy-saving policies for each of the clusters detected.

Similarly, by using panel data of China's 30 provinces from 1988 to 2007, Yu (2012) highlights that, when creating energy-saving policies, the Chinese government did not previously consider the regional variation in energy intensity. In fact, in the 11th Five-Year Plan period (2006–10), the central government stipulated that all provinces should reduce the energy intensity at a parallel percentage per year.

It seems that, as Chinese regions become more developed, energy use becomes more efficient and hence energy intensity falls. That is, the transformation of the economic structure has a positive effect on the way energy is consumed (Huang and Todd, 2010). Thus, national energy policies and regional strategies in China are inseparable. Also, as regions increase their level of economic development, an increase in energy consumption is expected. Thus, as Wu (2012) has recently stressed, in the coming decades, there is a need for urgent policy action to reduce energy intensity through structural changes in China's regional economies. To catch up with the leading eastern region, western and central China require special strategies to help gain much more advanced technology industries and the infrastructure that accompanies them. Investment from eastern China, as well as from abroad, is vital if this goal is to be achieved.

As we have tried to highlight, openness and reforms to investment ownership seem to be important drivers for the improvement in energy efficiency. Table 10.2 shows the regional distribution of FDI inflows (as percentage of GDP) during the period 1985–2009. As it is possible to observe, eastern provinces have received the highest amount of FDI.[12] Herrerias et al. (2013) confirm a differential regional impact of FDI on energy intensity. Specifically, their results confirm that foreign ownership has a negative effect on energy intensity in the eastern region, which includes those provinces that receive the highest amount of FDI. Table 10.3 also illustrates the higher concentration of foreign companies into the eastern region.[13] This last table shows the higher proportion of state-owned investments in the central (30.5%) and western provinces (42.4%) compared with the eastern provinces (24.1%). Most of

Table 10.2 Foreign direct investment as percentage of GDP

	1985	1990	1995	2000	2005	2009
East provinces						
Beijing	0.00	2.89	7.74	6.44	4.13	3.44
Tianjin	0.80	1.40	13.57	12.45	7.27	8.25
Hebei	0.03	0.23	2.28	1.68	1.53	1.46
Liaoning	0.10	1.22	4.18	4.52	3.62	6.93
Shanghai	0.43	1.22	10.81	5.48	6.03	4.78
Jiangsu	0.06	0.52	7.71	6.22	5.81	5.02
Zhejiang	0.12	0.28	2.94	2.17	4.64	3.23
Fujian	1.88	2.90	16.04	8.36	7.65	3.20
Shandong	0.03	0.52	4.38	2.95	3.91	1.61
Guangdong	2.86	4.89	14.27	9.43	4.46	3.38
Guangxi	0.22	0.35	3.72	2.09	0.75	0.91
Max East Prov.	2.86	4.89	16.04	12.45	7.65	8.25
Central provinces						
Shanxi	0.01	0.04	0.49	1.01	0.53	0.77
Jilin	0.08	0.75	6.60	2.09	2.57	3.35
Inner Mongolia	0.10	0.41	6.00	2.95	2.90	2.23
Heilongjiang	0.16	0.86	3.13	2.90	2.23	2.00
Anhui	0.02	0.08	2.22	0.91	1.03	2.64
Jiangxi	0.08	0.08	2.05	0.94	4.82	3.59
Henan	0.04	0.06	1.34	0.88	0.94	1.68
Hubei	0.00	1.07	4.37	2.20	2.70	1.93
Hunan	0.16	0.08	1.90	1.59	2.57	2.40
Max Central Prov.	0.16	1.07	6.60	2.95	4.82	3.59
Western provinces						
Sichuan	0.02	0.09	0.96	0.92	0.97	1.73
Guizhou	0.07	0.60	1.26	1.57	0.80	0.31
Yunnan	0.03	0.03	1.53	0.53	0.40	1.01
Shaanxi	0.14	0.54	2.60	1.32	1.34	1.26
Gansu	0.08	0.24	1.63	0.49	0.09	0.27
Qinghai	0.00	0.00	0.00	1.25	3.95	1.36
Ningxia	0.31	0.87	3.19	2.55	1.88	0.72
Xinjiang	0.04	0.14	0.68	0.12	0.15	0.34
Max Western Prov.	0.31	0.87	3.19	2.55	3.95	1.73
Max prov. Total China	2.86	4.89	16.04	12.45	7.65	8.25

Source: National Bureau of Statistics of China.

Table 10.3 Investment in fixed assets by status of registration and region in 2009 (percentage over the total in each province/region)

	Domestic									Foreign			
	State-owned	Collective-owned	Cooperative	Joint	Limited Liability	Share holding	Private	Others	Total Domestic	Hong Kong, Macao, Taiwan	Rest of the World	Total Foreign	Total
East provinces													
Beijing	33.5	1.5	0.2	0.1	45.9	3.2	4.7	1.4	90.5	3.8	5.7	9.5	100.0
Tianjin	37.1	4.8	0.3	0.4	29.9	9.7	7.8	1.9	91.9	2.5	5.6	8.1	100.0
Hebei	21.4	7.0	0.6	0.3	24.9	6.3	29.5	6.4	96.5	1.3	2.2	3.5	100.0
Liaoning	20.7	3.2	0.6	0.1	23.5	5.6	30.8	4.0	88.6	4.6	6.9	11.4	100.0
Shanghai	47.0	3.0	0.2	1.3	17.5	2.9	15.2	0.3	87.3	4.2	8.5	12.7	100.0
Jiangsu	17.8	3.7	0.3	0.2	20.0	4.1	36.1	3.7	85.8	5.3	8.8	14.2	100.0
Zhejiang	23.7	2.6	0.4	0.4	28.4	4.5	23.7	6.1	89.8	5.3	5.0	10.2	100.0
Fujian	33.2	3.8	0.2	0.4	16.2	3.7	22.9	5.9	86.3	8.3	5.3	13.7	100.0
Shandong	15.2	10.8	0.7	0.1	24.9	6.6	25.6	9.6	93.5	2.4	4.1	6.5	100.0
Guangdong	27.5	5.3	0.5	0.4	23.8	4.8	14.9	6.1	83.3	10.4	6.3	16.7	100.0
Guangxi	31.5	2.3	0.5	0.7	21.3	7.7	19.5	10.8	94.3	2.9	2.9	5.7	100.0
Hainan	32.8	0.1	1.0	0.1	28.6	11.1	10.4	4.0	88.2	5.7	6.1	11.8	100.0
Total East Prov.	24.1	5.1	0.5	0.3	24.2	5.4	24.3	5.6	89.6	4.7	5.7	10.4	100.0
Central provinces													
Shanxi	46.0	4.8	0.3	0.5	24.0	5.3	11.0	5.5	97.8	1.1	1.1	2.2	100.0
Jilin	27.6	0.9	0.3	0.1	36.8	6.9	19.2	4.5	96.2	1.3	2.5	3.8	100.0
Inner Mongolia	38.6	0.9	0.7	0.2	33.1	8.8	12.2	2.8	97.4	1.2	1.4	2.6	100.0
Heilongjiang	41.0	1.3	0.4	0.0	23.2	10.8	11.4	9.2	97.3	0.9	1.8	2.7	100.0
Anhui	26.9	1.8	0.5	0.3	26.1	6.1	25.6	7.9	95.2	2.7	2.1	4.8	100.0
Jiangxi	25.8	1.2	0.9	0.3	23.5	9.0	25.2	6.3	92.1	3.3	4.6	7.9	100.0

Continued

Table 10.3 Continued

	Domestic									Foreign			
	State-owned	Collective-owned	Cooperative	Joint	Limited Liability	Share holding	Private	Others	Total Domestic	Hong Kong, Macao, Taiwan	Rest of the World	Total Foreign	Total
Henan	17.9	6.5	1.0	0.3	21.0	8.0	30.0	13.1	97.9	1.0	1.1	2.1	100.0
Hubei	33.3	4.5	0.6	0.5	22.0	8.4	18.7	7.0	95.0	2.5	2.5	5.0	100.0
Hunan	35.8	2.1	1.4	0.4	19.8	8.5	19.8	9.5	97.4	1.3	1.3	2.6	100.0
Total Central Prov.	30.5	3.0	0.7	0.3	25.0	8.0	20.9	7.9	96.3	1.7	2.0	3.7	100.0
Western provinces													
Chongqing	33.3	0.7	0.2	0.8	28.4	5.2	21.4	4.1	94.1	3.6	2.3	5.9	100.0
Sichuan	38.3	0.8	0.4	0.2	27.3	6.7	12.6	10.1	96.4	1.4	2.2	3.6	100.0
Guizhou	45.3	0.5	0.8	0.8	22.1	3.6	16.7	7.3	96.9	0.8	2.2	3.1	100.0
Yunnan	46.1	2.1	0.3	0.1	20.9	7.1	14.0	6.7	97.3	1.5	1.3	2.7	100.0
Tibet	70.7	0.3	0.3	0.0	5.0	1.3	4.4	18.0	99.9	0.0	0.1	0.1	100.0
Shaanxi	46.9	4.9	0.4	0.3	21.4	6.0	11.1	5.9	97.0	1.7	1.3	3.0	100.0
Gansu	53.4	2.4	0.2	0.2	19.7	4.4	9.7	8.3	98.2	1.2	0.5	1.8	100.0
Qinghai	49.6	0.9	0.9	0.1	25.8	9.4	7.6	4.2	98.5	0.2	1.3	1.5	100.0
Ningxia	34.4	0.3	0.1	0.1	36.9	2.8	19.6	4.4	98.6	0.0	1.4	1.4	100.0
Xinjiang	46.0	0.3	0.1	0.1	18.9	17.9	10.1	5.4	98.8	0.6	0.5	1.2	100.0
Total Western Prov.	42.4	1.7	0.4	0.3	24.3	6.8	13.7	7.3	96.8	1.6	1.7	3.2	100.0
Total China	31.0	3.8	0.5	0.3	23.9	6.3	20.9	6.5	93.1	3.2	3.7	6.9	100.0

Source: National Bureau of Statistics of China.

the studies we referred to throughout Section 2 find that state ownership is associated with higher energy intensity (see Herrerias et al., 2013; Fisher-Vanden et al., 2004 and Sinton and Fridley for China). Therefore, regional heterogeneity in energy intensity across China could be also related to the structure of investment ownership.

4 Summing up and policy implications

Given China's economic size and high energyintensity, the analysis of energy efficiency policies in this country has a significant influence on the global effort to reduce energy demand and to improve the quality of the environment worldwide. In spite of the improvements in energy efficiency during the 1980s and most of the 1990s, there is much room for development in China's energy situation. We have tried to highlight throughout this chapter the relative contribution of those factors which might have major relevance in explaining changes in aggregate energy intensity in China. Similarly to most previous studies about this topic, we can conclude that structural change has made a marginal contribution to the decline in energy intensity. The potential effect of the relative stability in the industrial sector's share of energy intensity has been compensated by an increase in the importance of heavy industry. Thus, technology diffusion is a key factor in explaining the improvement in energy efficiency in China. Efficiency in the use of energy has improved mainly due to new processes, technologies and equipment, which were accompanied by the extensive application of energy-saving technologies and the development of management skills. This process seems to be mainly related to the openness process and the reforms in the structure of investment ownership in the country. These findings reveal the importance of fostering international diffusion of energy-saving technologies, encouraging research and development of energy-saving technologies and improving energy-saving legislation. In bringing in foreign investment, China should pay primary attention to the introduction of foreign advanced technologies, and experienced management and people to further shift the focus from investing in fossil energy resources to renewable resources. However, this process might not occur automatically. It probably requires active support from China's economic policy and the economic policies of China's trading partners, as well as support from international climate policy.

Changes in economic structure seem to have affected energy intensity modestly. Thus, there is considerable scope to reduce energy intensity through the structural transformations of the Chinese economy in the future (Wu, 2012). On the one hand, it is necessary to adjust the energy consumption structure in China. Coal is still the main energy consumed, being the main cause of smoke pollution, as well as the main source of greenhouse gases. Thus, it is necessary to improve the proportion of other sources of energy in the total energy consumption. On the other hand, and in spite of the improvements in this field, China's energy market system is yet to be completed, as the energy pricing mechanism fails to fully reflect the scarcity of resources, supply and demand, and the environmental cost. Moreover, rationalization in the structure of energy prices in China is necessary, as as is the reduction or removal of energy subsidies, which will result in increasing energy prices and will have significantly positive impacts on energy conservation and CO_2 reduction. Finally, the narrowing of regional differences in China's energy intensity seems to play a key role in reducing China's overall energy intensity. The Chinese government should develop a diversity of energy-saving policies to account for heterogeneity in energy efficiency across regions.

Acknowledgements

The authors gratefully acknowledge the financial support from the Spanish Ministerio de Economía y Competitividad and FEDER (ECO2011-28155), Generalitat Valenciana PROMETEO/2009/068, and Pla de Promoció de la Investigació Fundació Caixa Castelló-Bancaixa (P1.1B2013-22 and P1.1B2010-17).

Appendix: Business registration categories defined in China Statistical Yearbook, 2010

Registration status	Definition
Domestically Funded Enterprises	
State-owned enterprises: Non-corporate economic entities, where all assets are owned by the state.	
State-holding enterprises: Enterprises where the percentage of state assets (or shares by the state) is larger than any other single shareholder of the same enterprise.	
Collective-owned enterprises: Economic entities where assets are owned collectively. Ownership is considered to be public.	

Cooperative enterprises: Economic units set up on a cooperative basis, with funding partly from employees of the enterprise and partly from outside investment, where the operation and management is decided by all the members who also participate in the production.

Joint ownership enterprises: Economic units established by joint investment by two or more corporate enterprises or institutions of the same or different types of ownership.

Limited liability corporations: Economic units with capital from 2 to 49 investors. Limited liability corporations include state sole funded corporations and other limited liability corporations.

Share-holding corporations: Economic units with total registered capital divided into equal shares and rose through issuing stocks.

Private enterprises: Economic units invested or controlled (by holding the majority of the shares) by natural persons who hire workers for profit-making activities. Included in this category are private limited liability corporations, private share- holding corporations Ltd., private partnership enterprises and private sole investment enterprises.

Foreign Funded Enterprises

Enterprises with Funds from Hong Kong, Macao and Taiwan: All industrial enterprises registered as the joint-venture, cooperative, sole (exclusive) investment industrial enterprises and limited liability corporations with funds from Hong Kong, Macao and Taiwan.

Foreign Funded Enterprises: All industrial enterprises registered as the joint-venture, cooperative, sole (exclusive) investment industrial enterprises and limited liability corporations with foreign funds.

Source: National Bureau of Statistics of China.

Notes

1. See also Wolfram et al. (2012).
2. This variable refers to the amount of energy consumed relative to GDP.
3. China's total consumptions of coal and crude oil are about 34.4 per cent and 8.2 per cent of world consumption, respectively (Chai et al., 2009).
4. Chai et al. (2009) indicate that low coal price easily leads to high consumption of coal with a low efficiency resource in proportion to other energy types.
5. For simplicity throughout the paper we refer to the various components of the administrative division of China as provinces.
6. According to Lin and Jiang (2011), in 2007 the highest share of subsidy corresponded to diesel oil (26.52 per cent), followed by gasoline (21.66%); electricity (21.41%); coal (14.91%); natural gas (10.68%) and fuel oil (4.82%).
7. See IEA (2007).

8. See IEA (2007) and Dansie et al. (2010).
9. Heavy industry had been the principal beneficiary of trade protection and government subsidies (Fisher-Vanden et al., 2006).
10. Authors calculations based on World Development Indicators.
11. See for example Akkemik et al. (2012); Wu (2012) and Yu (2012).
12. Xu and Sheng (2012) also illustrate the geographic distribution of FDI inflows into China with the bulk of FDI concentrating in the easter region.
13. In 2009, the percentage of foreign investment over the total investment in fixed assets was 10.4 versus 3.7 for central provinces and 3.2 for western provinces.

11
Globalization and Energy Consumption in the Yangtze River Delta

Maoliang Bu and Huajiang Luo

1 Backgrounds

1.1 Yangtze River Delta in the globalization era

The Yangtze River Delta (also called Yangzi Jiang Delta, Tai Lake Region) is at the intersection of Chinese coastal regions and the lower reaches of the Yangtze River, including the triangular-shaped territory of Shanghai city, Jiangsu province and Zhejiang province. The urban build-up in the area has given rise what may be the largest concentration of adjacent metropolitan areas in the world (Gottmann, 1961). It covers an area of 99,600 km^2 and is home to over 105 million people as of 2010, of which an estimated 80 million are urban. Lo and Marcotullio (2001) referred the delta as a major player in the newly emerged "world manufacturing belt" of Asia, due to its huge manufacturing capacity. Scholars have focused on the Yangtze River Delta since the 1990s, when the region's economic performance and urban changes caught the world's attention (Zhang, 2006). Hall (2002) contended that the Yangtze River Delta provides a paradigm (the Yangtze paradigm) of the 21st century megacity in terms of economic growth and spatial expansion. Friedmann (2005) studied the Yangtze River Delta in an examination of China's urban transition and its bottom-up urbanization. More recently, the Institute for Yangtze River Delta Socioeconomic Development at Nanjing University has published a series of research reports on the Yangtze River Delta, including Liu and Zheng (2011, 2012).

The development of the Yangtze River Delta is closely related with China's overall open- door and reform policy since 1978. China has experienced fantastic changes since then (Naughton, 2007). Drawing foreign direct investment (FDI) to China has become an important part of market economy construction. And at the same time, it is also a positive initiative in response to the trends of economic globalization and international division of labour. The amount of FDI flow into China has reached new levels every ten years since 1987. China is now one of the countries that attracts the highest amount of FDI flow in the world. Figure 11.1 represents the FDI flows into China since 1984. The total amount of FDI in China was only USD 80,000 in 1979. It rose to USD 3,487 billion in 1990, 60-times that of ten years ago. The amount increased to USD 40,715 billion in 2000 an increase of nearly 11-times in ten years. The amount reached USD 106 billion in 2010 and China ranked second after United States. In the years 1979–2010, the total amount of FDI flow into China reached USD 1,063,583 billion, and China became the developing country that attracted the most FDI worldwide. Now China is the country that attracts the most FDI flows among developing countries Table 11.1 shows the top ten countries for FDI in the world in 1979, 2000 and 2010. In 1979, China ranked 126th with FDI flow only USD 0.8 million. China ranked 9th in 2000. And in 2010 China ranked second after United States. From these figures, we can see

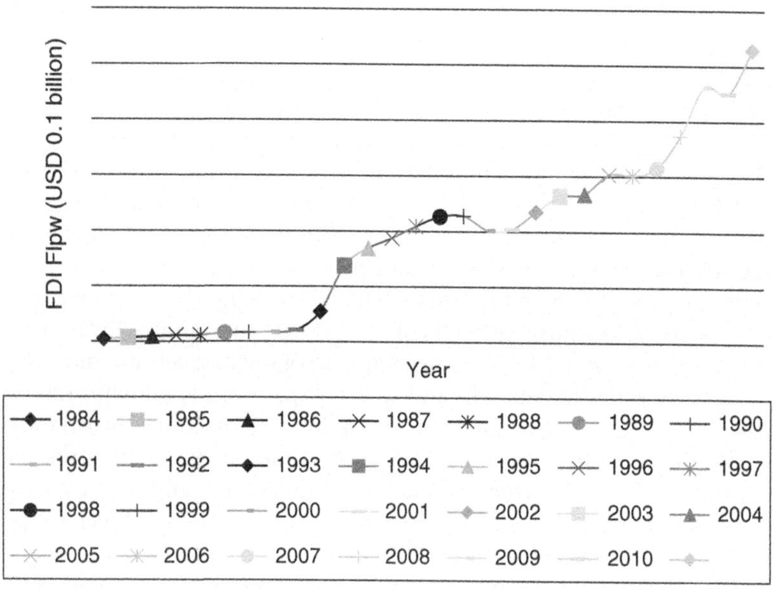

Figure 11.1 FDI flow into China, 1984–2010
Source: China Statistical Yearbook (2011).

Table 11.1 The top ten countries of inward FDI around the world (USD billion), 1979–2010

	1979		2000		2010	
Rank	**Country or region**	**FDI**	**Country or region**	**FDI**	**Country or region**	**FDI**
1	USA	8.7	USA	314	USA	228
2	UK	6.5	Germany	198.3	China	106
3	Canada	5.3	UK	118.8	HK, China	69
4	France	2.7	Belgium–Luxembourg	88.7	Belgium	62
5	Brazil	2.4	Canada	66.8	Brazil	48
6	Germany	1.7	Netherlands	63.9	Germany	46
7	Netherlands	1.7	HongKong, China	61.9	UK	46
8	Australia	1.5	France	43.3	Russia	41
9	Spain	1.4	China	40.7	Singapore	39
10	Egypt	1.2	Spain	39.6	France	34
126	China	0.0008				

Note: The data source is from China's National Bureau of Statistics. "Reform and opening up 30 years report", available athttp://www.stats.gov.cn/tjfx/ztfx/jnggkf30n/t20081117_402517351.htm.

that tremendous change has happened within China in attracting FDI. And FDI has kept a high growth rate.

The Yangtze River Delta, as the earliest region in China opening to the outside world, attracted FDI flows earlier than other places. And it also attracted a huge amount of FDI flows. Figure 11.2 shows the annual FDI flow in the Yangtze River Delta between 1984 and 2009 and Figure 11.3 represents the growth rate of FDI in the Yangtze River Delta. We can see that in middle 1980s and early 1990s, although FDI was limited, the growth rate was maintained at a very high level and FDI increased quickly. After that, the growth rate continued at about 10 per cent each year. The amount of FDI increased quickly. Figure 11.4 shows the share of FDI of the Yangtze River Delta in China. We know that the Yangtze River Delta is the most developed region in China, therefore FDI in the Yangtze River Delta plays a unique role in China. The share of FDI in the Yangtze River Delta is nearly half of the total for the whole country.

1.2 Energy consumption

As the largest developing country in the world, China is a large energy production and consumption country. Since the 1990s, the rapid

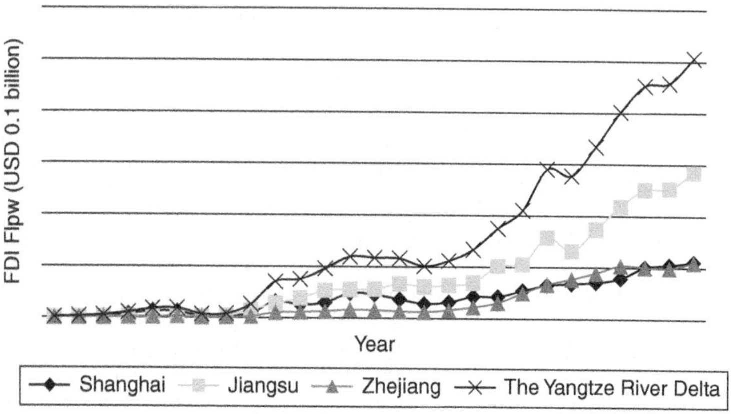

Figure 11.2 FDI flow in the Yangtze River Delta
Source: China Statistical Yearbook (2011).

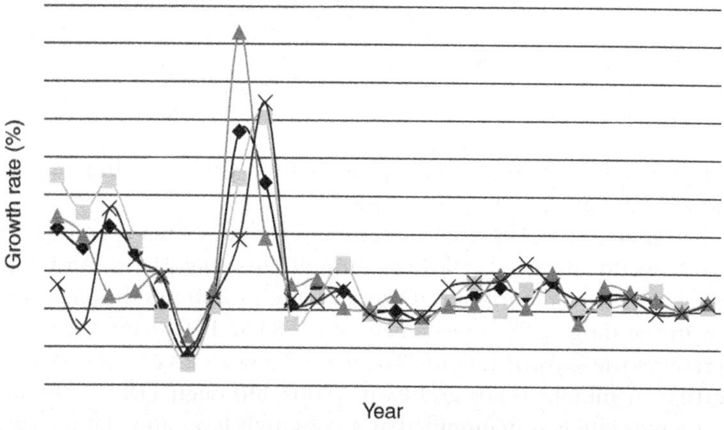

Figure 11.3 Growth rate of FDI flow in the Yangtze River Delta
Source: Statistical Yearbook series of Yangtze River Delta.

development of China's economy and the rapid improvement of people's living standards have led to a sharp rise in energy consumption. China has changed from a net energy exporter into a net energy importer since 1993. The energy demand has been greater than the energy supply. And energy demand is becoming the bottleneck in the development of China's

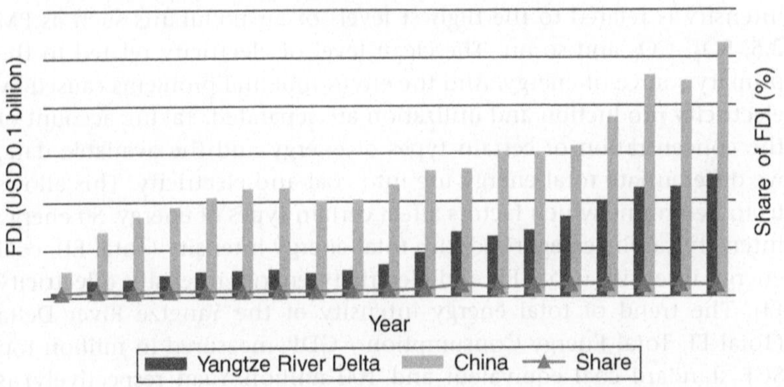

Figure 11.4 The inward FDI of the Yangtze River Delta and its share in China
Source: Statistical Yearbook series of Yangtze River Delta.

economy. In 2008 China's energy production ranked third in the world after the United States and Russia. While China's total energy consumption accounted for one-tenth of the world's total energy consumption, it ranked the second after the United States. According to the International Energy Agency (IEA), China overtook the United States to become the world's largest energy user in 2009. However, this growth in the consumption of energy resources is a relatively recent phenomenon; in 2000, Chinese energy use was only half that of the United States. The increase in China's energy consumption between 2000 and 2008 was more than four-times higher than in the previous decade (Herrerias et al., 2013). On the other hand, China's energy intensity has generally fallen since 1978, coinciding with the introduction of market-oriented and open-door reforms. Similarly with the national decrease in energy intensity, energy intensity in the Yangtze River Delta has fallen, too. And compared to Pearl River Delta, another developed area in China, the relatively later-developed Yangtze River Delta is more energy-efficient, although the energy efficiency is still only about one-tenth that of the US and one-fifth that of Japan despite the decrease in primary energy consumption per RMB GDP from 0.45 kg of standard coal equivalent (SCE) to 0.15 kg SCE in 1999 to 2009 (Sinton et al., 2004; RSEC, 2006; RSEC, 2007 and Fang et al., 2009). Further reducing primary energy consumption per unit of GDP and upgrading production technologies and managerial skills are long-term measures to save energy as well as reduce pollution.

The types of energy consumption, relate not only to energy efficiency but also to environmental performance. Generally, coal energy intensity is related to the highest levels of air pollutants such as PM 2.5, SO_2, CO_2 and so on. The clean level of electricity related to the primary source of energy. And the environmental problems caused by electricity production and utilization are separated. Taking account of the concentration of certain types of energy and the available data, we differentiate total energy use into coal and electricity. This allows us to determine which factors affect certain types of energy. So energy intensity can be categorized into total energy intensity (Total EI), coal energy intensity (Coal EI) and electricity energy intensity (Electricity EI). The trend of total energy intensity of the Yangtze River Delta (Total EI, Total Energy Consumption / GDP, measured in million ton SCE standard coal equivalent and 100 million Yuan respectively) is as described in Figure 11.5. We can easily see that total energy intensity was reducing from 1999 to 2010. The total energy intensity of Shanghai was 0.008091 in 1999, while it was only 0.0034583 in 2010, reduced by more than half on that in 1999. The total energy intensity of Jiangsu and Zhejiang in 2010 was also nearly half of that in 2000. We also reach a similar conclusion from Figures 11.6 and 11.7, being coal energy intensity (Coal Consumption / GDP, measured in million ton and 100 million Yuan respectively) and electricity energy

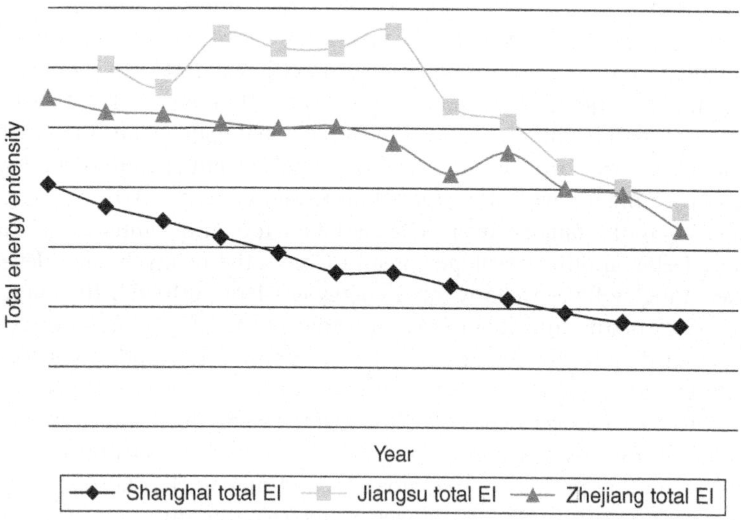

Figure 11.5 Total energy intensity of Yangtze River Delta
Source: Statistical Yearbook series of Yangtze River Delta.

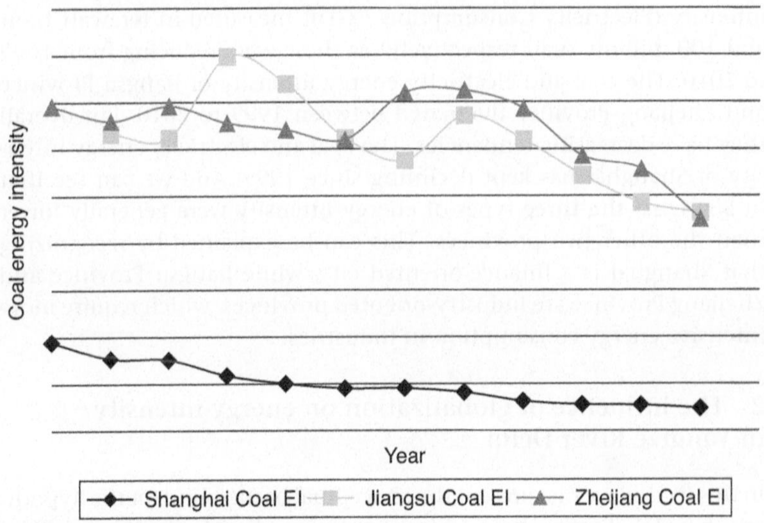

Figure 11.6 Coal energy intensity of Yangtze River Delta
Source: Statistical Yearbook series of Yangtze River Delta.

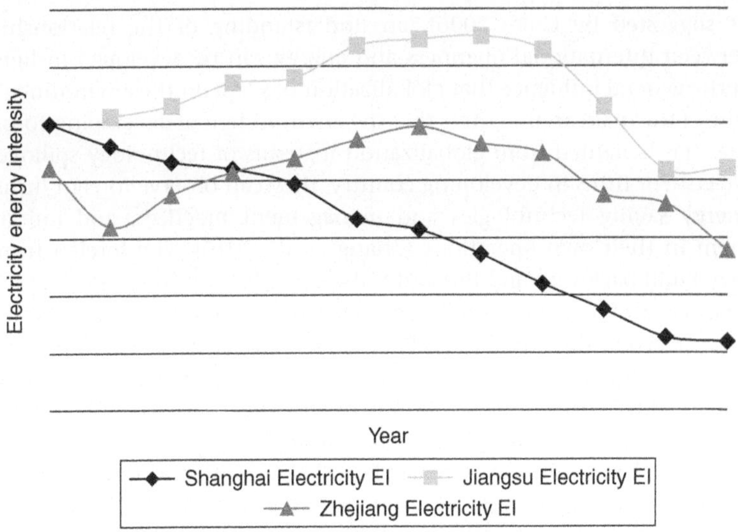

Figure 11.7 Electricity energy intensity of Yangtze River Delta
Source: Statistical Yearbook series of Yangtze River Delta.

intensity (Electricity Consumption / GDP, measured in terawatt hour and 100 million Yuan respectively) as these were reducing from 1999 to 2010. The coal and electricity energy intensity of Jiangsu Province and Zhejiang Province fluctuated between 1999 to 2010. But overall they have decreasing tendencies. The coal and electricity energy intensity of Shanghai has kept declining since 1999. And we can see that in Shanghai the three types of energy intensity were generally lower than the other two provinces. This can be explained by recognizing that Shanghai is a finance-oriented city, while Jiangsu Province and Zhejiang Province are industry-oriented provinces, which require more intensive energy consumption in industries.

2 The influence of globalization on energy intensity in Yangtze River Delta

In this section we first present the conceptual background for the hypothesis that globalization has an energy-reducing effect in the Yangtze River Delta. Special attention will be given to the possible mechanisms of the effect. Then we will perform an empirical test based on the city panel-data of Yangtze River Delta.

2.1 Theoretical mechanisms

As suggested by Cole (2006), an understanding of the relationship between international openness and energy can be developed in light of the general influence that globalization has had on the environment. One of the main arguments is that the environment of developing countries has benefited from globalization in terms of technology spillover effects. For firms in developing country, they can observe foreign firms' energy saving technologies and management practices, and imitate them in their own operations (Zhang et al., 2010). The foreign firms may build backward and forward linkages with firms in the developing country. And in these cases, knowledge from these foreign firms can be transmitted to the suppliers and distributors and ultimately to domestic firms which use the same suppliers and distributors (Spencer, 2008). As suggested by institutional economic theory, this process can be referred to as institutional isomorphism (Strang and Meyer, 1993). Dimaggio and Walter (1983) outline three major types of pressure that facilitate these isomorphic changes: coercive, mimetic and normative. In this way, the energy conservation capabilities of the firms in developing countries can be enhanced. Albornoz et al. (2009) point out some evidence for the existence of environmental spillovers.

Another mechanism of the energy-reducing effect of globalization is the exposure to more pressures from foreign customers, because energy pollution caused by suppliers could threaten the social legitimacy of foreign customers even when damage is limited to the export country. Bansal and Kendall (2000) point out individual firms respond to global norms to the extent that they are pressured to legitimize themselves by adhering to these norms even in the absence of specific government sanctions. The positive role of such pressures has been highlighted in prior published literature. Christmann and Taylor (2001) propose that such pressures force firms in developing countries to self-regulate. With self-regulation, firms go beyond the requirements of government regulations and improve their environmental performance. Other studies highlight the role of such pressures in "trading up" (e.g., Vogel, 1995; Young, 2003). Trading up is the idea that as exporters from countries with low environmental standards seek access to the markets of countries with higher environmental standards, they are forced to meet the more stringent environmental standards of their trading partners. Andonova (2003) points out those firms are under "reputation pressure" in international markets and that establishing a green image is important. The key points of this mechanism are: (i) the environmentally related pressure is imposed through the supply chain among different countries; and (ii) the pressure can be internalized by the exporting firms and changed into organic behaviour (improvement in environmental performance).

So far, there has been abundant research on the topic of globalization and the environment. But, researchers have not paid equal attention to globalization and local energy consumption. To the best of our knowledge, only a few studies have examined the influence of trade and FDI on the diffusion and implementation of energy conservation technologies and the adoption of better energy management. Eskeland and Harrison (2003) compare foreign plants and domestic plants, and find that foreign plants are significantly more energy-efficient and use cleaner types of energy. Batrakova and Davies (2012) analyse the consequences of becoming an exporter on a firm's energy consumption. They show theoretically and empirically with firm-level data that the increase in energy use when exporting is negatively correlated with energy intensity. This is because, although energy use rises with exports (due to production and transportation), the rise can be offset by adopting more energy-efficient technology. However, results obtained by Hübler and Keller (2010) for a sample of 60 developing countries (including China) do not find evidence for a general or uniform influence of FDI on energy intensity. More recently, Herrerias et al. (2013) suggest that openness to FDI and imports has been a driving force in the reduction of energy intensity in China.

2.2 Empirical analysis

We collect data from the statistical yearbooks of 16 cities in the core area of the Yangtze River Delta of China. The data cover total energy consumption, coal consumption, electricity consumption, foreign direct investment (FDI), import, export, energy price from 1999 to 2010.

Following the approach of Herrerias et al. (2013), we build the standard formulation of Time Series Cross-Sectional (TSCS) models under the assumption of pool ability to analyse the relationship between FDI and energy intensity for 16 cities in the Yangtze River Delta of China from 1999 to 2010. In Table 11.2, we report that part of the results that distinguishes between foreign and domestic investment as sources of potential reductions in energy intensity. In all these specifications we control for additional factors that may influence energy efficiency, such as domestic investment, the share of industry, import share, export share and energy prices. Results show that the coefficients of FDI and domestic investment are mostly negative. The coefficients of FDI are significant in the model taking total energy intensity and coal energy intensity as dependent variables. And the coefficients of FDI in the model taking electricity energy intensity as a dependent variable are not significant. It may be that the impact of FDI on energy intensity varies with certain types of energy. These findings support that foreign-invested firms use more energy-efficient technologies, and that access to foreign technologies has been a relevant factor in the reduction of energy intensity in Yangtze River Delta. As the foreign technologies have a different influence on certain types of energy, they have a different influence on certain types of energy intensity.

As different administrative regions in China have some differences in their policy, regional heterogeneity must be taken into account and

Table 11.2 Energy intensity and investment ownership by source of energy

Dependent variable	Total EI	Coal EI	Electricity EI
FDI	−0.0925***	−0.119**	−0.029
Domestic investment	−0.0787**	−0.0628	−0.0414
R-squared	0.638	0.446	0.135

Notes: * p < 0.10, **p < 0.05, *** p < −0.01. For brevity concern, Control variables, including the share of manufacturing industry, import share and energy price, are not presented in the table. However, the results are available upon requests. The same notes apply for Table 11.3.

further research is conducted. We divide the 16 cities of Yangtze River Delta into three groups according to their administrative division. Table 11.3 shows the regression results with regional heterogeneity. Similar findings are reached; that the impacts of FDI on total energy intensity and coal energy intensity are all negative and significant and the coefficients of domestic investment are negative but not significant in the three regions. However, the findings on electricity are a little different from those on total energy and coal energy intensity. The coefficient of FDI in Jiangsu is negative and fails to reach a significant level, while that in Zhejiang is positive and also fails to reach a significant level. We cautiously interpret this finding to suggest that the different influence of FDI in different cities in the Yangtze River Delta could be resulted the result of different administrative policies.

To sum up, foreign direct investment has undoubtedly been a driving force in the reduction of energy intensity in the Yangtze River Delta. However, the impact varies according to different energy types. Meanwhile, the impact also varies across regions within the Yangtze River Delta.

3 Implication and conclusions

In recent years, a number of papers have examined empirically the relationship between globalization and the environment (e.g., Bu et al., 2011, 2013; Cole and Elliott, 2003 and Grossman and Krueger, 1991). However, very few studies examine the impact of globalization on energy use and fewer still focus the role of foreign direct investment. As

Table 11.3 Energy intensity and investment ownership by source of energy with regional heterogeneity

	Total EI	**Coal EI**	**Electricity EI**
FDI*Grid1	−0.572***	−1.078***	−0.559***
FDI*Grid2	−0.136**	−0.177**	−0.0725
FDI*Grid3	−0.101***	−0.108*	0.0521
Domestic investment	−2312	−1893	−1313
R-squared	0.645	0.497	0.21

Notes: * $p < 0.10$, ** $p < 0.05$, *** $p < -0.01$.
Grid1 = 1 denotes Shanghai; 0 otherwise;
Grid2 = 1 denotes Yangtze River Delta cities belonging to Jiangsu Province; 0 otherwise;
Grid3 = 1 denotes Yangtze River Delta cities belonging to Zhejiang Province; 0 otherwise.

Source: Statistical Yearbook series of Yangtze River Delta.

pointed by Cole (2006), this neglect of energy use is very surprising since energy use, particularly the burning of fossil fuels, is the principal cause of most air pollutants. Other issues of wide public concern are the issues of energy pollution and climate change. Sanna-Randaccio (2012) argues that foreign direct investment may play a key role in the global effort to shift towards a low-carbon economy. Multinational enterprises can contribute in several important ways to climate change mitigation, by providing emissions-saving technologies, financial resources and managerial skills to resource-constrained economies. On the other hand, the fact that firms are internationally mobile may limit the possibility to implement unilateral mitigation measures, due to concerns about competitiveness and leakage. Thus, given the lack of explicit study on the relationship of globalization and energy, this chapter analyses the influence of globalization on energy consumption, by taking the case of the Yangtze River Delta, China.

The Yangtze River Delta not only contributes the most to China's manufacturing sector, it also possibly ranks first in terms of globalization involvement across Chinese regions. Therefore, the Yangtze River Delta provides a good case for the research of globalization and energy consumption, given that the remaining regions of China are mainly at a different level of economic development. That said, as China's reform policy depends highly on local government experimentation, the experience of the Yangtze River Delta can significantly influence the development route of the rest regions. In this sense, it is important to know what is happening in the Yangtze River Delta, to better know the future of China.

This chapter focused its analysis on cities across the Yangtze River Delta from 1999 to 2010 by using panel-data techniques. Specifically, we used panel-corrected standard errors models (PCSE), which allow us to consider the well-known heterogeneity both across regions and over time. The findings show that foreign direct investment has improved the energy efficiency of the Yangtze River Delta. The results are consistent across three sources of energy: total energy, coal and electricity. We made further empirical study to consider internal differences within the Yangtze River Delta and to capture the regional heterogeneity. The results maintain the energy-reducing effect in Shanghai, Jiangsu and Zhejiang, however, with small differences across regions.

We tend to explain this kind of energy-reducing effect of foreign direct investment in Yangtze River Delta by two main mechanisms. One is technology spillover; usually, foreign investors are equipped with superior energy saving technology and are more experienced with energy management. The second is increased pressure; with more inward foreign direct investment, Yangtze River Delta is exposed to more and more international public monitoring, which could encourage self-regulation to build a green image.

Given the large economic size and high energy intensity of the Yangtze River Delta, the analysis of energy efficiency policies in this region has a significant influence on the integral effect to reduce energy demand and to improve environmental quality across China. Therefore, in the long run, to save more energy, it is very important for China to foster international diffusion of energy technologies and increase its exposure to international public monitoring.

12

Institutional Barriers to China's Renewable Energy Strategy

Evan B. Hills and Zhengxu Wang

1 Introduction

China, soon to be the world's largest economy, is renowned for its impressive growth and development over the past thirty years. This has been mostly fuelled by fossil fuels, which, as has been widely discussed, have negative effects on the environment. As of June 2010, China was the largest carbon emitter in the world, and its emissions are only forecast to grow in the future (Zhang, 2010). These emissions have had wide-reaching negative effects upon the environment. On top of relying on fossil fuels, China's energy intensity – energy consumption per unit of GDP – is 2.4 times the global average, meaning that to produce one unit of GDP, China requires 2.4 times the amount of energy that the average state requires (Oxley et al., 2010). Even when compared to India, another developing country, China's energy intensity is 1.5 times greater (Mastny, 2010).

Needless to say, this combination of reliance on fossil fuels and lack of efficiency has led to major environmental issues in China. Acid rain, caused by an overabundance of SO_2 and other greenhouse gasses in the air, has been observed in 56 per cent of Chinese cities where measurements are conducted (Li, 2010). Additionally, the waterways in China are polluted to the extent of affecting marine life, "almost all the rivers are polluted in Shanxi Province, and no fish can exist in the [contaminated] water, and the water of the river cannot be [consumed] by humans and livestock" (Liu et al., 2010, p. 303). This is caused by the over-mining of coal, and presents a phenomenon all too "familiar in the whole [of] China" (Liu et al., 2010, p. 303).

Additionally, China is a net importer of both coal and oil, and its share of imported oil is only going to rise as China's economy continues to grow. This creates a major problem for China because it means that it has to rely on external states and actors to ensure that it can attain the energy it needs to survive and grow. This concept, known as energy security, is a major headache for the Chinese government, due to the volatile nature of most oil exporting states, which is amplified by the effects that a sudden disruption in supply could have upon the Chinese economy and society. The effects of this insecurity are compounded by the fact that in 2011, almost 50 per cent of Chinese oil imports came from the Middle East, a region plagued by conflict and instability (U.S. Energy Information Administration, 2011).

The Chinese government has taken measures to address the problems of pollution and energy security by increasing the role that sustainable or renewable energy production plays in China's future. In fact, ambitious targets have been set and great effort is being made to increase the share of renewable energy in China's energy consumption. China plans on becoming a major power in the renewable energy industry through both the domestic production of renewable energy to fuel the economy, as well as the mass-production of renewable energy products, such as wind turbines and photovoltaic solar panels. China foresees renewable energy as a two-pronged opportunity for technological advancement at home, as well as commercial success abroad, with its renewable energy products competing for a large share of the global market. This is especially true in OECD states like the United States or the European countries.

As will be discussed later in this chapter, the growth of China's domestic sustainable energy sector has been impressive and swift, though by no means without flaws. While China may be extensively working towards sustainability, factors within the government are holding its progress back. Inefficiencies within the institutional structure of the Chinese government and its entities have stymied China's otherwise impressive push to sustainability over the course of the past ten years.

This chapter will first establish a definition as to what constitutes renewable energy, and then trace the evolution of China's renewable energy policy. The evolution of China's renewable energy will be viewed through two lenses. One area of focus will be the evolution of China's thinking regarding the role that renewable energy will play in its technological and economic development, as well as its energy security. The other area that this chapter will focus on is the evolution of the legal and institutional framework within the Chinese government concerning renewable energy. Next, this chapter will examine the institutional inefficiencies present in the Chinese government that inhibit, or at least retard, the proper implementation of its renewable energy policy. The focal points of this analysis will be the lack of incentive for state-owned enterprises (SOEs), the weak authority of the central government due to the fragmentation of authority, as well as the conflict between central and local government that is endemic to the structure of the government itself.

2 History of China's renewable energy policies

Renewable energy is defined by the International Energy Agency as "Energy derived from natural processes (e.g. sunlight and wind) that are replenished at faster rate than they are consumed" (International Energy Agency, 2012). Renewable energy consists of many forms of energy, including solar, wind, hydroelectric, and biomass. China's continued economic development will require increasingly large amounts of energy to sustain itself and in the interest of its environmental and energy security, China will be forced to seek renewable sources of energy.

China's history with renewable energy technology has been brief, but its recent ascent has been swift. China's first pilot wind farm was established in Rongcheng City, in Shandong, in 1986, also known as the 863 program (Wang, 2010). The first major renewable energy initiative was the Bright Project, which was established in 1996, with the goal of bringing renewable energy to two million Chinese citizens (Zhang et al., 2009). The Tenth Five-Year Plan (2000–05) established goals for installed wind and solar energy capacity for 2005. These goals included an installed wind generation capacity of over 1.5 million kW, and installed photovoltaic (solar) generation capacity of 80 MW (Shi, 2000).

The next major piece of legislation was the Renewable Energy Law (REL), which was brought into effect in 2006. This law stipulated the long-term goals for renewable energy in China, along with how to implement them, including which institutions of the government were responsible for the various aspects of the plan. The REL was a major step forward in China's sustainable development, as it offered a holistic plan for how to utilize renewable energy, en masse, to satisfy China's energy needs. Evidence of the success of the REL lies in the numbers: in 2004, China's installed wind power capacity was 760.2 MW, whereas at the end of 2010 it was 41,827.3 MW, or in other words, average annual growth of more than 100 per cent (Fang et al., 2012). It goes without saying that this capacity to install new sustainable sources of energy at this rate is extremely effective and is no doubt a major boon for China's future aspirations.

In 2007, the National Development and Reform Committee developed the Medium- and Long-Term Development Plan for Renewable Energy (MLTPRE), which was designed to establish over-arching targets for China's renewable energy development. The MLTPRE established the means through which China was going to achieve the desired sustainability standards, by using hydropower, wind, solar and biomass, and by integrating those into social and economic objectives. Additionally, the MLTPRE set goals for the percentage of total energy consumption that is supposed to come from renewable energy, to be 10 per cent in 2010 and 15 per cent by 2020 (Campbell, 2011).

The recent 11th and 12th Five-Year Plans have both heavily addressed the issues of sustainability in a number of ways. The 11th Five-Year Plan allocated USD 172 million for various sustainability projects through the 863 Program. It also established and achieved a 20 per cent energy intensity reduction target from 2005 levels at the end of 2010 (Hilton et al., 2012). The 12th Five-Year Plan has been dubbed the Green Five-Year Plan, because much of it focuses on the sustainable development of China, and even reduces the government's GDP growth goals to 7.5 per cent annually – down from 8 per cent – to allow for more thorough and substantive development of China's green energy and environmental protection policies. The lowering of the GDP growth target aids greatly in the development of renewable energy infrastructure, because like most public goods, renewable energy has extremely high start-up costs, which, though valuable in the long term, often run counter to short-term economic goals. Therefore, by lowering the GDP target, investment in renewable energy carries less of an economic disincentive in the short-term because it is easier to hit a lower GDP target, and thus the high renewable energy infrastructure costs can be better absorbed without short-term economic consequences.

The main purpose of this section is to demonstrate that China has made great steps toward being at the forefront of the renewable energy revolution. During this period, China has become the largest producer of both wind and hydroelectric energy, with over 200 GW of installed hydroelectric capacity (Campbell, 2011). Additionally, China is the leading manufacturer of photovoltaic solar panels, many of which get exported to OECD states, offering a great amount of economic reinforcement for the value of renewable energy. In fact, in a recent study on the importance of policy to the development of renewable energy, China consistently ranked at or near the top in both production of renewable energy, and the manufacturing of renewable energy products (Barua et al., 2012). Additionally, many of the conclusions that the report established greatly supported China's current initiatives, including the need for a "comprehensive, predictable and targeted" policy with a scope that encompasses more than five years, something that China has worked strenuously to enact in its MLTPRE and REL legislation (Barua, 2012, p. 1). However, in the process of this development, some troubling signs have emerged that point to major institutional inefficiencies, which have stymied China's renewable energy growth from reaching its full potential.

3 Institutional inefficiencies in an authoritarian market promoter

This chapter will now evaluate some major issues regarding the implementation of renewable energy policy in China by examining the negative effects that institutional inefficiencies have on the process. For the purpose of this chapter, institutional inefficiencies will be defined as: the conflict that exists between and within the major government actors in charge of the implementation of renewable energy policy. As Christine Wong has noted, these inefficiencies are a product of the decentralization that took place in the 1980s and early 1990s during China's reform period (Wong, 2008). The major cause was the shrinking of the central government budget over this period, which placed emphasis on the local governments to grow in scope and size. This shift towards the local governments has led to long-term governance issues between the central and local governments, and the related state-owned enterprises (SOEs).

In addition to the process of decentralization, the Chinese policy-making structure itself is extremely convoluted, and often lacks any form of standardization of policy-making in favour of an informal system that is be categorized by large amounts of inter-agency bargaining. This process stems from what Kenneth Lieberthal refers to as 'fragmented authority,' in which "the structure of authority requires that any major project or policy initiative gains the active cooperation of many bureaucratic units that are themselves nested in distinct chains of authority" (Lieberthal and Oksenberg, 1988, p. 22).

To best understand the role that fragmented authority plays in the policy-making process, it is crucial to first gain an understanding of the organizational form of the Chinese government. To begin, delineation between the central government and local governments must be made. One way of understanding the relationship between the central government and the local governments is to view them as the structures of a western corporation. According to Lieberthal, the central government plays a role analogous to that of the corporate headquarters, while the local governments are the equivalent of the regional offices (Lieberthal and Oksenberg, 1988). The central government is in charge of determining broad policy initiatives, for instance the expansion of renewable energy capacity, which is then implemented by the local governments. Policy is generally initiated at the top level, then assigned to one or, more commonly, multiple ministries in the central government to oversee the implementation of the policy. The ministries then coordinate with the local-level governments, which actually implement the policy within their respective territories. Local governments begin at the provincial level, and scale all the way down to the village level, the smallest unit of government in the Chinese system.

This seems like a relatively straightforward organizational structure, with the hierarchy determining authority in the implementation of policy, however it is not as simple as it may at first appear. In Lieberthal's words, "what on paper appears to be a unified hierarchical chain of command turns out in reality to be divided, segmented, and stratified" (Lieberthal and Oksenberg, 1988, p. 137). The most salient cause of this is the existence of two distinct streams of authority within the government that often run in opposing directions, making the implementation of policy a much more time-intensive process. The Chinese refer to these streams of authority as being *tiao* and *kuai*. *Tiao* refers to the vertical system (*xitong*), specifically the ministerial chain of authority. This takes the form of, for instance, the ministry of finance, which runs from the ministry leader in the central government, all the way down to the Individual Township or village level of the ministry of finance. *Kuai*, on the other hand, refers to the territorial authority, which begins at the provincial level, for instance Guangxi, and continues down to the lowest level of government in the specific area, often the township or village level (Lieberthal and Oksenberg, 1988).

Tiao and *kuai* represent two conflicting levels of authority to which any individual branch of a ministry is responsible, and often these two branches of authority (vertical and horizontal) have conflicting goals. This is, in essence, the root of Lieberthal's "fragmented authority."

The result of "fragmented authority" upon the implementation of policy cannot be overstated. The Chinese government is thus categorized by a great level of organizational bargaining and consensus building, which can lead to major inefficiencies in the designing and implementation of policy. Additionally, the central government holds varying levels of bargaining authority over different provinces often determined by the province's wealth, strategic significance, personal connections (*guanxi*), ambition, and the provincial leader's acumen (Lieberthal and Oksenberg, 1988). This demonstrates the level of interdependence between the central and local governments, making it so that neither one can completely disregard the other. The local governments are relied on to take initiative and determine regional-specific ways of enhancing their economic standing, while the central government must play a large role, because without, it leads to "chaos" (Lieberthal and Oksenberg, 1988, p. 138). However, this often causes local governments to abuse the autonomy they're afforded, by seeking economic and personal success at the expense of the broad policy initiatives of the central government.

One common issue that arises during the implementation of policy is a conflict of interest between the local government and the central government, often rooted in the necessity on the part of the local government to pursue economic goals, which have a direct effect upon the operating budget of the local authority in future years. Additionally, the principle way to move up in the Chinese government is through economic success, so often the careers of leaders of the local governments are directly tied to the local government's economic performance. Another issue endemic in the system of "fragmented authority" is the amount of time necessary to establish sufficient consensus and support for a given policy. This is due, in large part, to the amount of inter-agency and regional bargaining that is required before a policy can be established. Indeed, for a policy to be implemented, it requires the support of multiple top leaders, often the heads of the relevant ministries involved in the various aspects of the policy itself, for instance the Ministry of Finance, the Ministry of the Environment and the National Development and Reform Commission. After this level of support for the policy is established, it is necessary to engage in the same process at the local-level of government, including the relevant branches of the local ministries, along with the provincial level leadership. As Lieberthal aptly puts it, no individual "decision" determines an issue, but "rather a whole string of mutually reinforcing 'decisions' are required in order to keep any one initiative on track" (Lieberthal and Oksenberg, 1988, p. 25).

Given the sheer number of individual entities that exist in the Chinese government, the process of establishing and then implementing a specific policy in China requires an immense amount of effort and time, and can subsequently be derailed very quickly if a specific organ or branch does not support the policy. In addition, the coordination required between the central ministries and local governments involves a myriad of individuals, each of whom has his or her own best interests to keep in mind, which can take precedence over the state's interest.

The major salient outcome of decentralization and the existence of "fragmented authority" is the crucial role that the local governments play in the enactment of policy dictated by the central government. The major institutional inefficiency that stems from this process is the difficulty that inherently arises when attempting to coordinate the planning and implementation of a given policy. This is only exacerbated given the interdisciplinary nature of renewable energy, which involves aspects of finance, planning, technological research, energy commissions, and environmental concerns among others. Another issue that this poses to policy implementation is the need to coordinate so many branches of each local government, which leads to a major hurdle simply due to the sheer magnitude of the agencies and individuals involved in policy implementation.

On the part of the central government, the process of decentralization led to a temporarily weakened central government that has regained its strength in a disorganized manner. The major symptoms of this process are shown by the number of agencies that play a role in most aspects of Chinese policy initiatives, especially renewable energy. This has led to a situation in which the goals of the agency or institution are placed above those of the government or state as a whole. This causes difficulties in the implementation of policies on the part of the Chinese Communist Party (CCP), because there is a lack of clearly defined roles and procedures that can be followed by the agencies in support of major planning initiatives. These inefficiencies on the part of the central government agencies have retarded China's otherwise impressive renewable energy policies, simply because no single ministry appears comprehensive enough to delegate responsibilities to each agency involved. Nor is any agency powerful enough to offer sufficient oversight to see the policy through from the top planning stage in the central government to the implementation of the policy at the local-level. In other words, if one agency falters in its implementation, there are ripples throughout the whole system.

The term "fragmented authority" can be applied to state-owned enterprises (SOEs) as well. As the central government decentralized during the reform period, SOEs became independent entities, meaning that as long as their financial results were good, and the SOEs followed the flow of major party initiatives, they were allowed to pursue effective independence. This has caused an institutional inefficiency because, like the local governments, as the SOEs have become accustomed to their newly afforded autonomy, the control that central government has over them has been eroding. This, again, leads to a difficulty on the part of the central government in implementing its policy. Because SOEs are ultimately judged by their economic success they're less reliant on the central government, and can choose to implement the policies that best serve the needs of the SOE, which are not always aligned with those of the government.

The following sections will examine some of the major issues facing the implementation of China's renewable energy policy through the lens of the SOEs, the central government and the relationship between the central and local governments.

4 State-owned enterprises

One of the most substantive issues facing China's renewable energy policy is the struggle to connect wind power to the national grid. In

2009, the Ministry of Industry and Information Technology reported that China's total installed capacity of wind energy was 25,805 MW, however, only 62.51 per cent of this energy potential is connected to the national grid (Fang et al., 2012). This means that slightly less than four out of every ten turbines are not actually generating useful electricity that reaches the Chinese end user.

The logical question to pose is: why does this happen? Though a simple question, the answer is not as easy to ascertain. One of the major contributors to this undesirable situation is the policy itself. Under the REL, "China's grid companies must accept subsidized wind power, but the costs of building transmission lines to connect to wind farms (especially those in remote regions) are not subsidized" (Campbell, 2011, p. 23). This is a troublesome omission in China's policy, because most of the available wind resources are located in the northeast, northwest and southwest, all of which have relatively low population density (Wang, 2010). This means that to connect the energy produced to the grid, somebody must build the infrastructure, however, in the law, there is no clear stipulation as to which entities cover what costs.

This is an institutional issue, as well as an example of vague policy, because the current system for building, establishing, and running renewable energy farms is almost completely dominated by SOEs. In China, there are five large power generation companies (Huaneng, Guodian, Datang, Huadian, Zhongdiantou), which play a major role in the generation of conventional and renewable energy, as well as two grid companies, all of which are accountable to the NEC, which is chaired by Wen Jiabao (Campbell, 2011). This means that each entity in this system is effectively controlled by the central government, and yet, there has been little progress to remedy what would seem like a minor issue. The simple solution is to force a state-owned grid company to build the connection to the grid, as most SOEs are ultimately controlled by the central government, yet this has not been the case.

This lack of central government authority demonstrates the issue that plagues most renewable energy policies, which is that SOE autonomy causes headaches for the central government because the SOEs are primarily concerned with their bottom lines, and less-concerned with any policy that might hamper its financial success. The different agencies involved in the oversight process of the REL include, but are not limited to, the State Electricity Regulation Commission (SERC), the Ministry of Finance (MOF), the National Development and Reform Commission (NDRC), all of which are under the broad oversight of the National Energy Commission (NEC). In 2009, the central government amended the REL, to state that national grid companies, which are ultimately under the scope of the National Energy Commission (NEC), must purchase all available energy generated though renewable sources, or face a penalty of less than the economic loss of the renewable energy generation company, in accordance with Article 29 of the REL. While this would appear to be a logical solution to the problem, it is difficult for the central government to keep track of how much electricity is generated through renewable sources, along with the responsibility of assessing tariffs being split between the State Electricity Regulation Commission (SERC) and the Ministry of Finance (MOF), with the National Development and Reform Commission (NDRC) offering oversight. This, again, points to a classic example of the negative effects of "fragmented authority", as simply assessing tariffs requires *three* separate agencies. Additionally, the updated REL still does not address the fact that it remains cheaper for the grid companies to pay the fines than to invest in the new infrastructure, with the fines not even equalling the economic loss of the generation company. This points to an inability on the part of the NEC to oversee every SOE and agency within its scope of authority, and displays obvious symptoms of the inefficiencies caused by the "fragmentation of authority".

The two SOEs in charge of grid management are the State Power Grid and the China South Power Grid. A lack of incentives for the SOEs to pursue renewable energy development leads to issues with connection to the grid. The first issue is that SOEs would need to cover the cost to connect remote areas to the grid. This is an extremely expensive venture, and something that would run against the financial best interests of the grid- controlling companies, which are more than happy with the status quo. Additionally, due to the small role that renewable energy plays in the grand scheme of Chinese energy generation, the lack of financial incentives are amplified, given the large sums the grid company would need to pay in order to connect these relatively minor resources to the national grid. In the best-case scenario, renewable energy would account for slightly more than 11 per cent of total power generation, which is a small share. This means that a grid company would need to pay for the connection cost up front, but the financial gain would remain relatively small, offering little to no incentive for the grid company to actually undertake such costly ventures.

For grid connection to become financially viable from the point of view of a grid company, without any external incentives, renewable energy would have to comprise a much higher share of total energy production. In turn, this means that there is less incentive to build renewable energy generation capability, because the grid company does not support connecting the generators to the grid, leading more and more renewable energy projects to lie unutilized. These result in an unprofitable situation for the renewable energy generation company, especially given the high start-up costs involved in building the renewable energy infrastructure (i.e., turbines, PV panels).

The salient issue here is that there is a lack of common incentive structure in the REL to encourage a holistic development of the renewable energy industry. The major cause of this is a disincentive inherent in building expensive renewable energy infrastructure, which is less profitable in the short-term than simply using fossil-fuel sourced energy. However, in the long run, renewable energy is cheaper, and eventually pays for itself. The Chinese government must therefore find a way to align its policies with this fact, by offering short-term monetary incentives that offset the initial financial burdens of renewable energy, and ultimately make it more profitable for the state grid companies. The system in place, though valid in its own right, does not incentivize the construction of infrastructure by the grid companies, but rather disincentivizes connecting renewable energy to the grid. Perhaps an approach that employed a positive reinforcement system (e.g., tax incentives) for renewable energy would aid greatly in aligning the incentive systems for all entities involved in the production of green energy.

The fact that these are SOEs, rather than actual organs of the government, only exacerbates this issue. As Lee demonstrated, sometimes, SOEs hold a higher status in the government than their actual rank (Lee and Wai, 2012). An examination of the case of the China Three Gorges Project Co (CTGPC) and the State Environmental Protection Agency (SEPA) is a good example. In 2005, the SEPA ordered the CTGPC to suspend its projects due to environmental violations. The CTGPC, an SOE, decided to ignore these orders, and went along and completed the project anyway.

The fact that the SEPA was unable to follow through with its policy and exercise its authority over an apparently lower-ranking SOE is what has been described as "institutional bridging" (Milhaupt and Lin, 2011, p. 4). Milhaupt and Lin define institutional bridging as: "widespread use of systematized fasteners uniting separate components of the system," meaning that members of one agency will be appointed to commissions in other agencies to encourage inter-agency collaboration (Milhaupt and Lin, 2011, p. 4). The most salient example of this is the State-owned Assets Supervision and Administration Commission (SASAC), which is in charge of drafting laws pertaining to SOEs, and is situated directly below the State Council.

Each year, the SASAC brings in managers from the major SOEs for a one-year period to serve as a member of the agency. This means that the agency in charge of the oversight of SOEs is actually partly comprised of senior staff from the SOEs. This creates an obvious conflict of interest that explains why SOEs are afforded such an ample amount of autonomy in their actions. Additionally, this institutional bridging can be used to explain why an agency such as the SEPA has such a difficult time enforcing policy upon SOEs, which are supposed to be ranked below the SEPA in the government organizational hierarchy, because the heads of the SOEs are also members of a high-ranking commission. Therefore, it makes sense that the grid companies are reluctant to spend the necessary capital to connect renewable energy potential to the grid, because they can simply affect the policy in a way that does not negatively impact the company's earnings, which are, after all, what the SOE managers are ultimately judged by. Given the senior authority awarded to the SASAC, and the members of the SOEs who are members of the council, it is plain to see why the SOEs are as powerful as they are.

The only obvious solution to this issue is to create an agency that is large enough in size, and comprehensive enough in scope, to design policy and then implement it, while being able to counter-balance the political clout of the SOEs. The Chinese government must strengthen the monitoring apparatuses in charge of renewable energy to realize its goals in this field. To use an English adage, the inmates are running the asylum, with regards to the SOEs, and the regulatory authorities are not afforded enough say or manpower to impact the status quo.

5 Central government

These inefficiencies are not constrained to SOEs, but rather pervade all aspects of the Chinese government system. Within the central government, a prime example of institutional inefficiency is the actual structure of the governing bodies in charge of any aspect of renewable energy. There are a number of government agencies that have a role in renewable energy, including the State Electricity Regulation Commission (SERC), the Ministry of Finance (MOF), and the National Development and Reform Commission (NDRC), along with the Ministry of Industry and Information Technology, the State Commission of Economy and Trade, Department of Agriculture, Department of Water Conservation, and State Forestry Administration, all of which are under the broad oversight of the National Energy Commission (NEC) on matters pertaining to renewable energy (Zhang et al., 2009). This means that at any potential given moment, as many as nine agencies are expected to coordinate their efforts and responsibilities with regard to the development of renewable energy.

Tam and Yang have examined the role that poor institutional framework and fragmentation of authority has had on the matter of food safety, and it's safe to say that those findings apply to renewable energy as well (Tam and Yang, 2005). Zhang et al. summarize this point best by stating that the vast amount of agencies with roles in the renewable energy sector, "substantially undermine the state macro-control" (Zhang et al., 2009).

The differences between these agencies create a situation where the goals of one agency might actually inhibit the realization of another agency's plans. An example of this was in 2009, when China cancelled the tariff for importing wind energy generators. However, at the same time, other sectors were attempting to support the Chinese manufacturing process by purchasing from local manufacturing plants (Zhang et al., 2009, p. 444). This lack of coordination actually undermined what the manufacturing sector was attempting to accomplish in creating domestically produced wind generators. For domestic renewable energy to take off, it is imperative that China develops a manufacturing industry for renewable energy generation. However, with the tariff being cancelled, importing these parts is cheaper and faster than setting up a whole business to design, build and distribute these parts. Essentially, what helps the growth of renewable energy in the short-term but hurts the long-term goal of domestic production of renewable energy equipment, a common thread throughout this analysis of China's renewable energy efforts.

Another example of an institutional inefficiency is the National Energy Administration (NEA), which was approved in March 2008, to act as an overseer to the central government's energy-related policies. It was created in response to the conflicts of interest mentioned above due to the sheer number of agencies involved in the renewable energy process. The issue with the NEA is the size of the agency.

When it was approved, the NEA had 112 seats. With no reference point, this seems like a sizable-enough agency. In comparison, however, the Agency for Natural Resources and Energy – the Japanese counterpart of the NEA – had 1,247 seats in 2007 (Li, 2010). This means that the Japanese version of the NEA has more than ten times the staff of the NEA, for a population that is one-tenth of China's, and a landmass of an even smaller proportion. In 2010, the NEA was replaced by the aforementioned National Energy Commission (NEC), which is a group of the ministers and chairmen of all of the major agencies, such as resources, finance, foreign affairs, and was designed to better coordinate the implementation of policy. This is all well and good, except for the fact that the actual agency became even smaller in size. Adding increased power and clout to the NEC will help, but the larger issue at play is the lack of size of the commission, which can only be remedied by adding people to the commission, not power.

As Wang et al. posit, the "Chinese government needs to strengthen its monitoring of [grid operators] to ensure that renewable electricity has guaranteed grid access as required by the REL" (Wang et al., 2010, p. 1877). This is proof that the key issue here is not the amount of political clout in the group, as it is clear the new NEC has about as many powerful individuals as any group in China, save for the Standing Committee, but rather the solution lies in an empowered and immense central government commission dedicated to monitoring renewable energy. It is unreasonable to assume that a group of ministers, whose real jobs are to focus on their respective agency or ministry, is going to place as much focus on renewable energy as a dedicated group would. Therefore, the main issue with the NEC as an oversight committee is that it lacks the necessary size to oversee the proper implementation of renewable energy policy. In addition to adding powerful individuals, the NEC must grow to a scale proportional to the amount of oversight required, which is to say, quite a bit.

6 Central versus local

Another salient example of the institutional inefficiencies that are endemic in the Chinese regulatory system is the separation of central and local governments. Article 5 of the REL states that, "Relevant departments of local people's governments above the county level are responsible for the management of relevant development and utilization of renewable energy within their authorities" (China, 2005, Article 5). However, again going back to Tam and Yang, there is a distinct conflict of interest when the central government entrusts a local government with any position of oversight (Tam and Yang, 2005). This occurs because often, the way to move up in the Chinese political system is to demonstrate one's worth through the generation of economic growth. As has been discussed above, in the short-term, fossil fuels are undoubtedly the cheapest and most effective means to achieving said growth. Therefore, furthering renewable energy, under the existing institutional framework is actually counter-intuitive to most local government officials' goals.

The roots of this problem date back to the end of the Cultural Revolution, when the gradual decentralization of power from the central government to local authorities began. This process, first referred to by Audrey Donnithorne as China's "cellular economy", stems from a push in post-Cultural Revolution China towards "self-reliance" of local polities from the central government (Donnithorne, 1972). Donnithorne points to the decision to eschew a form of "bureaucratic socialism," similar to that used by the Soviet Union, in favour of a more decentralized form of economic production, categorized by "a myriad of small discrete units" (Donnithorne, 1972, p. 605). The historical effects of China's cellular economy can be categorized by a large amount of local autarky, in the sense that instead of specialization of tasks, which has been proven to enhance state-wide efficiency greatly, each local entity was forced to produce its own grain and other goods of subsistence, before it could engage in industrial production. Thomas Lyons notes that in extreme cases, this led to the "dismemberment of the transportation network itself, with roads ending at county or provincial boundaries" (Lyons, 1985, p. 140). While the effects of China's cellular economy are not nearly as pronounced in modern China, their legacy is still felt today.

The local ministry branches are often in charge of collecting tariffs intended to supplement the creation of renewable energy and its connection to the grid. The Renewable Rural Electrification Program is a prime example of this. Independent village power systems are designed to bring reliable renewable energy to rural villages; however, the policy itself lacks specific guidelines regarding the collection of tariffs. This means that local governments collect tariffs, "without certain set criteria, and often they determine the tariff level and revenue distribution by themselves that many times led to chaotic situations" (Kumar and Zhang, 2011, p. 777). This is an obvious inefficiency in the renewable energy institution, because it relies heavily on the competence of local governments or ministries (or both) to subjectively determine the amount of an appropriate tariff that fully supports the creation and maintenance of the system.

The results of this inefficient means of governance over the implementation of renewable energy policy have led to a gap between tariffs and costs. This discrepancy has resulted in a system where the tariff "could not generate enough revenue for the salaries of operators, let alone system [oversight and management] and parts replacement" (Kumar and Zhang, 2011, p. 777).

On top of funding the upkeep of green energy systems, the actual oversight and maintenance of the systems is another issue facing the local governments, which suffer from a lack of prescription on the part of the central government, due to the existence of "cellular economies". The responsibility for the maintenance of these systems is not stipulated in the rural electrification program, which demonstrates a shortsighted approach, by appearing to ignore the constant maintenance necessary for the upkeep of such technologically advanced systems. Kumar and Zhang point to a greater level of clarity in the establishment of ownership and maintenance as being one of the crucial steps towards improving the efficacy of the Rural Electrification Program

(Kumar and Zhang, 2011). As it stands, the program establishes the bidding process for the contracts of the installation of the green energy components, however it fails to elaborate on who or what entity is in charge of system upkeep, which leads to a shirking of responsibility when issues arise. On top of a clearly established maintenance contract, the actual ownership of the equipment can be called into question since it is not stated in the contract (Kumar and Zhang, 2011). Ownership is especially difficult, because the funding for these systems comes from a wide variety of sources, including but not limited to the central government, the World Bank and other international donors under various carbon reduction programs. (Kumar and Zhang, 2011). Without proper documentation to stipulate which entities are responsible for various aspects of the renewable energy systems, this impressive program will suffer from a lack of organization that could easily be prescribed by the central government.

Another issue that can be attributed back to the "cellular economy" is the actual form of renewable energy used in the rural electrification program, which is not determined by an expert, but rather by a local official, who may or may not have previous experience in the renewable energy sector. This can lead to a "cookie-cutter approach" to the installation of renewable energy, that is to say an approach that leads to replicating solutions without regard to their appropriateness in particular circumstances, which results in suboptimal outcomes. For instance, solar power may be applied in an area where wind might be the more efficient option, or issues as simple as which direction a photovoltaic solar cell is facing may arise (Kumar and Zhang, 2011). This is not an isolated issue, but rather indicative of a larger problem endemic in many of China's green energy policies – a lack of central oversight, research and broad, prescriptive policies. Kumar and Zhang summarize this in their analysis of the rural electrification program, "there [is] no supervision mechanism," and without any supervision, the implementation of this admirable policy will always be afflicted by improper management, due to the autarkic nature that is endemic in China's "cellular economy" (Kumar and Zhang, 2011, p. 776).

The solution to this issue is, again, to implement an empowered central government agency with a size and scope capable of determining and implementing every detail of renewable energy installation and management. Without a proper agency that can plan and oversee the development of renewable energy throughout China, issues such as insufficient tariff collection and unspecified management roles will continue to hamper China's success in achieving sustainable development.

7 Conclusion

As has been covered throughout this paper, the conflicts between the various institutions within the Chinese government lead to a large number of inefficiencies that have inhibited China's growth in the renewable energy sector. For China's renewable energy initiatives to be realized to their full potential, the central government must establish an empowered agency in charge of every aspect of renewable energy development.

The reality is that China has a vast amount of renewable resources, and a vested interest in becoming a more sustainable society. Additionally, China benefits from a one-party system, and a consistency in implementing and fulfilling long-term policy that other, more democratic governments do not have. The role played by SOEs in China's energy sector should lead to an even easier transition, due to the fact that they are, in the end, accountable to the Chinese government. The effects that decentralization and fragmented authority have had on the central government's ability to dictate and enact policy has made it difficult to ensure that policy initiatives are realized to their full potential.

None of this is to say that China's green energy sector is truly lacking in any way. It leads the world in wind energy production and manufacturing, and is in the process of becoming equally powerful and influential in the solar energy sector. Additionally, China is a world leader in the use and generation of hydroelectricity. In fact, a working paper on the economic effects of renewable energy policy found China consistently to be at or near the top in the effectiveness of its renewable energy policy and sector (Barua et al., 2012).

However, as long as China maintains its aspirations of becoming a global power, it will be held to a higher standard, and along with this higher standard will come a greater level of scrutiny of its policies. With one-fifth of the world's population, and a sizable amount of territory as well, China will need to demonstrate its capacity for leading, as opposed to following. The renewable energy sector is an area where China can become a world leader. It is also in China's best interest to increase its reliance on renewable energy, because as a leading manufacturer of renewable energy components, it would be a financial boon, while also offering China an opportunity to ensure its future prosperity by reducing its reliance on foreign oil and improving its hazardous environmental issues. However, the only way for China to ensure that it reaches these goals, is to enlarge and empower the NEC so that it can better oversee the implementation of renewable energy policies, and act as an arbiter in the bargaining process between the various institutions.

13

Demand Effects on CO_2 Emission in China: A Structural Decomposition Analysis (SDA)

Chaoxian Guo and Yanhong Liu

1 Introduction

China's rapid industrialization has been accompanied by a fast growth in carbon emissions, which leaves it facing a serious challenge of carbon emissions reduction. Since the reform and open-up policy was launched, China's carbon footprint has gradually increased in two stages; the first stage before 2001 featuring low growth, and the second stage since 2002 featuring high growth. According to Figure 13.1, China's carbon footprint in 1980 was 1.5 billion tons, which then reached 3.36 billion in 1996. After that, it experienced extremely low growth due to the Asian financial crisis, which accounted for the 3.6 bn tons of carbon emission in 2001, only 0.25 billion higher than five years previously. There was an average annual growth rate of 4.3 per cent over the period of 21 years from 1980 to 2001. Since 2002, increase in carbon emissions started to speed up again, rising from 3.85 billion tons in 2002 to 7.7 billion in 2010, with an average annual growth rate of 9 per cent over eight years, which was two-times higher than the previous stage. During 2002–07, its average growth rate per annum recorded 12.2 per cent, surpassing the economic growth rate of 11.6 per cent for the same period (calculated in constant prices).

To effectively mitigate the carbon emission expansion, an important precondition is to figure out the causes for the continuous and fast growth of carbon emission in China, and it is the purpose of this chapter to explore the effects of consumption, investment and export as three final demands on carbon emissions in China.

Consumption, investment and export, as three engines of economic growth, are the major contributors to carbon emission. As final demands, they play their roles via a series of inducing effects. For this reason, input/output analysis has been widely employed as a preferred method to measure the effects of consumption, investment and export on carbon emission. Since the input/output table is well adapted to depict the relationship between the preliminary and intermediate inputs, and intermediate and final demands, if we put carbon emission as a "preliminary input", the effects on carbon emission caused by the changes of final demands can be calculated based on the equilibrium relations in an extended (including the carbon emission) input/output chart. In this respect, a structural decomposition analysis (SDA) can serve to decompose the effects caused by final demand expansion and their structural changes in a specific period. The revelation of various effects of final demands on carbon emission, will not only help us to better clarify the path of carbon emission growth in China, but can also provide important references to inform policy-making either for emissions reduction or for international negotiations.

2 Research method and data sources

The input/output analysis employed in this research was based on an expanding economy – subsequent expanding energy use – carbon emissions input/output table. Table 13.1 is a brief version of this table format. Since China has no separate input/output tables for domestic and imported goods, it is presumed that there is no difference between them and the (import) competitive economy – energy – environmental input/output table is therefore employed.

In Table 13.1, A is the input/output direct consumption coefficient matrix, X is the gross output column vector, and X^T is the gross input line vector (T denotes transposition). Y is the final demand matrix, composing three parts, that is the consumption vector (C), capital formation vector (I), and export vector (EX). IM is the import column vector. E denotes the line vector of energy intensity by sectors. $E\hat{X}$ denotes the amount of energy consumption by industrial sectors, where $\hat{X}$ denotes the diagonal matrix of X. F denotes the energy consumption mix matrix (referring to the proportions of coal, petroleum and gas). It can be deduced that aggregate carbon emissions $Q = cF\hat{E}X$, where c denotes the carbon emissions coefficient vector. By further making S=cF and writing S in the format of diagonal matrix $\hat{S}$, carbon emissions quantity Q can be written in the form of vector:[1] $Q = \hat{S}\hat{E}X$

Following the principle of data availability and compatibility, we employed the data of 1992, 1997, 2002 and 2007 across 29 industrial sectors, including one agricultural sector, 24 industrial sectors, one construction sector and three service sectors. The input/output tables

Table 13.1 (Import) Competitive economy – energy – environmental input/output table

		Final demand (Y)				
	Intermediate use	**Consumption**	**Capital formation**	**Export**	**Import**	**Gross output**
Intermediate input	AX	C	I	EX	IM	X
Value added	V	□	□	□	□	□
Total input	X^T	□	□	□	□	□
Energy consumption	$\hat{EX}$	□	□	□	□	□
Energy mix	F	□	□	□	□	□
Carbon emission	Q^T	□	□	□	□	□

Note: X^T and Q^T are the transpositions of X and Q respectively. $\hat{X}$ denotes the diagonal matrix of X. Where, $Q = S\hat{E}X$, $S = cF$, c is the coefficient vector of carbon emission.
Source: Author own elaboration.

of 1992, 1997 and 2002 were based on comparable prices sourced from *China Input/output Sequence Tables and Analysis Based on Comparable Prices from 1992 to 2005* by Liu and Peng. The 2007 table was worked out by authors based on the original data from China input/output table of 2007 (current prices) at comparative prices.[2] For energy consumption by industrial sectors, primary energy data were employed (coal, petroleum and gas), with original data from the *China Energy Statistical Yearbook* and *China Statistical Yearbook* over the relevant years. According to the principle of compatibility, we adjusted the number of energy-consuming industrial sectors to 29. Carbon emissions coefficients of different energies were taken from the default values provided by IPCC National Greenhouse Gas Inventory Guideline of 2006 complied by the Intergovernmental Panel on Climate Change (IPCC).

3 Horizon analysis

According to the input/output table, the relationship of total output and final demand can be expressed as $X = (I-\alpha A)^{-1}Y$, where $(I-\alpha A)^{-1}$ is the Leontief inverse matrix excluding the import; Y represents the final demand from domestic production, that is $Y = \alpha C + \alpha I + E$. Since, $Q = cF\hat{E}X$, $X = (I-\alpha A)^{-1}Y$, therefore, $Q = cF\hat{E}X\,(I-\alpha A)^{-1}Y$, wherein, if, $Y = (C, I, EX)$, then $Q = (Q_C, Q_I, Q_{EX})$, in which, the components of Q, Q_C£–Q£–Q_{EX} denote the carbon emission respectively caused by consumption, investment (capital formation) and export. The carbon emission caused by final demands respectively in 1992, 1997, 2002, and 2007 can then be calculated and illustrated in Table 13.2.

It reveals the following facts:

1. Prior to 2002, the growth of total carbon emission in China was relatively slow; afterwards it turned significantly fast, featuring the "high emission" character of China's new round of industrialization driven by tremendous expansion of the heavy energy-consuming industries. Reviewing the growth of carbon emission every five years, the amount in 1997 increased by only about 400 million tons, 14 per cent up on 1992; carbon emission in 2002 increased by only 300 million tons, 10 per cent up on 1997; however, carbon emission in 2007 increased by 2.7 billion tons, 80 per cent up on 2002.
2. With respect to the carbon emission expansion caused by three demands, the expansion caused by consumption was relatively slow. The amount of carbon emission was 1.317 billion tons in 1992, and 1.873 billion tons in 2007, rising less than 50 per cent over 15 years, during which the amount in 1997 even decreased compared to 1992. The expansion caused by investment and export, on the other hand, was fast. In the case of expansion by export, the amount was 491 million tons in 1992, rising up to 752 millions in 1997, and further up to 1.896 billion tons in 2007, nearly four-times as much as in 1992. In 2007, the carbon emission caused either by investment or export, all exceeded the amount of consumption, making the two former factors leading causes linked to carbon emission.
3. As far as the composition of total emissions is concerned, the share of carbon emission by consumption showed a downward trend, from nearly one-half in 1992, down to less than one-third in 2007. In contrast, the share of investment and export showed a rising trend. By 2007, both of the shares by investment and export surpassed the consumption.

4 Elasticity analysis

Elasticity analysis can serve to contrast the growth rates of two variables. The final demand elastic coefficient of carbon emission = growth rate of carbon emission / growth rate of final demands

Table 13.3 indicates the growth rates of final demands and carbon emission at various periods.

Based on the data in Table 13.3, the various demand elastic coefficients of carbon emission can thus be calculated and illustrated as in Figures 13.1–13.2.

Table 13.2 Carbon emission caused by final demand by years

	Carbon Emission (100 million tons)				Percentage (%)			
Year	In total	consumption	Investment	Export	In total	consumption	Investment	Export
1992	26.92	13.19	8.81	4.91	100	49.01	32.73	18.26
1997	30.77	12.88	10.37	7.52	100	41.87	33.69	24.44
2002	33.86	13.86	11.69	8.31	100	40.92	34.53	24.55
2007	61.10	18.73	23.42	18.96	100	30.65	38.32	31.03

Source: China Energy Statistical Yearbook (2008), China Statistical Yearbook (2008).

Table 13.3 Average annual growth of final demands and carbon emission

	Annual growth of final demands (%)				Annual growth of carbon emission (%)			
Period□	In total	consumption	Investment	Export	In total	consumption	Investment	Export
1992–97	10.48	8.07	11.75	16.74	2.71	–0.47	3.31	8.88
1997–2002	8.37	6.43	8.40	13.27	1.93	1.47	2.44	2.02
2002–07	12.00	7.74	13.35	17.80	12.53	6.21	14.90	17.93
1992–2007	10.27	7.41	11.15	15.92	5.62	2.36	6.73	9.42

Source: China Energy Statistical Yearbook (2008), China Statistical Yearbook (2008).

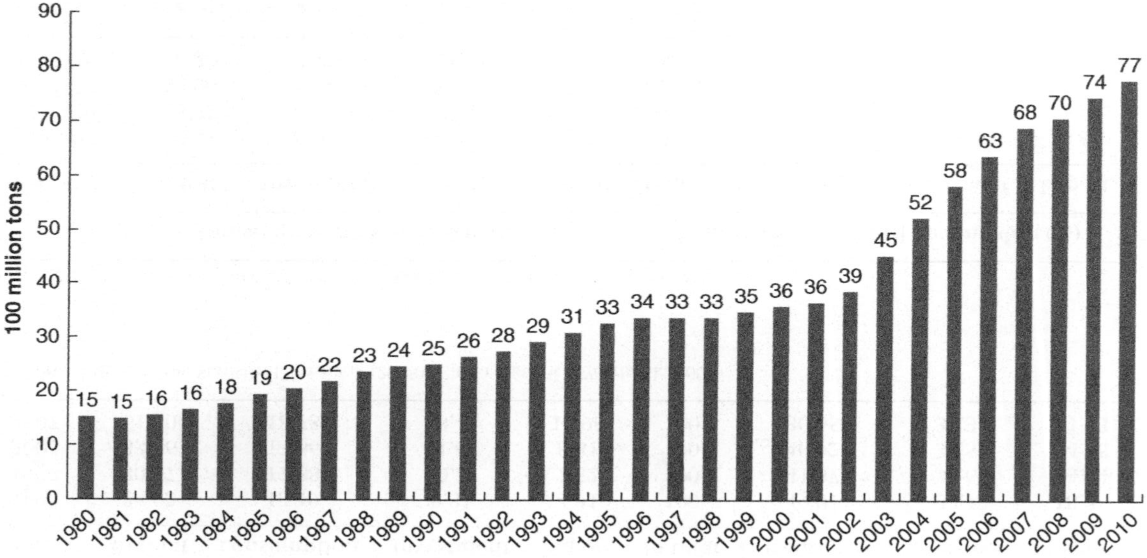

Figure 13.1 Carbon footprint in China, 1980–2010

Source: Calculated by authors based on yearly energy consumption by categories and the carbon emission factors provided by IPCC (2006).

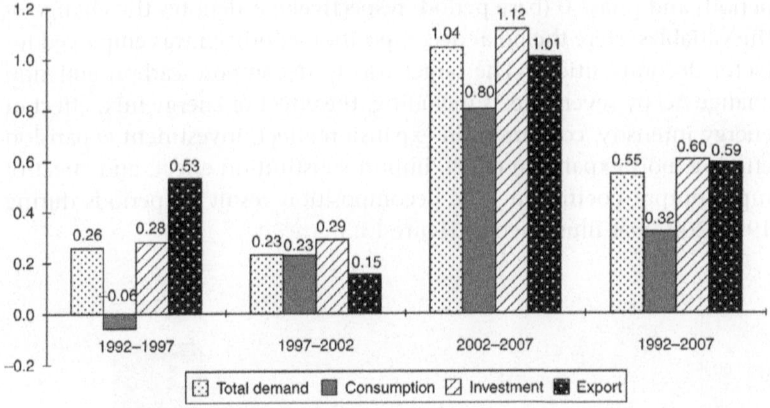

Figure 13.2 The final demand elastic coefficients of carbon emission by periods
Source: Generated by authors based on the data in Table 13.3.

As can be seen from Figure 13.2, (1) In terms of the change of total demand elasticity of carbon emission expansion, the elastic coefficient for periods 1992–97, and 1997–02, were all significantly smaller than 1, being 0.26 and 0.23 respectively, but the elastic coefficient went up to 1.04 during 2002–07. This illustrates again the "high emission" and "high carbonation" character of this new round of heavy-industrialized growth pattern in China.

In terms of the three varieties of final demand elasticity, the consumption elasticity of carbon emission expansion was generally small, its elastic coefficient, being 0.32 on average for the period of 1992–2007, was always lower than the level of total demand in each period from 1992 to 2007; in contrast, the investment elasticity of carbon emission, being 0.6 on average for the whole period, was generally larger than the level of total demands. The export elastic coefficient was relatively unstable, but still higher than the level of total demands for most of periods, with the level of 0.59 on average (compared with 0.55 of the total demand coefficient on average). It demonstrates again that, compared to consumption, investment and export were the more important contributors to the expansion of carbon emissions in China.

5 Contribution Analysis

According to $Q = \hat{S}\hat{E}X$, we could have $\Delta Q = Q_1 - Q_0 = \hat{S}_1\hat{E}_1X_1 = \hat{S}_0\hat{E}_0X_0$, where subscripts 1 and 0 denote variable values in phase 1 (reporting period) and phase 0 (base period) respectively; Δ denotes the change of the variables. Here the polar decomposition approach was employed for factor decomposition.[3] The target was to decompose carbon emission change ΔQ by seven effects including, the effect of energy mix, effect of energy intensity, consumption expansion effect, investment expansion effect, export expansion effect, import substitution effect, and effect of input/output coefficient. The decomposition result by periods during 1992–2007 was illustrated in Figure 13.3.

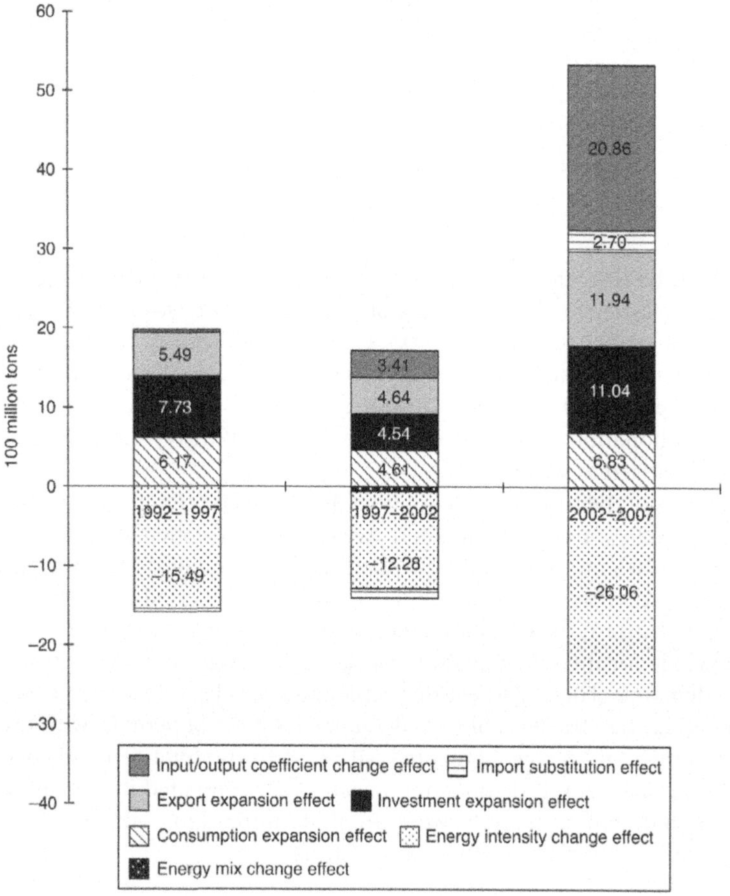

Figure 13.3 The structural decomposition of carbon emission expansion for 1992–2007

Source: China Energy Statistical Yearbook (2008), China Statistical Yearbook (2008).

The seven effects can also be divided as two categories, one is the effects caused by the scale expansion of final demands, including the expansions of consumption, investment and export; the other is the effects caused by other factors, such as the change in energy intensities, energy mix, and the change of the input/output coefficient (reflecting technological advance in broad sense). By this dichotomous approach, the structural decomposition of carbon emissions can be re-illustrated in Figure 13.4, which indicates that, the scale expansion of final demands was apparently the main force for the carbon emission expansion, while other factors tended to reduce this expansion effect. For the period of 2002–07, since the expansion effect of final demands was very significant, while the "counterforce" from other factors was weak, the consequence was the explosive growth of carbon emission.

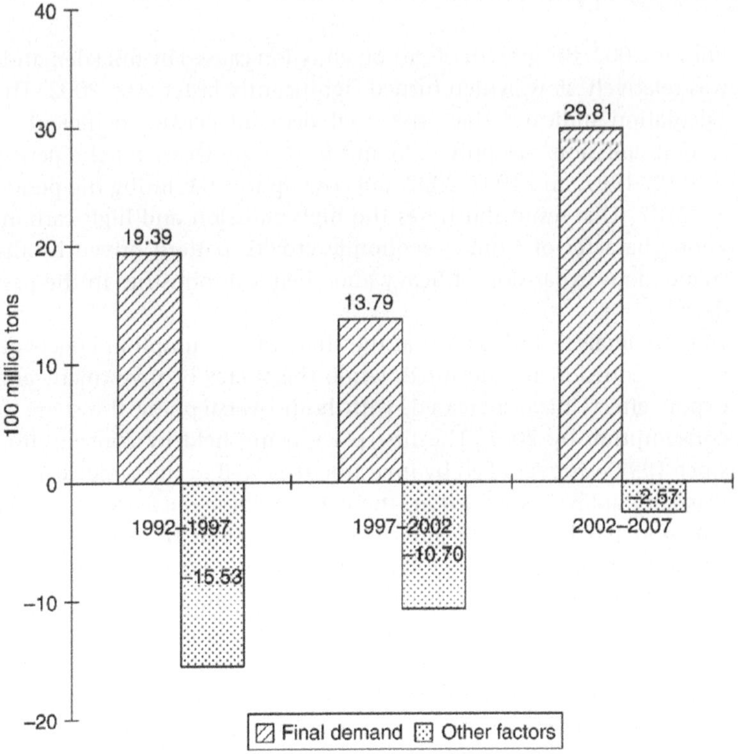

Figure 13.4 Carbon emission by final demand expansion and other factors
Source: China Energy Statistical Yearbook (2008), China Statistical Yearbook (2008).

In terms of the carbon emission effects caused by final demand expansion, consumption, investment and export played different roles as indicated in Tables 13.1–13.4. For the period of 1992–97, investment expansion was the leading force, which was followed by consumption, with export last. For period 1997–2002, the contributions of all three were roughly equivalent, with each accounting for around one-third of total effects. For 2002–07, the share of export effect jumped to the top, and the share of consumption dropped dramatically. An overview of the whole period of 1992–2007 shows that, export and investment played the key roles in the total effect of scale expansion, respectively accounting for 37.91 per cent and 37.72 per cent, while the role of consumption was much less important, with a share of only 24.37.

To summarize our findings from the above horizon, elasticity and contribution analyses based on the expanding economy-energy-carbon emission input/output model we constructed in this section:

1. Prior to 2002, the growth of carbon emission caused by final demands was relatively slow, which turned significantly faster after 2002. The calculation indicates that, the final demand elastic coefficient of carbon emission was only 0.26 and 0.23 respectively for the period of 1992–1997, and 1997–2002, but rose up to 1.04 during the period 2002–07. This result illustrates the high emission and high carbonation character of China's economic growth pattern driven by the tremendous expansion of heavy and chemical industries in the past decade.
2. Horizon analysis indicates that the share of consumption effects on carbon emission has declined, while the shares of investment and export effects have increased, with both overstepping the share of consumption by 2007. The first place being held by consumption since 1992 was overtaken by investment as well in the same year.
3. Elasticity analysis shows that, the consumption elasticity of carbon emission has been small and always lower than the level of total demand at all reporting periods. In contrast, the investment elasticity of carbon emission was generally larger than the level of total demand. The export elastic coefficient was relatively unstable, but still higher than the level of total demand for most of periods. It indicates that the growth of investment and export were the most important factors leading to the carbon emission expansion in China.
4. Contribution analysis also shows that, the scale expansion of final demands was apparently the main force for the carbon emission expansion, while other factors tended to reduce the expansion

Table 13.4 Expansion of three demands and their proportions in scale expansion effects by periods

□	1992–97		1997–2002		2002–07		1992–2007	
	Carbon emission (100 million tons)	Per cent (%)	Carbon emission (100 million tons)	Per cent (%)	Carbon emission (100 million tons)	Per cent (%)	Carbon emission (100 million tons)	Per cent (%)
Consumption expansion	6.17	31.84	4.61	33.43	6.83	22.91	25.60	24.37
Investment expansion	7.73	39.85	4.54	32.90	11.04	37.02	39.62	37.72
Export expansion	5.49	28.31	4.64	33.67	11.94	40.07	39.83	37.91
In total	19.39	100	13.79	100	29.81	100	105.04	100

Source: China Energy Statistical Yearbook (2008), China Statistical Yearbook (2008).

effects. Among three types of final demands, export was becoming more significant in the total effect of final demand scale expansion, accounting for the share over 40 per cent during 2002–07; while consumption was much less important, with the share of only 23 per cent.

6 Internal structure of each final demand and correlation with carbon emission

Carbon emission is not only determined by the growth and structure of total demand, but also by the internal structure of each of the three demands. To trace the changes of the contribution shares of the three demands to the total demand, and their shares of contribution to carbon emission during the period of 1997–2007, it can be illustrated as in Table 13.5 that, on the one hand, the share of investment and export in total demand kept rising over those years in which China's economic growth pattern was mainly driven by investment and export; on the other hand, the shares of both in contributing to carbon emission were rising even faster, leading to a larger contribution share to carbon emission than to total demand, which reflects the higher carbon intensity of investment and export.

One reason for the high carbon intensity in investment and export lies in the high proportions of carbon-intensive industries in the above two components of economy. From the perspective of final demands, the total input coefficient (TIC) of carbon emission is an ideal index for measuring the carbon intensity of an industry. According to the practical situation in China, we define industries with TIC greater than 3 tons per ten thousand Yuan in 2002, or 2.5 tons per ten thousand Yuan in 2007 as high carbon industries. According to this criteria, 14 industries including mining and washing of coal, extraction of petroleum and natural gas, mining and processing of metal ores, mining and processing of non-metal and other ores, processing of petroleum, coking, processing of nuclear fuel, chemical industries, manufacture of non-metallic mineral products, smelting and pressing of metals, manufacture of metal products, production and supply of electric power and heat power, production and supply of gas, production and supply of water, construction, and transport, storage and post, can be regarded as high carbon industries.

As illustrated in Table 13.6, the proportion of high carbon industries in consumption was only 8.83 per cent in 2002, and went up slightly in 2007, to 9.03 per cent. But the share of high carbon industries in

Table 13.5 Contribution shares of three demands to total demand and to carbon emissions

Year	Per cent in total demand (%)			Per cent in effects on carbon emission (%)			Difference (%)		
	Consumption	Investment	Export	Consumption	Investment	Export	Consumption	Investment	Export
1997	49.72	31.79	18.48	41.87	33.69	24.44	−7.85	1.90	5.96
2002	48.37	30.75	20.88	40.92	34.53	24.55	−7.45	3.78	3.67
2007	38.95	32.80	28.25	30.65	38.32	31.03	−8.30	5.52	2.78

Source: China Energy Statistical Yearbook (2008), China Statistical Yearbook (2008).

Table 13.6 Industrial structure in three final demands and carbon emission coefficients

	2002					2007				
	Direct coefficient (ton/ 10 thousand Yuan)	Total coefficient (ton/ 10 thousand Yuan	Per cent in consumption (%)	Per cent in investment (%)	Per cent in export (%)	Direct coefficient (ton/ 10 thousand Yuan)	Total coefficient (ton/ 10 thousand Yuan	Per cent in consumption (%)	Per cent in investment (%)	Per cent in export (%)
Agriculture, forestry, animal husbandry and fishery	0.12	1.46	14.82	2.42	1.53	0.11	0.99	8.73	1.84	0.70
Mining and washing of coal	4.19	6.91	0.30	0.36	0.51	3.42	5.87	0.11	0.03	0.24
Extraction of petroleum and natural gas	6.89	8.86	0.06	0.02	0.39	1.64	3.72	0.00	0.07	0.18
Mining and processing of metal ores	0.30	4.91	0.00	0.04	0.06	0.21	3.82	0.00	0.12	0.09
Mining and processing of non-metal and other ores	0.88	3.87	0.03	0.00	0.49	0.33	2.97	0.00	0.00	0.16
Manufacture of foods, beverages and tobacco	0.39	1.96	10.01	0.59	2.89	0.15	1.32	12.67	0.85	2.00
Manufacture of textile	0.33	2.63	1.20	−0.01	8.79	0.19	2.14	0.34	0.13	8.60
Manufacture of textile wearing apparel, footwear and caps, leather, fur, feather and related products	0.06	1.94	3.31	0.04	8.97	0.04	1.64	4.30	0.10	5.94
Processing of timber, manufacture of wood and furniture	0.13	2.65	0.56	0.25	2.15	0.07	1.96	0.39	1.12	2.54

Manufacture of paper products, printing, and manufacture of articles for culture, education and sport activities	0.57	2.90	0.59	0.22	3.19	0.48	2.51	0.32	0.08	2.37
Processing of petroleum, coking, processing of nuclear fuel	12.98	18.51	0.19	–0.10	0.85	7.09	9.84	0.57	–0.05	0.80
Chemical industries	1.62	5.73	2.02	0.53	7.03	0.76	4.06	1.78	0.44	7.58
Manufacture of non-metallic mineral products	3.17	7.14	0.78	–0.32	1.35	1.51	4.79	0.21	0.05	1.55
Smelting and pressing of metals	2.01	6.61	0.03	–0.02	1.49	0.86	4.07	0.00	0.58	5.40
Manufacture of metal products	0.08	4.21	0.52	0.72	3.44	0.03	3.07	0.31	0.98	3.72
Manufacture of general and special purpose machinery	0.12	3.14	0.10	14.03	4.22	0.05	2.34	0.05	14.60	6.00
Manufacture of transport equipment	0.18	2.81	0.95	6.59	2.11	0.06	2.02	1.86	9.24	3.44
Manufacture of electrical machinery and equipment	0.06	3.24	1.25	1.49	6.57	0.01	2.41	1.46	4.40	7.14
Manufacture of communication equipment, computers and other electronic equipment	0.03	1.81	1.70	6.54	16.05	0.02	1.30	1.47	4.01	22.38
Manufacture of measuring instruments and machinery for cultural activity and office work	0.60	2.85	0.12	0.60	4.79	0.04	1.56	0.14	1.03	3.39

Continued

Table 13.6 Continued

	2002					2007				
	Direct coefficient (ton/ 10 thousand Yuan)	Total coefficient (ton/ 10 thousand Yuan	Per cent in consumption (%)	Per cent in investment (%)	Per cent in export (%)	Direct coefficient (ton/ 10 thousand Yuan)	Total coefficient (ton/ 10 thousand Yuan	Per cent in consumption (%)	Per cent in investment (%)	Per cent in export (%)
Manufacture of artwork and other manufacturing	0.24	2.88	0.70	0.41	1.36	0.16	2.23	1.05	0.79	1.37
Recycling and disposal of waste	0.01	0.01	0.00	0.00	0.02	0.00	0.29	0.00	0.00	0.03
Production and supply of electric power and heat power	17.01	20.16	1.57	0.00	0.17	8.09	14.71	1.79	0.00	0.07
Production and supply of gas	5.94	11.96	0.22	0.02	0.00	2.97	5.45	0.24	0.00	0.00
Production and supply of water	0.12	4.80	0.20	0.00	0.00	0.05	3.74	0.24	0.00	0.00
Construction	0.04	3.44	0.00	59.86	0.34	0.02	2.79	0.71	53.05	0.43
Transport, storage and post	0.20	3.59	2.90	0.53	4.69	0.07	2.56	3.06	0.26	4.22
Wholesale and retail trades, hotels and catering services	0.07	1.63	8.74	2.40	9.33	0.05	1.08	10.24	1.79	4.97
Others	0.32	1.74	47.12	2.78	7.20	0.19	1.28	47.95	4.47	4.70
In total	–	–	100	100	100	–	–	100	100	100
Per cent of high carbon industries (%)			8.83	61.64	20.81	–	–	9.03	55.55	24.44

Note: High carbon industries are highlighted in bold.

Source: China Energy Statistical Yearbook (2008), China Statistical Yearbook (2008).

investment reached 61.64 per cent in 2002, and still maintained at 55.55 per cent in 2007. For export, the share was 20.81 per cent in 2002, and rose up to 24.44 per cent in 2007. Construction and chemical industries respectively took the biggest share as high carbon industries in investment and export.

7 Restructure three demands to slow the expansion of carbon emission

7.1 Demand 1: establish a long-term mechanism to expand consumption and change the status of the economic growth from over-reliance on investment and export.

To expand consumption demand, especially domestic consumption, is not only a necessary component in ensuring a sustained, rapid and healthy development of the economy, and the successful transformation of development pattern in China, but it is obviously an important measure for energy conservation and emission reduction as well. For a long period of time, China's economic growth was mainly due to the stimulation of investment. According to official data, in 2010, China's consumption rate was 47.4 per cent; much lower than the rate of 87.7 per cent in the US, 80.7 per cent in the EU, and 78.6 per cent in Japan, also significantly lower than the average level of middle-income countries, which was around 67 per cent. Although the potential of consumption is huge in China, it has yet to be effectively released. When it comes to current policy, measures to increase consumption are much more limited than those aimed to expand investment.

To change this situation, further reforms at the institutional level, particularly the reform of income redistribution system is needed to rationalize the redistribution structures and relations. The reform should target the matching growth of resident incomes and national economy, and the growth of labour remuneration and labour productivity, and the increase of the incomes of low-paid labours, and the proportion of middle-income earners. Also needed is an adequate social security system covering the pensions, health and unemployment, etc., and to provide the public with equal access to public services, to relieve the worries of entrepreneurs and employees.[4]

To expand consumption demand, the problem of so-called "double dual structures" should also be tackled. The term "double dual structures", refers to the dual structure occurring in the cities while the situation of dual structure between urban and rural areas has not been fundamentally changed, the former includes the difference between working and living conditions between urban residents and migrant workers and their families, and the living differences between the poor people living in shanty towns as the historical legacy of urbanization and the majority of the public. Urbanization has proved to be able to significantly bring domestic demand into full play. Some economists predicted that urbanization in China and high-tech in the US will constitute "two major engines" for the development of the world economy in the 21st century. Statistics shows that in 2010, the consumption level of rural residents in China was 4,455 Yuan, while the level of urban residents was 15,900 Yuan, which was 3.6 times that of rural residents. Based on this estimation, a newly transformed city resident is expected to increase his or her consumption by more than 10,000 Yuan each year. If the urbanization rate increases by one percentage each year, it can drag more than ten million rural people into the city, and thus stimulate ten billions in consumption demand accordingly. Therefore[5] removal of the "double dual structures" will be conducive to the coordinated development of urban and rural areas, will reduce social conflicts, and will further release the potential demands brought about by urbanization.

7.2 Demand 2: optimize the investment structure with priority being given to the new energy and circular economy

The optimization of the investment structure is impossible without the changing the status of over-production and over-investment. The change should start with eliminating backward production capacities. Meanwhile, increasing levels of new investment should be put into the areas of new energy, the technological transformation, and the development of the circular economy and clean production.

Accelerate the elimination of backward production capacities in the energy industry and heavy manufacturing sectors. Relevant analyses indicate that, the extensive pattern of economic growth with high carbonization trend in China has been maintained and even further intensified. This tendency is related to the fact that China's industrialization has entered into a stage dominated by heavy and chemical industries. Although heavy chemical industries do not necessarily produce heavy energy consumption and serious pollution problems, the backward production capacities definitely cause high energy consumption and high pollution. In essence, the current trend of high carbonation is mainly due to backward production within the energy industry and heavy manufacturing sectors. Therefore, high industry entry threshold should apply to ensure that new entrants comply with standards in terms of energy consumption, environmental protection, safety, technology, etc. On the other hand, various industrial policies of eliminating backward production capacities, including mandatory elimination and accountability mechanisms, should be strictly implemented to enable the effective shut-down of backward production capacities. The standards should also be unified nationwide to prevent the off-site transfer of backward productions.

Development of new energies and restructuring energy consumption. Previous analysis shows that changes in the energy structure have made only a small contribution to reducing carbon emission, revealing that China's energy consumption structure is relatively stable. This indicates that, it is unrealistic to expect effective emission reduction through adjusting the structure of traditional energies. Conversely, the development of new and renewable energies is the fundamental way to optimize the energy structure and emission reduction. At present, China is making great efforts to develop new energy industries. By focusing on the producing sector, however, many problems that exist in the consumption sector, such as the poor infrastructure for new energy consumption, have been neglected. More attention should be paid to the construction of new energy infrastructure, such as promoting the smart grid, and construction of new vehicle fuelling stations, to facilitate the convenient use of the new energies.

Actively develop circular economy, with particular emphasis on the promotion of cleaner production in the industrial field. Previous analysis proves that industry has always been the most important carbon emitter, particularly the energy industry and heavy manufacturing industry, while the service sector is on a trend of absolute reduction in carbon emission. Apparently, restructuring the industries by developing the service sector, and reducing the proportion of energy and heavy manufacturing industries, will be helpful to emission reduction. However, it is unrealistic for China at this stage to expect deep cuts in emission through industrial restructuring. The alternative is to actively develop a circular economy and promote cleaner production, especially in the industrial field. R&D concerning new processes and technologies in line with the principles of the circular economy should be encouraged to provide scientific and technical support for the development of the circular economy. More attention should also be given to clean production, to reduce the consumption of resources and energy, and the generation of waste from the resources.

7.3 Demand 3: optimize the export structure to reduce the embodied carbon emission exports

The foregoing analysis shows that, large carbon emission is embodied in China's exports, and export expansion effect is an important factor for

China's carbon emission growth. During 2002–07, among the total effects of scale expansion on carbon emission, export expansion accounted for over 40 per cent, which was even higher than its contribution share to total demand. This situation is to a great extent due to over-dependence on export and international markets in China's economic development, and its low-end position in the international division of industries. For this reason, lots of industries in China have had to participate in international competition at the expense of resources and the environment. For past decades, although China has been enjoying scale expansion of export, its export structure remains almost unchanged. To take chemical and related products as an example, although the amount of exports nearly doubled in the five years between 2006 and 2010, its share in total exports increased only by about one per cent, rising from 4.6 per cent from 5.6 per cent (see Figure 13.5).

To change this situation, China should accelerate the transformation of its economic development mode from relying on export and external demands to being led by consumption and domestic demands. Meanwhile, great efforts need to be made to change the low-end position of China's industries in the international rankings. By making full use of the strategic opportunities brought by the international financial crisis, China can fight for the first breakthrough in several manufacturing

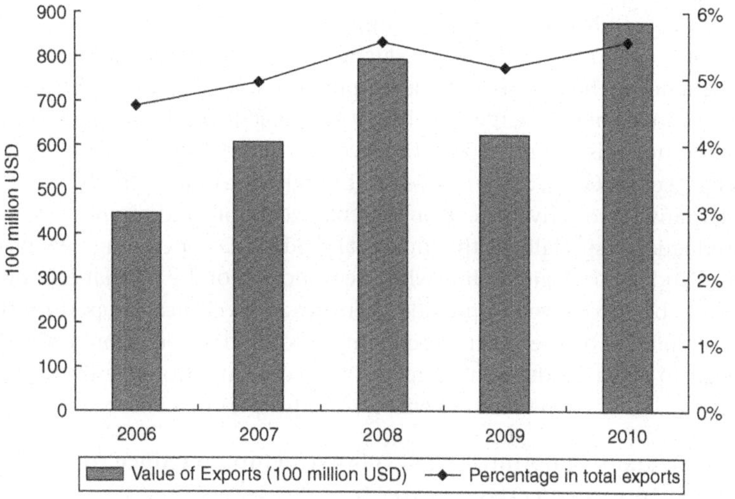

Figure 13.5 Chemical and related products exports, 2006–10
Source: China Statistical Yearbook (2011).

sectors, to form several strong industrial chains and value chains with international competitiveness on the one hand, and to reduce the excessive exploitation of resources and the environment of its industries on the other. In international climate negotiations, China should attach great importance to the issue of carbon emission transfer and actively advocate the carbon emission calculation mechanism based on the principle of common responsibility of both sides of production and consumption. This will help to ensure that the China's emission permits and emission rights are determined in a fair and reasonable framework.

In the past decade, China was able to maintain its fast economic growth at the expense of a faster increase in carbon emission and a rapid deterioration of the environment. The structural decomposition analysis (SDA) we employed in this chapter based on the 1992–2007 input/output data in China has revealed that, its economic growth pattern of over-dependence on investment and export, and internal structures of high carbon intensity, constituted the major determinants for the rampant carbon emission expansion in China since 2002. It is suggested that, to mitigate this problem, efforts should be taken in the directions of (1) effectively expanding domestic consumption, (2) restructuring investment with priorities on the new energy and circular economy, and (3) optimizing the export structure by developing manufacturing sectors and industrial chains with international competitiveness.

Notes

1. Considering that the carbon emission coefficients of different energy sources are normally stable, their contribution to aggregate effect is insignificant, we assume that the carbon emission factors remain constant and do not further single out the effect of changes in carbon emission coefficients.
2. For detailed formulation of the method, please refer to: Liu and Peng (2010) China input/output sequence tables and analysis based on comparable prices from 1992 to 2005, China Statistics Press.
3. The polar decomposition approach sets the mean value of the impact of changes in various factors decomposed from the first factor on dependent variable(s), together with the impact of changes in various factors decomposed from the last factor on dependent variable(s), as the impact of each factor on dependent variable(s).
4. Li (2012) 'Intensively Implement the Strategy of Expanding Domestic Demands in the Process of Reform and Opening-up', *Qiushi Journal* 4: 3–10.
5. Ibid.

14

Environmental Protection and Sustainability Strategies in China: Towards a Green Economy

Xiumei Guo and Dora Marinova

1 Introduction

With almost 20 per cent of the global population, China is the world's most populous economy (US Census Bureau, 2013) and the OECD (2013) anticipates that China will soon surpass the US to become the most economically powerful country. This large country already holds many other top positions but not all of them are encouraging. Since 2006, China has been the largest global greenhouse gases (GHG) emitter (PBL, 2008) and in 2008 its total ecological footprint became 2.9 billion gha – the largest for a single country (WWF, 2012). Although on a per capita basis, these statistics look better, particularly in comparison with developed economies such as the US and Australia, the impact of the Chinese economy on the globe is vast. However, China is now determined to become a significant player in tackling climate change and curbing environmental pollution. Since 2009, China has been the largest investor in new renewable energy technology (UNEP and Frankfurt School, 2013) and its current 12th Five-Year Plan is promoting a resource-efficient and environmentally friendly society.

The greening of the economy and transitioning to green growth should be at the heart of any development policies in the 21st century (OECD, 2013). This is also China's top national strategy on the road to sustainable development.

This chapter first examines China's dominant economic growth model associated with fast urbanization, increasing energy demand and pollution. It then presents China's growing concerns about the issues relating to climate change, including growing carbon emissions and industrial environmental problems. Through exploring the current government policies aimed at pollution control, we examine China's new development model set towards a greener economy. China's policy shift in environmental protection is then analysed and sustainability strategies for a green transformation are put forward.

2 Economic growth and environmental issues in China

Since 1978 when China initiated its open door and economic reform policies, the country has achieved high average annual economic growth at a rate of about 11 per cent (NBS, 2013). In 2012 the GDP growth rate was also high at 10.78 per cent (NBS, 2013) but it is expected that 2013 will become a turning point when China says goodbye to double-digit growth rates. China's economic growth was also accompanied by growing urbanization (see Figure 14.1). The share of urban population increased sharply from 17.9 per cent in 1978 to 52.6 per cent in 2012; thus more than half of Chinese citizens now live in urban areas. Both intensifying industrialization and fast-increasing urbanization drove

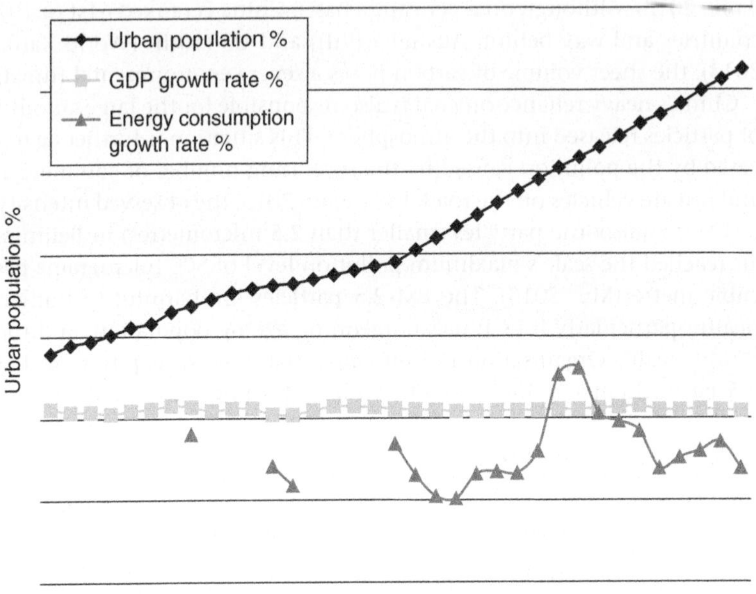

Figure 14.1 Urban population percentage, GDP growth rate and energy consumption growth rate in China, 1987–2012

Source: NBS (2013).

China's energy demand putting significant pressure on the country's limited natural resources and raising severe environmental concerns.

3 Environmental issues

Fossil fuels (coal, oil and natural gas) provide the basis for satisfying China's ever-growing energy needs (see Table 14.1). However, the energy mix has changed since 1978. Over the last 35 years, dependence on coal has increased due to the ample availability of this resource, despite the overall decrease in the reliance on fossil fuels (from 96.9% in 1978 to 89.9%) (NBS, 2013).

China's rapid GDP growth over the last three decades has caused serious airborne pollution in many cities and rural regional areas (Wei et al., 2012). In particular, the use of coal as well as other fossil fuels for energy supply is a serious environmental problem due to the associated high CO_2 (or carbon) emissions as well as air pollution. China is the leading carbon emitter (see Figure 14.2) with an annual generation of more than 7.5 billion tonnes of carbon dioxide emissions stemming from the burning of fossil fuels and the manufacture of cement (World Bank, 2013). Although on a per capita basis, China is ranked 61st of 197 countries and way behind Australia (9th) and US (10th) (World Bank, 2013), the sheer volume of carbon poses a severe environmental threat.

China's heavy reliance on coal is also responsible for the large amount of particles released into the atmosphere. This situation is further aggravated by the pollution caused by the increasing number of commercial and private vehicles on the road. In January 2013, the observed intensity of PM 2.5 (airborne particles smaller than 2.5 micrometres) in Beijing's air reached the scale's maximum pollution level of 500 micrograms per cubic metre (Mu, 2013). The PM 2.5 particles are harmful to human health, particularly for China's burgeoning ageing population, and the World Health Organisation recommends that 24-hour exposure to PM 2.5 be no higher than 25 (South China Morning Post, 2013). It was

Table 14.1 Energy mix in China, 1978–2012

	Coal	Oil	Natural Gas	Hydro/ Nuclear/Wind
1978	70.3	23.7	2.9	3.1
1990	74.2	19	2.0	4.3
2012	76.6	8.9	4.4	10.1

Source: NBS (2013).

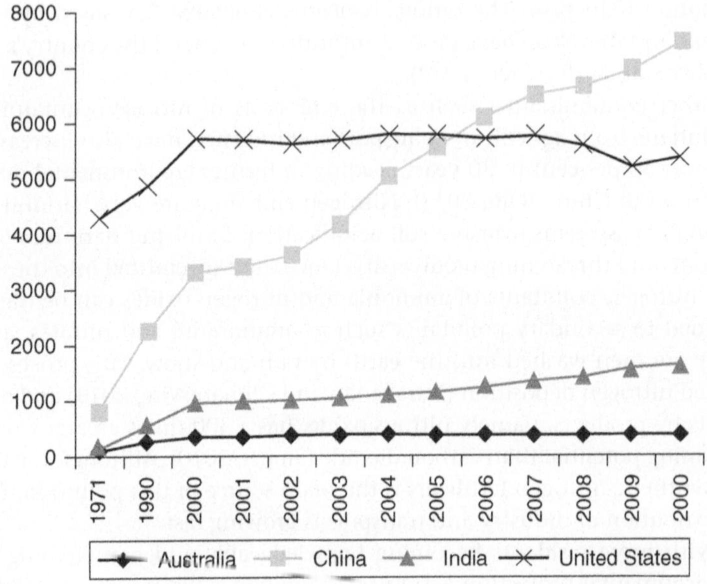

Figure 14.2 CO_2 emissions from fuel combustion, 1971–2010 (million tonnes) (GHG)

Source: OECD (2013b).

reported that the number of patients with respiratory illnesses sharply increased; some schools had to cancel their outdoor sports activities, and the wellbeing of city residents was jeopardized by the heavy smog. These particles are a major health hazard that can trigger cardiovascular and respiratory diseases (Chen, 2012). They are responsible for a significant reduction in average life expectancies, premature deaths, additional hospital admissions, increased use of medication and millions of days every year where human activities are restricted (CEC, 2005). Consequently, news about Beijing's air pollution was widely reported domestically and globally. The Chinese capital is just one of the many cities suffering from potent air pollution due to the country's increasing industrialization. Other cities affected include Shanghai, Guangzhou and Tianjin.

Recently, the Chinese public started to voice its concerns that people are paying for economic growth with their health (Economy, 2004). China's oldest and highly influential non-governmental organisation (NGO), Friends of Nature, has been playing a significant role in air pollution reduction. The serious concerns about PM 2.5 raised by the public and this NGO have pushed authorities to amend the country's air quality standards (Chen, 2012).

Other contaminants, such as the emissions of nitrogen-containing pollutants from agriculture, transport and industry, have also increased by over 50 per cent in 30 years, leading to further environmental deterioration in China (Qiu, 2013). Nitrogen emissions are very harmful to China's ecosystems, causing soil acidification, fertilizing harmful algal blooms and threatening biodiversity. Once they are emitted into the air, key nitrogen pollutants of ammonia and nitrogen oxides can be transformed to secondary pollutants such as ammonium and nitrates, and they are then washed into the earth by rain and snow. This process is called nitrogen deposition (Narayanan and ClimateWire, 2013) and one of its by-products, namely nitrous oxide, has a 300 times greater global warming potential than carbon dioxide (Smith, 2010). Although the use of synthetic nitrogen fertilizers is the main source of this pollution, the contribution of industry and transport is growing fast.

With more residents becoming knowledgeable and participating in environmental protection activities, the public is becoming a powerful force in influencing China's environmental protection. According to Friends of Nature (2012 and 2013), people have started to gradually understand their right to be involved and demand improvements in the government's decision-making efficiency in relation to air quality and pollution. This has triggered a range of important positive changes.

4 Enterprises strictly monitored for pollution and information disclosure

In 2008 and 2013, the Ministry of Environmental Protection of China published the names of enterprises which needed extensive supervision for pollution. These enterprises were encouraged to standardize their self-monitoring processes and provide information disclosure in relation to their operations. They were also urged to meet regulatory obligations with respect to environmental protection, take on social responsibilities and encourage public participation (Ministry of Environmental Protection of the PRC, 2013).

The self-monitoring entails that these enterprises undertake environmental monitoring activities according to existing environmental protection laws and regulations for the purpose of understanding their waste discharge situation and the ensuing impact on surrounding areas. They need to monitor discharged water pollutants, airborne pollutants and noise pollution, report and guarantee environmental quality according to their environmental impact assessment form. In 2008, the environmental authorities identified 3,472 enterprises as requiring strict monitoring for airborne pollution due to their heavy industrial wastes and negative impacts on agricultural land (Ministry of Environmental Protection of the PRC, 2009). The new list includes "more than 15,000 enterprises that discharge wastewater and gas, sewage treatment plants, heavy metal enterprises, and livestock and poultry farms" to be under state monitoring (Anon, 2013, n.p.).

With the introduction of environmental information disclosure in 2008 (Zhang et al., 2010), there was urgent need to standardize China's environmental laws and regulations. However, the best way to solve the environmental pollution problem was to strengthen administrative accountability. This meant that Chinese government officials from administrative organs were made responsible and consequently penalized for corruption or if they acted as an "umbrella" to protect those who continued with illegal discharge of waste into the environment. Local governments in particular are now expected to undertake full administrative accountability for environmental protection, including for enterprises that break environmental laws and regulations and need to face serious punishment and penalties (Xinhuanet, 2013c). The strictly monitored enterprises are part of the responsibility of local governments and environmental accountability is seen as the key to pollution control.

For a long period of time the performance of local governments was assessed primarily on GDP growth, so making local leaders accountable for environmental pollution is a major change in direction by the central government. Local government achievements are now assessed not only on pursuing economic growth but also on their environmental performance. Local governments are now acting as environmental watchdogs and regulators who have power to punish cities and enterprises for environmental pollution and they regularly release blacklists of cities and industrial enterprises that are penalized for failing to properly treat pollution discharges (Chen, 2012).

Information disclosure is becoming an important method for pollution control and encourages enterprises to take more environmental responsibilities. In 2008, according to their emissions of SO_2 and NO_2, over 80 thousand of China's enterprises were ranked by the Ministry of Environmental Protection, which named 3,472 enterprises of them as requiring to be strictly monitored for airborne pollution because their industrial emissions contributed 65 per cent of the total industrial pollution (Ministry of Environmental Protection of the PRC, 2009). With 2,069 or almost 60 per cent of the listed enterprises located in 899 counties of China, the contamination from these industries was having negative economic impacts causing agricultural loss due to airborne and other pollutants. For example, in spite of the ground-level ozone, the emissions of SO_2 by the strictly monitored enterprises reached 17.05 million tonnes in 2011, accounting for 84 per cent of total industrial SO_2 emissions (NBS, 2011).

In 2013, the list of strictly monitored enterprises was updated by the Ministry of Environmental Protection and became longer indicating that overall the number of big polluters has decreased with more enterprises accounting for 65% of the total industrial pollution. It comprises over 15 thousand enterprises to be strictly monitored for waste pollution, including 4,944 enterprises monitored for waste water discharge, 4,189 enterprises monitored for waste gases, 3,581 enterprises supervised for dirty water discharge, 2,834 enterprises for heavy metal discharges and 249 livestock and poultry farms (Ministry of Environmental Protection of the PRC, 2013).

There is a lot of publicity given to the performance of these enterprises. For example, the Guangzhou Municipal Environmental Protection Bureau published in the media the names of 67 strictly monitored enterprises and required them to disclose their data on pollutants. The list includes 18 enterprises monitored for waste gases, 28 for waste water and 21 for heavy metal, such as Guangzhou Petro-chemical Factory, Guangzhou Steel and Iron Factory, Zhujiang Beer and nine other large electricity-generating factories which are the main sources of major pollutants (Ifeng, 2013). For example, the Guangzhou Petro-chemical Factory emitted over 40 per cent of the volatile organic compounds (VOCs), the main cause of smog formation in the city. The power generating factories dominate the Guangzhou list emitting 20 per cent of the PM 2.5. Through strengthening and increasing the frequency of field investigations and supervising the environmental protection work, the listed monitored enterprises are requested to enhance their monitoring system capacity. They were also asked to report their data to the relevant environmental authorities on a regular basis and to report the measures taken. Eventually they were pushed to accept public supervision through online reporting of pollutants data (Ifeng, 2013) while also bearing the costs for any new technology and devices for conducting the self-monitoring tasks (Xinhuanet, 2013).

Despite the many measures put in place across many regions, pollution compliance continues to be a serious problem in China. The Ministry of Public Security and the Environmental Protection Bureau are actively prosecuting offenders who illegally discharge poisonous and other pollutants, including those who do this indirectly through agents in order to reduce their waste processing costs (Xinhuanet, 2013a).

Water pollution is also becoming a serious environmental problem. A constant monitoring survey for 118 Chinese cities shows that 64 per cent of their underground water was severely polluted, 33 per cent was slightly polluted and only 3 per cent of the underground water is basically clean (Xinhuanet, 2013b). Meanwhile, 88 enterprises from six northern provinces were fined over CNY 6 million for illegal pollutant discharge (Xinhuanet, 2013b).

Economic expansion causing growth in the consumption of fossil fuels is triggering increasing levels of emissions of sulphur oxides (SO_x), nitrogen oxides (NO_x), carbon dioxide, soot and fine particulates (Wang et al., 2007). China's industry and agricultural sectors are also contributing to environmental deterioration. Among serious concerns voiced by the public, the government started to put in place initiatives that attempt to control and curb pollution. Despite many challenges, China is slowly shifting onto a path to improve its environmental record and develop a greener economy.

5 Greening the economy in China

China's sustained economic growth contributed to fast industrialization, urbanization and improvements in the living standards of millions of people. The government has achieved enormous success in alleviating poverty. Official estimates indicate that between 1978 and 2010 the incidence of rural poverty fell from over 30 per cent to only about 3 per cent, and the size of rural population living in poverty decreased from around 250 million to 27 million (Household Survey, 2011). This however has come at a price for the country's natural environment and global ecology.

According to the Global Footprint Network (2013) assessment, China is operating in a state of biocapacity deficit as its per capita ecological footprint is 2.5 times the available per capita biocapacity in the country. It is also bigger than the global per capita biocapacity and has been on a steady rising trend in the last ten years (WWF, 2012). The growth in the total ecological footprint is triggered by the increasing total consumption of resources with the carbon footprint being the most rapidly expanding component (WWF, 2012).

The need for a change in this development pattern is recognized by the Chinese government, which is determined to put the country's economy on a green path. Since 1989, when the green economy concept was first put forward by Pearce (Pearce et al., 1989), many countries are taking actions in this direction. According to UNEP (2013, p. 31), a green economy is "one that results in improved human wellbeing and social equity, while significantly reducing environmental risks and ecological scarcities." Such "transition to a green economy not only generates increases in wealth, in particular a gain in ecological commons or natural capital, but also, over a period of six years, produces a higher rate of GDP growth" (UNEP, 2013, p. 32).

An evolving green economy helps improve ecosystem health and maintain its functionality and this is what China is set to achieve. It is expected that developing a green economy can put a brake on China's environmental deterioration. This economy is characterized by a resource efficient and environmentally friendly society as outlined in China's current 12th Five-Year Plan. The extensive development model characterized with high consumption of energy and raw materials, high pollution and GHG emissions needs to be transformed into a low-carbon and circular economy (centred around reduction, recycling, reusing and rethinking) which aims at reconciling the contradiction between limited natural resources and what appears to be unlimited human demand (Shen, 2010). This involves green industrialization and high technology industries with innovation playing a substantial and decisive role (Marinova et al., 2013).

This process of transformation comes with both challenges and opportunities. There is urgent need to look for solutions at a rate faster than the rate of environmental degradation (UNEP, 2013) while continuing to improve people's wellbeing. To achieve this, both private companies and governments are investing in innovation. Real growth spending on R&D in China has exceeded 18 per cent since 2000 with the aim of reaching 2.2 per cent of GDP by 2015 (McLean-Dreyfus and Bendemra, 2012). Investment in R&D is on an upward trend (see Figure 14.3) and in 2012, 47 Chinese companies were in the top global 1,000 largest R&D investors (Jaruzelski et al., 2012). In 2011, China became the world's top nation for domestic patent applications – surpassing both Japan and the United States. Its 12th Five-Year Plan (2011–15) sets the target of transforming China into an innovation-oriented society by 2020 and the evidence shows that this is already happening.

China announced an intention to voluntarily cut its emissions of carbon dioxide per unit of GDP by 2020 by around 40 to 45 per cent based on 2005 levels. Between 1990 and 2005 China reduced its carbon intensity by 44 per cent (40–45% reduction by 2020 in Copenhagen;

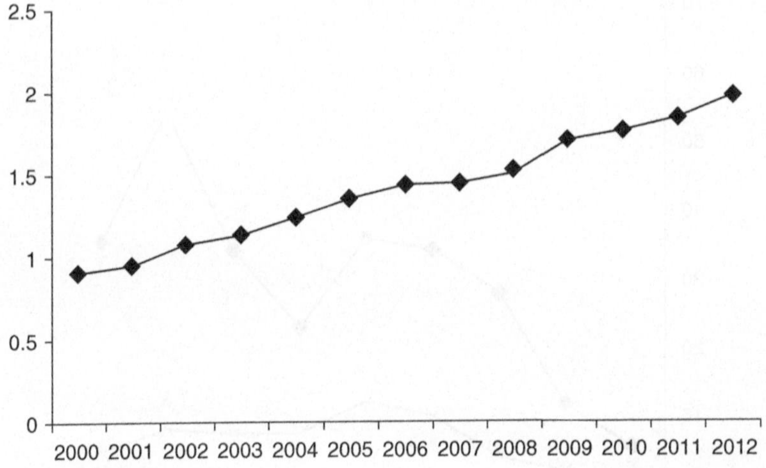

Figure 14.3 R&D intensity (the ratio of R&D expenditure over GDP), China, 2000–12

Source: National Bureau of Statistics of China.

17% reduction in China's current 12th Five-Year Plan by 2015). In 2009, China overtook the US in total installed energy capacity and new investment in renewable energy (see Figure 14.4); in 2013 it is the top renewables investor followed by Germany, US and India (UNEP and Frankfurt School, 2013). China also ranks 3rd (after France and Japan) according to the low-carbon competitive index (The Climate Institute, 2013). With commitments increasing by 22 per cent to USD 67 billion, mainly due to solar investment, China now hosts 27 per cent of the global renewable energy total (UNEP and Frankfurt School, 2013).

The concentration of clean energy, the flagship of the green economy, has now turned into Asia, particularly in China, Japan and South Korean through high technology exports and the large amount of public investment in the clean energy field (The Climate Institute/GE, 2013). In the transition to a green economy, the new jobs created over time exceed the losses in brown economy employment. This is the case with China where new jobs are constantly being created (Pan et al., 2011). Achieving this net gain, however, requires investment in re-skilling and re-educating the workforce where China also excels. According to the International Labour Organisation (ILO, 2013), the pursuit of a green economy will not cut employment opportunities overall, on the contrary, it will generate more and decent jobs. In China, with proper strategies, this

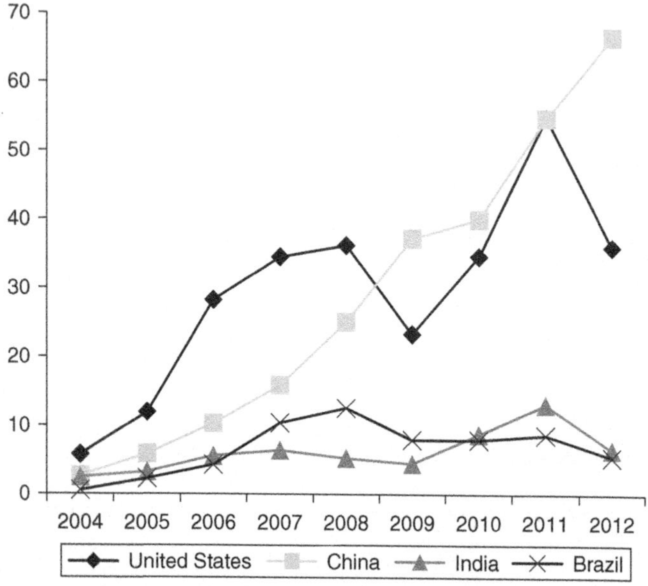

Figure 14.4 Trends in renewable energy investment, 2004–12 (USD billion)
Source: UNEP and Frankfurt School, 2013.

change will help reduce the environmental and resource pressure from economic development and create employment opportunities in enterprises that are more environmentally friendly, enhance innovation and attract investment. According to the Worldwatch Institute (2013), it is expected that China's fast-growing economy will create millions of new green jobs over the next eight years. China's energy, transportation and forestry sectors alone could provide at least 4.5 million green jobs by 2020 (Worldwatch Institute, 2013).

There is already evidence that the transition to a green economy is contributing towards reducing GHG emissions. Figure 14.5 compares China's provincial CO_2 emission intensities in 2003 and 2011. The trends show that all provincial CO_2 emissions per capita GDP dropped considerably at various levels (Jia et al., 2013). The central and western regions had overall higher annual decrease rates, which illustrates that the traditional regional disparity between the East and the rest of the country is gradually reducing as a result of the green economy.

China's national innovation system has been progressively enhanced by new knowledge, green technologies and growing R&D investment.

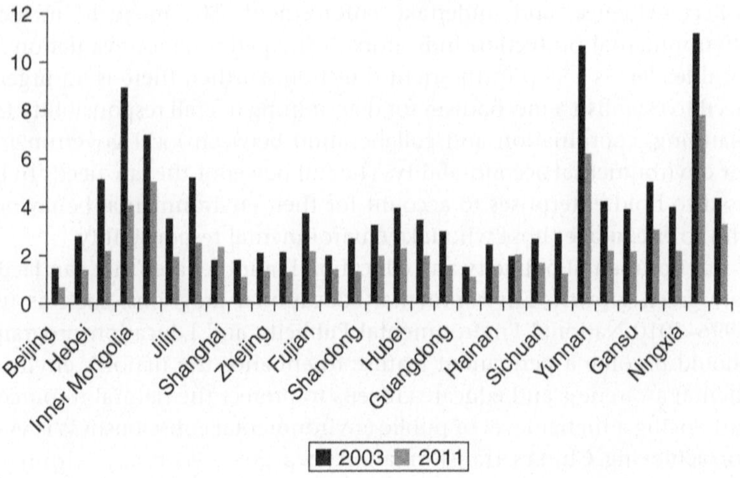

Figure 14.5 CO_2 emission intensities of China's provinces in 2003 and 2011
Source: Jia et al. (2013) and authors' calculation.

The country is evolving as a significant player in addressing global warming and tackling pollution, which is stimulating its transformation towards a green economy. As part of the emerging global green system of innovation (Marinova et al., 2013), China is now an important global player in green innovations.

6 Factors influencing the transformation to a green economy

There are many factors assisting the smooth transition to a green economy in China. However, government accountability, environmental education, public participation and environmental regulation all play a major key role in this process and we briefly examine them below.

Although environmental accountability has long been established, it has not been easy for all levels of governments to properly implement these regulations due to the gap between power and responsibility in local governments. Often faced with environmental incidents, relevant local governments avoid their responsibilities (China Environment, 2012). A more mature mechanism needs to be put in place with strengthened supervision to allow local authorities to demand accountability, collect evidence, and undertake enforcement. The move to include environmental protection indicators in the performance evaluation of local leaders is a step in the right direction. Further, there is an urgent need to establish a mechanism for determining overall responsibility for planning, coordination and collaboration between local governments for environmental accountability. The full power of the law needs to be used to hold enterprises to account for their environmental behaviour and to encourage those who take environmental responsibility.

Environmental publicity and education is another area that can facilitate green growth. Environmental educational programs, such as the 1996–2010 National Environmental Publicity and Education program, should become a permanent feature to enhance the nation's environmental awareness and educate citizens to protect the natural resources. Enhancing a higher level of public environmental consciousness is vital for achieving China's transformation to a green economy within an energy-efficient and environmentally friendly society. Such environmental education programs need to be carried out in adult education, mass media and through activities targeting business people, government agencies and pollution producers. China's effort to promote environmental protection will gradually increase people's environmental consciousness. Environmental training programmes, including developing a low-carbon economy, should be delivered to environmental experts, scientific, technological and managerial personnel to decouple economic growth from environmental pressure.

The mass media play an important role in increasing environmental awareness and particularly government-owned newspapers have been performing this role increasingly well. They not only trigger public concern for environmental damage but they also strongly create public consciousness. After an incident of environmental damage is disclosed in the media, this generates a lot of public opinion pressure on the polluter as well as on the local government to which they have to respond by taking appropriate measures. Positive environmental publicity on the other hand plays a significant role in public environmental education and guidance. The topic of environmental protection has increasingly been covered by media reports in all the provincial newspapers (see Figure 14.6), contributing to environmental publicity, supervision and disclosure of environmental incidents.

China's non-governmental organisations have also contributed in improving environmental awareness and behaviours. For example, Greenpeace and Friends of Nature have helped push the green transformation; the people's congress started to discuss and undertake laws and

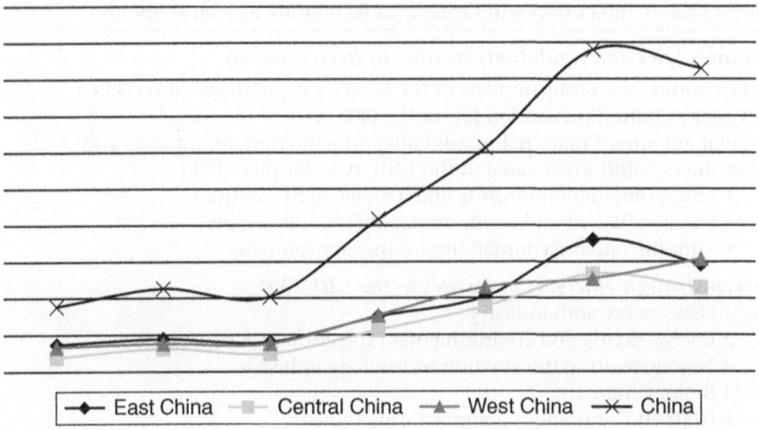

Figure 14.6 News/Articles related to environmental protection in provincial newspapers in China, 2003–09
Source: Guo and Marinova (2010).

regulations to control environmental pollution and China has added several environmental laws and regulations in the 12th Five-Year Plan. The environmental management mechanism in China has generally improved to prevent more polluting incidents happening. For example, in recent years, the number of environmental petitions and proposals submitted to the National People's Congress (NPC) and the Committee of the Chinese People's Political Consultative Conference (CPPCC) has been steadily growing, indicating that the level of public participation and consciousness in environmental protection is on the rise (Guo and Marinova, 2010).

China's significant efforts in battling pollution – more than CNY 3 trillion were recently allocated by the Chinese government to improve air and water quality in the next five years (Zhi, 2013) with CNY 1.7 trillion to be used for airborne pollution (Wee, 2013) – would not be achieved without strengthening and improving China's environmental laws and regulations. Current regulations and plans for this transformation are covered in Table 14.2. The country's environmental protection industries are expecting a golden period with many opportunities to improve key technologies and the provision of environment protection devices and services (Xinhuanet, 2013d).

China's first regulation of accountability for the environment was implemented in 2006. Its objective of building a resource-efficient,

Table 14.2 China's laws and regulations facilitating a green economy

China's laws and regulations relating to green economy

- Environmental protection law of the People's Republic of China (PRC)
- Water pollution prevention law of the PRC
- Total amount of main pollutants emission reduction, monitoring and assessment solutions covered in the 12th five-year plan (FYP)
  - Environmental monitoring and management solutions
  - Energy-efficient and environmentally friendly society
  - Administrative accountability for the environment

Seven strategic emerging industries in the 12th FYP

1 New energy auto industry
2 Energy-saving and environmental protection industry
3 New generation information technology industry
4 Biology industry
5 High-end equipment manufacturing industry
6 New energy industry
7 New material industry

Targets covered in the 12th FYP

- Reduce the energy-intensity of the economy by 16% and increase non-fossil energy to 11.4% of total supply
- Cut the carbon intensity of GDP by 17%
- Slower energy demand growth

Source: Compiled by the authors.

environmentally friendly and harmonious society represents the whole spectrum of sustainability goals.

7 Conclusion

This chapter analysed China's environmental transformation and its path towards a green economy, where balanced, mutually supportive and reinforcing relationships exist between economic development and the natural environment (Green Economy Taskforce, 2011).

China's astonishing economic rise in the last three decades has attracted a lot of global attention. However, the country is also criticized for its environmental deterioration, particularly for emitting the largest amount of carbon dioxide relating to global warming. As the world's largest country, China's development trajectory is vital to the global achievement of sustainability. Its growing investment in R&D, renewable energy, sustainable technology innovation and green jobs is making the country emerge as a green energy leader and helps to decarbonize its economy.

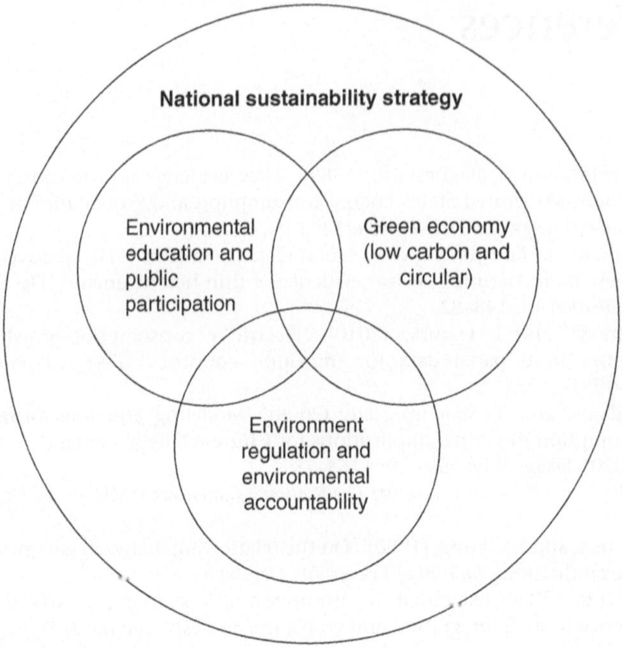

Figure 14.7 China's national sustainability strategy
Source: Developed by the authors.

Building a resource-efficient and environmentally friendly society is a long-term strategy and it is challenging for China to balance the basic sustainability goals of developing a green economy, ensuring ecological protection and accountability, and improving people's education and encouraging public participation (see Figure 14.7). China's government policy is shifting to these goals with the understanding that GDP growth is beneficial to many people, but all Chinese people will benefit from a good environment in a harmonious society. Building an energy-efficient and environmentally friendly society is very important for China's transition to a green economy. Committing to improving the quality of economic growth, which the green economy represents, is a prerequisite to maintain the long-term, steady and relatively fast growth of the Chinese economy.

Acknowledgement

The authors acknowledge the financial support of the Australian Research Council.

References

S. Abosedra, and H. Baghestani, (1989). 'New evidence on the causal relationship between United States energy consumption and gross national product', *Journal of Energy and Development* 14: 285–92.

F. Abraham, J. Konings, and V. Slootmaekers, (2010). 'FDI spillovers in the Chinese manufacturing sector: evidence of firm heterogeneity', *The Economics of Transition* 18: 143–82.

A. Acaravci, and I. Ozturk, (2010). 'Electricity consumption-growth nexus: evidence from panel data for transition countries', *Energy Economics* 32: 604–08.

G.F. Adams, and Y. Shachmurove, (2008). 'Modeling and forecasting energy consumption in China: implications for Chinese energy demand and imports in 2020', *Energy Economics* 30: 1263–78.

P. Aghion, and P. Howitt, (2009). *The Economics of Growth*. MIT Press. Cambridge, MA.

A.T. Akarca, and T.V. Long, (1980). 'On the relationship between energy and GNP: a re-examination', *Journal of Energy and Development* 5: 326–31.

A.E. Akinlo, (2009). 'Electricity consumption and economic growth in Nigeria: evidence from cointegration and co-feature analysis', *Journal of Policy Modeling* 31: 681–93.

E. Akhmadov, (2008). 'Uzbekistan: Central Asian Union destined to remain on paper', http://www.cacianalyst.org/?q=node/4850, date accessed 15 December 2012.

K. Akkemik, K. Göksal, and J. Li, (2012). 'Energy consumption and income in Chinese Provinces: heterogeneous panel causality analysis', *Applied Energy* 99: 445–54.

F. Albornoz, M.A. Cole, R. Elliott, and M. Ercolani, (2009). 'In search of environmental spillovers', *World Economy* 32: 136–63.

M.A. Al-Iriani, (2006). 'Energy–GDP relationship revisited: an example from GCC countries using panel causality', *Energy Policy* 34: 3342–50.

B. Algieri, A. Aquino, and M. Sucurro, (2011). 'Going "green": trade specialisation dynamics in the solar photovoltaic sector', *Energy Policy* 39: 7275–83.

M. Alguacil, A. Cuadros, and V. Orts, (2011). 'Inward FDI and growth: the role of macroeconomic and institutional environment', *Journal of Policy Modeling* 33: 481–96.

G. Altinay, and E. Karagol, (2004). 'Structural break, unit root, and causality between energy consumption and GDP in Turkey', *Energy Economics* 26: 985–94.

G. Altinay, and E. Karagol, (2005). 'Electricity consumption and economic growth: evidence from Turkey', *Energy Economics* 27: 849–56.

L. Anceschi, (2009). 'Energy governance and climate change: Central Asia's uneasy nexus', in: Anceschi, L. and Symons, J. (eds) *Energy security in the era of climate change, the Asia-Pacific experience*, Basingstoke: Palgrave Macmillan.

L.B. Andonova, (2003). 'Openness and the environment in Central and Eastern Europe: can trade and foreign investment stimulate better environmental management in enterprises?', *Journal of Environment & Development* 12: 177–204.

P. Andrews-Speed, (2007). 'China's coal-to-liquid plans: a good idea?', CEPMLP Gateway, http://www.dundee.ac.uk/cepmlp/gateway/index.php?news=29055.

Anonymous (Anon.), (2013). 'Enterprises urged to conduct self-monitoring, disclose information', http://news.xinhuanet.com/english/china/2013-07/31/c_132591344.htm (accessed 11 August 2013).

Asian Times, (2006). 'China cools down coal liquefaction', 04 October 2006, http://www.atimes.com/atimes/China_Business/HJ04Cb01.html.

N. Apergis, and J.E. Payne, (2009a). 'Energy consumption and economic growth: evidence from the commonwealth of independent states', *Energy Economics* 31: 641–47.

N. Apergis, and J.E. Payne, (2009b). 'Energy consumption and economic growth in Central America: evidence from a panel cointegration and error correction model', *Energy Economics* 31: 211–16.

K. Ari, and Y. Liu, (2010). 'Wind power in China: policy and development challenges', *Energy Policy* 38: 5520–29.

S. Aris, (2008). 'Russian-Chinese relations through the lens of the SCO', IFRI Russia/NIS Center, Paris 2008

S. Aris, (2009). 'Shanghai Cooperation Organisation: an anti-western alignment?', http://www.css.ethz.ch/publications/pdfs/CSS-Analyses-66.pdf (accessed 9 December 2012).

K.J. Arrow, (1962). 'The economic implications of learning-by-doing', *Review of Economic Studies* 29: 155–73.

J. Asafu-Adjaye, (2000). 'The relationship between energy consumption, energy prices and economic growth: time series evidence from Asian developing countries', *Energy Economics* 22: 615–25.

Alyson J.K. Bailes, P. Dunay, G. Pan, and M. Troitskiy (eds), (2007). 'The Shanghai Cooperation Organization', http://www.strategicstudiesinstitute.army.mil/pubs/display.cfm?pubid=1063 (accessed 8 July 2011).

T. Balmforth, (2011). 'Turkmenistan: China export deal undercuts Gazprom's leverage', www.eurasianet.org/node/64609 (accessed 1 December 2012).

P. Bansal, and R. Kendall, (2000). 'Why companies go green: a model of ecologicalresponsiveness', *Academy of Management Journal* 43: 717–36.

S. Batrakova, and R. Davies, (2012). 'Is there an environmental benefit to being an exporter? Evidence from firm-level data', *Review of World Economics* 148: 449–74.

P. Barua, (2012). 'Delivering the clean energy economy: why policy matters', *WRI Insights*, 15 November.

P. Barua, L. Tawney, and L. Weischer, (2012). *Delivering on the clean energy economy: the role of policy in developing successful domestic solar and wind industries*. Working Paper, World Resources Institute, World Resources Institute.

BBC, (2011). 'Russia-China pipeline opens', http://www.bbc.co.uk/news/world-asia-pacific-12103865.

A. Belke, C. Dreger, and F. de Haan, (2010). 'Energy consumption and economic growth. New insights into the cointegration relationship', Ruhr Economic Papers No. 109.

H. Bersager, (2012). 'China, Russia and Central Asia: the energy dilemma', http://www.fni.no/doc&pdf/FNI-R1612.pdf (accessed 5 December 2012).

Beyond Fossil Fuel, (2006). 'China leads the way to coal-to-liquid production', 12 February 2006, http://www.beyondfossilfuelcom/resources/liquid_coal_1202.html.

R. Bezdek, (2007). 'Looming oil problems: myths and realities', Keynote speech at Smart 2007 Conference, Sydney, June 2007.

S.C. Bhattacharyya, (2011). *Energy economics: concepts, issues, markets and governance*. Springer, UK, London.

F. Birol, and J.H. Keppler, (2000). 'Prices, technology, development and the rebound effect', *Energy Policy* 28: 457–69.

G. Blalock, and P. Gertler, (2008). 'Welfare gains from foreign direct investment through technology transfer to local suppliers', *Journal of International Economics* 74: 402–21.

S. Blank, (2010). 'The strategic implications of the Turkmenistan-China pipeline project', http://www.jamestown.org/programs/chinabrief/single/?tx_ttnews[tt_news]=36010&tx_ttnews[backPid]=414&no_cache=1 (accessed 8 December 2012).

H. Bloch, S. Rafiq, and R. Salim, (2012). 'Coal consumption, Co_2 emission and economic growth in China: empirical evidence and policy response', *Energy Economics* 34: 518–28.

Z. Bo, (2010). 'China's new national energy commission: policy implications', EAI Background Brief, No. 504, February.

N. Bowden, and J.E. Payne, (2009). 'The causal relationship between U.S. energy consumption and real output: a disaggregated analysis', *Journal of Policy Modeling* 31(2): 180–88.

K. Bradsher, (2010). 'China leading global race to make clean energy', *The New York Times*, January 31.

B. Brauer, (2011). 'Top of form rumors of secret land lease to China causes unease in Kazakhstan', http://www.jamestown.org/single/?no_cache=1&tx_ttnews[tt_news]=37645 (accessed 15 December 2012).

T.P. Brennand, (2001). 'Wind energy in China: policy options for development', *Energy for Sustainable Development* V: 84–91.

British Petroleum (BP), (2012). 'BP energy outlook 2030', http://www.bp.com/extendedsectiongenericarticle.do?categoryId=9048887&contentId=7082549 (accessed 21 October 2012).

British Petroleum (BP), (2012). *Statistical review of world energy*.

Brookings Institute, (2006). *Brookings foreign policy studies: energy security series: China*, NY, Brookings Institute.

M. Bu, Z. Liu, and Y. Gao, (2011). 'Influence of international openness on corporate environmental performance in China', *China and World Economy* 19: 77–92.

M. Bu, Z. Liu, and Y. Gao, (2013). 'Corporate social responsibility and the pollution haven hypothesis: evidence from multinationals' investment decision in China', *Asia-Pacific Journal of Accounting & Economics*. DOI:10.1080/16081625.2013.759175. forthcoming.

V. Bukarica, Z. Morvaj, and S. Robić, (2012). 'Energy efficiency master plan for Tajikistan. Energy efficiency for economic development and poverty reduction', http://europeandcis.undp.org/uploads/public1/files/vulnerability/Senior%20

Economist%20Web%20site/EEMP_Tajikistan_v1.pdf (accessed 12 January 2013).

K. Button, N. Ngoe, and J. Hine, (1993). 'Modeling vehicle ownership and use in low income countries', *Journal of Transport Economics and Policy* 27(1): 51–67.

J. Byrne, A. Zhou, B. Shen, and K. Hughes, (2007). 'Evaluating the potential of small-scale renewable energy options to meet rural livelihoods needs: a GIS- and lifecycle cost-based assessment of Western China's options', *Energy Policy* 35: 4391–401.

R.J. Campbell, (2011). 'China and the United States—a comparison of green energy programs and policies', ILR School, Cornell University.

A. Canas, P. Ferrao, and P. Conceicao, (2003). 'A new environmental Kuznets curve? Relationship between direct material input and income per capita: evidence from industrialised countries', *Ecological Economics* 46(2): 217–29.

F. Caselli, and D. Wison, (2004). 'Importing Technology', *Journal of Monetary Economics* 51: 1–32.

Central Asia Economy Newswire, (2012). 'Kazakh-Kyrgyz-Chinese pipeline saves Kyrgyzstan $30M', http://www.universalnewswires.com/centralasia/economy/viewstory.aspx?id=12560 (accessed 4 December 2012).

Centro Mario Molina, (2008). 'Low carbon growth: a potential path for Mexico', Centro Mario Molina para EstudiosEstratégicos de Energía y Medio Ambiente, México.

J. Chai, J-E. Guo, S-Y. Wang, and K. Lai, (2009). 'Why does energy intensity fluctuate in China?', *Energy Policy* 37: 5717–31.

T. Chang, W. Fang, and L. Wen, (2001). 'Energy consumption, employment, output, and temporal causality: evidence from Taiwan based on cointegration and error correction modeling techniques', *Applied Economics* 33: 1045–56.

R.H. Charlier, (2001). 'Ocean alternative energy: the view from China-small is beautiful', *Renewable and Sustainable Energy Reviews* 5: 403–09.

G. Chen, (2000). 'Development and reform of China's petroleum industry in the early 21st century', *International Petroleum Economics* 1, (in Chinese).

S. Chen, (2009). 'Marketization and China's energy security', *Policy and Society* 27: 249–60.

S.T. Chen, H.I. Kuo, and C.C. Chen, (2007). 'The relationship between GDP and electricity consumption in ten Asian countries', *Energy Policy* 35(4): 2611–21.

X. Chen 小沁, (2009). 'The preliminary study of the mechanism of energy cooperation in the SCO (上海合作 能源合作 初探)', *Education and Research (教学与研究)* 9: 56–61.

X. Chen, (2012). 'Public awareness of environment grows: report', *China Daily*, http://www.chinadaily.com.cn/china/2012-04/20/content_15094802.htm (accessed 8 August 2013).

B.S. Cheng, (1995). 'An investigation of cointegration and causality between energy consumption and economic growth', *Journal of Energy and Development* 21: 73–84.

J. Cherni, and J. Kentish, (2007). 'Renewable energy sources and electricity market reform in China', *Energy Policy* 35: 3616–29.

China Business Review, (2005). September–October.

Chinese Communist Party, (2011). 'China's 12th 5 Year Plan', Chinese Government.

China Daily, (2013). 'China sets emission reduction target', 24 January 2013, http://www.chinadaily.com.cn/china/2013-01/24/content_16172153.htm.

China Directory, (2012). Edited by Radiopress, Inc., Tokyo: JPM Corporation.

China Energy Statistical Yearbook, (2009–11).

China Environment, (2012). 'How to improve environmental accountability? (in Chinese)', http://www.cenews.com.cn/xwzx/gd/qt/201202/t20120215_712769.html (accessed 15 June 2012).

China Petroleum and Chemical Industry Federation (CPCIF) Annual Report, (2010).

China Statistical Yearbook, 1995–2011.

J. Chontanawat, L.C. Hunt, and R. Pierse, (2008). 'Does energy consumption cause economic growth? Evidence from a systematic study of over 100 countries', *Journal of Policy Modeling* 30: 209–20.

C. Clapp, K. Karousakis, B. Buchner, and J. Chateau, (2009). 'National and sectoral GHG mitigation potential: a comparison across models', Organisation for Economic Co-operation and Development (OECD).

Climate Action Tracker, (2013). 'China', http://www.climateactiontracker.org/countries/china.

P. Christmann, and G. Taylor, (2001). 'Globalization and the environment: determinants of firmself-regulation in China', *Journal of International Business Studies* 32: 439–58.

M. Clarke, (2008). 'China's integration of Xinjiang with Central Asia: securing a "Silk Road" to great power status?', *China and Eurasia Forum Quarterly* 6(2): 89–111.

The Climate Institute/GE, (2013), 'Factsheet low-Carbon competitiveness index global climate leadership review', http://www.climateinstitute.org.au/verve/_resources/TCI_GlobalClimateLeadershipReview_LCCIFactsheet_March2013.pdf (accessed 6 August 2013).

M.A. Cole, (2006). 'Does trade liberalization increase national energy use?', *Economics Letters* 92: 108–12.

M.A. Cole, and R.J.R. Elliott, (2003). 'Determining the trade-environment composition effect: the role of capital, labor and environmental regulations', *Journal of Environmental Economics and Management* 46: 363–83.

Commission of the European Communities (CEC), (2005). 'The communication on thematic strategy on air pollution and the directive on "ambient air quality and cleaner air for Europe"', Impact Assessment, Brussels, http://ec.europa.eu/environment/archives/cafe/pdf/ia_report_en050921_final.pdf (accessed 11 August 2013).

Compilation of Materials & Documents of Shanghai Five-Shanghai Cooperation Organization, (2003). Center for SCO (Shanghai Cooperation Organization) Studies, Shanghai Academy of Social Sciences.

T. Corn, (2007). 'The revolution in transatlantic affairs: perils and promises of a global NATO', http://www.hoover.org/publications/policy-review/article/6032 (accessed 9 December 2012).

V. Costantini, and C. Martini, (2010). 'The causality between energy consumption and economic growth: a multi-sectoral analysis using non-stationary cointegrated panel data', *Energy Economics* 32: 591–603.

P. Crompton, and Y.R. Wu, (2005). 'Energy consumption in China: past trends and future directions', *Energy Economics* 27: 195–208.

A. Cuadros, V. Orts, and M. Alguacil, (2004). 'Openness and growth: re-examining foreign direct investment, trade and output linkages in Latin America', *The Journal of Development Studies* 40: 167–92.

J.T. Cuddington, and D. Jerrett, (2008). 'Super cycles in real metals prices?', *IMF Staff Papers* 55: 541–65.

R. Cutler, (2012). 'China expands energy ties in Central Asia', http://www.atimes.com/atimes/Central_Asia/MI29Ag01.html (accessed 5 December 2012).

J. Daly, (2012a). 'Hydropower rich Kyrgyzstan and Tajikistan to go nuclear?', http://oilprice.com/Latest-Energy-News/World-News/Hydropower-Rich-Kyrgyzstan-and-Tajikistan-to-go-Nuclear.html (accessed 6 December 2012).

J. Daly, (2012b). 'Putin looking to modernize Russia's energy sector, bureaucrats fight back', http://oilprice.com/Energy/Energy-General/Putin-Looking-to-Modernize-Russias-Energy-Sector-Bureaucrats-Fight-Back.html (accessed 29 April 2014).

S. Dan, (2007). 'Regional difference in China's energy efficiency and conservation potentials', *China & World Economy* 15: 96–115.

G. Dansie, M. Lanteigne, and I. Overland, (2010). 'Reducing energy subsidies in China, India and Russia: dilemmas for decision makers', *Sustainability* 2: 475–93.

Z. Daojiong, (2006). 'China's energy security: Domestic and international issues', *Survival: Global Politics and Strategy* 48(1): 179–90

J. Dargay, and D. Gately, (1999). 'Income's effect on car and vehicle ownership, worldwide: 1960–2015', *Transportation Research. Part A, Policy and Practice* 33(2): 101–13.

J. Dargay, D. Gately, and M. Sommer, (1999). 'Vehicle ownership and income growth, worldwide: 1960-2030', *The Energy Journal* 28(4): 143–70.

A. Deaton, (1999). 'Commodity prices and growth in Africa', *Journal of Economic Perspectives* 13: 23–40.

C. De Gouvello, (2010). 'Brazil low-carbon country case study', The World Bank Group.

A. De la Torre, P. Fajnzylber, and J. Nash, (2009). 'Low carbon, high growth: Latin American responses to climate change: an overview', World Bank Publications.

K.S. Deffeyes, (2005). *Beyond oil: the view from Hubbert's peak*, New York: Hill and Wang, a division of Farrar, Straus and Giroux, LLC.

Y. Deng, R. Morck, J. Wu, and B. Yeung, (2011). 'Monetary and fiscal stimuli, ownership structure, and China's housing market', NBER Working Paper 16871, Cambridge, MA: National Bureau of Economic Research, March.

E. Dietzenbacher, and B. Los, (1998). 'Structural decomposition technique: sense and sensitivity', *Economic Systems Research* 10: 307–23.

P. Dimaggio, and P. Walter, (1983). 'The iron cage revisited: institutional isomorphism and collective rationality in organizational fields', *American Sociological Review* 48: 147–60.

D. Dollar, and S. Wei, (2007). 'Das (Waste) capital: firm ownership and investment efficiency in China', *IMF Working Paper Series* 07/9.

A. Donnithorne, (1972). 'China's cellular economy: some economic trends since the Cultural Revolution', *The China Quarterly* 52: 605–19.

S. Dougherty, R. Herd, and P. He, (2007). 'Has a private sector emerged in China's industry? Evidence from a quarter of a million Chinese firms', *China Economic Review* 18: 309–34.

E. Downs, (2006). *China's Energy Security Series*, The Brookings Foreign Policy Studies.

E. Downs, (2008). 'China's new energy administration', *China Business Review* November–December.

E. Downs, (2010). 'Business interest groups in Chinese politics: the case of the oil companies', *Brookings Institution Press*, July.

E. Downs, and M. Meidan, (2011). 'Business and politics in China: the oil executive reshuffle of 2011', *China Security* 19: 3–21.

E.I. Dumitrescu, and C. Hurlin, (2012). 'Testing for Granger non-causality in heterogeneous panels', *Economic Modelling* 29: 1450–60.

J. Eaton, and S. Kortum, (1996). 'Trade in ideas: patenting and productivity in the OECD', *Journal of International Economics* 40: 251–78.

J. Eaton, and S. Kortum, (2001). 'Trade in capital goods', *European Economic Review* 45: 1195–235.

E.C. Economy, (2004). *The river runs black: the environmental challenge to China's future*, Ithaca NY: Cornell University Press.

Ecoworld, (2007). 'China's coal-to-liquid', 06 March 2007, http://ecoworld.com/energy-fuels/chinas-coal-to-liquids.html.

Ecoworld, (2009). 'The elusive yet abundant hydropower in the Kyrgyz Republic', http://www.ecoworld.com/energy-fuels/the-elusive-yet-abundant-hydropower-in-the-kyrgyz-republic.html (accessed 6 December 2012).

Energy Information Administration (EIA), (2009). 'State renewable energy requirements and goals', update through 2008.

Energy Information Administration (EIA), (2011). 'International Energy Outlook', Washington DC.

Energy Information Administration (EIA), (2012a). 'China', version last updated September 2012, http://www.eia.gov/countries/analysisbriefs/China/china.pdf (accessed 30 November 2012).

Energy Information Administration (EIA), (2012b). 'Kazakhstan', version last updated September 2012, http://www.eia.gov/countries/analysisbriefs/Kazakhstan/kazakhstan.pdf (accessed 2 December 2012).

Energy Information Administration (EIA), (2012c). 'Uzbekistan', version last updated January 2012, http://www.eia.gov/countries/analysisbriefs/Uzbekistan/uzbekistan.pdf (accessed 2 December 2012).

Energy Information Administration (EIA), (2012d). 'Turkmenistan', version last updated January 2012, http://www.eia.gov/EMEU/cabs/Turkmenistan/pdf.pdf (accessed 3 December 2012).

Energy Resources Website, (2009). 'Chinese and Uzbek oil companies sign agreements on energy (中国石油与 兹 克斯坦油气公司 署能源)', http://www.nengyuan.net/200907/01-197444.html (accessed 05 December 2012).

P. Enkvist, T. Nauclér, and J. Rosander, (2007). 'A cost curve for greenhouse gas reduction', *EIA Quarterly* 1: 35–45.

P. Erickson, C. Heaps, and M. Lazarus, (2009). 'Greenhouse gas mitigation in developing countries', Stockholm Environment Institute, Working Paper WP-US-03, June.

U. Erol, and E.S.H. Yu, (1987). 'On the causal relationship between energy and income for industrialized countries', *Journal of Energy and Development* 13: 113–22.

G.S. Eskeland, and A.E. Harrison, (2003). 'Moving to greener pastures? Multinationals and the pollution haven hypothesis', *Journal of Development Economics* 70: 1–23.

Europe–China Clean Energy Centre, (2012). *Cooperation on energy security: China-EU Government and Business Perspectives*, Beijing, EC2.

European Commission, (2012). 'EU initiates anti-dumping investigation on solar panels from China', Memorandum, 06 September 2012, http://trade.ec.europa.eu/doclib/press/index.cfm?id=829.

Y. Fan, H. Liao, and Y.M. Wei, (2007). 'Can market oriented economic reforms contribute to energy efficiency improvement? Evidence from China', *Energy Policy* 35: 2287–95.

M. Fang, C.K. Chan, and X. Yao, (2009). 'Managing air quality in a rapidly developing nation: China', *Atmospheric Environment* 43: 79–86.

Y. Fang, J. Li, and M. Wang, (2012). 'Development policy for non-grid-connected wind power in China: an analysis based on institutional change', *Energy Policy* 45: 350–58.

M.J. Farrell, (1957). 'The measurement of productive efficiency', *Journal of the Royal Statistical Society* Series A: 253–90.

K. Fatai, L. Oxley, and F.G. Scrimgeour, (2004). 'Modelling the causal relationship between energy consumption and GDP in New Zealand, Australia, India, Indonesia, the Philippines, and Thailand', *Mathematics and Computers in Simulation* 64: 431–445.

K. Fisher-Vanden, G.H. Jefferson, H. Liu, and Q. Tao, (2004). 'What is driving China's decline in Energy Intensity?' *Resource and Energy Economics* 26: 77–97.

K. Fisher-Vanden, G.H. Jefferson, M. Jingkui, and X. Jianyi, (2006). 'Technology development and energy productivity in China', *Energy Economics* 28: 690–705.

A. Focacci, (2005). 'Empirical analysis of the environmental and energy policies in some developing countries using widely employed macroeconomic indicators: the cases of Brazil, China and India', *Energy Policy* 33: 543–54.

Forbes, (2009). 'Weakness in Chinese wind power', http;//www.forbes.com/2009/07/20/china-wind-power-business-energy-china.html (accessed on 5 February 2012).

Fortune Global 500 (2012).

C. Friedman, and T. Schaffer, (2009). 'India's Energy Options: Coal and Beyond', *South Asia Monitor* 2009 (August 24): 132.

J. Friedman, (2005). *China's urban transition*, Minneapolis: Univ. of Minnesota Press.

Friends of Nature, (2012). '2012 Green Book of the Environment', http://www.fon.org.cn/index.php/index/post/id/834 (accessed 8 August 2013).

Friends of Nature, (2013). '2013 Green Book of the Environment', http://www.fon.org.cn/index.php/index/post/id/1382 (accessed 8 August 2013).

X. Fu, C. Pietrobelli, and L. Soete, (2011). 'The role of foreign technology and indigenous innovation in the emerging economies: technological change and catching up', *World Development* 39: 1204–12.

M. Galeotti, A. Lanza, and F. Paulli, (2006). 'Reassessing the environmental Kuznets curve for CO_2 emissions: a robustness exercise', *Ecological Economics* 57: 152–63.

R.F. Garbaccio, M.S. Ho, and D.W. Jorgenson, (1999). 'Why has the energy-output ratio fallen in China?', *Energy Journal* 20: 63–91

A. Garg, K. Halsnaes, E.L. La Rovere, A.O. Pereira, A.F. Simoes, A.S. Pereira, C.B. Schmidt Dubeux, and R.C. da Costa, (2007). 'Development first: linking energy and emission policies with sustainable development for Brazil', UNEP Risoe Centre on Energy, Climate and Sustainable Development, Roskilde, Denmark.

R. Garnaut, (2012). 'The contemporary China resources boom', *The Australian Journal of Agricultural and Resources Economics* 56: 222–43.

J.A. Garrison, (2009). *China and the energy equation in Asia: the determinants of policy choice*, Boulder, CO: First Forum Press.

L. Geiver, (2011). 'China coal-to-liquid plant will use algae-based CO_2 capture'. Biodiesel Magazine, 19 October 2011, http://www.biodieselmagazione.com/articles/8111/china-coal-to-liquid-plant-will-use-algae-based-co2-capture.

K.H. Ghali, and M.I. El-Sakka, (2004). 'Energy use and output growth in Canada: a multivariate cointegration analysis', *Energy Economics* 26: 225–38.

S. Ghosh, (2002). 'Electricity consumption and economic growth in India', *Energy Policy* 30: 125–29.

S. Girma, and Y. Gong, (2008). 'FDI, linkages and the efficiency of state owned enterprises in China', *Journal of Development Studies* 44: 728–49.

S. Girma, Y. Gong, and H. Görg, (2009). 'Foreign Direct Investment, access to finance, and innovation activity in Chinese enterprises', *World Bank Econ Rev* 22: 367–82.

N. Gizitdinov, and A. Shiryaevskaya, (2012). 'Kazakhstan opens $6 billion link in Turkmen gas pipe to China',

http://www.bloomberg.com/apps/news?pid=newsarchive&sid=aX8pprcyD668 (accessed 07 December 2012).

Global Footprint Network, (2013). *Country trends: China*, http://www.footprintnetwork.org/en/index.php/GFN/page/trends/china/ (accessed 12 August 2013).

E. Gooseens, (2012). 'The downside of China's clean energy push', Business Week, 21 November 2012, http://www.businessweek.com/articles/2012-11-21/the-downside-of-chinas-clean-energy-p.

J. Gottmann, (1961). *Megapolis: the urbanized Northeastern seaboard of the United States*, Boston, MA: MIT Press.

Government.ru, (2012). http://government.ru/eng/docs/21739/ (accessed 10 December 2012).

Government of India, (2006). 'Integrated energy policy: report of the expert committee', Planning Commission, Government of India, New Delhi.

Government of India, (2008). 'National action plan on climate change', http://pmindia.gov.in/climate_change.php (accessed 23 August 2012).

Green Economy Taskforce, (2011). 'Development mechanism and policy innovation of China's green economy', CCICED 2011 Annual General Meeting, http://www.cciced.net/encciced/policyresearch/report/201205/P020120529371605387628.pdf (accessed 8 August 2013).

D. Greenaway, A. Guariglia, and Z. Yu, (2013). 'The more the better? Foreign ownership and corporate performance in China', *The European Journal of Finance*, DOI:10.1080/1351847X.2012.671785 (forthcoming).

C. Gross, (2012). 'Explaining the (non-) causality between energy and economic growth in the US – A multivariate sectoral analysis', *Energy Economics* 34: 489–99.

G.M. Grossman, and A.B. Krueger, (1991). 'Environmental impacts of a North American Free Trade Agreement', NBER Working Paper 3914.

A. Guariglia, X. Liu, and L. Song, (2008). 'Is the growth of Chinese firms constrained by internal finance?', Leverhulme Centre for Research on Globalization and Economic Policy, *Research Paper* 08/37.

C. Guo, (2010). 'An analysis of the increase of CO_2 emission in China: based on SDA technique', *China Industrial Economics* 12: 47–56.

S. Guo, (2007). 'The business development of China's national oil companies: the government to business relationship in China', The James A. Baker III Institute for Public Policy, Rice University.

X. Guo, and D. Marinova, (2010). 'Environmental education and awareness in China: facilitating the transformation to a low-carbon economy', *Transformations* 66–67(3–4): 157–70.

X. Guo, D. Marinova, and J. Hong, (2013). 'China's shifting policies towards sustainability: a low-carbon economy and environmental protection', *Journal of Contemporary China* 22(81): 428–45.

P. Hall, (2002). 'Yangtze paradigm', *City Planning Review* 26(1): 6–17 (Chinese).

Z.Y. Han, and Y.M. Wei, (2004). 'On the cointegration and causality between Chinese GDP and energy consumption', *Journal of System Engineering* 12: 17–21.

L. Hang, and M. Tu, (2007). 'The impacts of energy price on energy intensity: evidence from China', *Energy Policy* 35: 2978–88.

A. Harrison, and A. Rodriguez-Clare, (2010). 'Trade, foreign direct investment and industrial policy for developing countries', in: D. Rodrik and M. Rosenzwaig (eds) *Handbook of development economics*, Vol. 5 (North-Holland), 4039–198.

M.H. Hasan, T.M.I. Mahlia, and H. Nur, (2012). 'A review on energy scenario and sustainable energy in Indonesia', *Renewable and Sustainable Energy Reviews* 16(4): 2316–28.

K. He, H. Huo, Q. Zhang, D. He, F. An, M. Wang, and M. Walsh, (2005). 'Oil consumption and CO_2 emissions in China's road transport: current status, future trends, and policy implications', *Energy Policy* 33: 1499–507.

M.J. Herrerias, (2011). 'Weighted convergence and regional growth in China: an alternative approach (1952–2008)', *The Annals of Regional Science* 49: 685–718.

M.J. Herrerias, A. Cuadros, and V. Orts, (2013). 'Energy intensity and investment ownership across Chinese provinces', *Energy Economics* 36: 286–98.

M.J. Herrerias, R. Joyeux, and E. Girardin, (2013). 'Short- and Long-run causality between energy consumption and economic growth: evidence across regions in China', *Applied Energy* 112: 1484–92.

M.J. Herrerias, and G. Liu, (2013). 'Electricity intensity convergence in China: new evidence across Chinese provinces', *Energy Economics* 36: 268–76.

M.J. Herrerias, and V. Orts, (2010). 'Is the export-led growth hypothesis enough to account for China's growth?', *China & World Economy* 18: 34–51.

M.J. Herrerias, and V. Orts, (2011). 'The driving forces behind China's growth', *The Economic of Transition* 19: 74–124.

M.J. Herrerias, V. Orts, and E. Tortosa, (2011). 'Weighted convergence and regional clusters across China', *Papers in Regional Science* 90: 703–34.

I. Hilton et al., (2012). 'China's green revolution: energy, environment and the 12th Five-Year Plan'. ChinaDialogue.

A. Holland, (2011). 'Examination of possibly induced seismicity from hydraulic fracturing in the Eola Field, Gavin County, Oklahoma', Oklahoma Geological Survey, http://www.ogs.ou.edu/pubsscanned/openfile/OF1_2011.pdf.

Household Survey, (2011). *Poverty monitoring report for rural China, Department of National Bureau of Statistics*, China Statistics Press, Beijing.
R. Hu, (2012). 'A bright future for China's solar power industry', *Clean Energy Perspectives* 5: 2–3.
B.N. Huang, M.J. Hwang, and C.W. Yang, (2008). 'Causal relationship between energy consumption and GDP growth revisited: a dynamic panel data approach', *Ecological Economics* 67: 41–54.
J.K. Huang, J. Yang, H.G. Qiu, and Z.G. Xu, (2009). 'Sharp rise and fall of grain prices: reasons and trends', *Management World* 1: 72–78.
Y. Huang, and D. Todd, (2010). 'The energy implications of Chinese regional disparities', *Energy Policy* 38: 7531–38.
Huaxia, (2007). 'Sino-Kazakh bilateral relations (中國和哈薩克雙邊關係)')', http://big5.huaxia.com/zt/tbgz/07-074/523173.html (accessed 5 December 2012).
M. Hübler, (2009). 'Energy saving technology diffusion via FDI and trade: a CGE nodel of China', Kiel Working Papers No. 1479, January.
M. Hübler, (2011). 'Technology diffusion under contraction and convergence: a CGE analysis of China', *Energy Economics* 33: 131–42.
M. Hübler, and A. Keller, (2010). 'Energy savings via FDI? empirical evidence from developing countries', *Environmental and Development Economics* 15: 59–80.
Hydrocarbons-technology, (undated). 'Central Asia-China gas pipeline, Turkmenistan to China', http://www.hydrocarbons-technology.com/projects/centralasiachinagasp/ (accessed 6 December 2012).
Ifeng, (2013). 'Guangzhou disclosed the names of big polluting enterprises, with the petrol-chemical factory being the worst (in Chinese)', http://i.ifeng.com/news/dalu/news?aid=65679759&vt=2&mid=aqvYHG&m=1 (accessed 11 August 2013).
K.S. Im, M.H. Pesaran, and Y. Shin, (2003). 'Testing for unit roots in heterogeneous panels', *Journal of Econometrics* 115: 53–74.
Information Office of the State Council of the People's Republic of China, (2008). 'China's policies and actions for addressing climate change' . Information Office of the State Council of the People's Republic of China, Beijing.
Information Office of the State Council, (2012). 'China's Energy Policy 2012', Reproduced in full in English at http://www.chinadaily.com.cn/cndy/2012-10/25/content_15844539.htm.
Institute for Energy and Environmental Research Heidelberg in cooperation with Institute of Comprehensive Transportation of National Development and Reform Commission of China (ICT), (2008). 'Transport in China: energy consumption and emissions of different transport modes: Final report'.
Institute for Energy Research, (2011). 'China's coal-to-liquids program not allowed in United States', 28 June 2011, http://instituteforenergyresearch.org/2011/06/28/china's-coal-to-liquids-program-not-allowed-in-the-united-states/.
Institute for War and Peace Reporting, (2010). 'Uzbekistan: Mystery Surrounds Zeromax Collapse', http://iwpr.net/report-news/uzbekistan-mystery-surrounds-zeromax-collapse (accessed 4 January 2013).
International Atomic Energy Agency (IAEA), (2006). 'Brazil: A country profile on sustainable energy development', Vienna.
International Energy Agency (IEA), (2005). 'Monthly Oil Market Report', 11 August.

International Energy Agency (IEA), (2007). 'World Energy Outlook. China and India Insights (IEA)', http://www.worldenergyoutlook.org/.
International Energy Agency (IEA), (2011). 'World Energy Outlook, 2011', http://www.iea.org/weo/ (accessed on 6 February 2012).
International Energy Agency (IEA), (2008). 'Key World Energy, 2008', http://www.iea.org/textbase/nppdf/free/2008/key_stats_2008.pdf. (accessed on 2 February 2012).
International Energy Agency (IEA), (2010a). 'Medium-term oil market report', Paris: June, July.
International Energy Agency (IEA), (2010b). 'Medium-term oil market report', Update, Paris, December.
International Energy Agency (IEA), (2012). 'IEA - R. 2012', http://iea.org/aboutus/glossary/r/ (accessed November 2012).
International Energy Agency (IEA), (2012). 'Energy outlook', Paris: November.
International Energy Agency (IEA), (2012). 'Oil and gas security – emergency response from EIA countries. People's Republic of China', http://www.iea.org/publications/freepublications/publication/China_2012-1.pdf (accessed 20 November 2012).
International Labor Organisation (ILO), (2013). 'Green jobs', http://www.ilo.org/global/topics/green-jobs/lang--it/index.htm (accessed 13 August 2013).
International Monetary Fund, (2001). 'Oil scarcity, growth, and global imbalances', *World Economic Outlook* (April) Washington, DC: International Monetary Fund.
International Petroleum Economics, (2007). 'The statutes of the Shanghai Cooperation Organization Energy Club (上海合作 能源俱 部章程)', *International Petroleum Economics* 7: 60–62.
L. Jakobson, and D. Knox, (2010). 'New foreign policy actors in China', SIPRI Policy Paper No. 26, September.
B. Jaruzelski, J. Loehr, and R. Holman, (2012). 'The Global Innovation 1000: Making Ideas Work', Booz & Co., http://www.strategy-business.com/article/00140?pg=all#authors (accessed 13 August 2013).
G.H. Jefferson, A.G.Z. Hu, X. Guan, and X. Yu, (2003). 'Ownership, performance and innovation in China's large-and medium size industrial enterprise sector', *China Economic Review* 14: 89–113.
G.H. Jefferson, and J. Su, (2006). 'Privatization and restructuring in China: evidence from shareholding ownership, 1995-2001', *Journal of Comparative Economics* 34: 146–66.
R. Jia, X. Guo, and D. Marinova, (2013). 'The role of the clean development mechanism in achieving China's goal of a resource efficient and environmentally friendly society', *Environment, Development and Sustainability* 15(1): 133–48
B. Jiang, Z.Q. Sun, and M.Q. Liu, (2010). 'China's energy development strategy under the low carbon-economy', *Energy* 35: 4257–64.
Z. Jiang, (2008). 'Reflections on energy issues in China', *Journal of Shanghai Jiaotong University (Science)* 30: 164–65.
D. Jorgenson, (1984). 'The role of energy in productivity growth', *The American Economic Review* 74: 26–30.
C. Joseph, and K. Koleski, (2011). 'Backgrounder: China's 12th Five-Year Plan', U.S.-China Economic & Security Review Commission.

C.B.L. Jumbe, (2004). 'Cointegration and causality between electricity consumption and GDP: empirical evidence from Malawi', *Energy Economics* 26: 61–68.

R. Kaplinsky, (2006). 'China and the global terms of trade', *IDS Bulletin* 37: 43–53.

N. Kassenova, (2009). 'The Shanghai Cooperation Energy Club: purpose and prospects', in: I. Overland, H. Kjaernet and A. Kendall-Taylor (eds) *Caspian Energy Politics: Azerbaijan, Kazakhstan and Turkmenistan*, Routledge Taylor and Francis.

W. Keller, (2004). 'International technology diffusion', *Journal of Economic Literature* XLII: 752–82.

A.B. Kennedy, (2010). 'China's new energy-security debate', *Survival: Global Politics and Strategy* 52(3): 137–58.

T. Kemeny, (2010). 'Does foreign direct investment drive technological upgrading?', *World Development* 38: 1543–54.

A. Khodzhaev, (2009). 'The Central Asian policy of the People's Republic of China', *China and Eurasia Forum Quarterly* 7(1): 9–28.

L. Kilian, (2009). 'Not all oil price shocks are alike: disentangling demand and supply shocks in the crude oil market', *American Economic Review* 46(4): 871–909.

L. Kilian, and C. Park, (2009). 'The impact of oil price shocks on the U.S. stock market', *International Economic Review* 50(4): 1267–87.

P. Kobos, J. Erickson, and T. Drennen, (2003). 'Scenario analysis of Chinese passenger vehicle growth', *Contemporary Economic Policy* 21(2): 200–17.

B. Kong, (2005). 'An anatomy of China's energy insecurity and its strategies', Pacific Northwest Laboratory for the United States Department of Energy.

B. Kong, (2006). 'Institutional insecurity', *China Security* Summer: 65–88.

K. Kounetas, I. Mourtos, and K. Tsekouras, (2012). 'Is energy intensity important for the productivity growth of EET adopters?', *Energy Economics* 34: 930–41

J. Kraft, and A. Kraft, (1978). 'On the relationship between energy and GNP', *Journal of Energy and Development* 3: 401–03.

M. Krans, (2009). 'SCO energy club: what it will be like', http://infoshos.ru/en/?idn=5040 (accessed 14 December 2012).

A. Kumar, (2003). 'Energy intensity: aquantitative exploration for Indian manufacturing', *IGIDR Working Paper* No. 152, Indira Gandhi Institute of Development Research, Mumbai.

V. Kumar, A. Kumar, M. Åhman, A. Torvanger, and L. Zetterberg, (2009). 'A bottom-up approach for India', *European Review of Energy Markets* 3: 300–21.

A. Kumar, and X. Zhang, (2011). 'Evaluating renewable energy-based rural electrification program in western China: emerging problems and possible scenarios', *Renewable and Sustainable Energy Reviews* 15: 773–79.

La ComisiónIntersecretarial de CambioClimático (CICC), (2009). 'Programa especial de cambioclimático: versiónconsultapública 24/03/2009', SEMARNAT, Mexico.

J.H. Laherrère, (2001). 'Forecasting future production from past discovery', OPEC and the global energy balance: towards a sustainable energy future, 28 September.

M. Lai, S. Peng, and Q. Bao, (2006). 'Technology spillovers, absorptive capacity and economic growth', *China Economic Review* 17: 300–20.

M. Lanteigne, (2009). 'China, energy security and central Asian diplomacy. Bilateral and multilateral approaches', in: I. Overland, H. Kjaernet and A. Kendall-Taylor (eds) *Caspian energy politics: Azerbaijan, Kazakhstan and Turkmenistan*, Routledge Taylor and Francis.

C. Larson, (2012). 'China's shale gas potential and perils', Business Week.

M. Laruelle, and S. Peyrouse, (2009). 'China as a neighbor: Central Asian perspectives and startegies', web-hist.cohums.ohio-state.edu/osu/…/resource_origins_2-10.pdf (accessed 5 September 2012).

C.C. Lee, (2005). 'Energy consumption and GDP in developing countries: a cointegrated panel analysis', *Energy Economics* 27: 415–27.

C.C. Lee, (2006). 'The causality relationship between energy consumption and GDP in G-11 countries revisited', *Energy Policy* 34: 1086–93.

J. Lee, (2009). 'State owned enterprises in China: reviewing the evidence', Organization for Economic Cooperation and Development.

P.K. Lee, (2005). 'China's quest for oil security: oil (wars) in the pipeline?', *The Pacific Review* 18(2): 265–301.

C.C. Lee, and C.P. Chang, (2008). 'Energy consumption and economic growth in Asian economies: a more comprehensive analysis using panel data', *Resource and Energy Economics* 30: 50–65.

M. Lee, and H. Wai, (2012). 'Analyzing the influence of major actors in China's renewable energy policy process as a means of predicting future Chinese renewable energy policy trends', Thesis, Natural Resources and Environment, University of Michigan.

J.A. Legget, J. Logan, and A. Mackey. (2008). 'China's greenhouse gas emissions and mitigation policies', CRS Report, Washington DC: Congressional Research Service.

G.C.K. Leung, (2010). 'China's oil use, 1990-2008', *Energy Policy* 38: 932–44.

A. Lewis, (1954). 'Economic development with unlimited supplies of labor', *Manchester School of Economic and Social Studies* 22: 139–91.

I.J. Lewis, (2010). 'The evolving role of carbon finance in promoting renewable energy development in China', *Energy Policy* 38: 2875–86.

J. Lewis, and R. Wiser, (2007). 'Fostering a renewable energy technology industry: an international comparison of wind industry support mechanisms', *Energy Policy* 35: 1844–57.

F. Li, S. Dong, X. Li, Q. Liang, and W. Yang, (2011). 'Energy consumption-economic growth relationship and carbon dioxide emissions in China', *Energy Policy* 39: 568–76.

K. Li, (2012). 'Intensively implement the strategy of expanding domestic demands in the process of reform and opening-up', *Qiushi Journal* 4: 3–10.

K.W. Li, (2009). 'China's total factor productivity estimates by region, investment sources and ownership', *Economic Systems* 33: 213–30.

R. Li, and C.K. Leung, (2012). 'Coal consumption and economic growth in China', *Energy Policy* 40: 438–43.

X. Li, (2011). 'Ten years of Shanghai Cooperation Organization: successes, challneges and prospects (上海合作 合作十年：成就、挑 与前景)', http://www.siis.org.cn/Lunwen_View.aspx?lid=10000403 (accessed 7 December 2012).

Y. Li, and L. Zhang, (2008). 'Structural decomposition analysis of China's indirect household energy consumption', *Resources Science* 30: 890–95.

Z. Li, (2010). 'Quantitative analysis of sustainable energy strategies in China', *Energy Policy* 38: 2149–60.

M. Liao, (2009). 'Input-output and Extend Analysis', Capital University of Economics and Business Press.

K. Lieberthal, (1997). 'China's governing system and its impact on environmental policy implementation', China Environment Series, Environmental Change and Security Program.

K. Lieberthal, and M. Oksenberg, (1988). *Policy making in China: leaders, structures, and processes*, Princeton, NJ: Princeton University Press.

H. Liao, Y. Fan, and Y. Wei, (2007). 'What induced China's energy intensity to fluctuate: 1997–2006?', *Energy Policy* 35: 4640–49.

K. Liberthal, and M. Oksenberg, (1988). *Policy making in China: leaders, structures and process*, New Jersey: Princeton University Press.

K.C. Lin, (2006). 'Disembedding socialist firms as a statist project: restructuring the Chinese oil industry, 1997–2002', *Enterprise & Society* 7(1): 59–97.

K.C. Lin, (2008). 'Macroeconomic disequilibria and enterprise reform: restructuring the Chinese oil and petrochemical industries in the 1990s', *China Journal* 60: 49–79.

B. Lin, and Z. Jiang, (2011). 'Estimates of energy subsidies in China and impact of energy subsidy reform', *Energy Economics* 33: 273–83.

C. Liou, (2009). 'Bureaucratic politics and overseas investment by Chinese state-owned oil companies: illusory champions', *Asian Survey* 49(4): 670–90.

W. Lise, and K.V. Monfort, (2007). 'Energy consumption and GDP in Turkey: is there a co-integration relationship?', *Energy Economics* 29: 1166–78

L. Liu, (2008). 'Local government and big business in the People's Republic of China - Case study evidence from Shandong Province', *Asia Pacific Business Review* 14(4): 473–89.

L. Liu, Z. Wang, Y. Zhang, and Y. Xue, (2010). 'Solar energy development in China—A review', *Renewable and Sustainable Energy Reviews* 14: 301–11.

L.Q. Liu, and Z.X. Wang, (2009). 'The development and application practice of wind-solar energy hybrid generation systems in China', *Renewable Sustainable Energy Reviews* 13: 1504–12.

Q. Liu, and Z. Peng, (2010). 'China input/output sequence tables and analysis based on comparable prices from 1992 to 2005', China Statistics Press.

X. Liu, (2012). 'Prospects for regional cooperation', Energy Research Institute, http://www.unescap.org/esd/Energy-Security-and-Water Resources/energy/trade_and_cooperation/cooperation/epp8/documents/Agenda2-China-MsLiu.pdf (accessed 30 October 2012).

Z. Liu, (2008). 'Foreign direct investment and technology spillovers: theory and evidence', *Journal Development Economics* 85: 176–93.

Z. Liu, and J. Zheng, (2011). 'Growth of the service sector in the Yangtze River Delta', Enrich Professional Publishing.

Z. Liu, and J. Zheng, (2012). 'Conflict and harmony: development in the Yangtze River Delta', Enrich Professional Publishing.

F. Lo, and P. Marcotullio eds, (2001). *Globalization and the sustainability of cities in the AsianPacific Region*, New York: United Nations Univ. Press.

W. Lui, H. Lund, B. VadMathiesen, and X. Zhang, (2011).'Potential of renewable energy systems in China', *Applied Energy* 88: 518–25.

H. Lund, B. Mathiesen, X. Zhang, and W. Liu, (2011). 'Potential of renewable energy systems in China', *Applied Energy* 88: 518–25.

C. Luo, (2007). 'FDI, domestic capital, and economic growth: evidence from panel data at China's provincial level', *Frontiers Economics of China* 2: 92–113.

T.P. Lyons, (1985). 'China's cellular economy: a test of the fragmentation hypothesis', *Journal of Comparative Economics* (Academic Pres, Inc.) 9: 125–44.

C. Ma, (2010). 'Account for sector heterogeneity in China's energy consumption: Sector price indices vs. GDP deflator', *Energy Economics* 32: 24–29.

C. Ma, L. Oxley, and J. Gibson, (2009). 'Gradual reforms and the emergence of energy market in China: evidence from tests for convergence of energy prices', *Energy Policy* 37: 4834–50.

C. Ma, L. Oxley, and J. Gibson, (2010). 'China's energy economy: a survey of the Literature', *Economic Systems* 34: 105–32.

C. Ma, and D. Stern, (2008). 'China's changing energy intensity trend: a decomposition analysis', *Energy Economics* 30: 1037–53

H. Ma, L. Oxley, J. Gibson, and B. Kim, (2008). 'China's energy economy: technical change, factor demand and interfactor/interfuel substitution', *Energy Economics* 30: 2167–83.

H. Ma, L. Oxley, J. Gibson, and B. Kim, (2009). 'Modeling China's energy consumption behaviorand changes in energy intensity', *Environmental Modelling and Software* 24: 1293–301.

H. Ma, L. Oxley, J. Gibson, and W. Li, (2010). 'A survey of China's renewable energy economy', *Renewable and Sustainable Energy Reviews* 14: 438–43.

L. Ma, F. Fu, Z. Li, and P. Liu, (2012). 'Oil development in China: current status and future trends', *Energy Policy* 45: 43–53.

R. Maksutov, (2006) 'The Shanghai Cooperation Organization: a Central Asian perspective', *A SIPRI Project Paper*, 1–29.

A. Malhotra, (2012). 'Chinese inroads into Central Asia: focus on oil and gas', http://www.ensec.org/index.php?option=com_content&view=article&id=387:chinese-inroads-into-central-asia-focus-on-oil-and-gas&catid=130:issue-content&Itemid=405 (accessed 4 December 2012).

E. Marat, (2010). 'Kyrgyzstan boosts cooperation with China', http://www.jamestown.org/single/?no_cache=1&tx_ttnews[tt_news]=35918 (accessed 7 December 2012).

D. Marinova, X. Guo, and Y. Wu, (2013). 'China's transformation towards a global green system of innovation', *Journal of Science and Technology of China* 4(2): 76–98.

T.N. Marketos, (2009). *China's energy geopolitics: the Shanghai Cooperation Organization and Central Asia*, Routledge Contemporary China Series

C. Martenson, (2011). *The crash course: the unsustainable future of our economy, energy and the environment*, Wiley, USA.

E. Martinot, (2010). 'Renewable power for China: past, present, and future', *Frontiers of Energy and Power Engineering in China* 4: 278–94.

A.M.M. Masih, and R. Masih, (1998). 'A multivariate cointegrated modeling approach in testing temporal causality between energy consumption, real income and prices with an application to two Asian LDCs', *Applied Economics* 30: 1287–98

L. Mastny, (2010). *Renewable energy and energy efficiency in China: current status and prospects for 2020*, Worldwatch Institute, Danvers, MA: Worldwatch Institute.

A. Matusov, (2007). 'Energy cooperation in the SCO: club or gathering?', *China and Eurasia Forum Quarterly* 5(3): 83–99.

M.A. McLean-Dreyfus, and H. Bendemra, (2012). 'China moves towards an R&D eclipse', Business Spectator,

M. Meidan, P. Andrews-Speed, and M. Xin, (2009). 'Shaping China's energy policy: actors and processes', *Journal of Contemporary China* 18(61): 591–616.

http://www.businessspectator.com.au/article/2012/12/7/resources-and-energy/china-moves-towards-rd-eclipse (accessed 13 August 2013).

O. Mielnik, and J. Goldemberg, (2002). 'Foreign direct investment and decoupling between energy and gross domestic product in developing countries', *Energy Policy* 30: 87–89.

C.J. Milhaupt, and L. Lin, (2011). 'We are the (national) champions: understanding the mechanisms of state capitalism in China', Columbia Law and Economics Working Paper No. 409, Columbia Law and Economics Working Paper No. 409, Columbia University.

Ministry of Environmental Protection of the People's Republic of China (PRC), (2009). 'Solutions of self-monitoring and information disclosure for strictly monitored enterprises (in Chinese)', http://www.zhb.gov.cn/gkml/hbb/bgt/201001/t20100119_184559.htm (accessed 19 August 2013).

Ministry of Environmental Protection of the People's Republic of China (PRC), (2013). 'Solutions of self-monitoring and information disclosure for strictly monitored enterprises (in Chinese)',
http://www.zhb.gov.cn/gkml/hbb/bgth/201305/W020130509639333091992.pdf (accessed 11 August 2013).

V. Mishra, R. Smyth, and S. Sharma, (2009). 'The energy-GDP nexus: evidence from a panel of Pacific Island countries', *Resource and Energy Economics* 31: 210–20.

X. Mu, (2013). 'Beijing moves to curb prolonged haze pollution', http://news.xinhuanet.com/english/china/2013-01/13/c_124224746.htm (accessed 30 April 2014).

P.K. Narayan, and S. Narayan, (2010). 'Carbon dioxide emissions and economic growth: panel data evidence from developing countries', *Energy Policy* 38: 661–66.

P.K. Narayan, and B. Singh, (2007). 'The electricity consumption and GDP nexus for the Fiji Islands', *Energy Economics* 29: 1141–50.

P.K. Narayan, and R. Smyth, (2008). 'Energy consumption and real GDP in G7 countries: new evidence from panel cointegration with structural breaks', *Energy Economics* 30: 2331–41.

N. Narayanan, and ClimateWire, (2013). 'Massive nitrogen pollution accompanies China's growth', Scientific American,
http://www.scientificamerican.com/article.cfm?id=massive-nitrogen-pollution-accompanies-chinas-growth (accessed 11 August 2013)

National Bureau of Statistics of China (NBS), (2013). *China statistical abstract*, China Statistics Press, Beijing.

National Development and Reform Commission (NDRC), (2007). 'China's energy conditions and policies', Beijing, Information Office of the State Council of the People's Republic of China, http://en.ndrc.gov.cn/policyrelease/P020071227502260511798.pdf.

National Development and Reform Commission (NDRC), (2012). 'The notice about closing small coal mines in the last three years of the eleventh five-year plan', http://www.gov.cn/gzdt/2008-10/15/content_1122092.htm (accessed on 1 February 2012).

National Development and Reform Commission (NDRC), (2011). *The 12th five year guideline for national economic and social development*, People's Republic of China.

T. Nauclér and P.A. Enkvist, (2009). 'Pathways to a low-carbon economy: version 2 of the global greenhouse gas abatement cost curve', McKinsey & Company, 192.

B. Naughton, (2007). *The Chinese economy: transitions and growth*, Cambridge, MA: The MIT Press.

B. Naughton, (2008). 'SASAC and rising corporate power in China', *China Leadership Monitor* 24: 1–9.

P. Nolan, (2001). *China and the global business revolution*, Houndmills and New York: Palgrave.

P. Nolan, (2003). 'Globalization challenge for large firms from developing countries: China's oils and aerospace industries', *European Management Journal* 21(3): 285–99.

W. Oh, and K. Lee, (2004). 'Energy consumption and economic growth in Korea: testing the causality relation', *Journal of Policy Modeling* 26: 973–81.

Oil & Gas Eurasia, (02 March 2011). 'Turkmengas to receive Chinese loan', http://www.oilandgaseurasia.com/news/turkmengas-receive-chinese-loan (accessed 3 December 2012).

Oil & Gas Eurasia, (23 September 2012). 'Sizing up a new big brother. Kazakhstan plays out "Come here, go away" strategy with China, Inc.', http://www.oilandgaseurasia.com/tech_trend/sizing-new-big-brother-kazakhstan-plays-out-come-here-go-away-strategy-china-inc (accessed 5 December 2012).

Oil & Gas Eurasia, (6 December 2012). 'Kyrgyzstan considers joining Central Asia-China gas pipeline', http://www.oilandgaseurasia.com/en/news/kyrgyzstan-considers-joining-central-asia-china-gas-pipeline#sthash.G48LiJ32.dpuf (accessed 10 December 2012).

Organisation for Economic Co-operation and Development (OECD), (2013). 'OECD Economic Surveys: China 2013', OECD Publishing, doi:10.1787/eco_surveys-chn-2013-en.

Organisation for Economic Co-operation and Development (OECD), (2013a). 'Putting green growth at the heart of development', OECD Green Growth Studies, OECD Publishing, http://wwwdx.doi.org/10.1787/9789264181144-en.

Organisation for Economic Co-operation and Development (OECD), (2013b). 'OECD factbook 2013: economic, environmental and social statistics', http://www.oecd-ilibrary.org/content/book/factbook-2013-en (accessed 14 August 2013).

S. Oster, (2006). 'Illegal power plants coal mines in china pose challenge for Beijing', *The Wall Street Journal*, 27 December 2006: http://www.pulitzer.org/archives/7150.

X. Ou, X. Zhang, and S. Chang, (2010). 'Scenario analysis on alternative fuel/vehicle for China's future road transport: life-cycle energy demand and GHG emissions', *Energy Policy* 38(8): 3943–56.

L. Oxley, J. Gibson, H. Ma, and W. Li, (2010). 'A survey of China's renewable energy economy', *Renewable and Sustainable Energy Reviews* 14: 438–45.

I. Ozturk, (2010). 'A literature survey on energy–growth nexus', *Applied Energy* 38: 340–49.

J. Pan, H. Ma, and Y. Zhang, (2011). *Green economy and green jobs in China, current status and potentials for 2020*, World Watch report No. 185, Worldwatch Institute, Washington DC.

B. Pannier, (2010). 'Chinese-Central Asian relationship requires delicate balancing act ', http://www.rferl.org/content/ChineseCentral_Asian_Relationship_Requires_Delicate_Balancing_Act/2002215.html (accessed 11 December 2013).

J. Parikh, and K. Parikh, (2011). 'India's energy needs and low carbon options', *Energy* 36: 3650–58.

S. Paul, and R.B. Bhattachachrya, (2004). 'Causality between energy consumption and economic growth in India: a note on conflicting results', *Energy Economics* 26: 977–83.

J.E. Payne, (2010a). 'A survey of the electricity consumption-growth literature', *Applied Energy* 87(3): 723–31.

J.E. Payne, (2010b). 'Survey of the international evidence on the causal relationship between energy consumption and growth', *Journal of Economic Studies* 37: 53–95.

PBL Netherlands Environmental Assessment Agency, (2008). *China now no. 1 in CO2 emissions; USA in second position*, http://www.pbl.nl/en/dossiers/Climatechange/moreinfo/Chinanowno1inCO2emissionsUSAinsecondposition (accessed 9 August 2013).

D. Pearce, A. Markandya, and E. Barbier, (1989). *Blueprint for a green economy*, Earthscan, London.

P. Pedroni, (1999). 'Critical values for cointegration tests in heterogeneous panels with multiple regressors', *Oxford Bulletin of Economics and Statistics* 61: 727–31.

People's Republic of China, (2005). 'The Renewable Energy Law of the People's Republic of China', Beijing, 28 February.

People's Republic of China, (2008). 'China's policies and actions for addressing climate change', State Council Information Office, http://www.china.org.cn/government/news/2008-10/29/content_16681689.htm (accessed 20 November 2012).

People's Daily, (2010). 'China's oil production ranks 4th in world, only meets half domestic demand', http://english.peopledaily.com.cn/90001/90778/90860/6891500.html (accessed 11 December 2012).

M.G. Pereira, C.F. Camacho, M.A.V. Freitas, and N. Fidelis da Silva, (2012). 'The renewable energy market in Brazil: current status and potential', *Renewable and Sustainable Energy Reviews* 16: 3786–802.

R. Perkins, and E. Neumayer, (2009). 'Transnational linkages and the spillover of environment-efficiency into developing countries', *Global Environmental Change* 19: 375–83.

H. Pesaran, (2007). 'A simple panel unit root test in the presence of cross-section dependence', *Journal of Applied Econometrics* 22: 265–312.

S. Peterson, (2008). 'Greenhouse gas mitigation in developing countries through technology transfer? A survey of empirical evidence', *Mitigation and Adaptation Strategies for Global Change* 13: 283–305.

Pew Center on Global Climate Change, (2007). 'Climate change mitigation measures in the People's Republic of China', 9 April 2007.

S. Pfaffenzeller, P. Newbold, and A. Rayner, (2007). 'A short note on updating the Grilli and Yang commodity price index', *The World Bank Economic Review* 21: 151–63.

M. Philips, (2012). 'China's energy grab is about know-how, not resources', Business Week, 30 July 2012, http://www.businessweek.com/articles/2012-07-30/chinas-energy-grab-is-about-know-how-not-resources.

R.S. Pindyck, and D.L. Rubinfeld, (1997). *Econometric models and economic forecasts*, McGraw-Hill, Singapore.

I.I. Pop, (2010). 'China's energy strategy in Central Asia: interactions with Russia, India and Japan', *UNISCI Discussion Papers* 24: 197–220.

PRC Central Government, (2004). 'The joint announcement of the governments of the PRC and Kyrgyz Republic governments', http://www.gov.cn/gongbao/content/2004/content_63036.htm (accessed 5 December 2012).

PRC Ministry of Commerce, (2004). 'The framework for the cooperation between People's Republic of China and Kyrgyz Republic for years 2004–2014 (中 人民共和国和吉尔吉斯共和国二OO四至二O一四年合作 要)', http://tradeinservices.mofcom.gov.cn/b/2004-09-21/65643.shtml (accessed 5 December 2012).

R. Prebisch, (1950). *The economic development of Latin America and its principal problems*, New York: United Nations.

L. Price, M.D. Levine, N. Zhou, D. Fridley, N. Aden, H. Lu, M. McNeil, N. Zheng, Y. Qin, and P. Yowargana, (2011). 'Assessment of China's energy-saving and emission-reduction accomplishments and opportunities during the 11th Five Year Plan', *Energy Policy* 39: 2165–78.

J. Qiu, (2013). 'Nitrogen pollution soars in China, Nature', http://www.nature.com/news/nitrogen-pollution-soars-in-china-1.12470 (accessed 9 August 2013).

M. Radetzki, (2006). 'The anatomy of three commodity booms', *Resources Policy* 31: 56–64.

Report on the State of the Environment in China, (2006). China State Environmental Protection Administration, Beijing.

Report on the State of the Environment in China, (2007). China State Environmental Protection Administration, Beijing

Reuters, (2006). 'Acid rain affects large swathes of China', http://www.enn.com/top_stories/article/4948 (accessed 31 January 2012).

Reuters, (09 January 2012). 'Goldman sees China becoming biggest oil importer', http://www.reuters.com/article/2012/01/09/us-oil-china-imports-idUSTRE80815H20120109 (accessed 2 December 2012).

Reuters, (06 December 2012). 'China says to offer $10 billion in loans to SCO member states', http://www.reuters.com/article/2012/06/07/us-china-sco-loans-idUSBRE856029201206070 (accessed 2 December 2012).

RIA Novosti, (2006). 'Russia initiates SCO Energy Club', http://en.rian.ru/analysis/20060621/49855458.html (accessed 9 December 2012).

S.K. Roache, (2012). 'China's impact on world commodity markets', IMF Working Paper WP/12/115.

M. Romani, O. Soldatos, and A. van Benthem, (2006). 'Climbing the energy ladder: the role of growth and prices in determining energy demand', Conference presentation slides available at: http://www.usaee.org/USAEE2006/papers/mattiaromani.pdf .

D. Rosen, and T. Houser, (2007). 'China energy: a guide for the perplexed', China Balance Sheet, A Joint Project by the Center for Strategic and International Studies and the Peterson Institute for International Economic.

K. Rosner, (2010). 'China scores again in energy: Russia & Central Asia', http://www.ensec.org/index.php?option=com_content&view=article&id=230:china-scores-again-in-energy-russia-aamp-central-asia&catid=102:issuecontent&Itemid=355 (accessed 12 December 2012).

C. Rühl, P. Appleby, J. Fenema, A. Naumov, and M. Schaffer, (2012). 'Economic development and the demand for energy: a historical perspective on the next twenty years', *Energy Policy* 50: 109–16.

S. Sahu, and K. Narayanan, (2009). 'Determinants of energy intensity: a preliminary investigation of Indian manufacturing', *MPRA Paper* No. 16606, August.

Z.S. Saipov, (2012). 'China's economic strategies for Uzbekistan and Central Asia: building roads to Afghan strategic resources and beyond', http://www.jamestown.org/single/?no_cache=1&tx_ttnews[tt_news]=39873 (accessed 13 December 2012).

F. Sanna- Randaccio, (2012). 'Foreign direct investment, multinational entreprises and climate change', *Review of Environment, Energy and Economics*-Re3, 2012 (January).

R. Schaeffer, C. Cohen, A.C.J. de Aguiar, and G.V.R. Faria, (2009). 'The potential for electricity conservation and carbon dioxide emission reductions in the household sector of Brazil', *Energy Efficiency* 2: 165–78.

S. Schurr, and B.C. Netschert, with V.E. Eliasberg, J. Lerner, and H.H. Landsberg, (1960). *Energy and the American economy, 1850-1975*, Baltimore: Johns Hopkins University Press.

S. Schurr, (1982). 'Energy efficiency and productive efficiency: some thoughts based on American experience', *Energy Journal* 3: 3–14.

J. Seaman, (2010). Energy security, transnational pipelines and China's role in Asia, IFRI Centre Asie.

J. Shen, (2010). *Developing circular economy and low carbon economy coordinately*, http://www.europe1china.com/en/industry/2010051815444481.htm (accessed 14 August 2013).

R.W. Shephard, (1970). *Theory of cost and production Function*, Princeton: Princeton University Press.

D. Shi, (2000). 'China tenth five-year plan: renewable energy research and development', Speech, Department of High and New Technology and Industrialization, Ministry of Science and Technology, Beijing.

D. Shi, (2010). 'China's renewable energy development targets and implementation effect analysis', in: M. Parivizi Amineh and R. Yang (eds) *Globalization of energy: China and the European Union*, Leiden: Brill Academic Publishers, 201–26.

A. Shiu, and P.L. Lam, (2004). 'Electricity consumption and economic growth in China', *Energy Policy* 32: 47–54.

P.R. Shukla, A. Garg, S. Dhar, and K. Halsnaes, (2007). 'Balancing energy, development and climate priorities in India: current trends and future projections', UNEP Risoe Centre on Energy, Climate and Sustainable Development, Rosklide, Denmark, 67–75.

A. Shutov, (2012). 'China's growing economic importance to Central Asia', http://en.ria.ru/international_affairs/20120629/174304839.html (accessed 13 December 2012).

H. Singer, (1950). 'The distribution of gains between investing and borrowing countries', *American Economic Review, Papers and Proceedings* 11: 473–85.

Sinopec, (2010). Sinopec Corp. Annual Report.

Sinopec Annual Report, (2011). 'To be a world leading energy & chemical corporation', http://www.sinopecgroup.com/SiteCollectionImages/2012/en/reports/2011SinopecAnnualReportEN.pdf (accessed 2 December 2012).

J. Sinton, and D. Fridley, (2000). 'What goes up: recent trend in China's energy consumption', *Energy Policy* 28: 671–87.

J.E. Sinton, K.R. Smith, J.W. Peabody, Y. Liu, X. Zhang, R. Edwards, and G. Quan, (2004). 'An assessment of programs to promote improved household stoves in China', *Energy for Sustainable Development* 8: 33–52.

M.E. Slade, (1982). 'Cycles in natural-resource commodity prices: an analysis of the frequency domain', *Journal of Environmental Economics and Management* 9: 138–48.

K. Smith, (2010). *Nitrous oxide and climate change*, Earthscan, London

R. Smyth, Z. Qingguo, and H. Wenguo, (2001). 'Restructuring China's petrochemical enterprises: a case study of the Fushun Petrochemical Company', *Post-Communist Economies* 13(2): 243–61.

R. Smyth, and Z. Qinggguo, (2001). 'Reforming China's large-scale state-owned enterprises: the petrochemical sector', *Asia Pacific Journal of Economics and Business* 5(2): 82–118.

Solid Ground Magazine, (2013). 'China pushes coal-to-gas pilots', 19 April 2013, http://www.solidgroundmagazine.com/china-pushes-coal-to-gas-pilots/.

D. Solovyov, and R. Paxton, (2011). 'Kazakh leader to sack son-in-law after riots', http://www.trust.org/alertnet/news/kazakh-leader-to-sack-son-in-law-after-riots (accessed 3 January 2013).

R.M. Solow, (1956). 'A contribution to the theory of economic growth', *Quarterly Journal of Economics* 70: 65–94.

Source Watch, (2013). 'China and coal', https://www.sourcewatch.org/index.php/China_and_coal.

South China Morning Post, (2013). 'Pollution remains at hazardous levels in Beijing', http://www.scmp.com/news/china/article/1139530/pollution-remains-hazardous-levels-beijing (accessed 11 August 2013).

U. Soytas, and R. Sari, (2003). 'Energy consumption and GDP: causality relationship in G-7 and emerging markets', *Energy Economics* 25: 33–37.

U. Soytas, and R. Sari, (2006). 'Can China contribute more to the fight against global warming?', *Journal of Policy Modeling* 28: 837–46.

J.W. Spencer, (2008). 'The impact of multinational enterprise strategy on indigenous enterprises: horizontal spillovers and crowding out in developing countries', *Academy of Management Review* 33: 341–61.

D.I. Stern, (1993). 'Energy and economic growth in the USA: a multivariate approach', *Energy Economics* 15: 137–50.

D.I. Stern, (2000). 'A multivariate cointegration analysis of the role of energy in the U.S. macroeconomy', *Energy Economics* 22: 267–83.

D.I. Stern, (2011). 'The role of energy in economic growth', *Ecological Economics Reviews* 1219: 26–51.

D. Strang, and J.W. Meyer, (1993). 'Institutional conditions for diffusion', *Theory and Society* 22: 487–511.

D.G. Street, G.R. Carmicjael, and R.L. Arndt, (1997). 'Sulfur dioxide emissions and sulphur deposition from international shipping in Asian waters', *Atmospheric Environment* 31: 1573–82.

Y. Sun, (2009). 'The energy cooperation within the Shangahi Cooperation Organization (上海合作 的能源合作)', http://euroasia.cass.cn/news/110060.htm (accessed 05 December 2012).

R.G. Sutter, (2008). *Chinese foreign relations. Power and policy since the Cold War*, Plymouth: Rowman & Littlefield Publishers INC.

N. Swanstrom, (2007). 'Editors note – the SCO and the Bishkek Summit', http://www.silkroadstudies.org/new/docs/CEF/Quarterly/August_2007/Ed_Note.pdf (accessed 5 December 2012).

A. Szamosszegi, and C. Kyle, (2011). 'An analysis of state-owned enterprises and state capitalism in China', U.S.-China Economic and Security Review Commission, 26 October.

W. Tam, and D. Yang, (2005). 'Food safety and the development of regulatory institutions in China', *Asian Perspective* 29: 5–36.

N. Tanaka, (2008). 'Energy technology perspectives 2008: scenarios and strategies to 2050', International Energy Agency, Paris.

Z. Tao, and M. Li, (2007). 'System dynamics model of Hubbert Peak for China's oil', *Energy Policy* 35: 2281–86.

R.P. Taylor, C. Govindarajalu, J. Levin, A.S. Meyer, and W.A. Ward, (2008). 'Financing energy efficiency: lessons from Brazil, China, India and beyond', The World Bank, Washington, D.C.

The Energy and Resources Institute (TERI), (2006). 'Greenhouse gas mitigation in India: scenarios and opportunities through 2031', Center for Clean Air Policy.

M. Thoma, (2004). 'Electricity energy usage over the business cycle', *Energy Economics* 26: 463–85.

D. Tobin, (2008). 'From Maoist self-reliance to international oil consumer: a resource-based appraisal of the challenges facing China's petrochemical sector', *Journal of Chinese Economic and Business Studies* 6(4): 363–38.

D. Trenin, (2012). 'True partners? How China and Russia see each other', http://www.carnegieendowment.org/files/Trenin_CER_Eng.pdf (accessed 5 October 2012).

Tsinghua University of China, (2006). 'Greenhouse gas mitigation in China: scenarios and opportunities through 2030', Center for Clean Air Policy.

United Nations Framework Convention on Climate Change (UNFCCC), (2007). 'Investment and financial flows to address climate change', http://unfccc.int/resource/docs/publications/financial_flows.pdf (accessed 28 November 2012)

UNCTAD, (2007). *World Investment Report: Transnational Corporations, Extractive Industries and Development*, United Nations, Geneva.

UNEP, (2013). *Green economy and trade, trends, challenges and opportunities*, http://www.unep.org/greeneconomy/GreenEconomyandTrade.

UNEP and Frankfurt School Collaborating Centre for Climate and Sustainable Energy Finance, (2013). 'Global trends in renewable energy investment 2013', Bloomberg-new energy finance – UNEP, http://www.unep.org/pdf/GTR-UNEP-FS-BNEF2.pdf (accessed 3 August 2013).

United States (US) Census Bureau, (2013). *U.S. and World Population Clock*, http://www.census.gov/popclock/ (accessed 9 August 2013).

U.S. Energy Information Administration (EIA), (2011). 'China – Analysis', http://www.eia.gov/countries/cab.cfm?fips=CH (accessed November 2012).

U.S. Energy Information Administration (EIA), (2011a). 'International energy outlook 2011', http://www.eia.gov/forecasts/ieo/pdf/0484(2011b).pdf (accessed 12 October 2012).

U.S. Energy Information Administration (EIA), (2011b). 'Country analysis brief, China', URL: http://www.eia.gov/countries/analysisbriefs/China/china.pdf.

U.S. Energy Information Administration (EIA), (2012a). 'Annual energy outlook 2012 with projections to 2035', http://www.eia.gov/forecasts/aeo/pdf/0383(2012).pdf (accessed 12 October 2012).

U.S. Energy Information Administration (EIA), (2012b). 'Countries reports', http://www.eia.gov/countries/ (accessed 15 October 2012).

A.B. Vattenfall, (2007). 'Global mapping of greenhouse gas abatement opportunities up to 2030', http://www.schoonschakelen.nl/library_files/1_1253885146_Power%20Sector_Global_Mapping_of_Greenhouse_Gas_Abatement_Opportunities_up_to_2030-Vattenfall-2007%5B1%5D.pdf (accessed 18 November 2012).

V. Vivoda, (2009). 'Diversification of oil import sources and energy security: a key strategy or an elusive objective?', *Energy Policy* 37: 4615–23.

D. Vogel, (1995). *Trading up*, Cambridge: Harvard University Press.

R. Walsh, (1993). 'China and the new geopolitics of Central Asia', *Asian Survey* 33(3): 272–83.

D.Z. Wang, and Y.Y. Lu, (2002). 'Roles and prospect of nuclear power in China's energy supply strategy', *Nuclear Engineering and Design* 218 (1–3): 3–12.

F. Wang, H. Yin, and S. Li, (2010). 'China's renewable energy policy: commitments and challenges', *Energy Policy* 38: 1872–78.

H. Wang, (1995). 'China's oil policy and its impact', *Energy Policy* 23(7): 627–35.

H. Wang, (2011). 'China should actively promote the SCO mechanisms for multilateral cooperation on energy (中国 推 上合 多 能源合作机制)', http://www.chinareform.org.cn/open/view/201107/t20110728_117558.htm (accessed 4 February 2013).

S.S. Wang, D.Q. Zhou, P. Zhou, and Q.W. Wang, (2011b). 'CO_2 emissions, energy consumption and economic growth in China: a panel data analysis', *Energy Policy* 39: 4870–75.

Q. Wang, (2010). 'Effective policies for renewable energy—the example of China's wind power—lessons for China's photovoltaic power', *Renewable and Sustainable Energy Reviews* 14: 702–12.

Q. Wang, and Y. Cheng, (2010). 'Barriers and opportunities to using the clean development mechanism to advance renewable energy sources in China', *Renewable and Sustainable Energy Reviews* 14: 1989–98.

X. Wang, W. Manning, Z. Feng, and Y. Zhu, (2007). 'Ground-level ozone in China: distribution and effects on crop yields', *Environmental Pollution* 147(2): 394–400.

Y. Wang, Y. Wang, J. Zhou, X. Zhu, and G. Lu, (2011a). 'Energy consumption and economic growth in China: a multivariate causality test', *Energy Policy* 39: 4399–406.

Y.X. Wang, and M. Yao, (2007). 'Analysis of causality between energy consumption and economic growth in China', *Journal of Heifei University of Technology* 30: 1163–66.

C. Weber, G. Peters, D. Guan, and K. Hubaceck, (2008). 'The contribution of Chinese exports to climate change', *Energy Policy* 36: 3572–77.

S.-L. Wee, (2013). 'China to invest $277 billion to curb air pollution: state media', http://www.reuters.com/article/2013/07/25/us-china-pollution-idUSBRE96O01Z20130725 (accessed 15 August 2013).

J. Wei, R. Jia, D. Marinova, and D. Zhao, (2012). 'Modelling pollution control and performance in China's provinces', *Journal of Environmental Management* 113: 263–70

Y. Wei, and L. Liu, (2008). *'China energy report (2008): CO_2 emission research'*, Science Press, 2008.

R. Weitz, (2012). 'Is the SCO coming to life?', http://www.cacianalyst.org/?q=node/5812 (accessed 1 December 2012).

J. Westerlund, and D. Edgerton, (2007). 'A panel bootstrap cointegration test', *Economic Letters* 97: 185–90.

S.H. Whiting, (2000). *Power and wealth in rural China: the political economy of institutional change*, New York; Cambridge: Cambridge University Press.

C. Winzer, (2011). 'Conceptualizing energy security', Electricity Policy Research Group, EPRC Working Paper 1123, Cambridge Working Paper in Economics 1151.

E. Wishnick, (2006). 'Great powers compete for Kazakh energy', http://www.isn.ethz.ch/Digital-Library/Articles/Detail/?lng=en&id=108385 (accessed 10 December 2013) .

Wolfran, O. Shelef, and P. Gertler, (2012). 'How will energy demand develop in the developing world?', *Journal of Economic Perspectives* 26: 119–38.

C. Wong, (2008). *Rebuilding government for the 21st Century: can China incrementally reform the public sector?*, Oxford: University of Oxford.

World Bank, (2010). 'The World Bank Development Indicators', http://data.worldbank.org/indicator (accessed 1 September 2012).

World Bank, (2011). 'CO_2 emissions', http://data.worldbank.org/indicator/EN.ATM.CO2E.KT.

World Bank, (2013). 'CO_2 emissions (kt)', http://data.worldbank.org/indicator/EN.ATM.CO2E.KT/countries?display=default (accessed 9 August 2013).

Worldwatch Institute, (2013). 'Counting green jobs in China harder than creating them', http://www.worldwatch.org/counting-green-jobs-china-harder-creating-them (accessed 13 August 2013).

WTO, (2013). 'Dispute Settlement. DS452. European Union and certain member states- certain measures affecting renewable energy generation sector', Geneva, WTO. http://www.wto.org/english/tratop_E/dispu_E/cases_E/ds452_E.htm.

www.footprintnetwork.org/images/articles_uploads/China_Ecological_Footprint_2012.pdf. (accessed 26 July 2013).

G. Wu, Y.M. Wei, Y. Fan, and L.C. Liu, (2007). 'An empirical analysis of the risk of crude oil imports in China using improved portfolio approach', *Energy Policy* 35: 4190–99.

G. Wu, Y.M. Wei, Y. Fan, and L.C. Liu, (2009). 'Comparison of China's oil import risk: results based on portfolio theory and a diversification index approach', *Energy Policy* 37: 3557–65.

Y. Wu, (2012). 'Energy intensity and its determinants in China's regional economies', *Energy Policy* 41: 703–11.

K. Wuand, and I. Storey, (2008). 'Energy security in China's capitalist transition: import dependence, oil diplomacy, and security imperatives', in: C.A. McNally (ed.) *China's emergent political economy: capitalism in the dragon's lair*, New York: Routledge.

WWF, (2012). *China ecological footprint report 2012, consumption, production and sustainable development*, Global Footprint Network

Y. Xia, C. Yang, and X. Chen, (2009). 'Analysis on determining factors of energy intensity in China based on comparable price input-output table', *Systems Engineering: Theory & Practice* 29: 21–27.

Xinhua, (2008). 'Official says China's fuel prices will drop under new fuel-pricing system', 9 December.

Xinhua, (2011). *China announces first cuts in gasoline, diesel prices in 16 months*, 8 October.

Xinhua, (24 October 2012). 'Full text: China's energy policy 2012', http://news.xinhuanet.com/english/china/2012-10/24/c_131927649.htm (accessed 14 December 2012).

Xinhua, (06 September 2012). 'Chinese firm mulls cross-border power grid with Tajikistan, Kyrgyzstan', http://news.xinhuanet.com/english/business/2012-09-/06/c_131832091.htm (accessed 3 December 2012).

Xinhuanet, (2013). 'Guangzhou closed 116 pollution enterprises and rectified 2 enterprises' (in Chinese), http://www.gd.xinhuanet.com/newscenter/2009-09/05/content_17610024.htm (accessed 11 August 2013).

Xinhuanet, (2013a). 'Environmental pollution criminal cases solved, showing three characteristics of enterprises' illegal waste discharges' (in Chinese), http://news.xinhuanet.com/legal/2013-06/18/c_116191309.htm (accessed 12 August 2013).

Xinhuanet, (2013b). '88 enterprises of 6 northern provinces were fined more than 6 million Yuan for illegal waste discharges' (in Chinese), http://news.xinhuanet.com/politics/2013-05/09/c_115704305.htm?prolongation=1 (accessed 12 August 2013).

Xinhuanet, (2013c). 'Misconduct and corruption became protecting umbrellas for those guilty of environmental damage' (in Chinese), http://news.xinhuanet.com/legal/2013-06/03/c_124803310.htm (accessed 12 August 2013).

Xinhuanet, (2013d). 'Investment in air and water pollution will reach to trillion yuan, welcoming a golden period of environmental production industries' (in Chinese), http://news.xinhuanet.com/fortune/2013-07/28/c_116714127.htm (accessed 15 August 2013).

Q. Xu, (2012). 'The reality and prospects for energy multilateral cooperation at the SCO forum in the post-financial crisis period (后金融危机 期上合 框架内多能源合作 状及前景)', *Russian, Central Asian and East European Studies* 4: 56–62.

S. Xu, and Y. Sheng, (2012). 'Are FDI spillovers regional? firm-level evidence from China', *Journal of Asian Economics* 23: 244–58.

Y.C. Xu, (2008). 'Nuclear energy in China: contested regimes', *Energy* 33: 1197–205.

X. Yan, (1998). *The great restructuring of China's petrochemical industry—opportunities and challenges in the market economy (in Chinese)*, Petroleum Industry Publishing House, Beijing.

H.Y. Yang, (2000). 'Coal consumption and economic growth in Taiwan', *Energy Sources* 22: 109–15.

J. Yang, H. Qiu, J. Huang, and R. Scott, (2008). 'Fighting global food price rises in the developing world: the response of China and its effect on domestic and world markets', *Agricultural Economics* 39: 453–64.

W. Yang, Y. Gu, and J. Feng, (2007). 'Natural gas power in southern regions: research studies on price policy', *Energy Conservation and Environmental Protection* 1: 30–33 (Chinese).

A.T. Yalta, and H. Cakar, (2012). 'Energy consumption and economic growth in China: a reconciliation', *Energy Policy* 41: 666–75.

W. Ye, (2008). 'China's refined copper usage'. Presentation to the International Copper Study Group.

S.H. Yoo, (2006). 'Causal relationship between coal consumption and economic growth in Korea', *Applied Energy* 83: 1181–89.

A.R. Young, (2003). 'Political transfer and "trading up" – transatlantic trade in genetically modified food and US politics', *World Politics* 55: 457–84.

H. Yu, (2012). 'The influential factors of China's regional energy intensity and its spatial linkages: 1988–2007', *Energy Policy* 45: 583–93.

E.S.H. Yu, and J.Y. Choi, (1985). 'The causal relationship between energy and GNP: an international comparison', *Journal of Energy Development* 10: 249–72

E.S.H Yu, and B.K. Hwang, (1984). 'The relationship between energy and GNP: Further results', *Energy Economics* 6 (3): 186–190.

S.H. Yu, and J.C. Jin, (1992). 'Cointegration test of energy consumption, income and employment', *Resources and Energy Economics* 14: 259–66.

Y. Yu, (2011). 'Identifying the linkage between major mining commodity circle and China economic growth: its implications for Latin America', *IMF Working Paper* WP11/88.

J. Yuan, C. Zhao, S. Yu, and Z. Hu, (2007). 'Electricity consumption and economic growth in China: cointegration and co-feature analysis', *Energy Economics* 29: 1179–91.

J. Yuan, J. Kang, C. Zhao, and Z. Hu, (2008). 'Energy consumption and economic growth: evidence from China at both aggregated and disaggregated levels', *Energy Economics* 30: 3077–94.

J. Yuan, C. Zhao, S. Yu, and Z. Hu, (2007). 'Electricity consumption and economic growth in China: cointegration and co-feature analysis', *Energy Economics* 29: 1179–91.

J. Yuan, (2010). 'China's role in establishing and building the Shanghai Cooperation Organization (SCO)', *Journal of Contemporary China* 19(67): 855–69.

A. Zafar, (2007). 'The growing relationship between China and Sub-Saharan Africa: macroeconomic, trade, investment and aid links', *World Bank Research Observer* 22: 103–30.

M. Zamani, (2007). 'Energy consumption and economic activities in Iran', *Energy Economics* 29: 1135–40.

D. Zha, (2006). 'China's energy security: domestic and international issues', *Survival: Global Politics and Strategy* 48(1): 179–90.

J. Zhang, (2004). *Catch-up and competitiveness in China: the case of large firms in the oil industry*, London, New York: Routledge Curzon.

J. Zhang, (2011). *China's energy security: prospects, challenges, and opportunities*, Washington D.C: The Brookings Institution

L. Zhang, A.P.J Mol, G. He, and Y. Lu, (2010). 'An implementation assessment of China's environmental information disclosure decree', *Journal of Environmental Sciences* 22(10): 1649–56.

N. Zhang, N. Lior, and H.G. Jin, (2011). 'The energy situation and its sustainable development strategy in China', *Energy* 36: 3639–49.

P. Zhang, Y. Yang, J. Shi, Y. Zheng, L. Wang, and X. Li, (2009). 'Opportunities and challenges for renewable energy policy in China', *Renewable and Sustainable Energy Reviews* 13: 439–49.

T.W. Zhang, (2006). 'From intercity competition to collaborative planning – The case of the Yangtze River Delta region of China', *Urban Affairs Review* 42(1): 26–56.

X.L. Zhang, R.S. Wang, M.L. Huo, and E. Marinot, (2010). 'A study of the role played by renewable energies in China's sustainable energy supply', *Energy* 35: 4392–99.

X.P. Zhang, and X.M. Cheng, (2009). 'Energy consumption, carbon emissions, and economic growth in China', *Ecological Economics* 68: 2706–12.

Y. Zhang, (2010). 'Economic development pattern change impact on China's carbon intensity', *Economic Research Journal* 45: 121–34.

Y. Zhang, W. Han, X. Jing, G. Pu, and C. Wang, (2009). 'Development strategies for wind power industry in Jiangsu Province, China: based on the evaluation of resource capacity', *Energy Policy* 37: 2079–86.

Y. Zhang, H. Li, Y. Li, and L. Zhou, (2010). 'FDI spillovers in an emerging market: the role of foreign firms' country origin diversity and domestic firms' absorptive capacity', *Strategic Management Journal* 31: 969–89.

Y.T. Zhang, and W. Li, (2007). 'Study on causal relationship between coal consumption and economic growth in China', *Resources and Industries* 9: 89–93.

Z. Zhang, (2007). 'China is moving away the pattern of develop first and then treat the pollution', *Energy Policy* 35: 439–49.

Z. Zhang, (2010). 'Copenhagen and beyond: reflections on China's stance and responses', *East-West Center Working Papers* 111.

Z.Y. Zhang, (2003). 'Why did the energy intensity fall in China's industrial sector in the 1990s? The relative importance of structural change and intensity change', *Energy Economics* 25: 625–38.

H. Zhao, (2007). 'Central Asia in China's diplomacy', in: H. Zhao, E. Rumer and D. Trenin (eds), *Central Asia: views from Washington, Moscow, and Beijing, USA*, Armonk: M.E. Sharpe Inc.,

H. Zhao, (2008). *China's Central Asian Diplomacy* （中国的中 外交）, Shishi Publishing.

J.W. Zhao, and J.T. Fan, (2007). 'Empirical research on the inherent relationship between economy growth and energy consumption in China', *Economic Research Journal* 8: 31–42

X. Zhao, C. Ma, and D. Hong, (2010). 'Why did China's energy intensity increase during 1998-2006: decomposition and policy analysis', *Energy Policy* 38: 1379–88.

Z.Y. Zhao, J. Zuo, T.T. Feng, and G. Zillante, (2011). 'International cooperation on renewable energy development in China – a critical analysis', *Renewable Energy* 36: 1105–10.

C. Zhi, (2013). 'China to spend trillions on pollution battle', Xinhuanet http://news.xinhuanet.com/english/china/2013-07/28/c_132581008.htm (accessed 15 August 2013).

N. Zhou, M. Levine, and L. Price, (2010). 'Overview of current energy-efficiency policies in China', *Energy Policy* 38: 6439–52.

P. Zhou, B.W. Ang, and J.Y. Han, (2010). 'Total factor carbon emission performance: a Malmquist index analysis', *Energy Economics* 32: 194–201.

S. Zhou, and X.L. Zhang, (2010). 'Nuclear energy development in China: a study of opportunities and challenges', *Energy* 35: 4282–88.

Y. Zhou, (2010). 'Why is China going nuclear?', *Energy Policy* 38: 3755–62.

G. Zillante, Z. Zhao, Z. Jian, and L. Fan, (2011). 'Impacts of renewable energy regulations on the structure of power generation in China – a critical analysis', *Renewable Energy* 36: 24–30.

G. Zou, and K. Chau, (2006). 'Short- and long-run effects between oil consumption and economic growth in China', *Energy Policy* 34: 3644–55.

Index

The manufacturer's authorised representative in the EU is Springer Nature Customer Service Centre GmbH, Europaplatz 3, 69115 Heidelberg, Germany. If you have any concerns regarding our products, please contact ProductSafety@springernature.com

Printed and bound by CPI Group (UK) Ltd, Croydon, CR0 4YY
10/10/2026
02231232-0004